Date Due

APR 1 5 1999			

de Gruyter Studies in Organization 12

Laaksonen, Management in China

de Gruyter Studies in Organization

An international series by internationally known authors presenting current fields of research in organization.

Organizing and organizations are substantial pre-requisites for the viability and future developments of society. Their study and comprehension are indispensable to the quality of human life. Therefore, the series aims to:

- offer to the specialist work material in form of the most important and current problems, methods and results;
- give interested readers access to different subject areas;
- provide aids for decisions on contemporary problems and stimulate ideas.

The series will include monographs, collections of contributed papers, and handbooks.

Oiva Laaksonen

Management in China during and after Mao in Enterprises, Government, and Party

Walter de Gruyter · Berlin · New York 1988

Dr. Oiva Laaksonen
Professor of Business, Administration and Organizational Behavior
Helsinki School of Economics
Runeberginkatu 14–16
SF-00100 Helsinki

Library of Congress Cataloging in Publication Data

Laaksonen, Oiva.
  Management in China during and after Mao in enterprises, government, and party.
  (De Gruyter studies in organization ; 12)
  Bibliography: p.
  Includes index.
  1. Management—China.   2. Public administration—China.   3. China—Politics and government—1949–
  1. Title.   II. Series.
HD70.C5L23 1988
ISBN 0–89925–025–4   658'.00951   88–3584

CIP-Titelaufnahme der Deutschen Bibliothek

Laaksonen, Oiva:
Management in China during and after Mao in enterprises, government, and party / Oiva Laaksonen. – Berlin ; New York : de Gruyter, 1988
  (De Gruyter studies in organization ; 12)
  ISBN 3–11–009958–6
NE: GT

Acknowledgements

The research process during which I collected material for this study, began in 1973. As it contained several trips to China I have succeeded in completing this study only with the help of many different persons and institutions. Especially I would like to mention the following:

While I was completing this book in Beijing during the Fall of 1986 Professor Robert W. Hillman, School of Law, University of California, Davis, who was then a visiting professor at the University of International Business and Economics (UIBE), and Professor Kenneth Starck, School of Journalism and Mass Communication, University of Iowa, who was then a Fulbright Professor at the Chinese Academy of Social Sciences, kindly read my manuscript and made valuable and useful suggestions especially concerning the structure of the book. At a rather late stage I asked Professor Risto Tainio and Ms. Sinikka Vanhala (Lic. Econ.) from the Helsinki School of Economics to read the manuscript. They gave valuable comments.

Collection of research material from different localities and their enterprises required a local expert, who knew the enterprises and their representatives. In this sense I am deeply obliged to Professor Liu Yong Kang from Shanghai Jiao Tong University and Mr. Wang Xian-Chuan, Director of the Department of Chongqing City Economic Commission, and the Chinese writer Mr. Jiang Zi Long who helped to open for me the doors to enterprises in Shanghai, Chongqing, and Tianjin.

My research in China would not have been possible without the unexpectedly great help and hospitality of the Chinese People's Association for Friendship with Foreign Countries, which invited me and was my host-organization during my trips to China in 1973, 1980 and 1984. The Association provided me with very capable persons who acted as guides, interpreters, organizers and – may I add – valuable friends. These persons were: in 1973 Mr. Chen Lo-ming and Mr. Li Sing-mao, in 1980 Mr. Wang Xiutian and in 1984 Mr. Chen Shanmin.

I deeply appreciate the help I received from Mr. Philip Binham, a lecturer at the Helsinki School of Economics, who not only revised the English of my manuscript and checked the proofs, but also gave valuable hints concerning the writing.

In Beijing, while I was finishing the manuscript Mr. Larry Johnson, Ms. Frances Somers and Ms. Raija Starck helped me to check the data of the manuscript.

Especially great work has been done by Ms. Saini Lanu, who has several times typed and duplicated the manuscript. Also Ms. Leena Tapaninen has helped in typing, especially the many tricky tables. The help of Ms. Eija Savaja has also been valuable in carrying out the necessary data-processing.

When I was a visiting professor at the University of International Business and Economics (UIBE) in Beijing during the Fall term of 1986 Dean Gao Guopei kindly arranged for me to do organization research in different localities of China while teaching at the university. In the fall 1986 Mr. Zhou Jien-yuan from UIBE skillfully acted as an interpreter while I was interviewing in enterprises.

In this connection I should not forget to mention Professor Cornelis Lammers from the University of Leyden, who gave me the first impulse to write this book.

The following organizations have, by giving me financial support, made possible my research in China during different periods: The Academy of Finland, the Foundation for Economic Education, and the Helsinki School of Economics and Business Administration.

All the persons and institutions mentioned and many others who have not been named here, deserve my sincere and warm thanks.

Last but not least I would like to thank my wife and children who, for years, have borne a member of the family who has continually lived among his messy papers locked in his study.

Helsinki, November 1987   *Oiva Laaksonen*

Contents

5   Management During and After Mao

1 Introduction: The Management of the Colossus is Changing

1.1 Why Study Chinese Management?

During the history of the People's Republic of China, the management of enterprises as well as of government and of Communist Party (CPC) organizations has undergone great changes, reaching their culmination in the Cultural Revolution and afterwards under the administration which followed the late Chairman Mao Zedong. The main purpose of this book is to describe these changes and to analyze their causes and effects.

There are several reasons why knowledge of management in China is important in the comtemporary world. We shall mention four of them here.

1. From a practical and theoretical point of view, China during recent decades has been like a huge *management laboratory* where different kinds of management applications have been "tested" in huge natural environments. Some of them have been quite unique, like participation down the line, where managers work part of their time at shop-floor tasks with workers. These "experiments" have extended from strategic guidance and structure of organizations to leadership and motivation of employees. Although the Chinese societal environment differs considerably from that of many other countries, Chinese experiences can nevertheless throw more light on the great problem: how to manage organizations and people effectively and appropriately.

2. *Trade* with and within China presupposes knowledge of Chinese management, because managers of enterprises, government, and party organizations make the decisions about trade. Especially in the last few years the role of enterprise management has become more and more important. This is because according to the new economic reforms more decision-making power has been delegated to the enterprises, and many firms can now, although in a limited way, engage in international trade. China has moved towards a limited free-market system in order to activate the economic development of the country.

The purchasing power of a nation with one billion inhabitants can be enormous, and this has been observed by many countries, which are now trying to establish and develop trade relations with China. The country's economic development will probably be more rapid in the future, because

China has given up its earlier principle of not borrowing capital from abroad. The country has made large loan agreements, especially with Japan, to import modern technology. It should also be mentioned that China has large and versatile natural resources, which strengthen its position as a trade partner.

3. The political significance of the management of people who comprise one-fifth of he world's population should be mentioned. If China takes a more active role in *world politics,* its policies will have a great impact on the power balance of the entire world. This impact will be felt both in capitalist and socialist countries. The new Chinese "market socialism" will be especially important and interesting for other socialist countries,which are certainly following the impact of new Chinese management policies upon the economic, social, and political development of the country very carefully. Mao Zedong guided China towards a new socialism, developing, e.g., Marx's already old ideas about class designation and class struggle to better fit the changing situation in China. Mao's successors have again changed the content of socialism in their country.

4. The fourth reason to study Chinese management is the rapid *economic and cultural development* which has been characteristic of the People's Republic at least in comparison with other developing countries like India, for example. During quite a short period, the Chinese have succeeded in considerably reducing the illiteracy rate of the population as a whole, and also the standard of living has risen faster than on average in other developing countries. The improved standard of living has been brought about by the corresponding growth in the output of agricultural and industrial production. Chinese management in various fields has greatly contributed to these achievements. Thus, it is worth studying how Chinese management has functioned.

When one speaks about management in a capitalist country, one usually means management in industrial enterprises. However, in a socialist system enterprises do not act independently, but are strongly guided by party and government organizations. Enterprises, party, and government organizations at different levels form a tightly integrated entity. All the important strategic plans and decisions which the enterprises have to follow are (or have been) made at the central administrative top of the CPC and/or government. Thus, when one examines the management of China's economic organizations, one has also to study management in the CPC and the government.

The majority of Chinese people earn their living from agriculture and/or industrial and commercial organizations closely connected with agricultural production units. The share of the last-mentioned "side-line" industry forms a large part of China's total industrial production. Thus, we shall examine the management of rural organizations, in addition to the management of the CPC, government, and industrial enterprises, although our main focus is directed towards the latter.

During the history of the world different areas and countries have been at the center of development and worldwide interest. From the beginning of the Industrial Revolution succeeding centuries have been connected by researchers (McMillan 1985: 7; Macrae 1975) with special areas or countries where the development has been fastest or most advanced:

- British century 1775–1875
- American century 1875–1975
- Pacific century 1975–

Only some few years ago, of the East Asian countries of the Pacific Rim, usually only Japan, the two Koreas, Taiwan, Singapore, Malaysia, the Philippines, and Hong Kong, were mentioned; very seldom China. At present Japan is peaking, but there are already signs that China may be next.

1.2 Material of the Study

The material of this book has been collected by myself during four visits in China: the first during the Cultural Revolution in 1973, the second at the end of 1980 when the new rulers had already established their positions after Mao Zedong's death, and the third at the end of 1984, when the impact of the economic reforms could already be seen in the management of enterprises, CPC, and government agencies. While finishing the writing of this book, in the autumn of 1986, I was on my fourth journey to China as a visiting professor of international management at the University of International Business and Economics (UIBE) in Beijing. I could then test how well my descriptions, analyses, and interpretations, based on the material collected during my earlier visits to China fitted in with the situation in the country at the end of 1986.

During the first journey in 1973 I visited altogether 16 different organizations in Beijing, Guangzhou (Canton), Hongchow, and Shanghai. The organizations represented industry, commerce, agriculture, suborganizations of cities (street committees), and universities. The size and industry of those enterprise organizations which are included in the analysis of enterprise management are shown in Table 1.1.

I conducted the interviews in English with the help of a Chinese-English interpreter. Each interview took place in a group situation consisting of two to four persons where the main person interviewed usually represented top management. A person representing knowledge of organization and personnel matters was always present, because the firm had been informed beforehand that I would ask questions about the number of employees in different groups, salaries, social services, etc.

During my second journey to China in 1980 I visited 14 organizations, of which nine industrial enterprises are included in the data upon which the analysis of influence of different interest groups is based (Chapter 7). The firms were located in Beijing, Chongqing, Guangzhou, Yichang, Shanghai, and Wuhan. The size and industry of these enterprises appear in Table 1.1. The interview situations and the persons interviewed were very similar to those in 1973.

My third journey to China was made at the end of 1984. Then I visited 14 organisations, of which ten represented industry (Table 1.1), two universities, and two management training centers. The organizations were located in Beijing, Chongqing, Guangzhou, Shenzhen, and Wuhan. The interview situations were much the same as in 1980 and 1973.

Table 1.1. Size of enterprises according to number of employees, and type of industry

Number of employees	Number of enterprises		
	1973	1980	1984
200– 300	1	1	1
301– 1,000	1	1	1
1,001– 2,000	3	2	4
2,001–10,000	4	3	2
10,001–	1	2	2
All	10	9	10
Type of industry			
Metal and engineering	4	5	6
Textile industry	2	2	2
Other industry	4	2	2
All	10	9	10

During the beginning of my fourth visit to China, in the second half of 1986, which lasted five months, I was rereading the manuscript of this book, first, to make final corrections in my earlier descriptions and interpretations, and, second, to write the summary and concluding chapter based on my newest impressions of China right on the spot.

In going back to the empirical material I collected from Chinese firms during my earlier visits I should mention that the enterprises studied in

1973, 1980, or 1984 were not chosen at random, but by the Chinese authorities along the lines of my expressed wishes concerning the size and field of the firms. The enterprises were probably not the most "primitive" organizations in China with regard to technology and working conditions, but not all were the most modern either. Two of the enterprises included in 1973 were included in 1980, and four were the same in 1980 and 1984. Two of the same firms were studied during all three visits.

I must mention that the Chinese did not present any advance restrictions on my interviews in 1973, 1980, or 1984. They were very open. I had informed them beforehand only very generally that I intended to study the structure and management of Chinese enterprises. They did not require to see beforehand, e.g., my semistructured interview forms, nor did they, according to my understanding, control the content or results of my interviews before, during, or after the visits to the organizations.

My second source of material, in addition to my own interviews, has naturally been earlier studies concerning China, as well as other publications relevant for an understanding of the developments in this Far Eastern country.

Later on, in studying the influence of different interest groups upon decision-making in Chinese enterprises, the instruments used and the material collected concerning this special part of the analysis will be described in more detail. Then will follow a comparison of the decision-making of enterprises in China, Europe, and Japan.

1.3 Structure of the Book

This study is divided into seven main chapters. After this introductory chapter, there is in Chapter 2, "One billion human power units," a general description of the economic and societal environments in which the Chinese managers operate. The management of contemporary China is the heir of earlier generations. In Chapter 3, "Foundations of Chinese management: administration before Mao," we examine those periods of the history of China which it is believed have had great impact upon the nature of its present management practice. Thus, relevant aspects of "China of the emperors", briefly examine the early Chinese management thoughts and describe the storms of the short period of the republic.

In Chapter 4, "China in 1949: Mao's inheritance," the reader is offered a summary of the results of earlier developments in China which formed the basis and starting point for the new administration in 1949. To understand contemporary management practice in China it is important to have a picture of the elements upon which the present management has been built.

The main and largest chapter of the book is number 5, "Management during and after Mao." All the other chapters are in a way either supporting or concluding elements for this main chapter. It begins with an examination of the main stages of economic and political development of the People's Republic, and then studies management in government, the Communist Party, and also in agricultural organizations. The agricultural organizations are included in the study, first, because about 80% of Chinese live and work in these organizations and, second, because rural organizations, especially the people's communes, were like huge many-sided enterprises, engaged largely in industrial production and trade.

The management practice of the period of the "Cultural Revolution" is handled within the different subchapters. Originally I planned to describe the Cultural Revolution separately as one of the main chapters. However, when I proceeded with my writing I realized that this, although a special and turbulent period in the history of the People's Republic, actually was a continuation of earlier developments. The special management practices of that time, which the outside world has looked upon as being special features of just the Cultural Revolution, actually were nothing really new for Chinese communists. Mao and his colleagues had created many of the management practices, stamped in the West with the mark of the Cultural Revolution, already by the end of 1930s.

Because our main focus is management in industrial enterprises, quite a large part of Chapter 5 is devoted to management of industrial enterprises, first, during (section 5.5) and second after Mao (section 5.6). Chapter 5 ends with a description and analysis of the "opening the doors" policy of the People's Republic, which in practice terminated a period of separatism in China.

Chapter 6, "Chinese management in cross-national context: comparison with Europe and Japan," contains an analysis of the empirical material concerning the influence of different personnel and other interest groups of enterprises in the decision-making of firms. In addition to the European material, which includes 12 different countries, the Chinese material is also compared with data from Japan, Finland, and Sweden. We present in this chapter also the influence coalitions of enterprises in socialist China and capitalist Europe. In a way this chapter represents a summary, based on the empirical material, of the development of Chinese management after Mao. Chapter 7 contains the final summary and conclusions of the whole study. The chapter is divided into three parts: First, a summary is made of those developments during China's history which are believed to have had the greatest impact, on the one hand, upon the management practice of the next historical period and, on the other hand, upon contemporary Chinese management. Special focus is upon the management of enterprises. Second, the Chinese power struggle of the late 1980s is examined with the help of the theoretical frame presented in appendix. Third, those characteristics in Chinese management are pointed out which it is felt are in need of more research and elaboration in the future.

In appendix, "Concepts and instruments of analysis" beginning on page 339, we present a conceptual and theoretical frame, which we hope will help the reader to understand better what has happened in Chinese management during the last decades, and why. We have placed this chapter in the appendix firstly because many of the readers know well enough the concepts used and secondly we feel that a theoretical chapter at the beginning of the book would break up the presentation. In places in the text where we have used more of the concepts of our theoretical frame, we refer to this appendix.

I have to confess that it was difficult to find a satisfactory structure for this book because the deeper one studies this subject the more different aspects and historical events become important. For example, the period of the Cultural Revolution seemed at first to play quite a dominant role in China's recent history, but gradually, with more examination, this period melted down into a less dominant part of the entire stream of China's history.

The main "semaphore" in structuring this book has been Chinese management; how and why it has developed to its present stage. This requires not only studying management itself, but broadly also the factors that have affected it both historically and today. Managers may guide society, but society creates managers.

2 One Billion Human Power Units

In this chapter a general picture of the economic, cultural, and administrative environment in which Chinese managers act is presented in five parts: China's human resources, geography, economy, culture, and administration.

2.1 China's Human Resources

According to population, China is overwhelmingly the greatest country in the world. Its population reached 1,046 million in 1985; every fifth human being on our globe is Chinese. Although over 50 national minorities live in China, the country is nationally rather coherent, since 94% of the population belongs to the so-called Han nationality. The next greatest national group is the Zhuang tribe, comprising 13.4 million members, proportionally a small number in relation to China's whole population.

Although the Han tribe dominates in China, there are many dialects in the country. The people living in the north have great difficulty in understanding the Chinese from the southern part of the country. When I was interviewing in a Chinese enterprise in Guangzhou (Canton), in the southern part of the country in 1973, my Chinese-English interpreter, who was from the Beijing area, had to have a Chinese interpreter to translate from the Cantonese dialect into northern Chinese.

Some say that the main tribe of China, Han, has settled the same land longer than any other known nation. This has probably affected the national characteristics of the Chinese. The geography of China has both helped to protect its people and separated them from the other parts of the world. These factors have had great effect upon the development of the country and especially upon its economy. Traces of this separateness can still be seen in the management and structure of Chinese organizations.

China's growth to a nation of more than one billion inhabitants has created great problems. The national birth rate has, however, declined from 36 per thousand in 1949 to half this (17.5) in 1984 (Fig. 2.1). China is one of the very few developing countries which has really succeeded in its efforts to reduce the formerly ruinous birth rate by an effective birth control program. The grave population problem that existed in "old" China made

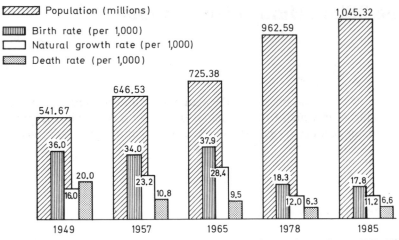

Fig. 2.1. China's population, birth rate, death rate, and natural growth rate 1949–1985. (*Beijing Review* (B.R.), January 1984; *China: A Statistical Survey in 1986*)

itself felt in massive unemployment in urban areas and in the impoverishment of the peasantry. It reduced the majority of the population to the level of starvation and poverty (Liu 1981: 7).

China's premier Zhao Zhiyang stated in his report at the Sixth National People's Congress in 1983 that

> "Stimulating production and improving the people's living standards both require that we continue to lay special stress on population control. This is our national policy, a policy of fundamental, strategic importance. We must persistently advocate late marriage and one child per couple, strictly control second births, prevent additional births by all means, earnestly carry out effective birth control measures and firmly protect infant girls and their mothers." (Zhao 1983: X–XII)

The statistics from the 10% sample survey of the third census in 1982 indicated that the median age of China's population was 22.9 years, which meant half of the population was below that age. From the age distribution of the two censuses (1953 and 1983) we can see that the proportion of children in the total population fell, while that of old people rose. In the 1982 census, 33.6% of the population was 14 years of age or younger. In the 1953 census the figure was 36.3% (B. R., January 16, 1984: 20–21/Population Census Office).

If and when the top of the Chinese age pyramid (Fig. 2.2) grows larger and thus the proportion of old people grows, the Chinese economy will have

Age distribution in the 1953 census

Age distribution in the 10% sample survey of the 1982 census

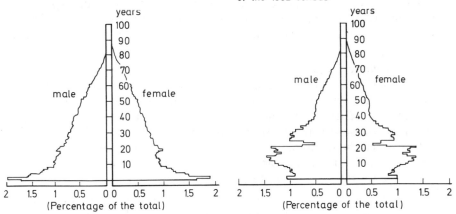

Fig. 2.2. Age distribution of China's population in 1953 and 1982. (B.R., January 1984: 20/ Population Census Office)

great problems, with the size of the active work force decreasing, and the number of old people who need support increasing. With time, this will also be felt in enterprise organizations and it could create serious personnel problems for management. The growing population of older people is also less educated and will be less successful in meeting the demands of, e.g., new and complicated technology. The ten years' period of the Cultural Revolution (1966–1976) still has a detrimental effect on the quality of human resources, because during that period higher education was practically stopped. Thus, one generation of potentially educated managers, now greatly needed, is in effect missing. This is one reason why the problem of management in contemporary China, which is striving towards the "four modernizations", is severe and acute.

2.2 China's Geography and Its Impact upon the Economy

China is according to area the third largest country in the world after the Soviet Union and Canada. China has a total land area of 9.6 million square kilometers, which makes the average density of population about 104 persons per km². However, the population is not evenly distributed all over the country.

It is estimated that 90% of the population lives in the eastern part of the country, which comprises only one-third of its total area. The reason for this uneven distribution is the topography of China. High in the west and low-lying in the east, China's topography varies from cloud-capped peaks to basins of varying shapes and sizes. Large deserts and wide expanses of grassland prevail over China's northwest, while rivers, canals and lakes criss-cross the extensive catchment area of the middle and lower reaches of the Changjiang (Yangtze River).

Because of the large mountainous area of the country only about 11% percent of China's total area is cultivated, and most of the cultivated area is located in the coastal region of the east and southeast. The bulk of the population is settled there, and it is estimated that the population density in that area is about 1,000 persons per km^2. It is also typical of the topography of China that the mountain ranges go from west to east, and although they become lower in the east near the sea they have been and still are a great hindrance to traffic in the north-south direction.

The topography of China has helped the isolation both of the whole country and of different parts of it. In the south and east the ocean has been an impassable obstacle to contacts with foreign nations until quite late in the history of China. In other words the distances, the location of the country, and its topography have prevented contacts with other great cultures of the world. In the border areas of China, no significant cultures which could have competed with the rich ancient Chinese culture developed. The sequestration and the high culture of the Han nation created a feeling of superiority in the ancient Chinese towards their neighbors and generally towards all non-Chinese people. This furthered the isolation of the country. The physical conditions of China have had and still have the following main impacts upon the economic system of the country:

1. The inclination to create independent, self-supporting economic units at all levels of the society
2. The great significance of water both in agriculture and in traffic
3. The dominating role of agriculture in the economy; the Chinese labor force is more than 400 million now, and of these about 300 million are engaged in agriculture (Liu 1981: 8)

It has been argued that the late Chairman Mao Zedong learned during the many years of the revolutionary fight to understand correctly the special natural characteristics of the country, in particular the special relation between the soil and man, and that he made good use of this understanding during the revolution and after it. These special physical conditions of the country still have a great impact upon the management of all of Chinese society and its organizations.

2.3 Economy

2.3.1 Changing the Course of Development

Although the Chinese consider their country a developing one, China has in some fields developed relatively advanced technology; e.g., space rockets, which are also used to launch foreign commercial satellites. The greatest hindrance to China's economic development is its technological backwardness in many areas in agriculture and industry as well as in transportation. The so-called Cultural Revolution during the years 1966–1976 meant ten years of stagnation, especially in the development of the nation's knowledge resources. During that time China followed the principle of developing everything itself, without relying on foreign technology and capital.

After Mao Zedong's death China changed its course completely in these matters; it is now inviting foreign experts to help in the country's various large development projects, and it now sends thousands of scholars and students abroad to study modern technology in every important field. China has opened its doors more widely also to foreign capital, and it encourages foreign firms to establish subsidiaries and joint ventures. For this China has created Special Economic Zones (SEZ), where foreign investors have an abundant variety of benefits and privileges.

It is relatively easy for China, although not unproblematic, to attract foreign investors and trading companies, because the country represents enormous potential purchasing power and it has rich natural resources.

2.3.2 China's Natural Resources and Production Capacity

China's most important natural resource is coal. The known coal reserves are about 1,500 billion tons; here China is third in the world after the Soviet Union and the USA. Most of the coal resources are located in the northern part of the country. China's iron reserves, which are also located in north China, are evaluated at 12 billion tons; thus, China possesses among the largest iron resources in the world (Fig. 2.3). China also has the world's greatest reserves of wolfram and antimony. There is also plenty of copper, manganese, and mercury in Chinese soil.

China's petroleum resources have been much discussed; the estimates are a little uncertain, but new wells have been constantly discovered since 1955, when the drilling of oil on a large scale began. China is now the world's seventh largest oil producer, after the Soviet Union, the USA, Saudi Arabia, Mexico, Iran, and Great Britain. But China is also the world's sixth

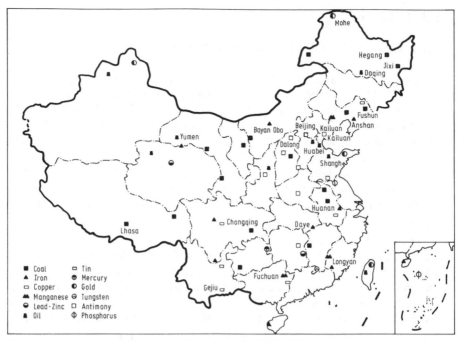

Fig. 2.3. The location of China's chief minerals. (Qi 1979: 116)

biggest oil consumer (*Time,* March 12, 1984: 42). China's oil needs are increasing more rapidly than is its domestic supply. According to one estimate, up to 30% of industrial capacity has been at a standstill between 1978 and 1984, mainly because of poor planning, but also because of inadequate energy supplies (*Time,* March 12, 1984: 42). To relieve its shortage of energy in September 1986 China signed a US$ 4 billion contract with foreign suppliers to build a nuclear power plant with two 900-megawatt reactors near Hong Kong (*China Daily,* (Ch. D.), September 24, 1986).

Table 2.1 shows the development of the production of major Chinese industrial products since 1949. It can be observed, that China has invested during the last 20 years in both energy production and in agricultural equipment, where light, so-called walking tractors play an important role. The demand for agricultural machinery has risen considerably during the past few years, because the relatively independent peasants are now allowed to buy agricultural machinery for themselves, and because they now often have enough money for this, thanks to the new contract-farming system.

Since the establishment of the People's Republic in 1949, China has tried especially to develop her heavy industry, although the focus has changed several times between agriculture, heavy and light industry during the last

Table 2.1. China's output of major industrial products in 1949, 1965, and 1985. (*China: A Statistical Survey in 1986*)

	1949	1965	1985
Coal (million tons)	32	232	872
Crude oil (million tons)	12	11.3	124.9
Natural gas (100 million m^3)	0.07	11.0	129.3
Pig iron (million tons)	0.2	10.8	43.8
Steel (million tons)	0.1	12.2	46.8
Rolled steel (million tons)	0.1	8.8	36.9
Electricity (100 million kwh)	43	676	4,107
– of which hydroelectric power contributes	7	104	924
Cars and trucks (units)	..	40,500	437,200
Tractors (over 20 HP; units)	..	9,600	45,000
Walking tractors (units)	..	3,600	822,500
Locomotives (units)	..	146	746

.. = No information

three decades (Table 2.2). The focus on heavy industry after 1949 was largely caused by the fact that the young People's Republic first strictly followed the Soviet development model, which stressed the importance of heavy industry. Now China tries to follow a more balanced development between agriculture, light industry, and heavy industry.

One of the main bottlenecks of China's economy is its transportation system. Although the volume of freight transport has grown considerably under the People's Republic, the different transportation networks have not grown sufficiently. For example the network of railways is still rather sparse. In 1949 it amounted to 22,000 km and in 1984, 52,000 km. Because of the geography and population of the country, the railways are mostly concentrated in the eastern and southeastern part of China. But also there the railway network is quite sparse; a great part of the country is altogether without railway connections (Fig. 2.4).

The inland navigable waterways have not been developed much either. Their length was 74,000 km in 1949, but had only grown to 109,000 by 1984. However, one major important improvement has been made in the waterways, with completion of the great new Getzhouba dam and locks on the Changjiang (Yangtze) river at Yichang at the beginning of the 1980s. Now the longest river in China is navigable from the sea-port of Shanghai up to Chongqing in central China.

Although the highway network is now more than ten times longer (927,000 km in 1984) than in 1949, it is far from good enough either quantitatively or qualitatively for the transportation needs of a quickly modernizing country (data from *China: A Statistical Survey in 1985*).

Table 2.2. Major figures of China's national economy, 1949–1985. (*China: A Statistical Survey in 1986; Statistical Yearbook of China 1985*)

Item	Unit	1949	1965	1978	1980	1985
Population	million	542	725	962	987	1,045
Workforce	million	–	287	399	419	499
Gross output value of agriculture	Index (1952 = 100)	67.4	137.1	229.6	259.1	451.5
Gross industrial output value	(1952 = 100)	40.8	452.9	1,601.6	1,888.9	3,147.5
– of which, light industry	(1952 = 100)	46.6	344.7	970.6	1,259.5	2,220.3
– of which, heavy industry	(1952 = 100)	30.3	651.0	2,780.4	3,036.4	4,808.8
National income	(1952 = 100)	60.8[a]	197.5	453.2	515.9	820.2
Volume of freight transport	100 million ton/kilo-meters	255	3,463	9,829	11,517	16,671
Total volume of imports	100 million yuan	21[b]	63.1	167.7	271.2	809.3
Total volume of exports	100 million yuan	2.0[b]	55.3	187.4	298.8	1,257.8

[a] Calculated from Ma 1983: 153
[b] Indicates 1950 figures (Ma 1983: 153)

Fig. 2.4. China's trunk railways. (Qi 1979: 137)

Although China sees itself as a developing country, its economy has developed better than most of the other developing countries. However, its per capita income is still low compared to other Pacific Asian countries (see Table 2.3).

2.3.3 Who Owns China's Industry?

One of the most important characteristics of socialism is that the means of production are owned by the people, or state. What is the situation in socialist China? In Table 2.4 we can see the development of the distribution of the output value of industry according to ownership.

It was natural that when the communists had won the civil war in 1949 the strategically important heavy industry was taken over by the state. Also other circumstances led in this direction, as we shall learn later. First, the proportion of state-owned industry grew rapidly until it reached its highest point in 1965; 90% of the output value of industries. After that the propor-

Table 2.3. Size of Pacific Asian economies, 1985. (*Asia 1987 Yearbook*)

	Population (million)	Per capita income (US$)	Merchandise exports (US$ m)	GNP real growth (%)
Australia	15.8	10,892	31,949	4.2[a]
China	1,050.0	220	31,300	12.3
Hong Kong	5.7	6,311	30,183	4.0
Indonesia	168.4	540	18,769	1.6[a]
Japan	121.5	8,316	175,638	4.2
North Korea	20.5	956	–	4.0
South Korea	43.3	1,954	26,441	5.1
Malaysia	15.8	1,574	14,460	– 1.5
Philippines	58.1	535	4,629	– 3.9
Singapore	2.6	5,847	22,800	– 2.1[a]
Taiwan	19.6	3,142	30.466	5.1
Thailand	52.8	579	7,065	4.1
Vietnam	62.0	..	646	..

[a] GDP (not GNP)

tion of collectively owned industrial enterprises began to grow constantly, until in 1984 it comprised 25% of the output value of industries. However, the collectively owned enterprises represent mostly small and medium-sized firms. It is interesting to note that the share of individually owned industry, which in 1949 was 23% and then dropped practically to zero for three decades, shows new although very small signs of life in 1986 (0.3 percent). This reflects the impact of the new economic reforms. If these tendencies go on, the share of individually and also privately owned industry will grow further.

The same trend appears in the growth after 1965 of retail sales for individually owned organizations as well as sales for peasants to nonagricultural residents (Fig. 2.5). In recent years China has decentralized 64,600 state-owned small commercial businesses by making them collectives or leasing them to individuals. This figure accounts for 75% of the country's state-run small enterprises (*China Daily* (Ch. D.), September 10, 1986). The retail sales of individually owned enterprises as well as those of collectively owned firms have steadily grown since the economic reforms made in 1978.

China has also made, especially in 1986, experiments among rural and township enterprises of issuing stocks which can be purchased by people both inside and outside an enterprise. The owners of stocks have the right to elect a board of directors, who select managers and set policy (Ch. D., September 20, 1986).

The changed proportions of different ownership forms in both production (Table 2.4) and retail sales (Fig. 2.5) show that China has in practice quite

Table 2.4. Changes in the form of ownership and output value of industries between 1949–1985; in percentages. (*Statistical Yearbook of China 1985; China: A Statistical Survey in 1986*)

Year	State-owned industry	Collectively owned industry	Joint state-private industry[a]	Privately owned industry	Individually owned industry	Other economic units	Total
1949	26.2	0.5	1.6	48.7	23.0		100.0
1965	90.1	9.9					100.0
1978	80.8	19.2					100.0
1980	78.7	20.7				0.6	100.0
1985	70.4	27.7			0.4	1.5	100.0

[a] The new joint ventures between Chinese and foreign enterprises are not included

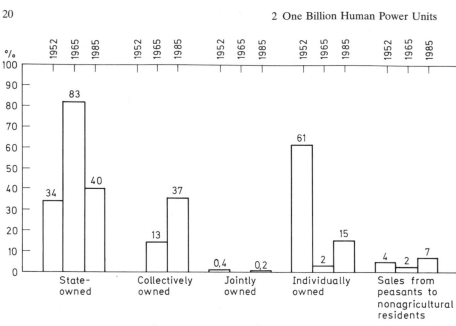

Fig. 2.5. Development of the value of retail sales according to ownership in 1952, 1965, and 1985; percentages. (*China: A Statistical Survey in 1986*)

largely realized her economic reforms since Mao. These changes in the ownership structure of China's economy will have great impact upon the management of enterprises.

To summarize China's economic conditions, the country has great human and natural resources. All this can give its leaders challenging targets at both the macro- and microlevels. China is still one of the developing countries, but it also has the advantage of being a late developer; it does not need to make all the same errors as the more industrialized countries have made.

Chinese managers are eager to develop their organizations especially now that the new top administration has given more autonomy and decision-making power to the enterprise organizations. But the managers are now also responsible of the efficiency and economic results of their organizations. In this striving for efficiency lies also a great danger, which is already well-known in practice in the more industrialized countries, namely pollution.

Until recent times Chinese enterprise managers have not thought too much about the consequences of rapid, "free" economic growth. But now the Chinese have suddenly become aware that their water, air, and soil are becoming rapidly and severely polluted. Very soon the Chinese authorities will have to give strict instructions limiting the pollution caused especially by the expanding industry. Already now all the great rivers are badly polluted. The official statistics show that every day Chinese cities let nearly 80 million cubic meters of untreated waste water into the water-courses. The situation is worst in Shanghai. This city cleans only 200,000 cubic meters of water of the five million cubic meters of waste water (*Helsingin Sanomat,* December 22, 1983).

Pollution is one of the great problems of contemporary Chinese managers on their way to greater economic growth. Other problems of the future will probably be caused by the management of human resources. As the ultimate goal of economic growth is to raise the living and cultural standards of the people, their needs and demands will change rapidly along with development. These new needs and demands require a new leadership style and guiding instruments of Chinese managers who must, however, take into account the special characteristics of China's culture. Not everything can be imported as such from the more industrialized countries, such as Japan and the USA. Luckily the Chinese top leaders have realized this, at least in their official speeches.

2.4 Culture

While organizations should satisfy the needs of their environments, i.e. match them, these organizations are the products of their environments, their societal and institutional settings, in other words, of the culture of the society. The managers of the organizations are mediators of the culture from earlier generations to the management, structure, and behavior of oragnizations. Mao Zedong and his administration managed however, in a few decades to change the ideology and institutions of China's society along the ideological lines created in nineteenth century Europe to an extent that foreign missionaries had dreamed of in vain.

Although Chinese institutional settings are now very different from those prevailing in pre-1949, the old values and behavioral norms cannot be wiped out in one generation. In recent years much research applying the so-called cultural approach to the study of organization and management has shown the importance and durability of so-called cultural variables (Lammers and Hickson 1979: 14, 402–416).

2.4.1 The Concept of Culture

Culture in the social sciences is a somewhat ambiguous concept. Many researchers use the terms culture and society synonymously, whereas others prefer to reserve the concept "culture" for patterns of roles and norms embedded in certain paramount values (Lammers and Hickson 1979: 6, 402–416; Kroeber and Parsons 1958: 582–583).

According to Kluckhohn (1951):

> Culture consists in patterned ways of thinking, feeling and reacting, acquired and transmitted mainly by symbols, constituting the distinctive achievements of human groups, including their embodiments in artifacts; the essential core of culture consists of traditional (i.e. historically derived and selected) ideas and especially their attached values.

Hofstede (1980: 25) gives the following condensed definition of culture as "the collective programming of the mind which distinguishes the members of one human group from another." According to this not only values and norms, etc., but also institutions, which further the individuals' and groups' programming of their minds in a certain way, belong to culture. In this sense especially the educational institutions play a crucial role.

2.4.2 Education

The educational level of the people has a great impact both upon the quality of managers and upon the quality of managed human resources. These again form the base of the development of the country.

One of the first and most important tasks of the government of the People's Republic of China created in 1949 was to develop the educational institutions. Before 1949, over 80% of the whole population was illiterate, while in the rural areas the illiteracy rate was over 95% (Qi 1979: 167). First, the government tried to give primary education for as many as possible, e.g., there were special campaigns for adults in factories and rural areas to teach them to read and write. Secondary and higher education was developed largely according to foreign, especially Soviet, patterns. Results were quick and favorable: in 1952 about 60% of school-age children were in school. In 1976, 96% of the nation's school-age children were enrolled, compared to about 20% in pre-1949 China; and 68% of primary school graduates have now the chance to continue their education in the junior middle schools (Qi 1979).

The Chinese state, however, that primary education has not yet been altogether popularized, thus permitting many school-age children, particularly girls, to drop out of the required elementary courses.

> This, in turn, leaves many young people and middle-aged illiterate or semi-literate. Furthermore, the quality of education in the rural areas

is generally low, with only 60 percent of the primary school graduates reaching the set standards. (Dai in B. R., May 12, 1986)

In his report to the Sixth National People's Congress, China's Premier Zhao Ziyang stressed the development of intellectual resources and culture, with emphasis on the promotion of education, science, and technology. This, he said, "is a prerequisite for invigorating China's economy" (B. R., June 20, 1983: 16). According to the five-year plan, enrollment in regular colleges and universities is to rise from 315,000 in 1982 to 550,000 in 1987, a 75% jump in those five years (B. R., July 4, 1983: XVII).

Most university courses last four years. University education is free and students with economic difficulties are provided grants by the state. Postgraduate study is also encouraged and can vary from two to four years in length (Qi 1979: 174).

In Fig. 2.6 it can be seen that the Chinese have, after the economic reforms were decided in 1978, really invested strongly in technical education (secondary technical schools) and higher education in universities and colleges. In later chapters we shall examine education in China in more detail.

The knowledge base of management personnel is among the most important factors affecting the efficiency of organizations and the development of the entire society. The training of Chinese leaders has long roots.

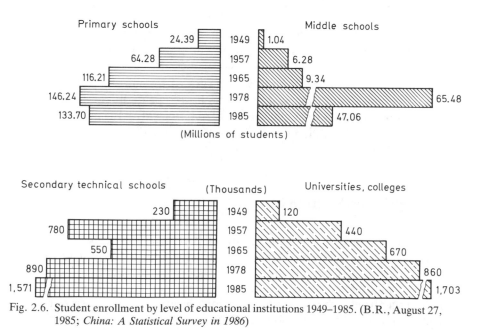

Fig. 2.6. Student enrollment by level of educational institutions 1949–1985. (B.R., August 27, 1985; *China: A Statistical Survey in 1986*)

They go back in Chinese history to the Tang dynasty (618–907 A. D.), because during that time the so-called Imperial Hanlin Academy was gradually developed, and the systematic training of civil servants was put on a permanent basis according to the philosophy of Confucius. This training system of Chinese civil servants lasted uniformly until 1905, when the examinations qualifying a person for an appointment to a public office were abolished. This damaged the status of civil servants and considerably lowered the qualitative level of local administrations (Lui 1981).

After 1949 the CPC administration established special schools for cadres of the party, in order to train them both in ideological matters and in management, especially of the party organization.

During the Cultural Revolution, from 1966 to 1976, there was a long period of stagnation in all higher education in China, but after the death of Mao Zedong the new wielders of power began rapidly to develop it. This also covered managers of industrial and government organizations.

The China Enterprise Management Association (CEMA) has especially concentrated on the training of managers of enterprise organizations all over the country. It has created abundant international contacts in the field of management training. Many foreign management training experts have visited and lectured in China: from European countries, the USA, and especially Japan. As Japanese culture is much nearer the Chinese than the Western cultures of Europe and the USA, and as Japan is geographically much closer to China, it is quite natural that the Chinese have leaned considerably on the Japanese when training their managers. Of course the Japanese do not do this quite unselfishly; they are very interested in getting involved in Chinese economic development programs.

However, the Chinese are very well aware of foreign interests and their bases, and moreover Chinese top leaders have repeatedly stated that China should not swallow everything offered from abroad. Also in management China has tried to apply new methods gradually and with careful advance experiments.

2.4.3 Religious Values in China

Religion has always been an important part of a country's culture. The values represented by a religion can develop into a forceful ideological power if the values belonging to the religion are so deeply rooted in the minds of individuals that this value system does not only act passively, helping actors to choose suitable options in exchange processes, but becomes an active force, a resource which can be used for certain purposes.

What kind of role has religion played in China? The earlier China has been described as a country of three different religions or philosophies: the ideas of Confucianism, Buddhism and Taoism. These religions have been living side by side in China for 2000 years. Confucianism and Taoism are of Chinese origin, while Buddhism has been brought in from India.

Although all the religions mentioned have had their own supporters, the great majority of Chinese people earlier satisfied their spiritual needs from all three religions. According to a Chinese proverb: "the three religions are one family"; they represent three different ways to the same goal. Confucianism, which mainly focuses on practical problems, has left plenty of room for the mysticism of Taoism and for the metaphysical ideas of Buddhism (Saarilahti 1960: 52–53). Thus, in old China the three "religions" formed together a kind of unity, a people's religion, which covered about 85% of the population. Because of this melting together of the main religious or philosophical thoughts, it has been difficult to produce any reliable statistics about the division of the Chinese between different religions. At any rate, it has been estimated that about 5% of the population is Moslem, while Roman Catholics are about 0.4% and Protestants about 0.07%.

The most characteristic feature of the Chinese religions has been the respect for and worship of ancestors. The hierarchically organized family played an important role in ancient China, and this still affects Chinese organizational behavior. The old and men have been most respected; females have been in an inferior position.

The revolution of 1949 changed the religious circumstances in China considerably. The Confucian temples were taken over by the state and the Buddhist monks were transferred to practical, productive work.

The worship of ancestors has been said to be the most common old religious feature which has prevailed most stubbornly in the new circumstances. In practical life the prominent status of men and old age have prevailed. This comes out clearly in the age and sex distribution of the top persons in the Chinese government and CPC hierarchy.

We can suppose that the old traditional values still play their special role in Chinese management. Values which have grown over a period of some 2,000 years cannot be wiped out in one generation. But this problem will be considered in more detail later on.

2.5 Administration

2.5.1 State Administration

As the main purpose of this book is to describe and analyze management in China both at the societal and organizational level, especially in enterprises, we shall here only briefly describe the main features of the state and CPC administration in China.

According to Article 1 of the Constitution of 1982:

> The People's Republic of China is a socialist state under the people's democratic dictatorship led by the working class and based on the alliance of workers and peasants.

According to Article 2:

> All power in the People's Republic of China belongs to the people. The organs through which the people exercise state power are the National People's Congress and the local people's congresses at different levels.

The National People's Congress is elected for a term of five years. It is composed of deputies elected by the people's congresses of the provinces, autonomous regions, and municipalities directly under the central government, and by the People's Liberation Army.

The composition of the Fifth National People's Congress, held in 1979, was as follows (in percent): workers, 26.7; peasants, 20.6; soldiers, 14.4; revolutionary cadres, 13.4; intellectuals, 15.0; patriotic personages, 8.9; returned overseas Chinese, 1.0.

There were altogether 3,497 deputies. Women deputies made up 21.2%. Minority nationality deputies accounted for 10.9%, with every minority nationality having its own deputies (Qi 1979; 46–47).

China is divided for administrative purposes into 21 provinces, 5 autonomous regions, and 3 municipalities, with Beijing, Shanghai and Tianjin, directly under the central government (Fig. 2.7). The administrative units under a province or autonomous region include cities, autonomous prefectures, counties, and autonomous counties. The total number of counties in China exceeds 2,000 (Qi 1979: 2–3).

The State Council, that is, the Central People's Government, is the executive highest organ of state power. It is responsible and accountable to the National People's Congress, or, when the Congress is not in session, to its Standing Committee. On the local level there are local people's congresses

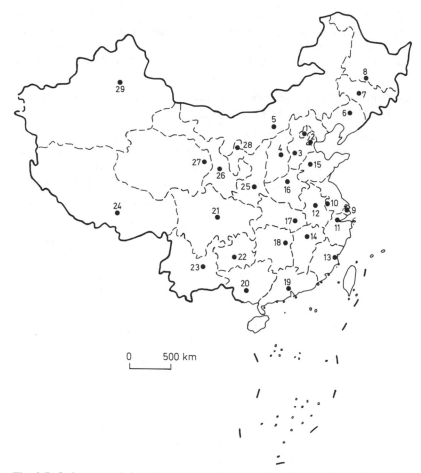

Fig. 2.7. Index map of the administrative division of the People's Republic of China. (*Administrative Division of the People's Republic of China* 1980: 1–3)

which represent state power, while the local people's government is their executive organ as well as there being other local organs of state administration.

2.5.2 CPC Administration

In a socialist country with a mainly one-party system, the state administrative organization gives only a part of the picture showing the administration and decision-making power of the country. The party, in China the Communist Party of China (CPC), plays a role whose impact extends to nearly every part of the life both of organizations and individuals. The significance of the party has changed to some extent since the communist revolution of 1949, but it has always been a dominant power in the People's Republic of China.

The Constitution of the State adopted during the Cultural Revolution in January 1975 stated in Article 2:

> The Communist Party of China is the core of leadership of the whole Chinese people. The working class exercises leadership over the state through its vanguard, the Communist Party of China. Marxism-Leninism – Mao Tsetung thought is the theoretical basis guiding the thinking of our nation.

In the new Constitution adopted in December 1982 there is no mention of the Communist Party in corresponding general principles of the Constitution. In a way the mention of the party is compensated indirectly by an enlargement of Article 1, which says:

> The People's Republic of China is a Socialist state under the people's democratic dictatorship led by the working class and based on the alliance of workers and peasants. The socialist system is the basic system of the People's Republic of China.

We can characterize the organizational system of the CPC as follows according to Article 10 of the Constitution of the CPC adopted by the Twelfth National Congress of the Communist Party of China in September 1982:

> The Party is an integral body organized under its program and Constitution, on the principle of democratic centralism . . . The basic principles of the democratic centralism as practiced by the Party are as follows:

> 1. Individual Party members are subordinate to the Party organization, the minority is subordinate to the majority, the lower Party organizations are subordinate to the higher Party Organizations, and all the constituent organizations and members of the party are subordinate to the National Congress and the Central Committee of the Party . . .

> 3. The highest leading body of the Party is the National Congress and the Central Committee elected by it. The leading bodies of local party organizations are the party congresses at their respective levels and the party committees elected by them. Party committees are responsible, and report their work, to the party congresses at their respective levels.

In China two parallel, hierarchical administrative structures, that of the state and of the CPC; run through the whole society from the highest societal top to the bottom of the microlevel organizations (Fig. 2.8). The two administrative lines are bound tightly together with many personal and organizational ties.

It is thus clear that CPC membership is a very important factor in the career of an individual, and especially of a manager in China, because the different party organizational units often make the final decision (or acceptance) concerning a nomination to an important vacancy in government, CPC, and enterprise organizations. To become a member of the CPC is not an automatic process, as membership is limited and requires a certain screening process. The number of members of the CPC has grown gradually, and was in 1986 44 million, or some 6% of the adult population.

The power relations between the government and CPC administrative systems have often changed during the history of the People's Republic. However, the most profound changes have occurred in recent years, when it has been decided that the CPC, government, and enterprise administration shall be separated. This decision, which greatly decreases the power of the

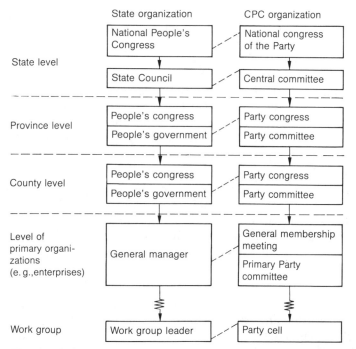

Fig. 2.8. The two administrative structures guiding the People's Republic of China

party, has already had profound effects upon the management of China's enterprise, state, and CPC organizations. The impact of this decision, concerning the limiting of the decision-making arena of the Communist Party, may in the course of time also have great effects upon the international environment of China.

2.6 Summary and Conclusions

The environments where the Chinese managers have to act offer both great possibilities and profound problems. China's human resources, with over one billion inhabitants, contain huge reserves of unused talent, while presenting a great employment problem for the future. The tremendous concentration of the population in the eastern and southeastern part of the country creates a state of imbalance in China as a whole.

The Chinese have succeeded surprisingly well with their birth control efforts, but one may ask what the effects will be in the long run: the age pyramid of the population will become dangerously "heavy" in its upper, old-age part.

According to area, China is the third largest country in the world. The country's topography varies very much, and because of the large mountainous area only about 11% of its total area is cultivated. The topography has contributed to the isolation both of the whole country and of different parts of it. The physical conditions have the following main impacts upon the economic system of the country: (1) The inclination to create independent economic units; (2) the great significance of water both in agriculture and transportation and (3) the dominant role of agriculture in the economy.

China's natural resources are rich. The most important of them is coal, but China also possesses iron ore resources which are among the largest in the world, as well as many other valuable minerals. The country's oil resources, partly still unidentified, are probably large. A major problem is caused by the fact that a great part of China's mineral resources is located in faraway areas in the western part of the country. Also the poor level of its own technology and lack of capital prevent the efficient use of China's rich natural resources.

China defines itself as a developing country. Its economy is quite unevenly developed. On the one hand, the country has created nuclear weapons and sent its own rockets into space, but, on the other hand, one can observe great backwardness both in urban and rural areas. After 1949 China began especially to develop its heavy industry, but during the past 30 years it has changed its focus more to agriculture and light industry. The main bottle-necks of China's economy are in its energy and transportation system.

Typically, for a socialist country, state-ownership dominates in industry, but during the past decade the share of collectively owned enterprises has grown considerably, and also individually owned industrial firms are now appearing in the picture again.

With regard to education, China's greatest problem in 1949 was her high rate of illiteracy, but the country succeeded surprisingly well in her primary education during the first decades of the Peoples Republic. Later on China has especially invested in secondary and recently in higher education. One of the main bottlenecks in China's modernization aspirations, however, has been the low educational level of the country's managers. Extensive train-ing programs have been created to strengthen the knowledge-resources of managers. In this area the China Enterprise Management Association (CEMA) with its wide network has done great work.

The value-environment in which Chinese managers function includes the legacy of the three old religions or philosophies: the ideas of Buddhism, Taoism, and most effectively, Confucianism. The main traditional values consist of worship of ancestors and the hierarchically organized family, with old people and men being most respected. The revolution of 1949 brought a new political ideology to the country, while the old traditional values still play their special role in Chinese management.

In China's administrative system we can also see traces of its history. China is largely organized geographically in the same way into provinces, prefec-tures, and counties as during the time of the emperors. The formally high-est state organ is the National People's Congress, which elects the members of the State Council, the executive highest organ of state power. Local people's congresses and correspondingly local people's governments repre-sent state power at the local level.

In China two parallel, hierarchical administrative structures, that of the state and of the CPC, run through the entire society. The Communist Party of China extends its influence to almost every part of the life both of organizations and individuals. Every medium-size and larger organizational unit contains also a unit of the party organization, which especially earlier controlled the operational management of the organization; this is also in the case in enterprises. Now, however, China's leaders have decided to separate CPC, government, and enterprise administration. This decision strengthens greatly the decision-making power of enterprise managers, and while it also profoundly lessens the power of the party, it can have unfore-seen consequences both for the whole of China and its international envi-ronment.

3 Foundations of Chinese Management: Administration Before Mao

In order to understand the characteristics of contemporary Chinese management we have to examine its roots: the socioeconomic history of China. The purpose here is not to try to give a whole picture of Chinese history, but to examine especially those factors which have affected Chinese management during and since the era of Mao Zedong, or since 1949.

3.1 China of the Emperors

3.1.1 Ancient Socioeconomic Developments

The oldest discovered Chinese culture existed along the Huanghe (Yellow) River. Approximately 5,000 years ago the tribes of the Huanghe and Changjiang (Yangtze) River valleys gradually entered the era of the patriarchal clan commune. During this time the people still lived under a primitive communal system with collective ownership and sharing, and the clans were held together by blood ties.

> The patriarchal clan commune represented a transitional social stage between primitive communal and slave society. Private ownership, polarization between rich and poor, class division, and the possession of slaves all made their appearance in the patriarchal clan commune period. (Bai 1982: 49)

From graves found by archeologists we learn that women were already in a subordinate position to males. For example, at the Huangniangniangtai site one joint adult grave was discovered containing one male and two females. The male lay face upward in the middle with a female on either side; both females lay on their sides facing the male with limbs bent, the lower limbs behind them and their two hands in front of their faces (Bai 1982: 49–51). Thus, the subordinate position of females, which has had throughout the centuries a great effect upon society and management – because half of the population was not according to the societal values "capable" of filling management positions – has really long roots.

The cultural unity of China was created during the so-called Shang dynasty (ca. 16th–11th century B. C.). It was during this period that historical records became consciously and systematically written instead of being spontaneous and fragmentary. "This was made possible by the emergence of two essential conditions, a written script and a calendar, during the Shang Dynasty" (Bai 1982: 62).

The state power of the Shang dynasty was exercised by the emperor and the slave-owning nobility. The emperors of the Shang dynasty were assisted by ministers and vice-ministers. Other officials with religious functions were the shamans, the recorders, and the diviners. Actually some of the ministers were also religious officials. Others took charge of military affairs, production, etc. "The numerous official posts were mostly hereditary for members of noble families" (Bai 1982: 68).

From the point of view of management ideology the third Chinese dynasty, Zhou, is important, because during that dynasty several important Chinese philosophical thinkers like Confucius, Mo Zi, and Lao Zi lived. In the beginning of the Zhou dynasty, which lasted about 900 years from 1,100–221 B. C., the slave system was well-developed. The king, vassals, and high officials owned slaves of different status and under different names and forced them to create wealth for them. The slave-owners held power and were also dominant economically (Bai 1982: 83).

The increase of productivity in agriculture which was largely caused by the newly invented farming tools gradually changed the nature of productive forces and the societal structure. The slave system gave place to feudalism. The slaves who had been engaged in collective farming were replaced as laborers by peasants each working on his own. The inadequate manpower resulting from the escape of slaves worried the slave-owners during the late stage of slave society. Land lay waste in many areas owing to the shortage of manpower. Under these circumstances slave-owners were compelled to give up the practice of using slave labor, as they realized that it was more advantageous to employ individual peasants.

Being relatively independent, the peasant could permanently cultivate his land according to his knowledge and energy. This gave birth to the concept of the family as a productive unit.

The individual peasant had two distinct features. First, he was tied to the land, unlike the relationship between slaves and land. Second, an individual family, where the husband tilled and the wife wove, became known as a "household" or a productive unit. All this further increased the peasants' dependence on the land (Bai 1982: 105). However, most of the land was owned either by the emperor or the landlords.

Thus, gradually some princes and dukes changed from slave-owners to landlords. Most of them acquired land through grants as a reward for their military deeds. Some of the individual peasants could also become land-lords. In places where land could be traded, merchants might also become landlords. Different landlords occupied different political and social positions. Such ranks were merely a reflection of different grades of land ownership. After its inception, feudal landownership in China always represented a hierarchy (Bai 1982: 106).

The hierarchy in landownership was, in order of importance, composed of the following strata when the system had reached its maturity in China in the first centuries A. D.:

1. The emperor was the supreme landowner and embodied a unity of land-ownership and political power.
2. The landed aristocrats with hereditary titles were next to the emperor; each of them had a feudal estate embracing a great number of house-holds.
3. The landowner of powerful families included the descendants of the nobility and influential local families.
4. The mercantile landowners generally got rich by branching out into the commerce of the handicraft industry (Bai 1982: 168–172).

The economic situation of peasants was difficult during that time. In addition to paying the agricultural tax in grain and different kinds of poll tax, peasants in the so-called Qin-Han period had to perform corvée and military service.

The growth of feudal relations in this period (ca. 206 B. C. to 220 A. D.) brought together people who were scattered over wide areas and who spoke more or less the same language and enhanced their national consciousness closer in economic life. It was under these historical conditions that the Han nationality came into existence (Bai 1982: 172–173). During the Han dynasties (ca. 206 B. C.–220 A. D.) the unity of China was for the first time really established.

Clan System

An institution which has had a great impact upon the practice and thinking of Chinese management is the clan system, which was composed of gentry families.

The clans developed gradually into closed, hierarchical systems, which set up rules of behavior and procedure to regulate all affairs to the clan and its branches without the necessity of asking the state to interfere in case of conflict. A new development of this period was the clan estates: Clans began to set apart special plots of land as clan land. The incomes of these clan estates were used for the benefit of the whole clan. They were controlled by clan-appointed managers and had tax-free status, guaranteed by the government, which regarded them as welfare institutions. "Technically, they might better be called corporations because they were similar in structure to some of our industrial corporations" (Eberhard 1977: 215).

The income of the clan estate was to be used also to secure a minimum of support for every clan member and his own family, so that no member could ever fall into utter poverty. Clan schools, which were run by income from clan estates, were established to guarantee an education for the members of the clan, again in order to make sure that the clan could remain a part of the élite.

Many clans gradually developed under the leadership of skillful and clever heads to become large economic and administrative systems. For example, in 1062 the chief house of the C'hen clan controlled more than 334 manors, all of which had their own branch families. The main house of the clan took care of contacts with the government concerning taxation, or special grants which a poor clan could obtain from the government (Eberhard 1962: 207).

A large clan needed an efficient management system to survive. One of the family members was nominated the head of the chief house of the clan and another the assistant head. They took care of the management of the clan estates (e.g., the measurement of the fields, permissions for business transactions) and decided rewards and punishments concerning behavior of clan members. In practice, the head of the chief house was like a little king, and he had also to be a good politician to be successful.

Responsible persons were nominated for all the main activities of the clan. There were special persons, elected because of their knowledge of finances, who kept books concerning the incomes and expenses of the clan. They also handled rewards and punishments, took care of official and private businesses, as well as of taxation and agreements of the clan (Eberhard 1962: 206–211). Along with the development of the clan system, the power of the family head gradually increased. "He was now regarded as owner of the property, not only mere administrator of family property. He got power over the life and death of his children" (Eberhard 1977: 206).

As a whole the clan institution strengthened the traditional Chinese hierarchical family system, where the father, the family head, had the top status, followed by the older sons. At the bottom of the family hierarchy were the females, mother and younger sisters. These old values at least indirectly still affect the behavior of individuals and organizations in contemporary China. The importance of the feudal period in Chinese history lies in the fact that this societal system remained to a high degree unchanging in China until our century. During this time the seed was sown for the revolution of 1949 and the complete changing of the societal and management system of the country. The seed lay in the growing dissatisfaction of the peasants: They had no, or very little, cultivated land of their own. The peasant was forced to become a tenant, and part of the crop, usually half of it, sometimes even more, was fixed as ground rent. In addition to this the small peasants had to pay different kinds of taxes and also to do extra work for their landlords. Units of different armies also often confiscated the peasants' products.

The peasants often had to face further adversities in the form of long dry seasons and heavy floods, by turn, which destroyed the crops. Swarms of grasshoppers could suddenly appear, destroying a crop which had seemed promising. Thus, the majority of agricultural population lived constantly on the brink of mere subsistence level, and was only just able to produce and feed a new generation.

This situation lasted until the present century, when Mao Zedong very cleverly used the dissatisfaction of hundreds of years in making the Chinese revolution, which gave birth to contemporary China in 1949.

3.1.2 Early Chinese Management Thoughts

Chinese philosophical thinking, which also contained management ideas, began to develop strongly during the Zhou Dynasty (1,100–221 B.C.). During that period, the "One Hundred Schools of Thought" flourished, four of which, Confucianism, Mohism, Legalism, and Taoism, were extensively studied and firmly established.

Confucius was the philosopher of ancient China who most affected the thinking and administrative behavior of later periods. His ideas have frequently been both condemned and praised, but they are still very much alive. Especially during the period of the Cultural Revolution (1966–1976) the ideas of Confucius were heavily criticized, but after the death of Mao Zedong the situation changed altogether, and in 1985 a special institute was founded in Beijing for the study of Confucian thought (B. R., August 26, 1985: 10).

The great problems of the time of Confucius (ca. 551–497 B.C.) were governmental. There were the questions of how to govern, to maintain order in the society, and how to guarantee happiness and prosperity for the people. Confucius' solution was that both the rulers and the ruled should be educated. Governing is in the first place education and training, and the ruler should first educate himself and govern with the help of virtues.

Confucius held that men were alike in nature, a teaching that was contrary to the basic concept of a slave society where social status was preordained. Speaking about politics, Confucius proposed that good and capable people should be appointed to official posts, a proposal that was contrary to the practice of hereditary rule. He emphasized the importance of benevolence and regarded it as the highest ideal of morality. But Confucius stressed also that benevolence should be practiced within the strict boundary of rites (Bai 1982: 110–111).

Confucius did not believe that noble status was preordained, but he defended the hierarchy of the nobility. He advocated the elevation of good and capable people, but he never raised objection to the official hereditary system, even advising good and capable men to be satisfied with their poverty and lowly position. Confucius saw a world in which harmony could best be achieved by everyone recognizing his place in the world. With sons obeying their fathers and subjects following the lead of the powerful, he thought there would be order and peace. In a way he legitimated the strong hierarchical order (power) which dominated in the family and in the whole society of his time. Traces of his thinking could be seen also in the People's Republic, where people were designated to special hierarchical groups by the new communist rulers after 1949. The new hierarchical pyramid was, however, set upside down, so that the poor peasants and workers came to the top and the former landlords and their descendants to the bottom.

A later Chinese school of thought which also had great influence was the school of Mohism founded by Mo Zi. He advocated universal love, the love for all without discrimination. In politics Mo Zi believed that people with ability should be elevated; he was opposed to inherited wealth or nobility. He said that a man with ability should become a government official even though he might be a lowly peasant or an ordinary worker. This was different from the ideas of Confucius, who did not clearly oppose the hereditary system in officialdom (Bai 1982: 112).

Mencius, who lived about 100 years after Confucius, gave further idealistic content to the ideas of the latter. The basis for Mencius' theory of a government by benevolence was that man was born with goodness. Man possessed the inherent qualities of benevolence, righteousness, propriety, and wisdom, which some people were able to preserve, others not. In Mencius' view every sovereign was able to rule by a policy of benevolence, and every citizen was able to accept it. Both the rulers and the ruled were able to be good (Bai 1982: 116).

If we compare these ideas, presented more than 2,000 years ago, with contemporary management thinking, we see here the same way of thinking as in the so-called X and Y theories of management. Theory Y emphasizes the positive sides of human nature. People are generally good and like to work and be active; supervisory methods should recognize this and offer their employees an opportunity for self-actualization (McGregor 1960).

A school of thinking which had a strong impact upon earlier management thinking in China was the Legalist school. During the beginning of the Zhou Dynasty the society was regulated by rites which ordered the life of the aristocracy, and by general laws which controlled the life of the peasants. When the fight between different states became more and more fierce, every state needed a strong, centralized governmental system. Precise and written laws, defining the rights and obligations of individuals, became necessary. According to Confucius the power of the ruler was based on benevolence. While, on the contrary, the Legalists believed that the ruler must rule through the law (norm power). If the law was followed correctly, order would exist in the society, and the benevolence of the ruler would not affect the situation in any way.

The Legalists taught also that the ruler should be given a status of authority, that the law could be applied in practice. Without the absolute power of the ruler the law had no meaning. The authority of the ruler was given to him by the aristocracy and the common people. Thus, in administration the Legalists considered it important to use together norm power (laws), hierarchical power, and the personal power of the ruler, the emperor. The form of using norm power, influencing, was generally coercion.

During the time of the Legalists the bureaucratic administrative system was also developing. Eberhard stresses (1977) that "Every feudal system harbours some seeds of a bureaucratic system of administration." When the administrative system had begun to develop, terms like "district" or "prefecture" began to appear, indicating that areas under a bureaucratic administration existed beside and inside areas under feudal rule. This process was sponsored by the representatives of the Legalist school, which was best adapted to the new economic and social situation (Eberhard 1977: 61).

The philosophy of the Legalist school was effectively applied in practice especially in the Qin province, which unified the country 221 B.C. and thus became the first feudal empire of China.

The Chinese imperial system, structured on the model of a vast bureaucracy, was intended to provide a strong central administration, whose authority extended through regional and local governments to the village level. Through periods of turbulence and stability, the Chinese bureaucracy managed to retain certain features common to other bureaucracies: the absoluteness of authority, hierarchy in structure, and rigidity in operation.

Administrative authority was exercised through a complex network of administrative units, clearly prescribed by offices and titles, and rigidly interpreted by a large body of law, codes, and decrees. Structurally, the central authority maintained a dedicated but elaborate organization, which provided a strong executive, policy-planning mechanism and a large central administration based on functional specialization. Chancellors (administrators of civil and military affairs) and secretaries (chiefs of staff of personnel and confidential matters) acted as the emperor's chief advisors. To provide for policy planning and debate, there were the political affairs council and cabinet meetings, where policy discussions and debates were held periodically. The ministries, or boards, were the line organizations which implemented the policies in six areas: personnel, finance, rites, war, justice, and public works.

Once the central authority was estasblished, detailed administration was left in the hands of the bureaucracy. One of its prime concerns was the establishment of a civil service system. This consisted of an education system for training civil servants, a public examination system for recruitment, a merit system for promotion, and minute regulations on classification, salary, and rotation.

Besides the training of civil servants in ancient China the general personnel management function was important. It was administered by the board of personnel, which office was responsible for appointment, dismissal, promotion, and discipline of civil officials. Position titles, salaries, and personnel records were carefully prescribed and kept (Chang 1976: 73).

The Chinese administrative tradition placed great emphasis on man. The Confucian idea of "government of man" was generally acknowledged in contrast to the Western idea of "government by law," which gives primacy to law over man. One of the most important tasks of management was to discover and develop "the rare commodity of administrative talent." According to the thinking of the time of the Legalists there were

> two levels of administrators: the virtuous (Hsien) and the talented (Ts'ai). Virtuous administrators were exceptional; they were intellectually superior, knowledgeable about both the past and the present, and were masters of strategy. Talented administrators were proven, experienced, and gifted. Thus, the virtuous were sought and the talented were nurtured. (Chang 1976: 73)

Management thought in early China was largely confined to governmental administration including the army and was conditioned by Chinese culture and ideology. Administrative strategy had deep philosophical roots and a broad application in China. It was a way of thinking, applied to politics, administration, and warfare. One of the most important Chinese strategists was Sun Tzu, who wrote the Art of War, said to have been used by leaders of the People's Republic of China in our time (Eberhard 1977: 64).

As the people who led the army during war and the government administration during peace were partly the same persons or in close contact with each other, the same strategic management principles were largely applied in peace and war. According to the writings of Sun Tzu the supreme aim of war was "Not to win one hundred victories in one hundred battles" but to "subdue the enemy without fighting." In competition either in politics or business, strategy should be aimed at disposing one's resources in such an overwhelming fashion that the outcome of the competition is determined before it gets started. This refers closely to the concept of covert power, and especially to he unconscious covert power dealt with in Appendix. In practice, the process of strategy-making accentuated assessment, calculations, planning, and execution.

> In military strategies, for example, there were five fundamental factors: the government, the environment, the terrain, the command, and the doctrine. Strategists studied these five factors to assess chances of success, and calculate their strengths and weaknesses vis-à-vis that of their opponents... Deception, speed, and concentration of forces were the rules of war. (Chang 1976: 74)

We can see that these principles of strategies of war can well be applied to a great extent to the strategic thinking of contemporary business management.

The person of the Legalist school who particularly dealt with management in his writings was Han Fei, who died in 233 B. C. He had studied especially political history, and made a political proposal for the purpose of strengthening feudal rule, a proposal that combined the use of law, tactics, and power. "Law", enacted by the monarch, consisted of written regulations whereby the people were subjected to his rule. "Tactics" were the means by which the monarch governed his citizens. In addition to law and tactics power was necessary. Power meant the monarch's supreme authority, which alone could make law and tactics effective. All three – law, tactics, and power – were indispensable tools for the monarchy. Han Fei proposed that all power should be concentrated in the hands of the monarch, who would then use a combination of the three to govern the people effectively (Bai 1982: 121).

In his writings concerning management, Han Fei noted four principles: (1) management by standards, (2) management of people, (3) organizational practices, and (4) prevention of usurpation.

1. *Management by standards.* Although "government of man" was the cardinal rule of administration, man must be safeguarded against arbitrary rule and self-seeking temptation. Law, rule-making, punishment and reward, responsibility, and accountability were the safeguards. Whereas law

and rule-making were to regulate conduct, punishment and reward were used as incentives to produce performance. Responsibility and accountability provided the means to achieve order and control. Rulers were advised to use plans and standards to induce and measure performance. Deeds not words, results not promises alone were the rules of management.

2. *Management of people.* This was based on the dual concepts of planning and controlling. The function of the chief executive was to plan strategy and to control people. Measurement of performance against rules and standards provided administrative safeguards. But control over the behavior of subordinates took precedence, for an absolute ruler needed to be particularly alert to the temptation his subordinates might have to usurp power.

3. *Organizational practices.* Authority was maintained through the application of law and punishment and reward was the fundamental principle. Law was to rectify conduct, punishment and reward were to safeguard authority. In structure, organization must be formed within clearly established boundaries. Departmental responsibilities and position descriptions must be rigidly prescribed; Jurisdictional encroachment was not to be tolerated. Administrative systems and official rankings were stringent in order to ensure proper delegation of authority and maintenance of order. Personnel appointments were made on qualifications, and promotion was given on merit. Within the bureaucracy, promotion and rotation were to follow the principle of promotion through the rank and file (Chang 1976: 75–76).

4. *Usurpation of power.* During the time of the Legalists to whom Han Fei also belonged, the political situation was very unsteady in China. There were many competing states and all of them were afraid of usurpation. "Like Machiavelli, he chose statecraft to prevent its occurrence and advised the use of ruthless means to eliminate usurpers" (Chang 1976: 76).

Many of Han Fei's principles of management are still deeply rooted, especially in the administration of state and communal offices. We must remember, as has been said before, that early Chinese management thoughts were mainly based on experiences obtained in public administration.

In this context we must describe the institution, the Hanlin Academy, which had a profound effect upon the training and career paths of the highest Chinese public servants for more than 1,000 years.

3.1.3 Hanlin Academy

The origin of the Hanlin Academy can be traced to the creation, in the Tang dynasty (618–907 A. D.), of a compartment situated inside the imperial palace precinct. Members of the compartment could be former heads of government departments or as low as junior officials, while for some time even farmers and scholars who made a name for themselves were invited to serve.

Under the Song dynasty (960–1279 A. D.) the posts of Hanlin readers and expositors were created to take charge of the classical and historical discussions with the emperor. This development marked the beginning of the extension of the Hanlin officials' influence into the literary and educational fields. It was under the Ming dynasty (1368–1644) that the Hanlin Academy received the name by which it is now known. Besides the compartment inside the inner court of the imperial palace, the Hanlin Academy now acquired its own building within the capital (Lui 1981: 1–3).

Under the Ming dynasty the Hanlin Academy became a fully developed government institution. The functions of the Hanlin members became more varied and included also those relating to the civil service examinations (Lui 1981: 3).

During the Ming-Qing period (1368–1911) the academy was not only the highest academic center, but it also served as a reservoir for potential senior ministers of the government. The staff members of the academy at no time numbered more than 200, yet from among them the majority of the Chinese grand secretaries and first-rank officials were recruited.

As industry and trade were little developed during those earlier times, the main area of management was in public administration. The Hanlin Academy has thus been a unique institution in training management for future high government officials. Its close contact with the emperor also made it a career path of the highest importance.

The uniqueness of Hanlin was in its long life, the limited number of its scholars (maximum 200 at a time), and close contacts to the highest top of the hierarchy as teaching and advisory body to the emperor. The activities of the Hanlin Academy lasted until its abolition in 1906. It had functioned as an independent institution from 1670, but, as mentioned, its origin can be traced back to the time of the Tang dynasty (618–907 A. D.). With the abolition of the Hanlin Academy in 1906, the long tradition of the training of civil servants with entrance examinations died also.

The Chinese traditional system of training and developing civil servants has had a profound positive impact upon public management. After its abolition at the beginning of the twentieth century the quality of local government and also the status of civil servants sank considerably in the society. This development probably made it easier later for the communists to take over in 1949. The government administration structure had become corrupt and weak without appropriate training and self-respect.

As we have noticed, the early management philosophy was mainly based on experience and training in the area of public administration. In the next section we shall examine the framework, the government administrative structure, in which this experience was gained.

3.1.4 China's Government Structure During the Imperial Period

China's long tradition of state administration is quite well documented. We know that from the beginning of the China of the emperors the imperial government was comprised of two parts: (1) the central government, located in the capital city, whose offices guided and controlled the whole country, and (2) local government administration, whose responsibility was limited to particular areas (Loewe 1965: 150–151). The same division still exists in the present Constitution of the People's Republic. Article 3 of the Constitution, "The Structure of the State", is divided into (1) the institutions of central government and (2) local people's government (Constitution of the PRC adopted by the Fifth National People's Congress (NPC), December 4, 1984). The contemporary local governments are divided into provinces and prefectures as in ancient China.

In imperial China there were two principal methods of governing the country: (1) the feudal and (2) the provincial system. The former contained an investiture of certain rights and responsibilities over defined areas, usually given to the members of the imperial family. They were in a way subordinated directly to the emperor rather than to the organizations of central government.

Under the provincial system the central government had appointed governors as salaried officials to administer defined areas, provinces. These governors were subordinated to the offices to the central government, which could replace them (Loewe 1965: 166). Gradually the provincial system became dominant − as early as with the establishment of the Qin dynasty (221 B. C.) − because it had certain advantages. For example, the system was flexible, because the size and number of provinces could be altered without seriously affecting the structure and functioning of the whole government system.

The provinces were divided into prefectures, and their senior official, called a magistrate, was the lowest official level of government administration to whom formal power of decision could be delegated. Local leaders of the country districts, e.g., members of the gentry families acted in the capacity of advisory elders capable of bringing considerable influence to bear in the community. Natural leaders of the villages acquired positions of honor and respect, without being recognized as men who held salaried posts; and they assisted the magistrates by compelling their flock to obey his orders and by reinforcing the rule of custom on which Chinese government so relied (Loewe 1965: 168–170).

Since the Chinese empire consisted during some periods of several hundreds of provinces, many of them located far away, sometimes a six or seven-weeks journey from the headquarters of the central government, it was not easy for the latter to keep the necessary contact with the distant provincial officials. These could easily become too independent, and use the great political and economic power, e.g., money, grain, arms, and manpower, of the area for their own interests.

To avoid this kind of misbehavior, as early as 106 B. C., the central government created a special system of inspection. The central government appointed some dozen independent officials as inspectors whose task was to ensure that the officials of local governments followed the norms and orders of the central government, and discharged their duties efficiently. For the purpose of inspection, the country was divided into larger units comprising several provinces under the control of particular inspectors.

In China there has always been the great problem of how to hold the different parts of the large country together. In imperial China the instrument of cohesion was the system of inspection; in Mao's China it was the powerful network of the Communist Party which had special commissions and commissioners for disciplinary inspection. The contemporary CPC has the same system.

Thus, the first great administrative problem of ancient as well as present China is how much power the central government can give to local administrative bodies, or to put it briefly: the problem of centralization or decentralization of decision-making power.

The second main problem of the imperial government was the difficulty of recruiting capable persons to serve the state. This often led to hiring foreign experts and professionals. This problem, hundreds of years old, exists again in comtemporary China, in its endeavor to develop its economy and management with foreign experts' know-how.

The third great problem of imperial China was that more attention was paid to form than to substance in government administration. It has been said that the old excessive training of civil servants led to strong conservatism, prohibiting innovative behavior. Because of the strict authoritarian bureaucracy, the civil servants did not dare to suggest to their superiors the kind of radical measures often needed to adjust the management of the country to the changing environment (Loewe 1965: 181–183).

Figure 3.1 presents the imperial government structure at the end of the Ming dynasty (1368–1644). The head of the state was, of course, the em-

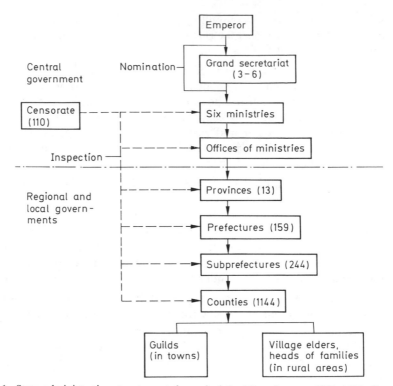

Fig. 3.1. State administrative structure at the end of the Ming dynasty, 1368–1644. (Loewe
1965: 159–179)

peror. His power was largely based on his privilege to select and appoint
the senior ministers of state. Directly under the emperor was the grand
secretariat, which consisted of between three and six grand secretaries, who
assisted the emperor in managing the six ministries. These were:
1. The ministry of personnel, responsible for appointments, records of service, and evaluation of performance
2. The ministry of revenue, which comprised 13 offices, each responsible of
   one province; the offices had the following sections: population and
   census, general accounts, special accounts, and granaries
3. The ministry of rites, responsible for ceremonies, sacrifices, reception of
   visitors, and provisions
4. The ministry of war, which had four offices: the first was responsible for
   appointment of officers, the second for supervision of operations, the
   third for equipment, and the fourth for military supplies
5. The ministry of justice
6. The ministry of works, responsible for schemes for construction, con-

scription of manpower for state service, manufacture of equipment for the government, land and water communications, and standardization of weights and measures

The censorate was an inspection unit controlling government in all parts of the empire. The power of the censorate was great, because it was in a position to criticize the activities of senior state servants and even the emperor himself (Loewe 1965: 159–160).

The basic unit of local government was the province. It was divided during different dynasties into one or more subordinate levels, prefectures, sub-prefectures, and counties, e.g., during the Ming dynasty.

At the lowest, grassroots level of administration, the government relied considerably on unofficial or semiofficial organizations such as the village leaders and heads of families. Thus, the old Chinese value system, within and between families, based on the power of the father over other family members and on respect for age, acted as an efficient, far-reaching unofficial instrument of the government at the grassroots level.

When the communists later tried to abolish the old Confucian value system, they had to create something to replace it. To a great extent the replacing (compensating) system was the CPC network and its ideology, which extended everywhere.

China had lived for over 1,000 years in a closed system, with very few influences from outside. However, the situation changed when Europeans began to move to the Far East. With the Europeans gradually came industrialization, and new enterprise organizations enlarged the concept of management in China.

3.1.5 European Invasion of China

There had been occasional contacts between China and Europe from ancient times, but during the thirteenth century, when the Yuan dynasty of the Mongols ruled China, a closer contact between China and the Western countries developed. During that time Marco Polo made his famous journey to China and received important offices from Kublai, the grandson of Tsingis-Kan; he acted inter alia as a governor of one province.

In 1516 the Portuguese came to the port of Guangzhou (Canton), and later received the right to establish a colony there. At the end of the same century tea and porcelain were exported to Europe. The Chinese tried, however, to keep themselves separate and forbade the Spanish, Dutch, and British to trade in China; the citizens of these countries were not allowed to settle in China.

European capitalism began in the nineteenth century to invade China. The Western industrialized countries had reached the situation where their industrialization process could no longer go deeper, but had to expand horizontally. The huge Chinese nation and its culture had earlier succeeded in absorbing foreign invaders, but the new Western invaders seemed to be superior. The Chinese rulers tried to limit contacts with Westerners, so that, for instance, foreign trade was concentrated in only one port, Guangzhou.

During the nineteenth century the British, Russian, German, French, Japanese, and American armies and navies threatened China. The Chinese rulers of that time had to accept their demands and were forced to underwrite many humiliating agreements. During that time the opium trade also developed, causing China many difficulties.

At the end of the nineteenth century the viceroys of northern and southern China began to develop the country according to the European model. Railways were built, the postal service was modernized, and industrial enterprises were established. But this modernization process was interrupted by a shortage of capital and the resistance of the people. In addition, a war broke out with Japan, which was competing with China over the supremacy of Korea.

Defeat in the war against Japan and the serious partition crisis caused by foreign forces awakened the Chinese people, and in 1898 bourgeois reformists initiated a modernization movement for reform and national revival. A wave of establishing factories swept the whole country after the Sino-Japanese War.

> Between 1895 and 1898, more than 50 enterprises, including textile mills, filatures, flour mills and other light industry, were established by Chinese merchants, their capital of about 12 million yuan exceeding the total Chinese investments in the twenty years prior to the Sino-Japanese War. (Bai 1982: 475–476)

The reformists thought that if China would learn from the West the foreign powers would give up their aggressive schemes. But the reformists were isolated from peasants and other lower classes, and when a heavy drought occurred in China in 1900 the Boxer Rebellion broke out. The Boxers were mainly composed of peasants. During the Boxer Rebellion railways were destroyed, mission stations were burned down, and missionaries as well as Chinese Christians were killed. When the German ambassador to China, von Ketteler, was killed and the Chinese began to attack the legation quarter in Beijing, a 20,000-strong eight-power allied force was sent to Beijing, and foreign troops were placed at several points between Beijing and the sea. Foreign countries, especially Russia, Japan, and Great Britain, tried in competition with each other to take advantage of the weakness of China. According to the changing political balance they sometimes attacked China, sometimes fought with each other, and sometimes allied again.

At the beginning of the twentieth century modernization was beginning again in China, but it developed so slowly that dissatisfaction grew in the country. The growing dissatisfaction was also caused by the reactionary rule of the Dowager Empress Tzǔ Hsi, who is still regarded as responsible for the sufferings that China had to experience for half a century. Together with the Empress Lü in the early Han period, and the Empress Wu in the Tang era, she became the symbol of evil: What would become of a country under the rule of a woman? This may well be one of the reasons why still so few women are in high positions and recognized as capable in the People's China (Eberhard 1977: 312). In contemporary China these memories and stories may have helped to remove the "Gang of Four" from power after Mao Zedong's death, because its leader was supposed to be Mao's widow, Jiang Qing.

The Empress Tzǔ Hsi died in 1908, but before her death she had assassinated the captive Emperor Te Tsung. As the latter had no children, she nominated the two-year-old prince Pu Yi as emperor on the day of her death. When the Chinese realized that a child was to reign and a new regency to act for him, and when they also remembered all the failures that had been made in domestic and foreign policy, revolutionary thoughts were strengthened.

The undisputed leader of the revolutionaries was Sun Yat-sen. As a young Chinese physician who had been living abroad he took on after 1898 the leadership of the reformist movement mentioned earlier, the leader of which, Khang Yo-wei, went to Europe after his failure to lead the movement.

The revolutionary movement had been split into many different groups. Sun Yat-sen and other "group leaders" realized that the situation required a national, unified political party to lead the revolutionary movement. As a result of this development Sun Yat-sen succeeded with the help of other revolutionary leaders in amalgamating part of the membership of different revolutionary organizations to form the Chinese Revolutionary League in Tokyo in August 1905.

Sun Yat-sen who was elected president of the League, wrote in its published program the following "Three People's Principles": (1) The principle of nationalism was to overthrow the government of the Manchu aristocracy, the elite group around the emperor; (2) the principle of democracy was to overthrow the monarchical autocratic system and establish a republican government; and (3) the principle of people's livelihood was to appraise and fix land prices that would result from the development of the social economy after the revolution, and gradually allow the state to purchase land from landowners (Bai 1982: 496). These principles belonged to a political program by means of which the Chinese bourgeois hoped to establish a republic and to develop a capitalist economic system according to the European and American model.

After many attempts to overthrow the imperial regime, the revolutionaries at last succeeded in 1911. The revolutionary groups of Hubei province, which had contacts with the Chinese Revolutionary League, persuaded some of the emperor's soldiers, who were located in the city of Wuhan, to rise in rebellion and occupy the city. The revolt spread quickly over the whole country, and on December 29, 1911 the establishment of the Republic of China was proclaimed in Nanjing; Sun Yat-sen was elected its president.

Meanwhile the chief of the imperial army, General Yuan Shikai, tried fruitlessly to suppress the uprising. When he realized that he could not succeed, Yuan Shikai told the imperial house that the monarchy could no longer be defended because his troops were too unreliable. He induced the government to issue an edict on February 12, 1912, in which they renounced the throne of China and declared the republic to be the constitutional form of the state. On the news of the abdication of the imperial regime, Sun Yat-sen resigned in Nanjing and recommended Yuan Shikai as president. He was forced to do this because the latter was backed by the army, and many of Yuan Shikai's supporters had infiltrated the groups around Sun Yat-sen.

The revolution of 1911 had defeated the Qing dynasty, which had ruled China for more than 260 years. The revolution also ended the monarchical feudal system which China had had for over 3,000 years. However, although the form of government was changed, not much was changed in the life of the lower social classes. China continued as a semicolonial and semifeudal state. Foreign powers interfered constantly in Chinese internal affairs, and tried to benefit from the chaotic situation of the country. China's future looked very turbulent when it entered the period of the Republic.

3.2 Storms of the Republic

The history of China during the Republic from 1912 until 1949 is very turbulent, full of external and internal wars and campaigns of different groups of power in this huge but during that period, internally weak country. In the analysis of this period, those historical events have been selected that had a decisive impact upon the formation of the new societal system as it appeared after 1949, and in addition attention will be focused on those events which affected the Chinese future management system and economic development.

The industrialization process which had begun much earlier in Europe gradually found its way to China. It has been estimated that in 1870 there were barely 10,000 industrial workers in the country. Their number grew to between 500,000 and 600,000 before the 1911 revolution, and it had increased to more than two million by 1919. China's industry was mostly concentrated in mines, railways, and textiles, match, cigarette, and steamship enterprises. These were mostly located in a dozen or more large cities such as Shanghai, Wuhan, Tianjin, Guangzhou, Qingdao, Dalian, and Harbin. It has been estimated that in Shanghai alone there were 300,000 to 400,000 industrial workers.

This high degree of concentration of industry was typical of China, and was important from the point of view of the possibility of Chinese industrial workers to form power alliances and unite at a comparatively early stage. This concentration of industrial workers had its special impact upon the development of the Chinese communist movement later on (Bai 1982: 523).

As mentioned earlier, the great Western countries had tried to take advantage of the weakness of China, but none of them could have tried to occupy the whole of China because of their mutual rivalry and jealousy. The Second World War, which absorbed the energy and resources of the fighting Western powers in Europe, gave China a breather and offered its national industry a chance to grow. To the same degree as the European powers withdrew from China and stopped exporting commodities to the country, China's industry and handicrafts grew. Chinese export of wheat, cotton yarn, and textiles grew so much that China was close to reaching a balance in its foreign trade. At the same time, many new industrial enterprises were established.

But this peaceful time did not last long. When the Japanese realized that the European states were fully occupied with their war in Europe, they tried to use the situation to their advantage. During the First World War they presented China in 1915 with the so-called twenty-one demands to make China a Japanese colony. In this situation, in order to avoid the Japanese threat, China joined the Allied forces in the First World War, and in this way came to be on the winners' side at the end of the War. China expected the Peace Talks in Versailles to give the country economic and political independence. But these hopes were fruitless; Japan was given the former German possessions in China, and the Chinese demands were not even included on the agenda of the conference.

Meanwhile things had begun to happen in Russia in 1917. "The salvoes of the October Revolution brought us Marxism-Leninism" wrote Mao Zedong (Mao 1977: IV, 413). Because of the success of the Russian October Revolution, Chinese intellectuals began to study Marxist ideas and the process of revolution in Russia. Its success gave some groups new hope of solving the turbulent situation in China.

On May 4, 1919, students of the National University in Beijing demonstrated against the government and their pro-Japanese adherents. When the police attacked the students and put some in jail, the demonstrations and students' strike spread all over the country and resulted in a general boycott of Japanese imports. Some university professors also gave their strong support to these events, known as the "Movement of May Fourth." It has been said that this movement awakened in the Chinese workers a feeling of their own potential power, and the ideas of Marx as well as the thoughts developed in the Soviet Union during and after the revolution of October 1917 spread all over China.

Later Mao Zedong wrote that the following characteristics were typical of the Movement of May Fourth:

1. The strikes organized because of the movement were purely political; there were no demands for higher wages. This was an indication of high political awareness.
2. The merchants, shopkeepers, and other small capitalists helped the movement financially and also took part in the demonstrations with students and workers. In this way a uniform front was formed, based on a multiclass movement.
3. The Movement of May Fourth showed that a great and powerful mass action could develop in China. (Hultcrantz et al. 1974: 14)

The Movement of May Fourth was important because, owing to the great power of this action, Mao Zedong's ideas about the mass-line strategy began to develop. These thoughts were still more strengthened by the peasants' revolts in 1925–1927. The mass line strategy was later one of the main factors leading to the successful revolution in 1949 which created the People's Republic of China. The mass line stratey had a great impact later on also upon management at the macro-, meso- and microlevel.

One can also say that the Movement of May Fourth had a great impact upon the founding of the Communist Party of China in July 1921. Then twelve men came together in a school in Shanghai. One of them was a young library assistant, Mao Zedong. The new party had from the beginning two wings: The one adhered to the Western communist program, which said that a revolution must to be led by the urban proletariat — though at that time only Shanghai had so many industrial workers that it could form a "proletariat" group. The other wing held that without the help of the peasants, who were the vast majority of all Chinese, no revolution could succeed, an idea which Mao Zedong later accepted (Eberhard 1977: 325).

The new Communist Party of China began to organize the working class. The secretariat of the Chinese Workers Union was established. Schools for workers were established, and Marxist classical works were published in the Chinese language. The labor movement was developing fast: in 1922 there were more than 100 strikes all over China, and the number of workers involved was about 300,000. But the working class at that time was relatively small; it had little more than two million workers. However, it became the most politically conscious group in China, because it was heavily exploited by the often foreign owner-managers of industry, and it was working during that time with quite advanced production technology.

The workers mostly came from rural areas and were descendants of poor peasants. The working class then had close ties with the peasant class. This became a very important factor for the later development of China towards a socialist revolution because the working class was so small that it would have been impossible for them to win with only their own resources (Hultcranz et al. 1974: 15–16).

The political development of China during the three decades before the victory of the communists in 1949 was very turbulent. At the time of the establishing of the Communist Party of China in the early 1920s, Sun Yatsen changed the former Chinese Revolutionary League to the National People's Party, generally called Guomindang. Twenty years earlier, Sun Yat-sen had published the well-known three principles for development already mentioned: (1) nationalism, (2) democracy, and (3) people's livelihood. He now presented the way in which China could realize these three principles: cooperation with the Soviet Union, cooperation with the Communist Party of China, and support for the movement of workers and peasants. On this basis it would be possible to unite the forces of the two parties.

The status and power of the Communist Party changed markedly. In 1925 the number of party members grew tenfold, up to 10,000, and at the beginning of 1927 the number of members was 57,000. The number of workers who joined the workers' union was nearly three million. The movement spread out also to the rural areas, especially in the province of Hunan. At the end of 1926 more than one million peasants had organized themselves in peasants' associations in Hunan (Franzen 1977: 32).

Especially Mao Zedong was very enthusiastic about this strong development of the revolutionary forces both among industrial workers and peasants. But not all were satisfied with the revolutionary wave, which seemed to go on very strongly. Among the People's Party (Guomindang) there were powerful groups representing the owner class, and they were really uneasy because of the direction of the development. Especially after the death of Sun Yat-sen in 1925 their power apparently increased, and Chiang Kai-shek became their leader. He had succeeded in becoming the commander-in-chief of the National Revolutionary Army.

Meanwhile the generals of the different armies in northern and central China were fighting for power. The People's Party, under Chiang Kai-shek and with the support of the communists, began a great war against the north in July 1926. At first they had success. When Chiang Kai-shek reached the gates of Shanghai with his southern army, he had to make an important decision which meant choosing between two alternatives. As mentioned earlier, there were two wings in the People's Party: left and right. Should the party and the army follow the ideas of the leftists, the great capitalists of Shanghai would suffer expropriation as would the gentry. If Chiang Kai-shek should form an alliance with the capitalists, limits would be set to the expropriation of landed estates.

However, Chiang Kai-shek, through his marriage with Sun Yat-sen's wife's sister, had become allied with one of the greatest banking families in the country. Before attacking Shanghai, Chiang Kai-shek decided, after discussions with his closest colleagues, to ally himself with the capitalists. Because of this, Shanghai fell into his hands without struggle, and the rich Shanghai capitalists as well as foreign capitalists began to finance his troops and his administration.

The important decision of Chiang Kai-shek and his friends to ally with the capitalists did not remain unopposed. The communist left group formed a rival government in Hankow, while Chiang Kai-shek placed his government in Nanjing. This location was a strategic decision, because the bulk of China's young industry lay in the same Changjiang River (Yangtze) region, and that region was also the center of the agricultural production of the country.

After Chiang Kai-shek's troops had executed thousands of communists in Shanghai in 1927 and attacked them in other places, Mao Zedong went to Hunan province with his supporters and established the first units of a peasants' and workers' army. In the mountains of Chingkang on the boundary between Hunan and Jiangxi provinces, a revolutionary base area was established. This area was gradually enlarged, and other similar base areas were established in various parts of the country. A central government for these areas was formed.

In the territories occupied by communists the land was divided in a new way among the agricultural people, and collective activity was encouraged on a large scale. In 1933 there were more than 1,000 collectives, following the Soviet model, in Jiangxi alone. It has been said that in these areas unemployment, the opium trade, prostitution, child slavery, and compulsory marriage were eliminated. Also the living standard of the poor peasants was greatly improved in these areas.

Mass education was very lively in these quite peaceful areas, and in some places the communists succeeded in raising literacy in the countryside to the highest level in centuries (Franzén 1977: 35).

3.2.1 The Long March

In the following the so-called Long March is described in some detail, because it was decisive for the communists victory and thus for the establishing of the People's Republic of China. The experience "collected" during this famous march also had a great impact on China's later management practices.

Thus began the Long March, which lasted 368 days. During this time the Red Army marched 12,500 km. It went through 12 provinces, over 18 suggested an alliance against the Japanese to Chiang Kai-shek, but Chiang wanted first to crush the communists. In danger of having to fight Chiang Kai-shek's army on one side and the Japanese on the other, Mao Zedong with his army decided to leave their basic areas in southern China and move to the north, where they would be safer from the threat of Chiang Kai-shek's army and could fight against the Japanese occupying troops.

Thus began the Long March, which lasted 368 days. During this time the Red Army marched 12,500 km. It went through 12 provinces, over 18 mountain ranges, and 24 rivers. The average distance of one day's march was nearly 40 km. The Red Army reached its new base area in Yan'an in the province of Shaanxi in October 1935. In Shaanxi there was already a communist base area, established in 1933. The communists had created their own economic system with its special banking system and postal service in the area. Land reform had been accomplished, and cooperatives had been established.

Mao Zedong used the Long March for propaganda purposes on behalf of the communist movement very skillfully. During the March, meetings were held in cities and villages, and theater performances were given. The communists explained to the people their view about the necessity of revolution, and tried to create favorable contacts between the Red Army and the local people. The peasants and other ordinary people had now seen the

Red Army, the soldiers of which were friendly towards them. This was something new for the people who had learned always to be afraid of soldiers.

At the same time the Red Army gave weapons to thousands of peasants and left its own personnel to train new Red partisans. These again tied down a great part of Chiang Kai-shek's troops with their guerilla activities (Franzén 1977: 35–371).

During the long fighting Mao Zedong had summed up his experiences and come to the conclusion that in China communists had to follow a different fighting strategy from that applied in capitalist countries: first, occupy the cities, and after that attack the rural areas. The only way for the communists, according to Mao, was to establish strong rural revolutionary bases, then surround the cities from the countryside, and finally capture the cities (Qi 1979: 38).

The Long March was not only important because it saved the communist army from being crossed by Chiang Kai-shek's troops; during the march the Red Army came into contact with millions of Chinese − peasants and urban people − and taught them their ideology. The communists also showed in practice the kind of land reform and other social changes they would apply if they gained power in the country.

In the liberated areas the communists really did accomplish great social reforms. The profiteers no longer had the opportunity for speculation based on the poor situation of the peasants. The latter could now borrow money from the government at low interest rates. The land of the landlords was divided up, but they themselves could have as much land as they could cultivate "with their own hands." Many large estates were owned at that time by government officials, tax collectors, and absentee landlords. The land of these people was confiscated and divided among poor peasants and families who owned no land at all.

The peasants formed mutual-aid groups, cultivated larger areas together, and divided cattle and farming implements among themselves. Small industrial cooperatives were established, and trade was handled by cooperatives and not by speculators. In villages the peasants elected their own representatives to the so-called soviets, and those who had had it worst − tenants, rural workers, partisans, etc. − now had the majority in these collective units.

During the Long March the communists, as earlier mentioned, gave the peasants weapons and taught them to use them. Everywhere Mao Zedong's army sowed a revolutionary seed, which could begin to grow when the circumstances would become favorable. Later on during the fight with

Chiang Kai-shek's army, Mao Zedong's communist troops could harvest what had been sown earlier.

For communists the only strategy to fight and win was guerilla warfare, because both the Japanese and Chiang Kai-shek's armies outnumbered them and the Japanese were much better armed both technically and quantitatively. Chiang Kai-shek had strong financial circles backing him also.

During the civil war, the fight between the communists and Chiang Kai-shek's troops, as well as in the war against the Japanese, Mao Zedong and his colleagues learned that the most important and in the final analysis the most powerful group in Chinese society was the rural population. Without its support the administration of the country would be very difficult if not impossible.

3.2.2 War Against the Japanese

From the period between 1932 and 1933, when Japanese troops occupied northeast China, the Chinese people felt strongly that all the Chinese forces should unite to fight against the Japanese. Despite this, the civil war between the communists and Chiang Kai-shek's troops went on.

At last in the spring of 1937 an agreement was made according to which the communist troops were joined to Chiang Kai-shek's forces as a separate army. However, the two sides did not trust each other, and therefore a great part of the Chinese troops was idle, watching each other, when the Japanese started their great attack.

Japan first occupied Beijing and Tianjin (Tientsin), and wide regions between them and south of them. Gradually the whole of northeast China fell into the hands of the Japanese, although the Chinese put up heavy resistance. The superior Japanese forces had by 1940–1941 attained their war aim: China was no longer a dangerous adversary. The Japanese had set up puppet governments in Beijing, Guangzhou, and Nanjing, and the invaders expected that these governments would gradually induce supporters of Chiang Kai-shek to come over to their side.

But China was only a part of the Japanese strategy to take over dominance of enormous areas of Asia. These great territorial goals gradually became a threat to Japanese imperialistic policy: their troops were soon divided over too many different fighting fronts. At first the Japanese had success. After the initial victories of Hitler's Germany in 1939–1941, Japan thought the time had come to attack the positions of Western European countries and the United States in southeast Asia.

In these circumstances the situation of Chiang Kai-shek's government in Chongqing seemed hopeless. Although the Chinese had succeeded in building small industries all over western China, and although roads and railways were built, these resources were not enough to push the Japanese out of China. Everything had to wait until the situation cleared up in Europe. Even in the spring of 1945 when the war ended in Europe, there were no signs that it would end in Asia, although Japan had also become the target of bombing. The atomic bombs dropped on Hiroshima and Nagasaki brought the war to an end.

But unfortunately the war did not end in China. The final struggle of power between Chiang Kai-shek's and Mao Zedong's supporters still remained. It was an irony that when China after many decades was suddenly at last free of foreign occupying powers, the Chinese had to begin a civil war. The birth of the new China did not occur without great pains.

3.2.3 Second Civil War

After the defeat of Japan the Chinese communists were very well aware that the people of China wanted peace after so many years of continuous wars. Mao Zedong also knew that Chiang Kai-shek had not given up his plans to destroy the Communist Party and take over the territories under communist administration. To clear up the situation, the communist leaders Mao Zedong and Chou En-lai went to Chongqing, headquarters of Chiang Kai-shek's government, to negotiate in August 1945. There both parties came to an agreement that they would try to avoid a civil war, and that they would cooperate on the basis of "peace, democracy, solidarity, and unity." However, Chiang Kai-shek demanded that all the territories under the communist regime should come under his administration. The communists could not accept this, and so the fighting began again.

At the beginning of the second civil war, Chiang Kai-shek's troops were superior both in numbers and quality. He had more than four million men under arms, and their weapons were modern. They had received tanks, airplanes, and warships from the USA. The communist troops numbered about 1.2 million.

Chiang Kai-shek began the civil war by attacking the territories administered by the communists on a wide front. Although Chiang Kai-shek's troops were numerically and materially superior they had great difficulties in fighting against the communists. One of the main reasons for their poor success was the attitude among the majority of the Chinese population. When the Nationalist government took over the administration, it lacked popular support in the areas liberated from the Japanese. The Nationalist soldiers, most of whom had been separated for years from their homes and families, were not willing to fight other Chinese in the civil war that was now well underway; they wanted to go home and start a new life. The communists, however, were now well-organized militarily and were constantly strengthened by deserters from Chiang's troops (Eberhard 1977: 336–337).

It should be mentioned that the communists received some material help from the Soviet Union although that country had occupied some Chinese territories after the war in Europe was over. The Soviet Union entered the war against Japan and among other places occupied Manchou (Manchuria) and Chengde. Although the Russians looted Manchou, which was one of the most industrialized parts of China, they supplied the Chinese communists with weapons they had taken from the Japanese. This enabled the communists to move into Manchou and parts of north China.

When Chiang Kai-shek moved his troops to Manchou, he was opposed by communists who were well equipped with Japanese arms, and cleverly led by Lin Piao. The communists won the battle and Chiang Kai-shek lost his best troops. It has been said that with this defeat, general demoralization began among Chiang Kai-shek's troops. The communists began to march from victory to victory, and in October 1949 the whole Chinese mainland was in the hands of the communists. Thus, on the first of October 1949 Mao Zedong, as Chairman of the Central People's Government, proclaimed the establishment of the People's Republic of China on Tiananmen Square in Beijing.

3.3 Summary of Developments to 1949

In this chapter Chinese developments until 1949 which have had a special impact upon the culture and structure of contemporary Chinese society and management thinking have been summarized. In Chapter 4, "China in 1949," the Chinese economic and cultural situation and the material and immaterial resources upon which the new communist administration was founded are described in more detail.

To start from the very beginning, the cultural unity of China can be said to have been created already during the Shang dynasty ca. 16th–11th centuries B. C. During this slave system period the state administration with a king assisted by ministers and vice-ministers was developing rapidly.

From the point of view of management thinking the third dynasty, Zhou (11th century to 221 B. C.) was important. Such important philosophers as Confucius, Mo Zi and Lao Zi lived then. Of these the ideas of Confucius were the most lasting. Confucius did not believe that noble status was pre-ordained, but he defended the hierarchy. Thus, Confucius' ideas strengthened the use of hierarchical instrumental power by the rulers, emperors and their vassals, whose resource powers were economic and arms power, and the method of exercising power, or influencing, was mainly coercive (see Appendix, p. 342).

During the Zhou dynasty the fight between different states became more and more fierce. Therefore, every state needed a strong centralized governmental system. Precise and written laws, norm power, which defined the rights and obligations of the individuals, became necessary. In these circumstances the so-called Legalist school, which had a strong impact upon earlier Chinese management thinking was born. According to the legalists, the ruler had to rule through the law. The ruler should be given a status of authority, so that the law could be applied in practice. Without the absolute power of the ruler the law had no meaning.

During the time of the Legalists the bureaucratic administrative system was also developing upon the feudal societal system, which gave it a good base to grow from. The philosophy of the Legalist school was effectively used in the Qin province, which unified the country in 221 B. C. and this thus became the first feudal empire of China. The Chinese imperial system had a strong bureaucratic central administration whose authority extended through regional and local governments to the village level. The basic characteristics of the later Chinese administrative system were then established. Thus, the Legalists added to the power arsenal of the central administration the norm power (laws), and the strengthened personal power of the ruler (emperor). The hierarchical power was centralized at the top of the state administration.

During this time public administration became a prestigious profession where admission was highly competitive, and graduates were required to take public examinations for entry into the civil service. The tradition of the training of civil servants, with entrance examinations, lasted uniformly until 1905, when the examinations were abolished altogether.

During the legalist period strategical thinking in administration and warfare was well developed. Strategy should be aimed at disposing of one's resources in such an overwhelming fashion that the outcome of the contest was determined before it got started. The process of strategy-making accentuated assessment, calculations, planning, and execution.

During the Zhou dynasty, Chinese society hanged gradually from a slave-owining society to a feudal one, and this period gave birth to the concept of the family, household, as a productive unit.

During the Qin and Han dynasties (ca. 221 B. C. to 220 A. D.) the feudal system was established, and the peasants were oppressed and exploited. Thus, about 2,000 years ago, the seed of growing dissatisfaction was sown which finally led to the 1949 revolution — largely a revolution of poor peasants.

Early Chinese management thought was mainly based on experience obtained from public administration. When industrialization led to more industrial and commercial enterprises, the management of economic organizations enlarged the concept of management in China. This development was in close contact with the coming of Europeans to China.

In 1516 the Portuguese came to Guangzhou (Canton) and later received the right to establish a colony there. European capitalism did not begin to invade China until the nineteenth century. The Western industrialized countries had reached a situation where their industrialization process could not go any deeper but had to expand horizontally, and one object was China.

During the nineteenth century the British, Russian, German, French, Japanese, and American armed forces threatened China and the country had to underwrite many humiliating agreements. Also the opium trade, which caused China many difficulties, developed during that time.

At the end of the nineteenth century the viceroys of the northern and southern part of China began to develop the country according to the European model. This development was interrupted by war with Japan. Defeat in this war and partition caused by other foreign forces "awakened" China, and in 1898 bourgeois reformists initiated again a modernization movement. A wave of factory establishment swept over the whole country after the Sino-Japanese War.

As a country China was, however, still very weak, and foreign powers, especially Russia, Japan, and Great Britain, tried in competition with each other to take advantage of the situation. During the rule of the Dowager Empress Tzŭ Hsi dissatisfaction grew rapidly in the country, and when she died in 1908, and the successor was to be a two-year-old-child, the country was ripe for a revolution.

The revolt began in the city of Wuhan and spread quickly all over the country. On December 29, 1911 the establishment of the Republic of China was proclaimed in Nanjing, and Sun Yat-sen, the leader of the Chinese Revolutionary League, was elected President of the Republic.

The revolution of 1911 ended both the 260 years rule of the Qing dynasty and the monarchical feudal system which had lasted for over 2,000 years.

The October Revolution in Russia brought Marxism-Leninism to China, and these ideas were studied in the country, especially in universities. In one of the universities, the National University in Beijing, the famous Movement of May Fourth (1919) began; this had far-reaching consequences for China. Because of the great power of this movement Mao Zedong began to develop the so-called mass-line strategy. The Movement of May Fourth also had a great impact upon the establishment of the Communist Party of China in July 1921.

The new party began to organize the workers. The Secretariat of the Chinese Workers' Union was established, and the number of workers who joined the union grew fast, so that in 1927 they numbered nearly three million. Also the peasants began to organize themselves into peasants' associations.

After Sun Yat-sen's death in 1925 Chiang Kai-shek became the leader of the People's Party. With the support of the communists he began a great war against the generals and their armies in northern and central China. Chiang Kai-shek was successful, and when he entered the gates of Shanghai he had to make a choice between the left and right wing of the People's Party. He chose the right wing and executed great numbers of communists in Shanghai.

In the meantime Mao Zedong went with his communist supporters to Hunan province and established the first units of the peasants' and workers' army, and they began to divide up the land in a new way to peasants and encouraged collective activity. Under the constant attacks of Chiang Kai-shek's army, Mao Zedong and his troops began the Long March through 12 provinces. During this March they succeeded in creating a positive attitude among the peasants towards them and communist ideology. In the areas the communists had occupied they also accomplished great social reforms.

In 1937 the Japanese started an offensive against China on a broad front. The Japanese were successful at first and by 1940–1941 they had attained their war aim: they had occupied the most important parts of China. However, the war did not end in China in 1945 as in Europe and Japan, but continued as a civil war between communist and Chiang Kai-shek's troops. The latter were quantitatively and qualitatively superior, but Mao Zedong had on his side the support of the majority of the Chinese people, especially in the rural areas. This was of crucial importance for the guerilla warfare his troops mainly waged. The morale of the communist troops was also much better than in Chiang Kai-shek's army. Thus the communists gradually succeeded in pushing Chiang Kai-shek's troops out of mainland China to the island of Taiwan.

On the first of October 1949 Chairman Mao Zedong proclaimed the establishment of the People's Republic of China.

4 China in 1949: Mao's Inheritance

The China which had come under the rule of the communists in 1949 was a gigantic, sick country with enormous economic problems. The people, who had suffered decades of constant internal and external wars, to a great extent still lived under feudal conditions. The majority (89%) lived in the rural areas in primitive mud huts with earth floors. They lived together with their domestic animals: chickens, pigs, and, during bad weather, even water buffaloes.

In order to examine management during and after Mao, a summary is first necessary of earlier developments which were the starting point and basis for the new administration in 1949. In this description a somewhat simplified form of the theoretical frame (Fig. A.3 on page 353) is used because the focus at this stage is mostly on phenomena at the societal level. Thus, we proceed through the following steps in Fig. 4.1: (1) Inherited value system; (2) inherited resources; (3) inherited guiding and controlling structures; (4) management resources and functions in 1949; and (5) as a consequence of the factors mentioned, we should have a picture of the state of the society in 1949.

4.1 Chinese Traditional Values

4.1.1 Religions in Old China

In every part of the world religions have represented ideological power resources, which all rulers, or persons who would like to become rulers, have to take into account. Some have tried to get the religions under their

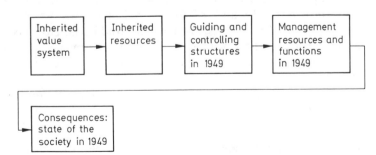

Fig. 4.1. Frame and skeleton for analysis of China's starting point in 1949

control to help attain their own goals; some have tried to destroy a certain religion if its values have not supported the attainment of the goals of the rulers. An example from the contemporary world is Poland, where the Roman Catholic church has strongly kept alive Polish traditional and not only religious values. The Polish church has been a great and constant problem for the government and party administration of the country. What was the situation in China in 1949?

For long periods of Chinese history the ancestor cult has been the oldest and most important phenomenon in Chinese religious life. The rituals connected to the ancestor cult were an obligation to all societal classes from the emperor to the commoner during the classic period of Chinese history and even during the time of the Republic (1912–1949) these rituals represented the most active part of Chinese religious life. The ancestor cult has in a way formed the main river to which the side streams of other religions have joined.

As mentioned earlier, China has traditionally been characterized as a country of three religions, where three different religious systems: Confucianism, Buddhism, and Taoism have lived together for over 2,000 years, though not always without mutual competition and conflicts, but in general having friendly relations with each other. Although all of these have had their own special supporter groups, the majority of the people have within their lifetimes followed all three religions.

It should also be mentioned that religion had both strongly societal as well as individual meaning in ancient China. It contained rituals and activities which belonged to the necessary obligations of an individual towards his family and society. In this sense the ancestor cult has had a very vital significance in Chinese society. It has strengthened family ties and helped to integrate and unite the society. It has also helped preserve the traditional Chinese institutions.

Was Chinese religion in 1949 for or against the ideas of the new rulers? From the standpoint of the social reforms which the CPC had in mind, the terminal and instrumental values of Confucianism were most important. These included especially the ancestor cult and traditional customs. Since Confucianism represented the values of the old China of the emperors, it was no wonder that its ideas were frequently heavily attacked in Mao's China. One reason for this was that Confucianism was especially the religion of civil servants and the intelligentsia. The CPC thought therefore that Confucianism represented values which belonged especially to a class society.

Mao's regime could, nevertheless, accept some of the thoughts of Confucius: the idea that the family was a hierarchically organized basic unit of society. According to this belief some family members had more power and privileges than others. Eberhard submits that the Communist administration tried to put the party in the place of the family in this value system. Although members of the party are officially equal, it is organized in a strongly hierarchical way.

One of the main characteristics of Confucianism was the requirement of loyalty to the Son of Heaven, the emperor, who was looked upon as the representative of heaven and the law of nature. It has been argued that the CPC have tried to "move" these values to the party and its leader. The cult of the emperor was changed to the cult of Mao. One of the thoughts of Confucius which Mao could easily accept and use was the appreciation of education and knowledge, and the idea also of seeing the leader as a teacher (Eberhard 1977: 360–361).

In judging the impact of religions upon the changes and reforms which the CPC intended to introduce into Chinese society, they, however, probably counted more on its negative effects than on the positive ones. They therefore tried to lessen the impact of religions after 1949. As mentioned in Chapter 2, the temples of Confucianism were taken over by the state, and Buddhist monks were shifted to practical work. Taoism itself had degenerated with time. The ancestor cult may be the form of religion which has still been persistently preserved in communist China.

4.1.2 Values and Attitudes Concerning Age

As mentioned previously, respect for tradition, ancestors, and age, largely stemming from the thoughts of Confucius, was among the main values of the people in old China. The respect for age was manifested especially in family life. Since the family has been the key basic unit in old Chinese society, its "organization" and function have had a profound effect upon other parts of societal life.

The hierarchical relations of a Chinese family were to a great extent determined by age. This has been manifested, e.g., in the nomenclature of sisters and brothers; their "names" follow the age-order of the family members. Thus, every member has a special "name" (word) according to his/her age in relation to other family members in the Chinese language. For example an older brother is called "gēge" and a younger sister "mèimei". It would be very impolite if a younger brother called his older brother by his given (first) name. Only parents call their children by their given names. One reflection of the minor importance of the given name is perhaps in the Chinese way of telling a person's name: the family name is written first, and after it the given name, the meaning of which is often connected with nature. For example, my guide in the city of Chongqing in 1984, who was about 25 years old, was called "Young Red Tiger". In a village community the hierarchy does not only follow age; before that the generation comes into the status system. Always the representative of an older generation comes into the status system of a village before the person of a younger generation.

When speaking of the importance of age, it should be noticed also that the average age of Chinese top leaders, both in government and in the Communist Party, has been rather advanced.

4.1.3 Values Concerning Hierarchy and Authority

The dominant values and attitudes of a particular country tend to result in dominant behavior patterns concerning managerial authority, responsibility, and superior-subordinate relationships in industrial and business enterprises. Barry Richman (1969: 243–244) gives a good description of the former situation in China:

> In old China the dominant attitudes toward authority, responsibility, and subordination were shaped largely by Confucianism and other traditional historical values which defined interpersonal relationships and obligations almost wholly in terms of the family system. One's duties to others typically derived from one's status, rather than from the contractual type of relationships, and also from one's relationship to others as represented normally as in the ties of kinship.
>
> ... Business and industrial enterprise in old China typically functioned as an extension of the family system, placing high value on family-type obligations and personal relationships. What held the organization together were personal relationships rather than a contractual Weberian type of legal national system. The managers were not simply overseers; they were personal representatives of the board of directors and usually had considerable financial interest themselves in the firm.

Because of the hierarchical family system and the thought of Confucianism, the industrial workers in old China did not typically question higher authority or strive for much authority themselves, thus, reinforcing the subordinate's subservience and the dependence on superiors. Authority in industry and business was typically viewed as an absolute right of owners and the managers in control. Higher-level managers tended to feel that their authority and power were based on some type of natural law, rather than on a clearly defined contractual type of role in the organization, or on specific skills and knowledge. Superior-subordinate relationships were typically personal, subjective, and viewed as father-son or master-servant relationships (Richman 1969: 244–245).

We may conclude that because of the hierarchical order of the family and of the society no two persons were equal in relation to each other. This inequality was reflected generally through three criteria; an older person had more rights than a younger one, a man had more rights than a woman, and a superior had more rights than a subordinate. However, in Chinese culture there also existed other values which have greatly affected the behavior of managers and their subordinates. One of these values was related to face-saving behavior, which we shall deal with in the following chapter.

4.1.4 Role of "Face" in China

In studying the behavior of Chinese managers overseas, Gordon Redding and Michael Ng argue that "face" plays a dominant role in guiding the work and management behavior of oriental people and thus also of Chinese. Face is defined as "the positive social value a person effectively claims for himself by the line others assume he has taken during a particular act" (Redding and Ng 1982: 203; Goffman 1955).

Redding and Ng made an empirical study of 102 Chinese middle-level executives in commercial, trading, and engineering firms in Hong Kong. To the question "What portion of people would often perceive face to be important?", the response yields a figure of 85%, thus indicating the great importance of this factor in the society (1982: 205). Table 4.1 shows a number of aspects of face.

Redding and Ng also found (1982: 209) that the nature of "face transaction" was reciprocal. This was indicated in responses to questions about how a person normally reacts.

Table 4.1. Perceived aspects of face among 102 Chinese managers working in Hong Kong. (Redding and Ng 1982: 208)

Face-related perceptions	Mean	Standard deviation	Range
1. People can have varying amounts of face	4.84	0.36	4–5
2. Perceived difference between prestige and face	4.79	0.45	3–5
3. There are many kinds of face, some better than others	4.22	0.66	3–5
4. Perceived difference between respect and face	3.83	0.82	3–5
5. Perceived difference between esteem and face	3.83	1.00	2–5

Scaling: 1 to 5 Likert scales

> If you are being given face, then 100 percent of the sample would give it back in return. If one's face is being challenged or attacked, then the response of 80 percent is to retaliate by destroying the other's face in return, and 20 percent by simply not giving face.

We can see that the model of socioeconomic exchange can be applied also to this face-related behavior. Giving and not giving face are felt as positive or negative sanctions, and correspondingly positive or negative exchanges.

There seem to be two main areas where the significance of face is especially noteworthy. One is in the field of social relationships between colleagues, the other is that involving negotiation, either in the marketing context where the transaction is likely to be selling, or in financial, legal, or purchasing negotiations. Areas of management in which its effects are indicated are leadership behavior, organizational climate and motivation, organization structure, marketing, financial decision-making, and management control (Redding and Ng 1982: 210, 217).

One may ask to what degree face was an important factor also in mainland China in 1949. Have the value systems in Hong Kong and mainland China been similar among Chinese? With regard to the geographical differences, one must remember that many Hong Kong Chinese, or at least their ancestors, have moved to Hong Kong from mainland China. That the Chinese in Hong Kong have maintained the special Chinese values and habits of life can be clearly seen in contemporary Hong Kong when one moves in the Chinese parts of the city.

4.1.5 Chinese Organizational Values Found Outside the People's Republic

As there are no reliable empirical studies concerning Chinese organizational values in 1949 we must try to approach the matter indirectly and look at research made among overseas Chinese, as we did in the preceding chapter. For this purpose Geert Hofstede's studies give some help. He used the results of a survey made in 1968 and 1972 within subsidiaries of one large multinational business organization in 40 countries. Later on Hofstede extended his material to 50 countries (Hofstede 1980: 11). Among these "countries" were also Hong Kong, Singapore and Taiwan, where the great majority of inhabitants are Chinese: in Hong Kong and Taiwan more than 90%, and in Singapore about 75%. In the following we shall especially focus upon these "countries" as representatives of Chinese traditional culture inherited from before 1949.

When Hofstede compared the values of his matched samples and looked for national patterns in these values, he found that value patterns dominant in the 50 countries varied in the following four main dimensions: (1) Individualism versus collectivism; (2) large and small power distance; (3) strong or weak uncertainty avoidance; and (4) masculinity versus femininity (Hofstede 1985: 5). The three "Chinese regions" mentioned in the sample were distinguished in the same way from the other countries especially in the dimensions: (1) Individualism versus collectivism and (2) large and small power distance. They all belonged to the group representing countries of large power distance and low individualism, or high collectivism.

The fundamental issue involved in power distance is how society deals with the fact that people generally are unequal. In organizations, the level of power distance is related to the degree of autocratic leadership. High power distance means that things like centralization and autocratic leadership are rooted in the mental programming of the members of a society, "not only of those in power but also of those at the bottom end of the power hierarchy" (Hofstede 1985: 7). These results from the Chinese regions of Hofstede's study match the traditional value system well, which resulted in hierarchical power both in family relations and the state administration in old China as described earlier.

The individualism-collectivism dimension, where the Chinese regions of Hofstede's study lie clearly on the side of low individualism, or correspondingly of high collectivism, represents the closeness of the relationship between one person and other persons. At the individualism end of the scale we find societies in which the ties between individuals are very loose; everybody is supposed to look after his or her own self-interest. This is made possible by a large amount of freedom which society leaves to individuals.

At the collectivism end of the scale, where the Chinese group belongs, there are societies in which the ties between individuals are very tight.

> People are born into collectivities or in-groups which may be their extended family (including grandparents, uncles, aunts, and so on), their tribe, or their village. Everybody is supposed to look after the interest of his or her in-group and to have no other opinions and beliefs than the opinions and beliefs of their in-group. In exchange, the in-group will protect them when they are in trouble. (Hofstede 1985: 6)

As we can see this description by Hofstede concerning collectivism reminds one considerably of the family and clan system in old China.

In Hofstede's third value dimension, strong or weak uncertainty avoidance, the Chinese group lies on the side of weak uncertainty avoidance. Singapore represents the utmost end of weak uncertainty avoidance; It is 40th of 40 countries which belonged to the original sample. Hong Kong was 37/40 and Taiwan 20/40 (Hofstede 1980: 165). Uncertainty avoidance represents the idea that

> We are all caught in the reality of past, present and future and we have to live with uncertainty because the future is unknown and will always be so. Weak uncertainty avoidance societies teach their people to accept this uncertainty and not to become upset by it. They take risks rather easily. (Hofstede 1980: 279)

When we earlier described Chinese traditional values, we stated that women in old China were in a subjugated position in relation to men, who usually had superior roles both in the family and society. Women were in the more service-oriented and caring roles. This would represent more masculinity-oriented values in Hofstede's dimension of masculinity-femininity. Japan was first in masculinity orientation in Hofstede's original 40-country sample, Hong Kong was 17th, Singapore 24th, and Taiwan 27th (Hofstede 1980: 279). Thus, the Chinese group did not belong to the extremes in masculinity, but were clearly more oriented in that direction compared to the more "feminine" Scandinavian countries, where the roles of males and females in the society are most equal compared to the other countries of Hofstede's sample.

In summary, we can say that the values of the Chinese capitalist societies of Hong Kong, Singapore, and Taiwan seem in the 1960s and 1970s to represent strongly the values of old China concerning in particular the importance of hierarchy and centralization (high power distance), and collectivism, where ties between individuals are tight, especially inside families and larger family systems (clans). Probably the same kind of values strongly prevailed also in mainland China in 1949.

4.2 Knowledge Resources of China in 1949

4.2.1 Problem of Knowledge in a Developing Country

The educational level of a nation and its overall educational system have a great impact upon management and especially its possibilities to manage the enterprises effectively and profitably.

In particular it has a great bearing on the entire staffing function, the size of industrial enterprises and their overall organization structures, degrees of work specialization, types of processes, techniques and technology used, costs of production, and the overall productivity of firms and their managements. (Richman 1969: 69)

In a truly underdeveloped country such as China was in 1949, the problem of literacy and primary education was of vital importance. By literacy we mean here the ability to read, write, and do simple arithmetical computations with reasonable accuracy.

The organization of a literate firm would tend to be very different from one using a large proportion of illiterates, mainly because the possibilities open to an enterprise with literate personnel are so much greater than one operating with many illiterates. It is typical that industry in developing countries contains mostly small enterprises. That is because large enterprises need an enormous amount of horizontal, upward, and downward communication to be able to function at all. A great part of this communication must be in written form. If a large proportion of the workers, foremen, and other supervisors are illiterate, they all have to be instructed orally. This is a very difficult and time-consuming task for the few literates who should also take care of their own jobs. As we all know, instructions given orally, especially if they are complex, can seldom be remembered completely; many errors and thus inefficiency occurs.

When a developing country where a great proportion of the labor force is illiterate must base its economy mostly upon small firms, advantages of economies of scale cannot be obtained. For the same reason, large-scale decentralization of industry is impossible in an illiterate country, because decentralization always requires great amounts of written communication (Richman 1969: 70).

4.2.2 Educational Level of Pre-Mao China

Actually there is very little accurate knowledge of the educational level of the people in earlier times. Some authors have estimated that before 1800 probably all upper-class sons and most daughters were educated, and that men in the middle and even in the lower classes often had some degree of literacy. This means that they could read classical poetry and essays written in literary Chinese, which was not the language of daily conversation.

"Literacy" means different things to different authors, largely depending on what matter they are considering and what time point they are referring to in Chinese history. About the circumstances in China around 1935, Eberhard argues that if a person could read and write some 600 characters, it was enough to conduct business and to read simple stories. Some argue that a farmer or a worker could at that time manage well with a knowledge of about 100 characters (Eberhard 1977: 342). This meant, however, a very simple life.

According to what one means by literacy, we come to very different conclusions concerning the literacy level of pre-1949 China. Barry Richman argues that prior to 1949 over 90% of the Chinese population was illiterate, and among industrial personnel illiteracy was about 80%. But his requirements of "literacy" are much higher than Eberhard's, probably because he starts from the requirements of more modern industry and a generally higher standard of living. Richman says that a Chinese urban citizen

> is considered basically literate if he comprehends about fifteen hundred to two thousand characters – about half the number required for completion of primary education. This is adequate for reading newspapers and magazines of the mass media type. Peasants are considered literate if they comprehend about fifteen hundred characters. (1969: 133–134)

There is also another dimension of "literacy" which should be mentioned, namely literacy in foreign languages. Since China was a quite backward, developing country in 1949 it needed knowledge from abroad written in foreign languages, particularly in English, Russian, German, and French. The lack of knowledge of these important foreign languages was certainly a great constraint on managerial effectiveness and industrial progress. If the Chinese industrial enterprises wished to make use of the experiences and technical knowledge of the advanced nations, scarce educated manpower had to be used to translate the relevant written material.

Probably those persons who knew foreign languages belonged to the upper classes and/or the management-level personnel in the enterprises of pre-1949 China. A large number of them left the country because of the communists' victory. In these persons China lost valuable knowledge resources needed to develop the country after the civil war. As we will see later, the communists tried to keep these persons, especially enterprise managers, in the country by promising them that they would not lose their managerial positions at the beginning of the People's Republic.

What was the capacity of the Chinese educational system in 1949 with the help of which the CPC had to begin to build the knowledge resources of the country? It should be mentioned that Mao's troops had already during the civil war before 1949 begun to teach the adult population to read and write in the "liberated" areas which were under their control.

In Fig. 2.6 it can be seen that the primary schools were by far the greatest source of education, and the role of the middle schools and universities was of minor importance. The enrolment in universities was only 120,000 in 1949, in a country with a population of 542 million at that time. Thus, one of the main problems of the new People's Republic was to strengthen the educational system of the country and thus the knowledge resources of China.

4.3 Human and Economic Resources of China in 1949

4.3.1 Human Resources

The years before 1949 were very difficult for the Chinese people. The feudal living conditions, wars, epidemics, and famines resulted in innumerous casualties among the Chinese. The life expectancy for a Chinese person is estimated to have been only 27 years at the turn of the century (Hultcrantz et al. 1974: 18; Tregear 1965: 106).

As mentioned earlier (Fig. 2.1), the estimated population in 1949 was 542 million. Although the proportion of the urban population was relatively small, it amounted to over 50 million. Only 8 million were working as workers or clerical employees; some 3 million of these were industrial workers. It has been estimated that 4 million were unemployed, without taking into account all those unemployed and young people who had never really worked or who could not find the means to go to school (Hultcrantz et al. 1974: 29; Ten Great Years 1960: 177–178). According to the calculations, of the 8 million workers and clerical employees only one million or 0,2% of the total population worked in an industry which one could call modern.

What was the quality of the population as a workforce? Eberhard argues that the quick development of the People's Republic was not astonishing. Both Taiwan and mainland China have developed extremely quickly since 1949. The reasons do not seem to lie solely in the form of government. Eberhard thinks that the preconditions for a "take-off" existed in China as early as the 1920s, if not earlier; it was, however, prevented primarily for political reasons. One of the main preconditions for the later rapid development of the People's Republic was that a large proportion of the population was inured to hard and repetitive work. The Chinese farmer was accustomed to such work. To train the Chinese was easy, and absenteeism was never a serious problem, as it has been in other developing nations (Eberhard 1977: 341).

4.3.2 Condition of Agriculture

It has been estimated that during the first half of this century the landlords and rich peasants, who together formed only 8% of the rural population, owned more than 70% of the cultivated land. The peasant class, whose share of the rural population was more than 90% owned the other part, 30% of the remaining cultivated land (Hultcrantz et al. 1974: 19–20; Kuan 1960: 3–4).

With regard to the productivity of agriculture before 1949, we must remember the great damage which the long wars caused to the rural areas. For example the dikes (embankments) of rivers were destroyed in many places, as well as irrigators. The wasted rural areas were destroyed by noxious insects which quickly also spread over the still-cultivated parts of the country. Invasions of locusts, which had appeared every three to four years for thousands of years, appeared still more frequently. The accumulated effects of the wars, natural catastrophes, and other destructive factors had reduced the grain harvest to 75% of the level before the wars, the cotton harvest to half, and the number of farm implements to 70% of the level before the wars (Hultcrantz et al. 1974: 17–18; *Agriculture in New China* 1953: 2, 26, 39).

Fig. 4.2 shows that agricultural products formed the main part (45%) of China's total production at the beginning of the People's Republic in 1952 (reliable data for 1949 are not available). Their share had decreased to 23% in 1978, but increased again to 28% in 1983.

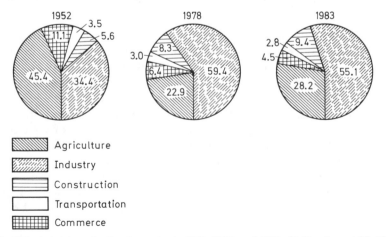

Fig. 4.2. China's total production by sector in 1952, 1978, and 1983. (B.R., August 27, 1984)

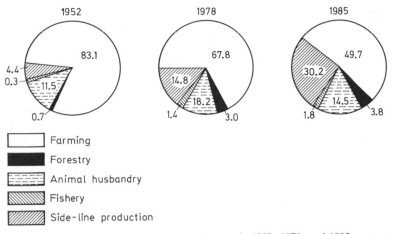

Fig. 4.3. Composition of China's gross agricultural output in 1952, 1978, and 1985; percentage values by contributing field. (*China: A Statistical Survey in 1986*)

In 1952 the share of farming was dominant (83%) in China's gross agricultural output, but also the share of agricultural side-line production, which later was to play an important role in the Chinese economy, at the starting point of the People's Republic was considerable (4.4%), as Fig. 4.3 shows.

4.3.3 Chinese Industry in 1949

Before we begin to examine the condition of Chinese industry before the communist victory in 1949 we must consider a factor which greatly affected the development of industry and the whole Chinese economy during the last war years, namely inflation. It has been said that China's rampant inflation, one of the worst in world history, which began around 1939 and reached its peak at the end of the 1940s, was undoubtedly also a major factor in the communist victory in 1949.

The grossly inept banking system with highly ineffective monetary policies and extremely adverse fiscal policies contributed greatly to China's huge inflation and severe economic crisis. The Nationalist regime completely lost control over the country's fiscal and monetary situation. In 1938, prices rose an average of 3% per month, but from mid-1940 to the end of 1944 10% per month, and 20% until the end of the Japanese war in 1945. In the "final months before total collapse and the Communist victory the price index took off and disappeared into the great beyond . . ." (Richman 1969: 478–479).

Also corruption and bribery within the government and among bankers, as well as the great extravagances of many officials, became pervasive with the inflation, further aggravating the economic situation and hindering productive efficiency and economic progress. The spiraling inflation made it virtually impossible for industrial managers to plan ahead or to organize, staff, or control activities efficiently (Richman 1969: 479).

As has been said earlier, China before 1949 was a truly underdeveloped country. Its economic system was basically capitalistic, although a number of public-sector enterprises were established and operated by the government during the Republican era. There were a number of large-scale heavy industrial enterprises, mostly under foreign control, and primarily in north China. Shanghai and Tianjin (Tientsin) were also fairly large industrial centers primarily involved in light industry such as textiles and food processing. But both in absolute and per capita terms, China's level and diversity of industrialization were low; considerably lower than in India, for example (Richman 1969: 125).

With regard to the development of Chinese industry before 1949, it must be pointed out that the relatively modern and most productive sector had before 1937 been in the hands of foreigners as follows: coal 56%, cast iron 82%, shipping tonnage 48%, cotton yarn 29%, and cotton fabrics (cloth) 61%. During the years of war this modern industrial sector came almost wholly under Japanese control, and after their defeat in 1945 the Guomindang government took over these enterprises; or rather – it has been said – the capitalists of the bureaucracy along with the family of Chiang Kai-shek and three other rich families. It has been estimated that of the total industrial output value in 1949, the state sector accounted for 35%, the joint state-private sector 2%, and the private sector 63% (Xue 1981: 19).

We have already described generally how much the wars and political restlessness as well as other adversities damaged the Chinese economy before 1949. Concerning industrial production in 1949 it has been estimated that it had on average dropped to half of the volume of the highest level before the war. The variations between different industrial fields were, however, quite large, as we can see from Fig. 4.4.

In Chapter 2.3 Chinese production capacity was described and Table 2.1 shows how modest China's output of major industrial products was in 1949. To get a somewhat larger view of the situation of industrial production before Mao took power, we present in addition in Table 4.2 the output figures of some other products important for the Chinese. These also show that China, taking into account its population of 542 million, had to start its industrial production after 1949 almost empty-handed.

On the whole industry played quite a small role in China's national economy before 1949. The factories were ill-equipped and the level of technol-

100 % = highest level before 1949

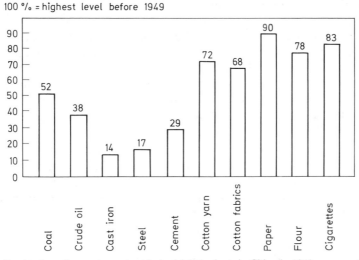

Fig. 4.4. Production of some important industrial products in China in 1949 compared to the highest level before the war; percentages, highest level = 100. (Based on Hultcrantz et al. 1974: 21; *Ten Great Years* 1960: 2)

Table 4.2. Output of some industrial products in China in 1949 and 1985. (*Statistical Yearbook of China* 1985; B. R., March 24, 1986)

Product	1949	1985	Units
Cloth	18.9	143.0	100 million meters
Sugar	20.0	445.0	10 thousand tons
Bicycles	1.4	3,235.0	10 thousand
Sewing machines	6.6[a]	986.0	10 thousand

[a] in 1952

ogy was low. The industries were unevenly developed and distributed. Light industry, mainly the textile and food industries, accounted for upwards to 70% of the total value of industrial output. Heavy industry contributed very little, and the machine-building industry accounted for only 1.7% of the total values of industrial output.

Industry was concentrated mainly along the eastern seaboard. In the interior, Wuhan, Chongqing, Taiyuan, and a few other cities were the only centers with any modern industry. In the vast border regions of the north, northwest, west, and southwest inhabited mainly by minority nationalities, even handicraft industries were to all intents and purposes nonexistent (Qi 1979: 102–103). In 1949 industry accounted for 25% of the gross social product compared with 55% in 1983 (Lu 1984: 18).

4.3.4 Transportation in 1949

Right from ancient times, one of the great problems of China's economic development has always been transportation. The main reason for this has been the topography of the country. The main region of China is very mountainous and the mountain ranges go from west to east, and although their height becomes lower in the east near the sea, they have formed and still form a great obstacle to transportation, especially in the north-south direction.

For freight, the inland water routes consisting of rivers and canals formed an important transportation system. However, the railways took care of most freight transportation at the beginning of the 1950s, although they were not as long as inland water routes (Fig. 4.5). We see from Fig. 4.6 that in later years water transportation has become more and more important. This development is largely due to the engine-driven boats and ships, which can move quite quickly also upstream in great rivers. Earlier this was difficult, and transport by sailing vessel or tugging was very labor- and time-consuming. Now great passenger boats also move rapidly up and down the Changjiang (Yangtze) River, as I myself have experienced.

The whole transportation system in China was greatly damaged during the wars, since transportation is one of the most important strategic factors in warfare. Both the aggressors and the defenders tried to destroy the transportation system to hinder the moves of the enemy. Thus, for the leaders of

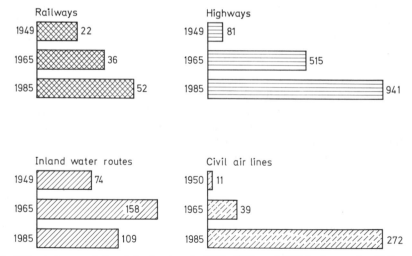

Fig. 4.5. Chinese transportation infrastructure in 1949, 1965, and 1985 in thousands of kilometers. (*China: A Statistical Survey in 1986*)

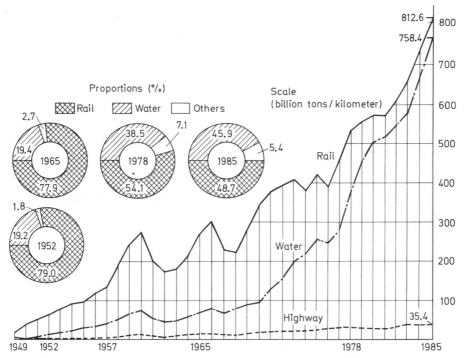

Fig. 4.6. Scale and proportions of freight transportation in China in 1952, 1965, 1978, and 1985. (B.R., August 27, 1984; *China: A Statistical Survey in 1986*)

the new People's Republic the repair and development of the transportation system was one of the most urgent tasks when they began to build up the country again.

4.3.5 Trade in 1949

The Chinese have always been known as skillful traders. In countries where they have emigrated they have soon created their "own" system of trading and handicraft. It is difficult to get a clear picture of commerce in China in 1949. Probably the local trading activities were relatively lively, but the trade between different parts of the country was probably in a bad state of stagnation because of unsettled conditions and damage caused to the transportation system. Of course, there are no reliable statistics from that time. The first figures are for 1952. Probably the number of trading companies as well as individual traders was relatively larger (in relation to the size of the population) before 1949 than after it, because the socialist system concentrated trade in the hands of the state and collectives. The impact of a free-

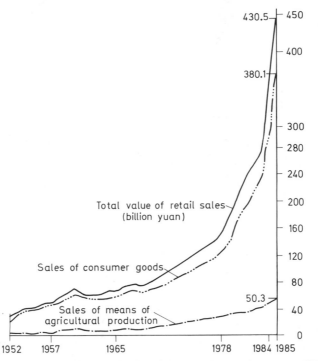

Fig. 4.7. Retail sales in China 1952–1985, (*China: A Statistical Survey in 1986*)

market system, especially upon trade, can be seen in Fig. 4.7, where the curve indicating the sales of consumer goods goes sharply upward after 1978, when the new Chinese leaders opened the doors for a limited local free-market system.

It has been estimated that of the total retail sales in 1950, private commerce accounted for 85% and state commerce 15% (Xue 1981:19). The former was to a great extent in the hands of family enterprises.

Because of the wars, foreign trade was also in a depressed state in 1949 and the preceding years. The main foreign trade was probably in war materials, which again only helped to damage the domestic trading system.

4.4 Administrative Resources in 1949

When we try to describe the administrative resources or systems that Mao inherited on October 1, 1949, we must divide our description into two parts; first, those administrative practices which had been applied traditionally in old China, and, second, those new administrative experiences or experiments that the communists applied in the areas occupied by them in the late 1930s and 1940s. At the end ot this section we focus more precisely upon those human managerial resources available to Mao after the revolution in 1949.

4.4.1 China's Traditional Administrative System

The old Chinese administrative system will be described here with the help of our theoretical frame, analyzing separately the exercise of (1) hierarchical, (2) norm, and (3) communication powers (see Appendix pp. 346–348).

Hierarchical Power

As described earlier, the human relationships in old China were sharply hierarchical according to the Confucian way of thinking. This actually meant in practice obedience to those owed respect because of their position and the virtues associated with it. The superior virtues and capacities assigned to certain social and political positions were the property of males in general, of the father who was the head of the family, of the emperor who was the head of the government and the state, and of the officials who were the emperor's representatives.

Here we must mention the so-called mutual responsibility groups, which gave powerful support to Confucian moral and ideological authority. This system, originally initiated by the early unifiers of the Qin dynasty (221–207 B.C.), held the family responsible for the public acts of its members. It was able to exert great social pressure on each individual, inculcating obedience to the government and to the social order through the family (Andors 1977: 28).

From the point of view of the whole society, the Confucian bureaucracy was necessary for the agrarian economy, supervising, controlling, and coordinating the productive labor in isolated peasant farms and villages. Without the bureaucracy the whole state would have disintegrated and there would have been no central authority. Production and distribution of goods would have been very difficult. On the other hand, without the hard work of the peasantry and the skills of the small class of urban merchants and artisans, the bureaucracy and the central authority would have had no material base for its privileged existence in the towns. The bureaucrats' monopoly of knowledge in political and economic coordination made them indispensable. Thus, the economic (work) resources of a very large group and the knowledge resources of a proportionately very small group held up the society; however, the latter group had a controlling and privileged status. The bureaucracy had the hierarchical power positions to guide and control the society.

Although the bureaucracy was important for the economic and political system, its functioning did not make it efficient or creative. The traditional value system and rule by moral example affected the officials in that they could not risk their privileged positions by upsetting old routines, challenging entrenched privilege, or embarrassing their superiors (Andors 1977: 29).

During the years before 1949 the traditional hierarchical power structure with its officials held China or its different parts in some way together. Dissatisfaction with it had, however, become very acute, not least because of the inefficient and corrupt behavior of the officials, which grew worse and worse with wartime insecurity.

When we turn to examine the state of the hierarchical power in China in 1949, we see clearly that the administrative structures were badly damaged because of the wars both at the levels of macro- and mesomanagement. The country had been divided into parts for a long time, beginning with the Japanese occupation which was followed by the civil war, when part of the country was under the Chiang Kai-shek administration and another part under communist rule. Thus macromanagement for the whole of China was not functioning, although both parties, both Mao's and Chiang Kai-shek's, tried to establish their own kind of administration in the areas they were occupying. On the whole we can say that both meso- and macrolevel organizational structures were damaged for so long that the communist regime could begin to build its own guiding organizational structures – hierarchical power – from scratch. The building of new organizational structures was helped by the experiments the communists made in the area of administration of those parts of the country that were occupied by them. We examine these experiments later in this chapter.

With regard to the situation at the level of micromanagement, especially the small family enterprises tried to function also during the difficult war years – people had to live. Because of this, and because both parties were trying to win the war, both groups tried to maintain production, especially in those enterprises vital for warfare. Probably some of the medium-sized industrial enterprises were functioning, and a great number of the smaller family enterprises. It was probably the family institution with its strict hierarchical structure, the father at the head, that maintained the lower-level Chinese organizational structures during the difficult war period.

Norm Power

Every country has a legal code, written or traditional, which greatly affects the operation of industrial enterprises and of the whole society at every level of management. "It is common to find in underdeveloped countries that much or most of the law has not yet been formally codified, and this tends to make business activity subject to considerable uncertainty" (Richman 1969: 94).

As China before 1949 was still much more a developing country than now, its legal system was accordingly very underdeveloped. In particular there was very little formal codification of laws affecting business and industry. Managers in old China, as also today, had a deep sense of obligation to do their best to fulfill the agreements and conditions that they entered into voluntarily with other parties in the course of doing business. The concept of "loss of face" which we have described earlier plays an important role here. Bad and dishonest business behavior could ruin a manager's reputation, which could be disastrous for his future activities in the business community. In general the absence of effective contract law resulted in great uncertainty and risks, which seriously hindered such important managerial activities as planning and control (Richman 1969: 367).

What has been said concerns mostly the "normal" time and circumstances before 1949. When we add to the underdeveloped state of the legal system the disruptive effects of the constant wars, when different rulers in different parts of the country had different guiding and controlling norms, the whole picture becomes more or less chaotic, and one must ask how life could actually have functioned in these circumstances. The nature of the legal system and the nonexistence of coordinated uniform norm power in pre-1949 China was probably one additional negative factor that led to the communist victory.

Communication Power

Communication is the cement holding the hierarchical organizational structures together, whether it is the organization or the whole society. Before the Revolution, written communication could not be very efficient because the majority of Chinese were illiterate. Mass communication through a radio network was also difficult, because radios were a rarity even in cities. Thus, most communication had to be spread orally through personal contacts.

As has been mentioned, relationships between different hierarchical levels in the administration depended greatly upon personal contacts. Because transportation and communication were very slow, and important messages could be lost on the way, local officials were quite independent of their superiors in provincial or state government centers. The only way to get a message to its destination and to be sure that the orders communicated would be fulfilled, was to send the message with armed forces, and to use coercion if necessary.

We described how important the family system has been in strengthening the government administration system. One important task which the family and the clan system also had to fulfil in an illiterate society was to spread and collect information through the network of personal contacts.

The official communication network in China was badly damaged in the years before 1949 because of the war against the Japanese and because of the civil war between Mao Zedong's and Chiang Kai-shek's troops. All of these different forces naturally had their own formal and informal communication systems in the areas they ruled, but one must realize that the communists had already very early begun to build their own member as well as communication networks. This we describe a little later when we examine the communists' management experiments before their final victory.

4.5 Communist Management Practices Before Their Victory

4.5.1 New Experiments with Hierarchy

Since the old central and provincial level management structures were more or less destroyed before the communist victory, Mao and his colleagues were in a way in a fortunate position to begin to build new hierarchical management structures, for there were few to compete with.

However, the communists themselves did not need to begin to build their new management system altogether from scratch. The creation of a new management system had actually begun long before 1949 in the areas occupied by the communists. When the remnants of the Red Army reached the hills of northern Shaanxi province after the Long March in December 1936, they established their headquarters in the small, poor city of Yan'an, where the population lived in caves carved out of the hard soil. Though a good place to hide and recuperate, the poverty and isolation of the area presented the communists with severe problems; the production and distribution of the necessities for survival were top priorities. Here in these hard conditions the basis for the administration and management system of

Mao's People's Republic at the state, provincial, and organizational level, which still has a great impact upon management in China, was established. After 1940 Yan'an's poverty and isolation were compounded by the Guomindang blockade of the communist-controlled areas, making self-reliance even more necessary for raising the collective standard of living and preventing the communist revolutionaries from becoming an unwelcome burden. Cooperatives and mutual-aid groups were started in both industry and agriculture. Yan'an military, educational, and governmental institutions became models of austerity and self-support. "Participation in productive labor by intellectuals and officials was a consequence of necessity that was to have far-reaching political effect" (Andors 1977: 35; Schran 1975).

To shift the power from the old elites, the communists had to create new organizations. The associations of peasants and women, trade unions and youth organizations were all strongly influenced by communist leadership. A "three-thirds" system, whereby candidates representing the old Guomindang government, the communists, and various mass organizations shared administrative power in the new "government", was also important in institutionalizing and legitimatizing this shift of power (Andors 1977: 37).

To wage guerilla warfare with a technologically superior enemy the communists needed close relationships with the local impoverished peasants. There developed a markedly egalitarian and cooperative society with an attitude toward human relationships heretofore unknown in China, one which was later to be incorporated into the theory of the mass line. The mass-line principle was stated by Mao (1975b: III, 117–119) in the following way:

> The two methods which we communists should employ in carrying out any task are, first, the linking of the general with the specific, and second the linking of the leadership with the masses . . . but there is no possibility of testing . . . general directives and of making them more specific and concrete, and there is danger of them coming to nothing, unless the leaders, instead of contenting themselves with issuing directives, personally carry out the tasks on hand in a concrete and thorough manner.

> Within each unit a leading group should be formed comprising a small number of active workers united around the head of a given unit, and this group should maintain close contact with the masses . . . The activity of this leading group unless combined with that of the masses will dissipate itself in the fruitless efforts of a handful of people.

As the experience obtained by the communists in Yan'an and in their other areas before 1949 had a profound effect upon the management of enterprises, government, and the Communist Party in the People's Republic these effects are summarized here:

1. The old hierarchical structure of society with authority centralized in the hands of inherited ruling classes was destroyed, and a new, more egalitarian and cooperative society was developed. At the same time attitudes towards authority changed as legitimate power was shifted from traditional bureaucrats to the revolutionary cadres participating in the hard work of agriculture and industry.
2. There developed a new hierarchical system of strong leaders and central authority, which, however, was striving towards flexibility in case of emergency.
3. Production, education, and the military became interrelated in the same organizational units. This was later on typical in enterprise organizations in the People's Republic.
4. Production units became self-reliant economically.
5. Different organizational forms of cooperatives were developed both for agriculture and industry.
6. Different kinds of participation systems were created:
   (a) The "three-thirds" system, where representatives from three different interest groups shared administrative power, was later used in different forms, especially during the Cultural Revolution in 1966–1976. They then represented, e.g., special kinds of project groups in which representatives of the workers, cadres, and technicians actively participated.
   (b) During the period before 1949 the participation down the line system was largely developed. Usually we mean by participation that subordinates take part in decision-making which "normally" belongs to their superiors. In participation down the line, superiors, intellectuals, and cadres take part in productive labor on the shop floor both in industry and agriculture.
7. Symbols of hierarchical power and signs of rank, were abolished, because making the leaders highly visible would have endangered them before 1949. The abolition of symbols of power occurred again during the Cultural Revolution when all signs indicating military rank were removed; in the 1980s they are back again.
8. The "mass line principle" which linked the leaders' ideas and behavior with the masses was created as a necessity in the hard conditions of Yan'an. This principle later played a central role in Mao's thinking and in Chinese management principles.
9. Finally, there was the changed status of women at every level of societal

and organizational hierarchy. Their hierarchical power changed radically from a very subjugated status to a much more egalitarian role which represented a great contrast to traditional Chinese cultural values.

As the communists in Yan'an had a strong leading group, with Mao Zedong at the top, and as this group remained in power after their victory in 1949, the Chinese could transmit the administrative and managerial experiences they had tested in Yan'an further on to the managerial system of the new People's Republic of China.

4.5.2 CPC Communication and Norm Power Before Their Victory

Well before their final victory, the communists had begun to build up their own communication system, which was based on both interpersonal contacts and mass media. One thing which greatly helped the communists to obtain accurate information wherever they went was the support of the local people, especially the peasants. As mentioned before, the communist troops had tried to create friendly ties with the local common folk. This support from the "masses" helped the communists very much in gathering information.

The communists began to build their own communication network based on personal contacts long before their final victory in 1949. The " formal" side of the network consisted of the members of the Chinese Communist Party. Membership grew from about 40,000 in 1937 to over 800,000 in 1945 (Andors 1977: 36). When the communists took over in 1949 they could relatively quickly develop an effective communication network on the basis of the membership network, and especially on the hierarchical structures already mentioned. Organizational hierarchy also is a communication channel, and the group with the hierarchy in its hands has also at the same time great communication power, which is especially important when starting to build a new societal and administrative system based on a new ideology.

But the communists depended not only on personal contacts in their communication. The value of the mass media has also always been recognized by them. The Xinhua News Agency began in 1931. The communists' first radio station near Yan'an began broadcasting in 1945, and the first edition of the *People's Daily* was published in June 1948 (Campbell 1981: 59).

Because the great majority of Chinese were illiterate before the revolution, the most effective communication was done orally through personal contacts. But personal networks and oral communication are not enough to manage large organizations effectively in the long run. One needs written norms which can be communicated in the same form to everybody; the state administration needs a broad legislation system, and microlevel organizations require written work rules, etc. The legal system in old China was very undeveloped, and became "ruined" during the wars. Thus, the communists had enormous tasks in the areas of communication and legislation in 1949. Mao and his colleagues soon realized that to make communication and norm power effective, to be able to really have influence through them, the ability to read and write was vital. Therefore, great education campaigns were launched throughout China, first, to wipe out illiteracy, and, second, to begin to modernize the country.

4.6 China's Managerial Resources in 1949

In this section we examine the sources from which Mao had to recruit managers for organizations of the new People's Republic in 1949. The groups of potential sources were as follows: (1) the managerial body of existing Chinese enterprises in 1949; (2) the members of the Communist Party; (3) the People's Liberation Army; and (4) universities and other higher educational institutions.

4.6.1 Managers of Enterprises

As mentioned before, the "modern" sector of China's industry was proportionately small and mainly owned by foreigners. The industrial labor force not assimilated into the modern sector often worked in small workshops or in machinery repair and maintenance plants associated with mining and railroads. People gained experience and learned technical skills working in these small workshops, and Chinese entrepreneurs often began in these. Management was also trained in them.

Although these small workshops were important as producers and employers, they remained small and were limited to light industrial machinery and spare parts. However, these workshops, often family enterprises, formed an important managerial source for the organizations of the People's Republic.

Among Chinese managers of larger firms, hired by rich businessmen to produce profit, loyalty to the owner was more important than competence. Therefore, administrators often had to delegate primary authority for operations to skilled, experienced workers known as gang bosses. Sometimes management hired a professional labor contractor who, for a fixed price, would recruit workers and take responsibility for their behavior and performance. This policy was used prominently in foreign-owned companies, in Chinese companies with foreign experts as managers or technical specialists, among female workers, and in mines.

Both the contract labor system and the gang-boss system were open to grave abuse, since labor was abundant and cheap in a poverty-stricken agrarian society. Females were considered to be surplus, and since there were few or no laws regulating working conditions, female workers were especially abused (Andors 1977: 33).

This extract gives an idea of the difficulties the communist rulers had with the existing managerial resources in 1949. Although there were people who had been in managerial positions for many years, their attitudes and behavior as superiors were in great contrast to the socialist ideology, which stressed equality at work and worker-centered values. The lack of managerial resources in 1949 was enormous, but to make direct use of a great proportion of the available managers trained in pre-1949 circumstances would have caused great trouble. Against this background some of the communist measures, e.g., to train the "old" managers ideologically, become understandable.

An "extra" source in industry, from which the Chinese communists could draw for revolutionary leadership in the industrial sector, comprised skilled, literate workers who, with the blessing of the Communist Party, were quickly promoted to positions of leadership in the factories by the trade unions.

> These workers were especially important as replacements for the old gang bosses, chiefs of secret societies and religious sects, and Kuomintang labor leaders. They helped to destroy the influence of the urban criminal underworld, formerly pervasive in many Chinese factories, which had often operated through those same gang bosses and sect leaders. The number of workers suitable was not great, however, because of the very poor educational level of the working class. (Andors 1977: 48)

Thus, the Chinese had really great difficulties in the area of management resources concerning industry. The existing managers, though skillful, were often badly corrupted, and thus ideologically unreliable. The ideologically suitable skilled workers, who were not illiterate, were relatively few in number, and had often no managerial experience and/or capability. Thus the communists had to rely on other resources; one of them was the party.

4.6.2 CPC as a Managerial Resource

What was missing in ideology among the group of industrial managers and government officials before October 1949, was being compensated by Communist Party members, whose number had grown from 40,000 to over 800,000 between 1937 and 1945.

> Many of the new members had not assimilated the intellectual or moral attributes of the Communist guerilla leaders because of previous social experience, ignorance, or illiteracy. Thus a great effort was placed on leadership training and ideology. As in traditional learning, political morality was the core of such training, but the Marxist value system and epistemological theory replaced the Confucian. (Andors 1977: 36)

With regard to the members of the Communist Party as a management resource, it must be said that their function was more in the area of ideology; they seldom had any practical or theoretical experience of management. But without them the change in power and the adoption of new values in management practice would have been impossible. Alone they did not have any real power resources upon which they could base their influence. The People's Liberation Army was the power behind them.

4.6.3 People's Liberation Army as a Managerial Resource in 1949

As mentioned before, the prevailing conditions in Yan'an brought about a situation where economic, productive, educational, and military activities became interrelated. As army units were active in production and also in training, it was natural that the army became an important source of potential managers. There was also strong ideological training in the army along the lines of communist thought.

Thus, from the point of view of ideology the soldiers were almost as suitable for managerial positions in industrial enterprises as the cadres of the Communist Party, but the former, especially officers, had more experience in organizing and personnel administration, as they had been leading guerrilla troops, often in extremely difficult circumstances. They had also been trained through this fighting in independent decision-making based on skills in analyzing different situations and problems themselves.

Because of these qualities, many of the army officers became managers of enterprises after 1949. Even in 1980 I found army officers in top management positions, especially in large strategically important industrial enterprises. It may be that their managerial position was partly a reward for well-performed military service, and partly because they looked after the interests of the government, CPC, and army.

4.6.4 Government Organizations as a Managerial Resource

In a capitalist economic system government organizations normally function quite separately from the industrial and business enterprises, but in a socialist country economic, government, and party organizations are tightly bound together. There is actually no gap as in capitalist countries between higher government and party hierarchical structures and local level enterprise organizations. The government structure continues unbroken from the highest peak of government at state level, to provincial, municipal, county, and district levels, and then to individual industrial enterprises.

Thus, the civil servants of pre-1949 government organizations were greatly needed, both directly to fill managerial positions in enterprises under reconstruction after the war, and, as government organizations became tightly linked with industrial organizations under communist rule, in the new tasks of governmental units guiding and controlling industrial enterprises under them. Tasks of industrial management awaited them both in enterprise and government organizations. What kind of resource did the 1949 body of civil servants form in this sense?

As has been mentioned, before 1905 China had had a well-developed training system for civil servants with entrance examinations; the quality and esteem of government officials were high then. With the abolition of the famous Hanlin Academy, this system, which had lasted in a relatively uniform shape some 2,000 years, died. With this abolition the quality of local government dropped sharply, and also the status of civil servants sank considerably in Chinese society.

During the insecure times before 1949, corruption spread more and more among civil servants, and their moral status sank further. The moral corruption weakened the governmental machinery and thus made it easier, and perhaps we can say even possible, for the communists to win the civil war. On the other hand, the body of civil servants which Mao Zedong inherited was not of great use qualitatively for the purpose of building a new socialist society based on altogether different values from the old one. Against this background it seems a miracle that Mao Zedong succeeded in establishing and developing the administrative structure of the new People's Republic.

4.6.5 Higher Educational Institutions as a Managerial Resource in 1949

Traditionally the most valued career path in China was that of a public official. It has been estimated that as late as the 1930s, more university students were in political science and law than in science, engineering, or business (Andors 1977: 32).

Gradually the Chinese intellectuals awoke to see the technological backwardness of their country in comparison with the Western countries, which had continually threatened China with technologically superior military forces. The impact of Western technology on intellectuals led to a broadening of the field of studies. Quite soon technology, engineering, business management, accounting, and economics became the subjects on which an increasing proportion of a growing but still relatively small group of privileged urban dwellers concentrated.

There was also to some extent an exchange of knowledge between China and foreign countries. Chinese students went abroad to Japan, the USA, and Europe as well as to the USSR, and foreign educators, specialists, technicians and missionaries came to China. Many of them were associated with American universities or large foundations.

Several Chinese universities trained economists in Western, non-Marxist economic and business management theory as well as in Western political and social science theory. The university graduates, who were exposed to these Western-liberal concepts, were often criticized by the conservative Chinese for their Western views. "However, these engineers, social scientists and economists trained by Western methods were to be crucial to the educational, political, and economic establishment after 1949, when trained technical manpower was at a premium" (Andors 1977: 38–39).

The Western and the traditional Chinese educational systems were similar in that they were very competitive. Both systems were based on values which held that formal degrees constituted legitimate indicators of a person's knowledge and expertise, and that these degrees should bestow power and privilege on those who held them, especially in relationship to those who had gained their knowledge through experience or practice. In Western and traditional Chinese systems there was a complex status hierarchy among degree-holders.

In Yan'an, however, the communists had developed another type of educational system, which had a great impact as part of the general political mobilization, and which helped to overturn entirely the old Chinese system. Wedded to the urgent need to solve the problems of mere existence by the use of technical knowledge was a commitment to a long-term educational process which had no less a goal than transforming the way the Chinese had traditionally related to one another. Marxist concepts provided the theoretical and moral basis for this philosophy, wherein labor was not simply an economic necessity but a major source of human knowledge. It was through labor, according to this idea, that human beings were related to one another and also to the environment. In this relation Mao Zedong's essay "On Practice", in which he explained the unity of theory and practice, knowing and doing, mental and manual work, became important. It was used as a major study document in Yan'an's universities and also in the vast ideological education campaign of the early 1940s of the Communist Party of China (Andors 1977: 39).

Quantitatively the higher Chinese educational institutions formed a relatively modest source for potential managers in relation to the size of the population, which was 542 million in 1949. From Table 4.3 we see that the enrollment in higher educational institutions dropped in 1949 quite considerably from the pre-1949 peak year, and did not begin to grow faster until after 1952.

Table 4.3. Entrants, enrollment, and graduates in Chinese higher education pre-1949 and 1949–1954; in thousands. (Richman 1969: 164)

Year	Entrants	Enrollment	Graduates
Pre-1949 peak year	. .	155	21
1949–1950	. .	117	18
1950–1951	35	137	19
1951–1952	35	153	32
1952–1953	66	191	48
1953–1954	71	212	47

The development of China has often been compared with that of India. In the latter country the enrollment in higher educational institutions was 383,000 in 1949–1950, more than three times that of the Chinese figure. However, enrollment in India increased by about 350% during 1949–1963 as compared with about 700% in China (Richman 1969: 165).

As a whole, in 1949 Chinese higher educational institutions formed both quantitatively and qualitatively a very modest management source. The number of graduates was small in relation to the large population of China and, as we have realized, the class and ideological background of the graduates was to a great extent contradictory to the ideological principles according to which the communists wished to develop the new People's Republic of China.

4.7 Summary and Conclusions

As our main focus is management, we will try now to summarize the resources at the societal, organizational, and individual level with the help of which Mao had to begin to create and manage the new People's Republic.

During the long period of wars Chinese society was badly damaged. This was not only a bad thing for the communists, because they could begin to build a new society from scratch. There were no strong resources ready and available to help Mao, but there were not many resources against him either.

At this point we must stress that though the Communist Revolution in China was especially famous because it was made mostly with the help of peasants, this was actually nothing new in that country. When one analyzes Chinese history, one can see revolutionary features in the establishing of every new dynasty, and the revolutionary group has most often been of the peasant class; thus also in ending the last (Chiang Kai-shek) "dynasty" in 1949. Actually Mao did not invent anything new when he performed his revolution with the help of peasants. History was only repeating itself.

The following is an attempt to summarize the positive and negative factors Mao inherited when he and his comrades began to build the new China in 1949. According to our theoretical frame (Fig. A.3) we begin with values.

4.7.1 Old Values and New Ideological Power

The traditional Chinese value system was largely associated with the three religions: Confucianism, Buddhism, and Taoism, which had "lived" together in China for over 2,000 years. Confucianism had been most influential in old China, and some of its thoughts were heavily attacked by the communists. These were especially the ancestor cult and traditional customs, which represented a hierarchical view of society and people. As Confucianism was in addition a religion of the civil servants and the intelligentsia its values were according to the communists typically those of a class society. Confucianism also saw the family as a hierarchically organized basic unit of the society, which was against the communists' ideas.

The cult which has perhaps most clearly remained in Chinese society during the communist regime is the ancestor "cult". The old hierarchical system, based upon age, has been difficult to root out, because it expresses itself everywhere; also in the Chinese language, i.e., in the "names" of family members. One can see that the value of age comes out also in the high average age of Chinese top leaders.

Thus, values concerning authority, responsibility, and subordination were largely shaped by Confucianism and the family system. Business and industrial enterprises typically functioned in old China as an extension of the family system. Subordinates were generally expected to be unquestioningly loyal, obedient, and subservient in executing the orders and instructions issued by their superiors. Under this system there was little worker participation in managerial decision-making, and individual initiative involving risk was significantly constrained.

When examining interpersonal relations in China, one must take into account the great role of "face". The social exchange process of face-giving has been and probably still is – according also to this author's own experiences with Chinese people – an important factor regulating human behavior.

When one speaks of values in 1949 China, one must of course take into account the communist ideology which Mao and his colleagues had been planting in China since the 1930s; first, as an underground activity, later on openly in the areas under communist rule. The communist ideology differed greatly in many points from Chinese traditional values, especially from those concerning status, authority, and hierarchical order. However, Mao could, consciously or unconsciously, transfer some of the old Chinese values to CPC ideology. The family was replaced by the party as a central institution of the society, and one can see that the later great personal cult of Mao fitted in well with the old Chinese emperor cult. However, this was with the great difference that Mao's personal cult was also largely based upon his own, impressive personality.

Thus, the communists had already long before 1949 begun to create a strong ideological power base closely assimilated to Mao's growing personal power. Ideology and personality themselves were not enough to make a revolution; the force behind the victory and the party was the People's Liberation Army, or arms power. The method of influencing others was thus indoctrination when using ideological power, and coercion when using arms power.

4.7.2 Knowledge Resources

The knowledge resources of 1949 China were not great. One of the main constraints on China's industrial development after 1949 was the high illiteracy rate; 90% of the 1949 population. The staffing problems in enterprises as well as those of communication were overwhelming. The high illiteracy favored development of small enterprises and made difficult the establishing of large, modern industrial firms, which China needed badly.

A great constraint on managerial effectiveness and industrial progress was also the lack of knowledge of important foreign languages. Probably a large proportion of the management-level personnel who knew foreign languages belonged to the upper classes and left China because of the communist victory.

4.7.3 Economic Resources

China's whole economy was in a chaotic situation in 1949 because of several factors, of which the main destructive factor had been for several years the constant wars: the war against the Japanese and then the civil war between Chiang Kai-shek's and Mao Zedong's armies. The war brought with it other devastating effects on the economy. A very serious one was the massive inflation. Spiraling inflation made it virtually impossible for industrial managers to plan ahead or to organize, staff, or control operations efficiently. Also corruption and bribery within the government and among bankers, as well as the great extravagance of many officials, became pervasive with the inflation, further aggravating the economic situation and hampering productive efficiency.

The long wars also brought with them and/or enhanced the natural catastrophes of the times. The rural areas wasted by the war were finally ruined by noxious insects, which quickly also spread over the still-cultivated parts of the country. Locusts also invaded the land more frequently than formerly. Thus, of China's economic sectors, agriculture, which was and is the backbone of the economy, was badly damaged. The accumulated effects of the war, natural catastrophes, and other destructive factors had reduced the grain harvest in 1949 to 75% of the level before the war.

The most modern and productive sector of Chinese industry had been in the hands of foreigners before 1937. During the war with Japan this modern industrial sector came almost completely under Japanese control, and after their defeat in 1945 the Guomindang government took over these enterprises. It has been estimated that of the total industrial output value in 1949, the state sector accounted for 35%, the joint state-private sector 2% and the private sector 63%. The wars, political restlessness, and other adversities had also badly damaged Chinese industry before 1949. It has been estimated that the industrial production had on average dropped to half of its highest level before the war.

Because of China's typical topography, transportation problems have always been great there. During the wars the whole transportation system was greatly damaged, since it was an important strategic factor both for aggressors and defenders.

Commerce in 1949 was mostly in the hands of private enterprises, whose share of the total retail sales accounted for 85% in 1950. Because of the war, trade between different parts of the country was stagnant in 1949, but local trade, mainly in the hands of family enterprises, continued to be relatively lively despite the restless times.

During the last years of the war the main proportion for foreign trade consisted of war materials, which did not help in building up the new People's Republic.

4.7.4 Guiding and Controlling Instruments

Norms

The Chinese legal system was quite underdeveloped before 1949, and legal norms did little to improve managerial effectiveness or spur industrial progress. Rather there was an absence of laws in critical areas, and often the dishonest enforcement of laws tended to lead to considerably more uncertainty, greater risks, and less efficiency for firms than would have been the case with a better legal system.

However, already before 1949 the communists began to build up their own legal system by the Yan'an administration. These new informal and formal norms, applied in the areas occupied by communists, were sturdy seed for the norm system of the People's Republic.

Communication

The official communication network in China was badly damaged during 1949 and before it. All partners of the war had their own communication systems in the areas occupied by them. However, as the communists had begun to build up their party membership network long before 1949, and they usually had the support of the local people, their communication network covered a large part of China, including the areas occupied by the enemy. The members of the Communist Party, who numbered over 800,000 in 1945, formed an effective communication network which helped the new rulers to strengthen their administrative power after 1949.

Although the communists had mostly relied upon personal contacts in communication, they had also recognized quite early the importance of mass media. The Xinhua News Agency began its operations in 1931, and the first radio broadcasting was started near Yan'an in 1945. However, because the great majority of Chinese were illiterate and there were very few receiving sets, the effects of mass media were limited.

Hierarchy

According to the deeply rooted Confucian thinking, human relationships in China were sharply hierarchical before the revolution. The hierarchically organized family system was the base of this phenomenon. Although the hierarchical bureaucracy was important in maintaining the economic and political system, its functioning did not make it efficient or creative.

In 1949 the macro- and mesolevel controlling and guiding structures (hierarchical power) were badly damaged because of the war. However, both parties in the civil war established their own administrative system in areas occupied by them. After the communists' victory it was only natural that the new China inherited to a great extent those administrative and hierarchical structures which the communists had first established in Yan'an. The forming of these structures was considerably affected by the poor environmental conditions of the Yan'an area. As these structures greatly differed from traditional Chinese practice, and as they had a profound impact upon the administrative hierarchical structures of enterprises, government, and CPC organizations after 1949, they are summarized again here:

1. When the old hierarchical authority of the hereditary ruling classes was destroyed, it shifted into the hands of revolutionary cadres who participated also in the workers' tasks. A more egalitarian and cooperative society was established.
2. A new hierarchical system of strong leaders and central authority developed.
3. The economy, production, education, and the military became interrelated in the same organizational units, also in enterprises.
4. Production units became self-reliant economically.
5. Different forms of cooperative organizations were developed.
6. Different kinds of participation systems were created. Participation down the line, which became so well-known during the Cultural Revolution, was already created in Yan'an before 1949.
7. Symbols of hierarchical power, e.g., signs of rank in the army, were abolished; a practice which was applied again during the Cultural Revolution.
8. Mao's well-known mass line principle, which linked the leaders' ideas with the behavior of the masses, was created.
9. The status of women was radically changed, and they came to have a more egalitarian role in the society.

It is interesting to note how many of the organizational solutions, which were made later on during Mao's time in macro-, meso-, and microlevel management were applied in practice long before 1949 by the communists

Table 4.4. Main influence structure of prerevolution China in 1949 as seen from the communists' viewpoint

Values	Resources	Methods of influence
• Old Confucian: hierarchy, age and male dominated • New communist: equality and collectivism dominated	• 50% of industrial production • 75% of grain production • Peasants' human resources • People's Liberation Army	Manipulation, indoctrination and coercion – especially among lower hierarchical levels

in Yan'an. Without this experience the structure and management of Chinese organizations would have probably looked quite different.

In Table 4.4 the main influence systems available to the communists in 1949 when they began to build the new People's Republic are presented. Mao and his colleagues had to find a balance between two sets of values: the old traditional Confucian values, dominated by a great sense of hierarchy in state, organizational, and individual relations, in addition to, and related to hierarchy, respect for old age and the male sex. On the other hand there was the communist ideology, which had been enhanced by the Chinese Yan'an experience, and included a striving towards equality and collectivism.

The resources Mao inherited were not overflowing. With regard to economic resources, industry worked at only 50% capacity, and grain production was at 75% capacity. Knowledge resources were very poor, and Mao's personality, assimilated with communist ideology, at that time only affected his closest supporter groups. What were available in overflowing quantities were peasant human physical resources. When Russian and other arms were added to them, the decisive resource of revolution was ready: the People's Liberation Army (PLA), which resolved the civil war, the revolution, and the growing power of the Communist Party.

Depending on the circumstances, the main methods of influencing individuals, groups, and organizations were manipulation, indoctrination with communist ideology, and coercion with the help of armed forces. The latter played a decisive role in old China and during difficult times in Mao's reign. The new era of China since Mao has also begun with Deng Xiaoping as the chairman of the party's military commission, which controls the PLA.

4.7.5 Managerial Resources

We have grouped the potential managerial resources of 1949 as (1) the existing managerial body of enterprises, (2) members of the Communist

Party, (3) the People's Liberation Army, (4) higher educational institutions, and (5) the civil service.

Qualitatively the main body of those potential managers who had some experience, and whom the Chinese could use when beginning to rebuild their economy, came from small enterprises. The managers of large enterprises were often professionals who had been hired by the owners of their firms. These administrators had often delegated the supervision of actual production work to skilled workers, "gang bosses", and also to labor contractors. These often abused the workers. Neither the gang bosses, labor contractors, nor their managers were ideologically suited to a communist regime. One group the communists had to rely on as a superivisory source was skilled literate workers; but they seldom had supervisory skills and/or experience.

Probably the bulk of 1949 China's managerial experience was in business related to the operation and sales of foreign firms. We must, however, remember that many of the potential experienced managers in 1949 were highly corrupt, and managerial proficiency was not sufficient for the development of the new China with its new terminal and instrumental values. As the potential experienced managerial body from enterprises was small and ideologically unreliable, the communists had to rely on other sources, e.g., the party.

The party members filled the ideological gap between the old managerial morals and the values of the new communist government. The number of the members of the CPC had grown rapidly after 1937, and was up to 800,000 in 1945. As the members of the party were the only ideologically reliable persons, they had to be used everywhere in managerial positions or positions controlling the managing of organizations. But they often had no practical or theoretical knowledge of management. Thus, as they had no knowledge resources to rely on, and their ideology was not widely accepted, their own power-base was weak. The real "power" backing them and the building of the People's Republic was the People's Liberation Army, which also formed a great managerial source.

In the economically very difficult conditions of Yan'an the Communist army was deeply involved in production and the training of the people. It was therefore natural that the army became an important source of potential managers. As the army also had strong ideological training, and as the soldiers, especially officers, had good experience in organizing and managing people in difficult circumstances, the representatives of the army were placed in almost every enterprise of any importance. In their managerial positions they acted as experts in some matters, ensured that the correct ideological line was followed, and perhaps also received rewards because of their earlier service in the army.

The contribution of higher educational institutions to management was quite modest in volume compared, e.g., to India. The quality of their contribution had become more suitable during the years before 1949, because the main field of studies had shifted from literary or political subjects to technology, engineering, economics, and business management. However, several Chinese universities trained economists in Western, non-Marxist social science, and economic and business management theory. This Western educational philosophy also reinforced the Confucian tradition that purely intellectual work was superior to manual labor. This widened the disruptive mental-manual labor gap in enterprises.

The fact that in 1949 almost all the students in Chinese universities and higher level technical schools were from the middle and upper middle classes, traditionally not very sympathetic towards communist ideology, presented problems for the new communist regime after 1949.

In the area of Yan'an the communists had developed before 1949 another type of educational system, stressing Mao Zedong's ideas about the unity of theory and practice, mental and manual work. These thoughts later had profound effects upon education in China.

The civil service had traditionally been highly esteemed in China. With the abolition of the training and entrance examination system for governmental positions at the beginning of this century, the quality and status of civil servants sank considerably, and still more during the years of widely spread corruption before the communist victory in 1949.

The civil servants were, however, even more needed after October 1949 than before, as in the socialist system the government and enterprise organizations are tightly bound together, the former controlling and guiding the latter. Governmental managers had to become capable of managing economic organizations also in a much wider sense than before. As especially provincial and local level governmental organizations are vital in China to hold the whole state structure together, it was really a miracle that the communists were able to rule and manage this large country and begin to develop it.

It has been necessary to describe China in 1949 in some detail, because this was the base upon which the later development of the whole of China as well as its management was grounded.

5 Management During and After Mao

5.1 Main Stages of Economic and Political Development of the People's Republic of China

To be able to examine Chinese management in enterprises, government, and the CPC after 1949 we must first describe how the main societal environments developed in the country. Thus, we will not need to repeat these developmental stages every time we examine the development in the three sectors mentioned. As agriculture forms the most important sector in the Chinese economy, and as people's communes with their vast industrial activities in fact represented one kind of enterprise, we have included agricultural organizations in our later analysis.

There are plenty of difficulties when one tries to divide the economic and political development into meaningful temporal stages. On the one hand, there have been so many different kinds of developments, each with their special waves, that an "objective" picture of these waves is difficult to form. On the other hand, when the time is historically relatively near, the observer can very easily focus his attention on phenomena and/or persons which are more clearly visible during his own time, but whose significance in the stream of history may become less and less important, representing only a by-product of greater historical development trends.

Historians say first that historical research gives meaningful order to past phenomena, and second that it answers the question: what is historically important? And it is historically important for a researcher to throw light on those historical factors which help to solve one's own research problem (Kalela 1972: 85).

Our "problem" is to examine Chinese management and its development. We are focusing especially upon economic organizations, but as government, CPC, and enterprise organizations form an integrated entity in socialist China, we must examine all of these to understand the development in any one of these sectors. Thus, we must find here such developmental trends that help to throw light on developments in each of the sectors mentioned. We, so to speak, must see the ground-swells of the society, and describe them first, and then examine the smaller waves of the development typical of individual sectors; this will be done in corresponding subsections.

Thus, we see the following main developmental stages in China after the creation of the People's Republic:

- Period of economic rehabilitation, 1949–1952
- Period of socialist transformation, 1953–1956
- Period of readjustment, 1957–1965
- Period of the Cultural Revolution, 1966–1976
- Period of economic reforms after Mao, 1977–

In this main chapter we will first examine these periods more closely to give adequate background for the later analysis of management in government, CPC, and enterprises.

5.1.1 Economic Rehabilitation (1949–1952)

As mentioned earlier, China's economy as well as its administrative machinery was in chaos after the communist victory in 1949. One of the most needed resources to rebuild the country was knowledge concerning both workers and management in nearly every sector of the society. But to develop knowledge the Chinese badly needed one basic knowledge: the ability to read and write.

The Chinese communists also realized very clearly that they had to first wipe out illiteracy, especially in industry. They succeeded in doing this quite rapidly through a pervasive spare-time adult literacy program. In 1957 the premier of China, Chou En-lai, estimated that the illiteracy rate had fallen to 70% (Richman 1969: 134). This estimate seems to strengthen the previously mentioned estimate by Richman that the illiteracy rate of the 1949 population was 90%.

We stated earlier that management resources that existed in 1949 were small and mostly to be found in industrial, commercial, and government organizations of old China. These potential managers had, however, a quite different societal ideology from that of the communists, at least for the purpose of beginning to build a socialist economy from which the private capitalist enterprise system should be abolished. What should and could the new communist rulers do to get the country on its feet again? Fortunately, the idea for an appropriate strategy had already matured among the communists well before October 1, 1949. Three months before this date Mao Zedong gave a speech during the celebration of the CPC's

28th anniversary, where he explained the economic and political strategy for rehabilitation:

> To counter imperialist oppression and to raise her backward economy to a higher level, China must utilize all the factors of urban and rural capitalism that are beneficial and not harmful to the national economy and the people's livelihood; and we must unite with the national bourgeoisie in common struggle. Our present policy is to regulate capitalism, not to destroy it. But the national bourgeoisie cannot be the leader of the revolution, nor should it have the chief role in state power. (Mao 1977b, IV: 421)

The macromanagement strategy applied during the period of economic rehabilitation, 1949–1952, had a profound impact upon China's later development. The strategy thus contained the following principles: The remaining imperialist and feudal characteristics of Chinese society should be abolished. This, however, should not occur in such a way that everything which could be called capitalist should be destroyed. Instead the communists should at first cooperate with the national capitalists, and at the same time change the economy gradually in order to obtain resources both to get the economy on its feet again, and to begin later in more stabilized political and economic circumstances to develop the society toward socialism.

The same kind of strategy should be applied in agriculture, where the rural economy based on rich peasants should partly be defended, developed, and controlled to secure the livelihood of the people. The system of the feudal landlords should, however, be abolished. There could be exceptions concerning the more enlightened landowners during a period of changeover, especially concerning capitalist industrial production which they had taken an interest in parallel with their landownership (Chao 1960: 95, 114).

It was planned that only after the rural economy, based on the controlled activities of rich peasants, on the one hand, and national capitalism, on the other, had made enough economic progress, could the socialist rebuilding of the society step by step be accomplished. The actions which took place during the period of rehabilitation 1949–1952 – land reform, confiscation of bureaucrat-capitalist and imperialist enterprises, establishment of a handicrafts cooperative, enlarged control of trade, etc. – can be seen as necessary preparations for the socialist changeover of production conditions. Even the most critical assessors of the history of the People's Republic have, regarding the rapid initial growth, seen the period of rehabilitation as decisive for the continuous economic development of China (King 1968: 175).

Industrial and agricultural production grew during the years of economic rehabilitation in the following way: Farm output rose by 48.5%, averaging 14.1% a year. Industrial output went up by 145%, averaging 34.8% a year.

In industry, the average yearly increase in light industry was 29% and that in heavy industry 48.8%. Of course, the high rates were peculiar to a period of recovery and could not be attained in normal times (Xue 1981: 7–8).

China had experienced, as we have noted, hyperinflation which had lasted more than 12 years. Control of the high inflation was necessary to revive the national economy. To put an end to the great fluctuations in market prices, in the spring of 1950 the CPC leaders took the decisive step of unifying the management of all financial and economic work. Until that point, because of the demands of the wars, each strategic area had been independent financially and economically. Unification meant centralizing the control of financial and economic work for the country as a whole and balancing the nation's income and expenditure.

> By balancing the financial budget, restricting the purchasing power of government organizations and the army, and making an inventory of all warehouse stocks, in less than six months China had successfully controlled inflation and stabilized market prices throughout the country. (Xu et al. 1982: 5–6)

When we examine as a whole the strategy the CPC applied during the period of rehabilitation it seems clear that this successful strategy was based on a careful analysis of the class structure of the Chinese society, and also the tensions between the classes. As agriculture was the key sector of the Chinese economy, and as the class conflicts in this sector had given power to the communist revolution, it was only natural that the economic reform began in rural areas. We examine this reform in more detail later.

5.1.2 Period of Socialist Transformation (1953–1956)

After the period of rehabilitation during which the land reform had been introduced and the bureaucrats' capital, which had been in the hands of the Guomindang government, had been confiscated, the Chinese economy consisted of three main sectors: (1) the state-run economy; (2) the individual economy of the peasants and handicraftsmen; and (3) the capitalist economy of the national bourgeoisie. The next step of the communist leaders included further advancing towards socialism by transforming agriculture and handicrafts under individual ownership into a collectively owned sector, and changing national capitalist industry and commerce into part of the state-run economy (Xu et al. 1982: 6).

The collectivization of agriculture went through several phases which we will describe later in more detail. The transformation process advanced at higher speed than expected; at the end of the period of socialist transformation, in 1956, 96% of agricultural households were already organized into cooperatives. Parallel to this development was the cooperativization of handicrafts. By the end of 1956, 92% of all handicraftsmen had joined producer cooperatives (Xu et al. 1982: 7).

In industry the socialist transformation proceeded step by step from 1953 when the first five-year plan started. During the period of rehabilitation (1949–1952) the communist government had taken those enterprises which had been under the control of the Guomindang government into its hands. In addition to these firms there were private enterprises which had been partly owned by Guomindang officials through ownership of shares. The communists confiscated these shares and joint state-private enterprises appeared already at the time of the establishing of the People's Republic (Xue 1981: 29).

It has been estimated that the output value of socialist state industry accounted for 67.5% of the gross industrial output value, the share of joint state-private industry was 32.5%, and the share of private capitalist industry was practically nonexistent at that time.

The socialization process proceeded in trade along the same lines. State and joint state-private commerce accounted in 1956 for 97.2% of the turnover in wholesale trade, whereas private commerce accounted for only 2.8%. In retail trade the share of state commerce was 68.3%, joint state-private and cooperative commerce 27.5%, while private commerce accounted for only 4.2% of the retail turnover (Xue 1981: 31).

Private family-owned small stores and vendors had played an important role in distributing goods in pre-1949 China.

> Until 1956, the socialist transformation of China's small stores and vendors was carried out mainly by making them retailers of goods distributed by state commercial enterprises and letting them earn the differences between wholesale and retail prices. During the upsurge of socialist transformation in 1956, the co-operative movement was extended to small stores and vendors. In fact, many small stores were incorporated into state stores. Other small stores and vendors were organized in co-operative stores or co-operative groups, while a considerable number of small stores and vendors continued to operate on their own. (Xue 1981: 42)

The process of socialist transformation which occurred in China from 1953 to 1956 was a huge undertaking; it would have been a difficult task to plan even for experienced specialists. The communist leaders had little experience, if any, in this kind of very complicated development. Thus, this transformation process brought with it many unintended consequences (see Fig. A.3), causing serious problems for the entire society.

One example concerned transportation. Private businessmen had previously taken care of the long-distance transportation of commodities between the countryside and cities. With the disappearance of private businessmen, because of the socialization process, these vital transportation channels were cut off. The supply and marketing cooperatives could not handle thousands of different kinds of products. The result was that many kinds of local products, especially in mountainous areas, rotted in the valleys or fields, because there was nobody to transport them away; the income of the peasants dropped, as did supplies to the cities (Xue 1981: 43).

Although most of the socialization of the Chinese economy had been carried out by 1957, the situation in the society was quite unstable, and the many unintended consequences had caused serious problems. Thus, a period of readjustment was needed, although this also contained sudden, poorly planned changes, as we will learn in the next section.

5.1.3 Period of Readjustment (1957–1965)

The period of readjustment, as the Chinese call it, contained in some areas, e.g., agriculture, a clear organizational process towards more advanced socialism, but in some areas the period can be characterized by a kind of double readjustment, where contradictory forces were marching back and forth.

Hundred Flowers Movement

Before going on to examine what happened to the economy during the period of readjustment, let us briefly look at an episode at the beginning of this period, which especially concerned intellectuals. After 1949 the communist government tried to use well-educated people who had remained in China to industrialize the country and to develop the economy in the best possible way. The status of the more highly educated intellectuals attained its acme during 1956 and 1957 under the so-called movement of the Hundred Flowers, or of free speech.

> A vigorous effort was made to use their talents to the "fullest possible extent," and they were encouraged to put forth their candid opinions and criticisms. At that time the social scientists who had been trained prior to 1949 and particularly the Western-educated social scientists were the most outspoken critics of the regime and the party. (Richman 1969: 218)

The period of free speech, or the changing of the use of communication power, did not, however, last a long time. The following period of the Great Leap Forward included a nationwide, strong antiintellectual campaign, the aim of which was levelling out class distinctions based on formal educational qualifications. Thus, China in a few years moved from one extreme, the great appreciation of higher education and intellectuals, to the other: accusing the intellectuals

> of being Expert at the expense of Red, of favoring individualism rather than collectivism, self-interest rather than collective interest, of being specialists rather than generalists, of placing technical, economic and other non-political issues above politics and ideology. (Richman 1969: 218)

Thus, to keep the general power resources and corresponding power to influence in their hands, the relatively new communist government actively regulated the use of the communication network – the instrumental power – first to allow free speech, and then to prohibit it. Through the use of this instrumental power, the Communist Party and government prevented the intellectuals and their knowledge power from becoming a threat to their ruling status. Looking back, one feels that ending the Hundred Flowers movement was an exaggeration of self-defence, but we must remember that the communists had only a few years before achieved their victory after many years of bloody wars. Against this background their behavior, although often changing and contradictory, becomes understandable.

The Great Leap Forward and Its End

The period of readjustment began with great enthusiasm. The first five-year plan (1953–1957) had been successful. During that period the gross value of industrial output had increased by 128%, and the corresponding percentage for agriculture was 24.8. National income rose during the period at an annual rate of 8.9%, with industry growing at 19.6% and agriculture at 3.8% (Xu et al. 1982: 8–9). In addition, the harvest for 1958 was a record one, 90% bigger than in 1957. All this created an atmosphere of too much optimism, which led the leaders to make wild plans for the future. The famous campaign of the Great Leap Forward was launched by Mao Zedong in February 1958, calling for a doubling of output within one year.

But there soon appeared several drawbacks, which suddenly halted the favorable economic development. Agriculture was hit in 1959 and 1960 by great natural catastrophes. In 1960, for example, more than half of the cultivated land was badly damaged. Had the organizational structure of agricultural production not been changed just before these catastrophes, their results could have been still more devastating for China. In 1958 a great proportion of Chinese agriculture was organizationally changed from producers' cooperatives to large people's communes with tens of thousands of people. These great organizations had a large distribution network covering dozens of villages and thousands of households. With their wide-reaching organization the communes could help the more hard-hit villages and households, and distribute government catastrophe aid.

Because of the great setbacks the Chinese economy had suffered during the Great Leap Forward, a hectic discussion emerged about future economic strategy. This ended in a temporary victory for the so-called Liu Shao-chi line, which proposed enlarging the size of private plots of land which the peasants could cultivate for their own needs. There were other measures to motivate industry, which we shall describe later. It is difficult to find the main reason why the Chinese economy took a favorable turn again, as is evident from Fig. 5.1. At all events, the bad years were over, at least for a while.

The victory of Liu Shao-chi and his supporters did not last long; the struggle went on and reached its climax later during the Cultural Revolution. In agriculture the greatest change concerning management during the period of readjustment was indisputably the organizational change from producers' cooperatives to people's communes. This move greatly changed not only management practice and the modes of production in rural areas, but also the content of life for hundreds of millions of Chinese.

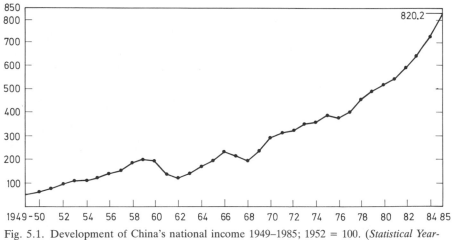

Fig. 5.1. Development of China's national income 1949–1985; 1952 = 100. (*Statistical Yearbook of China 1985*; *China: A Statistical Survey in 1986*)

Period of Readjustment in Industry

The great optimism created by the successful first five-year plan affected the plans for industry. When the Great Leap Forward campaign was launched in 1958, one of its enthusiastic slogans concerned industry in particular: "Exceed Britain's production in the most important industries within 15 years." The central authorities gave arbitrary directions in industry, and set excessively high targets for production and construction. Since these were further raised at local levels, the process led to serious imbalances in the economy (Xu et al. 1982: 9). Later the natural catastrophes which hit agriculture worsened the development of industry. During the second five-year plan (1958–1962) the annual rate of growth of the gross value of industrial and agricultural output was only 0.6%. The industrial average was 3.8%, as compared with 18% during the first five-year plan (Xu et al. 1982: 8–10).

Another bad setback hit Chinese industry in 1960, when Soviet aid ended suddenly, and the Russian technicians and experts were withdrawn from China. Soviet aid was based on a 30-year agreement of "friendship, alliance, and mutual assistance" made in 1950. The Soviets had chosen, with or without purpose, an extremely critical time-point for their withdrawal: a severe economic crisis was then emerging in China because of the ideological fanaticism of the Great Leap Forward campaign, and because of the natural catastrophes which had hit agriculture. As there had been between 10,000–20,000 Soviet experts and industrial advisers in China during the 1950s, their withdrawal with their detailed plans was deeply felt in Chinese industry for a long time afterwards.

However, the Soviet pull-out did not altogether stop the wheels of industry, and it gradually began to recover in 1962. A general improvement occurred in 1965 after three years of readjustment. During these years, 1963–1965, the average annual increase in the gross value of industry was 17.9% and of agriculture 11.1% (Xu et al. 1982: 11). This positive development can clearly be seen in Fig. 5.1.

The positive development mentioned was made possible by several factors, including a new economic strategy. The demand for a new industrial strategy after the failure of the Great Leap Forward required, according to the line of Liu Shao-chi and his supporters, the replacing in industry of the quantitative production targets with profit targets for every enterprise. One part of the new strategy contained the forming and developing of small and medium-sized enterprises in the countryside. Their operations should also be based upon their own responsibility concerning profit and loss, and their production targets should be set to meet the needs of the individual households. As mentioned, the sum of several positive measures probably had a favorable effect upon the national economy until the beginning of the Cultural Revolution in 1966.

Before we proceed to examine the general development of the Chinese economy during the last ten years of Mao Zedong's rule, let us briefly consider the readjustment of commerce during 1957–1965. As has been mentioned, during the period of socialist transformation the cooperative movement was extended to small stores and vendors. The socialization process continued in 1958, when the Chinese began to incorporate many cooperative stores and groups into state stores. As a result of these developments small stores and vendors responsible for their own profits and losses were almost nowhere to be found. "Thus people had to stand in long lines to get a meal or some groceries" (Xue 1981: 42).

It seems that the contemporary Chinese leaders have taken advantage of the poor experiences of the too rapid socialization of the Chinese economy in the 1950s and 1960s – experiences which were felt deeply among the common citizens especially in the area of trade. Thus, these misfortunes of some 25 years ago may have influenced the contemporary Chinese leaders to move towards market socialism, giving the enterprises relatively greater independence and responsibility for profits and losses. We must remember that the most influential Chinese leaders of the 1980s, such as Deng Xiaoping, had reached leading positions already in the 1950s and 1960s, and thus have their own personal experiences of those times.

5.1.4 Cultural Revolution (1966–1976)

When I originally planned the structure of this book, I had reserved for the period of the "Great" Cultural Revolution one of the main chapters. However, when I began to write the book, and especially when I examined the different longer periods of Chinese history, including those during the dynasties before 1911, I began to realize that the Cultural Revolution was a short episode in the history of China. It was a very painful episode for many prominent contemporary Chinese, but the period itself did not actually change the flow of history; perhaps only slightly slowing it down for a while.

Historians argue that there have always been more or less turbulent periods between the different dynasties in China's ancient history. The pains of the birth of a new dynasty have usually been greater, the greater the changes the new ruling system has brought to the society. The antenatal pains of the new People's Republic were hard, with many bloody battles between 1911 and 1949. But this long and painful struggle gave birth to triplets: first, a new communist ideology, second, a new socialist organizational system, and, third new rulers, Mao Zedong and his supporters.

In a way, the period of the Cultural Revolution can be seen as the last death throes of Mao's era. The result, as well as a probable cause, of the ten-year struggle was the change of leaders. The main ideology as well as the main macrostructure of the society have not changed since that period, or at least not yet. At the organizational level there have been more changes, which we will examine later.

What were the reasons for launching the Cultural Revolution? As we have seen, the setbacks of the Chinese economy created during the Great Leap Forward awakened lively discussion in the Central Committee (CC) of the CPC concerning the strategy, best suited to develop the economic and social development of the country. Liu Shao-chi, at that time the President of China, had gathered around him a group of party members who heavily criticized the societal policy applied during the Great Leap Forward. As a result of these discussions, the emphasis in the development of the three main economic sectors was changed: agriculture was placed first, light industry second, and heavy industry was given last place in the development strategy.

At the same time China was beginning to create a free-market system for rural areas, and was also increasing the number of small and medium-sized enterprises guided by their own profits.

This tendency towards a free-market economy worried Mao Zedong. He stressed that the Chinese should not forget the class struggle, and began a strong counterattack, which gradually incurred many unintended and uncontrollable consequences. In a nutshell, we can see the following as main reasons for the Cultural Revolution:

1. The fear of Mao Zedong and his supporters concerning the results of the new strategy, which they thought could lead China back to a capitalist society. The new strategy was personalized in Liu Shao-chi.
2. A fight between a decentralized economy, defended by Mao, and a centralized economy according to the Soviet model. It should be remembered that Liu Shao-chi had received his education in the Soviet Union.
3. A conflict between the Maoist and Soviet Communist ideology. It was thought that Liu Shao-chi represented the latter.
4. The age structure of China was weighted very much towards youth. It has been estimated that in 1966 more than half of the Chinese population was under 22 years of age. Mao was worried that these young people would not grow up in a correct ideological and societal environment. China would therefore need repeated "revolutions" after a certain interval; these would keep the masses on the right ideological road.

5. Mao was afraid that an elite group had already been formed in the upper levels of Chinese society; a group supplementing itself, and separated sharply from the masses. This group should be brought back into contact with the broad masses.
6. Connected with the previous reason, there was demand for a reform of the educational system, because it had become more and more difficult for the children of peasants' and workers' families to enter higher educational institutions. It was thought that universities and other higher educational institutions should become closer to the masses and to practical work.
7. Last but not least it should be mentioned that the Cultural Revolution was closely connected with a fight over the power inheritance of the old Chairman Mao Zedong.

Mao and his supporters thought that, especially in points 3, 4, 5, and 6, ideological reeducation was needed. That is perhaps why the period was named the "Great Cultural Revolution." In reforming the content of the education there were three basic objectives: (1) to intensify ideological education to raise the political consciousness of the students; (2) to integrate theory and practice in the educational process – this would better satisfy the immediate production needs of the country; and (3) to popularize education, so that it would reach the rural areas of the country. Thus, the most culturally deprived elements of the population would no longer be subordinate to or dependent on an elite technocracy primarily serving its own interests.

It has been estimated that in 1965–1966 approximately 30% of Chinese children were not covered by a system of primary education. Thus, 30 million school-aged children, most of them living in rural areas, were not at school. Especially opportunities concerning higher-level education were unduly concentrated in big cities (Wang 1975: 760, 762).

The entrance procedure of universities during the Cultural Revolution was changed altogether, and contained the following steps: (1) the applicant voluntarily made a personal application for admission; (2) he had to get recommendations from the mass organs with which he was affiliated; (3) the application had to be ratified by the leadership concerned (i.e., the Party Committee); and (4) the university granting admission reexamined the candidate. "It was a system combining recommendation and some degree of selection" (Egashira 1975: 993).

In the process of levelling out class differences and of bringing the intellectuals closer to the masses, thousands of university professors and other teachers were sent for years to rural areas to do physical work in agriculture. Teaching in universities practically stopped for years. When I was visiting the Beijing University in Beijing and the Sun Yat-sen University in

Guangzhou (Canton) in 1973, I learned that not a single new teacher had been appointed there from 1967 to 1973. The Chinese did not during that time altogether ignore training, knowledge, and skill, but they especially stressed the importance of political "purity." Thus, when they considered the placing of persons in various tasks, the Chinese preferred the politically pure all-rounder to the nonpolitical technical expert (Laaksonen 1975: 16).

The Cultural Revolution shook all of Chinese society profoundly, and often individually very painfully. However, not many of its "innovations" remained alive after Mao Zedong's death in 1976. Also the changes concerning, e.g., management of organizations were not new innovations, but had already been experimented with earlier. They were reintroduced and intensified, because they suited the ideological and practical goals of the movement that has been described. In my opinion the most important changes accomplished during the Cultural Revolution in the area of management were the following:

1. The earlier more or less one-man management system was replaced by a system of collective management. So-called revolutionary committees were created for large and small organizations and/or their units in government, agriculture, industry, and commerce, and also, e.g., in educational and health organizations.
2. A system of participation down the line was greatly intensified and made systematic. This meant that persons in superior positions in organizations had to participate with and work alongside workers at shop-floor level.
3. According to the dominant ideology and levelling policy of the time the communist leaders abolished the bonus system earlier connected with salaries and wages as a device to improve work motivation. The economic power in management of employees was compensated by ideological power, which took the form, e.g., of highly intensified ideological training.

In a way one might say that the Cultural Revolution was a repetition of the 1949 revolution, although on a minor scale. After 1966 the Chinese society was again torn apart from its earlier entity and the pieces were put together again in a partially new form. The fact that the Chinese society did not altogether collapse during the storms of the Cultural Revolution was at least partly because of the same factor as in 1949, the People's Liberation Army. The PLA first looked at the development of the Cultural Revolution from the sidelines, but when it began to bring about unintended, too violent consequences, the PLA checked its temper and gradually brought back order to the society.

How developed was the economy during the Cultural Revolution? At the beginning of the period from 1966 onward, economic activity slowed down greatly. There were at first huge demonstrations of workers, students, and other youth groups. The large-scale transport of great masses of Red Guards to different parts of the country stopped the transportation needed by the economic system almost completely. This was soon felt in the form of a great shortage of raw materials and other commodities. Because of this, the majority of factories had to close their doors for shorter or longer periods during 1967.

In 1967 the output value of industry fell by 13.8%, and in 1968 by a further 5%. In 1968 agricultural production declined by 2.5%. The production figures began to rise in 1969 and 1970, as can be seen from Fig. 5.1. During the turmoil and fight for power of the last years of Mao Zedong's life, or during the period of the Fourth Five-Year Plan (1971–1975), the annual growth rate of industry dropped to 9.1% (the corresponding figure for 1963–1965 had been 17.9%), and in agriculture to 4% (for 1963–1965 it was 11.1%, Xu et al. 1982: 11–12).

If we examine the Cultural Revolution from the point of view of how different powers were used, we observe (Fig. 5.2) that during this turbulent period Mao took advantage of his own personality power, and the ideological power created by himself and his supporters to activate the young Red Guards. The latter again used coercion to dissolve the former hierarchical structures (power) and their representatives, or Liu Shao-chi's supporters. The activity of the Red Guards, however, brought about unintended disruptive consequences. Strong coercion can often be overcome only by still

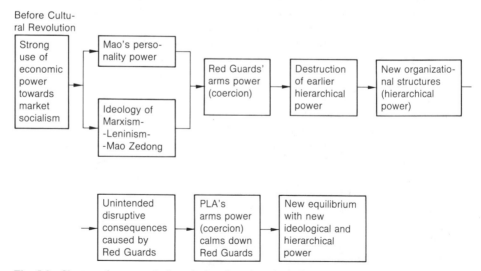

Fig. 5.2. Change of power relations during the cultural revolution

stronger counter-coercion. This came from the People's Liberation Army, which quickly calmed down the Red Guards, and stabilized the situation; not, however, to the level before the Cultural Revolution, but to a great extent to the level Mao had aimed at.

It is still difficult to close the accounts of the Cultural Revolution. It seems now, a decade after Mao Zedong's death, that the seemingly great changes or "experiments" made, e.g., in the area of management remained largely provisional.

However, it is important from the viewpoint of management that China during the Cultural Revolution was like a huge management laboratory, where different experiments, concerning tens of thousands of organizations and their managers, and hundreds of millions of people, were tried out in natural circumstances. The sad problem from the point of view of management research is that very few empirical studies have been made in China concerning these experiments and their outcome. The death of Mao Zedong on September 9, 1976 practically finished the Cultural Revolution. New leaders soon stepped into power and a new era began in the history of the People's Republic of China.

5.1.5 Reforms After Mao: The Giant Ship Turns

Changing the Leaders

The year 1976, which spelled the end of the Cultural Revolution and Mao Zedong's reign, was in many ways dramatic. During the same year several powerful Chinese leaders died. The first was the long-time premier of China, Zhou En-lai, Mao's close friend and fellow soldier from the time of the Long March. His death on January 8, 1976 removed a steadying influence on Chinese politics and sparked off a series of political earthquakes. It was anticipated that Deng Xiaoping, who presided over the memorial service on January 15, would succeed to the premiership. But this did not happen. Instead, on February 7 there came the surprising announcement that a relatively little-known person, the minister of public security, Hua Guofeng, had been made acting premier.

The fight for power went on. Mao Zedong himself or the forces behind him stepped in. On April 7, "On the proposal of our great leader Chairman Mao," the Party Politburo dismissed Deng Xiaoping from all posts both inside and outside the party, but not from his party membership. At the same time Hua Guofeng was appointed first vice-chairman of the CPC Central Committee and premier of the government. In this way Zhou En-lai's carefully arranged succession plans, which envisaged the accession of a pragmatist to power for the benefit of China's economy and polity alike, had been thrown away (Clubb 1978: 470).

There were certain events that followed during the same year, which might well have been taken by the Chinese as bad omens. In June there was an official announcement that Chairman Mao Zedong would no longer receive foreign visitors. Then another important person in the Chinese polity died, Chu Teh, founder of the People's Liberation Army and chairman of the standing committee of the National People's Congress.

> There had been a serious earthquake in Yun'an Province in May; now at the end of July, a devastating earthquake hit North China. Its epicenter was the important mining town of Tangshan, which was effectively destroyed, with heavy loss of life. This was followed in August by yet another quake in northern Szechuan. Those imbued with traditional Chinese superstition might well have concluded that the natural disasters presaged political calamity (Clubb 1978: 470).

And the old prophecies proved to be true: on September 9 "the Great Helmsman" Chairman of the Communist Party of China, Mao Zedong, died. Although a relatively short time has elapsed since his death, the general opinion is that he will be seen in history as one of the great earthshakers (Clubb 1978: 470–471).

The death of Mao was an event that was felt long before and after its occurrence. The Cultural Revolution was in a way the death struggle of the creator of the People's Republic. With his last energies Mao tried to ensure that his ideological and societal inheritance – the ever-continuing revolution and class struggle – would be passed on to future generations. But during the Cultural Revolution so many powerful persons and groups had been hurt that a strong opposition had grown up, just waiting for a suitable moment to take over and change the policy.

The fight over power, over the "right" political ideology and the development strategy, began immediately after Mao's death. Mao's powerful widow Jiang Qing and the other three radicals, the "Gang of Four," were arrested quite soon after Mao's death, and were later on brought to court. The trial in 1980 was televised throughout China, and as I was at that time in Guangzhou (Canton) I could follow the defence of Jiang Qing herself on TV. She defended herself very forcefully, and attacked the new leaders for their behavior while Mao was living, and their antisocialist policy after 1978.

But the new policy appeared also in the way the new leaders treated the old ones. In earlier times they would have normally been executed immediately, but now they were taken to court. However, one can see in this behavior an instinct for self-preservation. The condemned persons still had plenty of supporters all over the country.

The actual turning point in China's economic and political strategy was the Third Plenum of the Eleventh Central Committee of the CPC in December 1978. It discarded the slogan "Take class struggle as the key link," which had become unsuitable in a socialist society, and made the strategic decision to shift the focus of work to socialist modernization during the remaining 21 years of this century. The afterwards often-cited "four modernizations" concerned: (1) industry, (2) agriculture, (3) national defence, and (4) science and technology. The meeting declared that attention should be paid to solving the problems of serious imbalances between the major fields of the economy. Beginning from 1979 China should first tackle the existing imbalances and carry out a policy of "readjustment, reform, consolidation and improvement" (Xu et al. 1982: 13; *Resolution on CPC History* 1981: 50; Field 1984: 743–745; Yeh 1984: 696).

The development according to the new economic strategy was slower than anticipated, however; it was especially difficult to overcome problems of economic imbalances and the overextension of capital construction. Thus, after two years' effort it was decided to carry on with the policy of readjustment for another five years or more, beginning from 1981 (Xu et al. 1982: 13).

It is difficult, if not often impossible, to radically change a development strategy for a nation without at the same time also changing the leaders for those who really wholeheartedly support the new way of thinking. Hua Guofeng, the premier of the country, had been chosen by the late Chairman Mao Zedong for the leading posts of both government and party in April 1976, at the same time as Deng Xiaoping was dismissed from all posts "inside and outside" the party. In the late 1970s Mao Zedong's ideas and policy during his last years had already been strongly criticized. Thus, there were probably ideological, power, and personal reasons why Hua Guofeng had to step aside when Deng Xiaoping and the ideas represented by him had regained power.

In his speech to an enlarged meeting of the Political Bureau of the Central Committee of the CPC in August 1980, Deng Xiaoping said that

> Changing the leadership of the State Council will be a major item on the agenda of the forthcoming Third Session of the Fifth National People's Congress. This change will cover the following: Comrade Huo Guofeng will no longer hold the concurrent post of Premier, which will be assumed by Comrade Zhao Zhiyang. (Deng 1984)

Deng also said that he and six other vice-premiers would leave their posts so that "more energetic comrades can take over."

Other changes concerning the heads of important positions of the government were announced. Deng gave the following main reasons for these great personnel changes:

1. To avoid overconcentration of power, which is liable to give rise to arbitrary rule by individuals at the expense of collective leadership. The concentration of power was, according to Deng, also an important cause of excessive bureaucracy under those circumstances.
2. To avoid proliferation of concurrent and deputy posts. "There is a limit to one's knowledge, experience and energy ... Too many deputy posts will lead to low efficiency and contribute to bureaucracy and formalism."
3. Deng's statement of the need to distinguish between the responsibilities of the party and the government and to stop substituting the responsibilities of the former for those of the latter was a profound change of policy, and it may have unforeseen consequences for the power structure in a socialist country.
4. To change the older persons in leading posts for new and younger ones in order to smooth the succession of leadership. (Deng, B.R. October, 1983)

Deng summarized that the main maladies concerning leadership and the cadre system of the party and state are bureaucratism, the patriarchal way of doing things, life-long tenure of leading posts, various kinds of privileges, and overcentralization of power.

To change the course of a nation of over one billion inhabitants, it is not enough to change only the top leaders in the party and government. The "cleaning" had to go down to the lower levels of management, and in the party down to the grassroots level, or to the ordinary members of the party. Thus, in October 1983 the CPC Central Committee made a decision on party consolidation.

The tasks of party consolidation were first the achievement of ideological unity concerning the new course of the party; second, rectifying the party style; third, strengthening the party discipline; fourth, purifying the party organizations by sorting out elements which persist in opposing and harming the party, "and expel them from the party in accordance with the Party Constitution."

> To meet the needs of Party Consolidation, the Party Central Committee has decided to edit and publish A Must Book for Party Members, A Concise Edition of Important Documents Since the Third Plenary Session of the 11th Party Central Committee, Comrade Mao Zedong on the Party's Style of Work and Party Organization. These

three books and the Selected Works of Deng Xiaoping will be the documents for study during this Party consolidation. (Decision of the CC, October 11, 1983)

Relying greatly on written official material (norm power), and publications of the top leaders themselves seems to be a part of Chinese culture. Earlier it was the "Red Book" of Mao; in the 1980s it is the *Selected Works of Deng*. Naturally in a party of 40 million members it is impossible to communicate correct information only orally. Colsolidation needs a uniform, solid, and thus written knowledge base distributed to everyone in exactly the same way.

At the time of the Central Committee meeting in October 1983 the party had 40 million members, about 2.5 million party organizations at the grass-roots level and above, and altogether more than 9 million cadres working in them. It was decided by the Central Committee that the party consolidation would be completed in two stages and over three years, beginning in the winter of 1983. To ensure that the consolidation work would be brought to a satisfactory conclusion, the CC also decided on a reregistration of party members. All 40 million party members had to reapply to the party over the following two years, or until the end of 1986 (B.R., December 17, 1984).

The consolidiation program also contained a rejuvenation operation among the top leaders of the party. Thus, in 1985 altogether 131 aging party veterans resigned from the Central Committee, the Central Advisory Commission, and the Central Commission for Discipline Inspection. Younger technocrats occupied their positions. Among the retired persons were ten members of the powerful Political Bureau of the Central Committee; they were replaced by six new younger members.

The concept "young" in Chinese leadership positions is a relative concept. The average age of the six new "younger" members was 60; the youngest was 56 and the oldest 68. The traditional Chinese value system honoring age seems still to have a strong effect.

As the Standing Committee of the Political Bureau remained unchanged, the average age of its five members is 74. The oldest, Deng Xiaoping, was at that time (1985) 81, and the youngest, Premier Zhao Ziyang 66.

To summarize this section, we can state that to be able to really change the course of development in a human system one needs to change the leaders who have to implement the new strategy in practice. This applies to macro-, meso-, and micromanagement. Later we will see how there has been a big changeover in enterprise managers in China since 1978.

The same kind of development has occurred in the Soviet Union since Gorbachev came to power. He also had new ideas about how to develop his country and saw that it was necessary to change many of the older leaders for new ones whom he was sure would support his program. In a way, the two greatest socialist powers have both begun a new development program in their countries. It is interesting to note that in China, where the program of change is more radical – at least at the present stage – the initiator of the change process is over 80 years old, whereas Gorbachev, whose program is much milder, is more than 20 years younger. Of course we must remember that the societal starting points for these two countries and persons are different.

Economic Reforms after Mao

The process of economic reforms after Mao actually began before his death in 1976. The discussion of economic policy in China was centered before and after Mao's death around the Marxist analysis of the relationship between the forces of production and on the relations of production. The latter issue of the transformation of the relations of production was at the forefront during the Cultural Revolution and was represented by the "Gang of Four." During 1975 and 1976, when the struggle between Deng and his supporters and the "Gang of Four" was going on, Deng gave primacy to the major determining role of the productive forces, practice, and the economic base in general historical development.

After Mao's death and the arrest of the "Gang of Four", Deng's analysis won more and more support. There was press support already before Deng was rehabilitated. Thus, the door was gradually opened for a new economic policy aimed towards technological modernization and an acceleration in the rate of output. The process of transformation did not, however, proceed quickly. After 1976, economic policy passed through several distinct phases, each involving an intensification of the process of change (Gray and White 1982: 90–91). We shall divide the periods after Mao into the following phases concerning economic change:

- Launching of the "Four Modernizations", 1976–1977
- Breakthrough of the reforms, 1978
- "Green Revolution", 1979
- Opening up to the world, 1980

Launching the "Four Modernizations" (1976–1977)

The first phase began in October 1976 and lasted until the Fifth National People's Congress in February 1978. During that time the process of introducing new economic policies, which largely followed Deng's ideas, began. Especially the slogan concerning the "four modernizations" was often in the foreground in official speeches (Xu et al. 1982: 13). The policy at that time stressed the strengthening of management, restoring the status of engineers and technicians, and, e.g., increased import of foreign technology. It has been said that the very ambitious goals contained in the ideas of the "four modernizations" were very reminiscent of the atmosphere before the Great Leap Forward in the late 1950s.

Breakthrough of the Reforms (1978)

The year 1978 can be seen as representing the second phase of the reform process. An official turning point was the Third Plenum of the Eleventh Central Committee of the CPC in December 1978, which shifted China's course towards market socialism. The ideas, which found their official expression in the Plenum, had been introduced earlier by both Hua Guofeng and Deng Xiaoping. These ideas included a complete reevaluation of the economic policies implemented during Mao's time.

Opinions about how to develop China's industrial planning and management further differed greatly, however. Gordon White (1983) has summarized the different viewpoints in three main groups:

1. The centralizing position argued that earlier too much decision-making concerning industrial enterprises was in the hands of local administrations. Since these local authorities largely controlled financial revenue and resources, they did not take into account the central planning priorities. The overall system was poorly coordinated, and thus a reassertion of central guidance was needed. According to our concepts the hierarchical power was much too decentralized at the mesolevel, and a move towards macrolevel centralized control was needed.
2. The position regarding decentralizing was opposite to that mentioned above. Too much power had been in the hands of central departments, and the local authorities had to constantly consult with the central government on every issue. As there was very little real freedom of initiative, the main purpose of the reform would be to create possibilities for greater initiative. According to this viewpoint the hierarchical power lay too much in the hands of macromanagement, and should be transferred to the mesolevel.

Although the two viewpoints were very different, the first stressing macromanagement and the second mesomanagement, a common idea to both was that they saw the economic management system mainly as administrative relations in a very complex system of hierarchical bureaucracy.

3. The third position stressed the importance of micromanagement, not only in terms of administrative decentralization, but also in terms of how

to look at the relationships between state agencies and industrial enterprises. These reformers saw these relationships as being more economic than administrative. Previously enterprises had very little decision-making power of their own and very little opportunity for initiative in economic matters. This created general passivity and inefficiency. According to these people the most important thing was to give more decision-making power to enterprises – to micromanagement (White 1983: 485). This position also represented a clear step towards so-called market socialism.

The new ideas about how to develop China's economy during the last part of the twentieth century were officially crystallized in the Central Committee of the CPC in December 1978.

The standpoint taken at the meeting was clearly in favor of the third position mentioned above, stressing the importance of micromanagement and economic before administrative relationships. As the decisions made affected the behavior of enterprises in particular, we will examine them later in more detail. The main steps taken towards market socialism can be summarized briefly here:

1. The right to market freely part of the products of enterprises
2. The right to reserve part of the profits
3. The right to export independently part of their products and to reserve part of the foreign exchange earnings for their own purposes
4. The right to issue bonuses at the enterprise's own discretion, and hire and dismiss employees more independently (Tian 1982: 94–95)

In October 1978 Sichuan province had already begun to experiment in granting extended autonomy to some enterprises. One of the main initiators in this was Zhao Ziyang, later premier of the country, who acted as party secretary in Sichuan province in 1978, and made investigations concerning enterprise management in his province. He also went abroad to study management.

The experiments in greater autonomy for enterprises spread widely in the country during the following year. Although the new reform program was published, there was much disagreement among the reformers on how to proceed and at what speed and on what were the final targets of the reforms. Many asked how the reforms decided upon fit in with a socialist system. Deng Xiaoping's statement that "it doesn't matter if the cat is black or white, as long as it catches mice," was typical of his thinking.

Deng's other famous remark to foreign correspondents, that China has already gone so far in her reforms that there is no turning back, actually represents a real strategy of change: to change quickly so much that it would be too costly to withdraw.

The Green Revolution (1979)

The economic reform, which affected the majority of the Chinese population, was the establishment of the so-called contract responsibility system in rural areas. In this system the peasant households became relatively independent commodity producers. A two-tier management system which integrated peasant household with collective management was established. In May 1983 already 93% of rural production teams had instituted the system (B.R., September 5, 1983).

Under the contract system the production brigades or production teams conclude contracts with individuals, households, or groups composed of several households. The contracted household organizes its work on its own. This is a break from the past, when the brigade and team leaders organized all the work and the peasants were paid by the working day.

There are various forms of payment. The most typical one is the fixing of quota contracts. Under this arrangement, the peasants keep what is left of their output after turning over the state's purchasing quotas, paying agricultural taxes, and contributing to the collective's welfare funds. Later in 1985 the reform continued; the state stopped using fixed quotas for purchase of farm products from the peasants. Instead the state will purchase under contracts signed with the peasants and purchase in the market.

Public ownership of the means of production has not been changed. The peasants have rights to till the land owned by the collective and to use the collective's farm tools and water conservation facilities, but they are forbidden to sell or buy them and transfer them to others. The peasants hand part of their yield over to the collective for developing production, improving public welfare, and helping households in difficulties.

One of the main reasons for the agricultural reform was to motivate the peasants to achieve higher productivity, based on the idea that their income was mostly dependent upon their own efforts. The results were promising, because grain output rose from 305 million tons in 1978 to 407 million tons in 1984, a 33.6% increase. During the same period cotton output went up from 2.17 million tons to 6.08 million tons, a 180% increase. Peasants' incomes increased from 133 yuan per capita in 1978 to 355 yuan in 1984 (B.R., June 24, 1985).

In the new system the peasant households are relatively independent commodity producers. The household has again become the basic organizational unit in rural areas. Thus, the development has come full circle during the time of the People's Republic, as can be seen in Fig. 5.19. Before and at the beginning of the new China, the peasant household was the basic unit. The trend was gradually towards the huge people's communes, which have now been abandoned; the relatively independent households have come back and are marching towards a market system.

One factor which greatly increased the peasants' incomes in China after Mao and especially in 1978–1979 was domestic side-line production. This is a wide concept, covering such functions as: cultivation of private plots of land allocated on a per capita basis by the collective; raising domestic animals and fowl, including pigs, sheep, chickens, and ducks; engaging in handicraft production such as braiding, weaving, sewing, and embroidery; and undertaking subsidiary activities such as collecting medicinal herbs, fishing, hunting, growing fruit and other plants alongside the house. Domestic side-line production was quite modest until 1977, when this activity was strongly promoted as an important way of increasing rapidly both the supply of nonstaple foods and small goods, and improving the material standards and morale of peasant households (Croll 1982: 235–236).

During the following years side-line production grew rapidly, so that about 100 million peasants have switched from grain production to other lines of production such as poultry and fish breeding, farm and side-line product processing, small industrial undertakings, transportation, and commerce. Of these, approximately 30 million peasants, or 10% of the total labor force in rural areas, are employed in small factories and enterprises (B.R., March 28, 1983). Thus, gradually the peasants began to establish their own small enterprises, and switched from farming to entrepreneurship in trade and small industry.

But the situation of the peasants changed gradually also in that they were allowed to own farming machinery, e.g., tractors and trucks privately or collectively. It has been estimated that Chinese peasants owned privately 2.12 million tractors by the end of 1983. Of the tractors owned by peasants, 69% belonged to individual households; the rest were bought collectively by several households. In 1983 almost 90% of the new tractors were under 20 horsepower, a size especially suitable for family production and transportation (B.R., July 2, 1984: 8–9).

The economic reform was deliberately begun in agriculture, because 80% of Chinese work in this field. Through the rising standard of living and consequent satisfaction in rural areas the Chinese leaders formed a solid base for the continuing of reform in other areas, industry, and cities.

The "Green Revolution" can be said to represent in agriculture a decentralization process down to the microlevel from the large mesolevel people's communes, which often covered wide geographical areas. In this way the trend was the same as in industry.

Opening to the World (1980)

In 1980 China took an important step towards a new foreign trade policy by beginning to build the so-called Special Economic Zones (SEZ) in Shenzhen, Zhuhai, and Shantou in Guangdong province, and in Xiamen in Fujian province. The idea was already put forward at the end of 1978, when China began its modernization drive, but the final decision was made in August 1980.

There were many reasons for beginning China's open trade policy in this limited way. Through these first experiments China could learn how to do trade with capitalist countries and how to use modern technology without suddenly disturbing the total economic and social balance in China. The aim was to bring new ideas, technology, etc. to China through these narrow gates, melt down the experiences first, and only then begin gradually to introduce the new knowledge and experience in a form suitable for China to other parts of the country.

The economic development of the Special Economic Zones has been rapid. For example Shenzhen's industrial output value in 1979 was US 20 million; in 1984 the figure had jumped to US 600 million (B.R., August 26, 1985). How then do the Chinese entice foreign capital and technology to these Special Economic Zones? The following are the main ways:

1. The income tax rate for enterprises is set at 15%, which is lower than in Hong Kong, where it was 18.5% in 1985.
2. Foreign import to the zones is tax-free.
3. Cheap labor: the average wage of workers is less than half of that in Hong Kong. Enterprises are allowed to pay floating wages and salaries or to pay piece-work rates. Enterprises also operate under the labor contract system, according to which they can recruit qualified workers through exams. Both enterprise and worker sign a contract.
4. The price of land is cheap. The ground rent at the end of 1984 was on average 40 Hong Kong dollars per year and the rent agreement was made for 25–30 years at a time.
5. The management system is independent. The enterprises run exclusively by foreign or overseas Chinese capital have the right to manage themselves, provided they observe Chinese laws and regulations. Joint ventures and cooperative enterprises are managed by their own board of directors.
6. Entry and exit procedures and other formalities are simplified for foreign businessmen and visitors.

The Special Economic Zones have not been developed without heavy basic investment. The Chinese have made great efforts to develop a good environment for investors. The first thing was to launch a coordinated urban development program with emphasis on the infrastructure. For example in three years, starting in 1980, the Chinese spent US $ 1 billion on urban construction in Shenzhen, including a housing project with some 3.3 million square meters of floor space.

The results can clearly be seen in Shenzhen. In the center of the city dozens of skyscrapers stretch towards the sky, and in the harbor great enlargement projects are in progress. An international airport is being planned for the area. The small village of some 3,000 fishermen had by the end of 1984 grown to a town of 23,000 inhabitants, and will later develop into a city with 50,000–60,000 people (from this author's interview in Shenzhen at the end of 1984).

After three years' experience of the Special Economic Zones, China's leaders dared to open more doors to the outside world. In 1984 China decided that flexible economic policies would be practiced in 14 more Chinese coastal cities, among them Beihai and Guangzhou (Canton) in the south, Shanghai in the middle, and Tianjin and Dalian on the north coast (see Fig. 5.3).

One year later, in February 1985, the government decided to open up three more areas to foreign investment. These were the Changjiang (Yangtze) River delta, the Zhujiang (Pearl) River delta, and the Xiamen-Zhangzhou-Quanzhou delta. It was planned that the three new zones would be opened up gradually, with emphasis first on the cities in the area and their 50-odd surrounding counties or key industrial satellite townships. In the second phase the opening would reach out to the vast countryside of these areas.

At the same time it was planned that the Liaodong and Jiaodong Peninsulas would be opened up later at an opportune time, making the entire east China coast a new economic beachhead that would in time be extended gradually to inland cities. According to the strategy applied, proceeding step by step will provide China with opportunities to sum up its experience, thus enabling the opening up policy to expand in a healthy way.

The coastal areas are extremely important for China in its search for economic growth. The total area embraces 200 million people with a higher economic and cultural level than in the hinterland. Chinese leaders are counting on the coastal areas soon to be opened up wielding considerable influence by speeding up structural reform, absorbing advanced technology from abroad, and adopting modern management methods which conform to socialist production. They will first become economically and culturally advanced areas, and then spread their technology and experience to the less-developed hinterland.

How are the coastal areas attracting foreign investors? Foreign businessmen who invest in these areas will be given preferential treatment. For

Special Economic Zones: a-c, Shanton, Zuhai, Shenzhen;
                        d, Xiamen

Open coastal cities: 1, Dalian; 2; Quinhuangdao;
                     3, Tianjin; 4, Yantai; 5, Quingdao; 6, Lianyungang;
                     7, Nantong; 8, Shanghai; 9, Ningbo; 10, Wen-
                     zhou; 11, Fuzhou; 12, Guangzhou; 13, Zhanjiang;
                     14, Beihai

Open delta areas: A, Changjiang; B, Zhujiang, and
                  C, Xiamen-Zhangzhou-Quanzhou delta

Open peninsulas: I, Liaodong; II, Jiaodong

Fig. 5.3. China's open economic areas

example many joint ventures, cooperative enterprises, and foreign-owned businesses which are productive or research-oriented and whose products are for export, will benefit from a 20% income tax reduction.

Energy, transportation, and technology-intensive projects with direct foreign investments or productive projects with a foreign investment of over US $ 30 million and a long production cycle will be taxed at an income tax rate of 15%. When remitted overseas, the legitimate profits shared by foreign businessmen will be duty free. When the products of these enterprises are exported, they will be exempted from export tax and consolidated industrial and commercial tax.

After giving a general picture of the main economic and political developments in China since 1949, we examine in the following sections how Chinese management has developed in government, the CPC, and in industry and commerce in more detail. Since government organization and its management system have largely remained the same before and since 1949, and since government organization, especially as a geographical organization, forms the frame also for the whole party and enterprise organization and management system, we begin our examination with government.

5.2 Management in Government

5.2.1 Problem of Centralization vs. Decentralization

In China, government administration has often been left in the shadow of CPC administration, because the party has played the top role in important decision-making concerning the whole country. However, the state organization structure, in which all citizens can at least formally participate, e.g., through elections, has the important task of carrying out the "daily" administration of the country.

The whole structure of the state can be divided into three levels: (1) center, (2) regional and local level, and (3) level of basic organizations. This division into three levels is especially important when we examine the problem of centralization vs decentralization. By decentralization we mean here that a certain amount of decision-making power is transferred downward to lower level organizational units from some central point. Schurmann has divided the acts of decentralization into decentralization I and II. Decentralization I means that certain decision-making is delegated all the way down to the production units themselves. In decentralization II the delegation reaches some level of regional administration (Schurmann 1971: 175–176). According to our definitions we here call decentralization I microdecentralization (see Appendix p. 339).

Schurmann's decentralization II corresponds closely with our concept of meso- or regional level (mesomanagement); thus we call it mesodecentralization, which is perhaps easier to remember. Mesodecentralization can be divided according to the different mesolevels, i.e., province, prefecture, and county level.

As mentioned earlier, the great problems of Chinese management at the macrolevel, from ancient times to the present day, have been concerned with the question of centralization or decentralization between central and local governments. The tendencies have fluctuated considerably through known Chinese history.

5.2.2 Central Government

National People's Congress (NPC)

According to the Constitution (1982), the National People's Congress "is the highest organ of state power" (Article 57). The National Congress is composed of deputies elected by the provinces, autonomous regions, and municipalities directly under the central government – Beijing, Shanghai, and Tianjin – and by the armed forces. In the Fifth NPC in December 1982, 2,978 deputies took part. The following percentages describe the composition of the NPC. The share of female deputies was 21%. Members of the Communist Party accounted for 37%; far more than their share of the adult population. Intellectuals, industrial managers, and engineers had a relatively large representation, with 41%. The share of army delegates was also relatively large, 9% (White 1983: 24). The status of the Standing Committee of NPC is in many ways central, because it convenes Congress once a year, and is responsible for its administrative and legislative tasks when the NPC is not in session. According to the Constitution "The National People's Congress and its Standing Committee exercise the legislative power of the state" (Article 58, 1982).

The powers of the Standing Committee further include, e.g.:

1. Interpreting the Constitution and supervising its enforcement
2. Examining and approving, when the NPC is not in session, partial adjustments of the plan for national economic and social development and of the state budget
3. Supervising the work of the State Council, the Central Military Commission, the Supreme People's Court, and the Supreme People's Procuratorate
4. Deciding when the NPC is not in session, on the choice of ministers in charge of ministries or commissions
5. Deciding on the enforcement of martial law throughout the country

The entire structure of the Chinese state is officially divided into three main branches: (1) government, (2) army, and (3) judiciary (Schurmann 1971: 180). These three branches are headed (see Fig. 5.4) by: (1) the State Council, (2) the Central Military Commission, and (3) the Supreme People's Procurate and the Supreme People's Court. The members of these bodies are elected by the National People's Congress, as well as also the presidents and vice-presidents of the country. The power of the President is rather nominal. He promulgates statutes and makes appointments in accordance with the decisions of the NPC and its Standing Committee.

The administrative working body of the central government is the State Council and ministries and commissions subordinated to it.

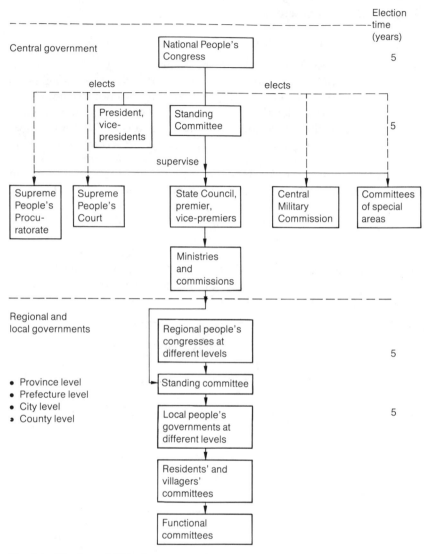

Fig. 5.4. Structure of China's government

State Council

According to the Constitution of 1982, Article 85: "The State Council, that is, the Central People's Government of the People's Republic of China is the executive body of the highest organ of state power; it is the highest organ of state administration." The State Council is composed of the premier, four vice-premiers, ten state councillors, and a secretary-general.

The ministries are formed according to functional fields, e.g., industries. In addition to ministries there are special commissions directly under the State Council responsible for activities in some special area. The most important commissions are in the area of economics: the State Planning Commission, which is in charge of long-range and short-range economic planning, and the State Economic Commission, which has the task of compiling short-range plans and coordinating current economic activity. Third is the Commission for Restructuring the Economic System, headed by the premier himself.

The number of ministries has often changed during the People's Republic. At the beginning of 1982, for example, there were 98 ministries, commissions, and agencies under the State Council. This was certainly heavy machinery to administer. Therefore, the Standing Committee of the NPC in March 1982 approved a plan according to which the ministries should be merged and the number cut down to 52, and the number of staff members in these bodies reduced by one-third. The target has been reached; the number of ministries and commissions, etc. was under 50 in 1983.

If we compare the contemporary central government of China to that of imperial times, we can see some historical connections, albeit weak ones. During the Ming dynasty (Fig. 3.1) there were ministries and their offices and the emperor plus the grand secretatiat corresponded somewhat to the present State Council, the Standing Committee of the NPC, and the president as an entity. But the resemblance becomes greater if we take into account the central Party administration, where the top hierarchy of the party has in a way stepped into the place of the former emperor, both ideologically and as a ruling center.

Relationship Between Central Organizations of Government and CPC

Now we approach an interesting and important question: which is the actual ruler, the government or the CPC? Beyond dispute it has been and is the CPC in the People's Republic of China. The party constitution of September 1982 states: "The focus of the work of the Communist Party of China is to lead the people of all nationalities in accomplishing the socialist modernization of our economy ...."

The ties between the CPC and government administration are strengthened through forming so-called "leading party members' groups" in the leading bodies of central or local state organs and economic and cultural organizations. These groups have to ensure that the party's principles and policies are implemented in the organizations in question. The groups, the forming of which is officially mentioned in the party constitution (September 1982, Article 46) act as a powerful instrument of the party in managing the organizations and the country. Thus, no party member in a leading position in the government or other nonparty organization can make important decisions without informing colleagues in the leading party members' group.

The economic reform which began at the end of 1978 is closely related to the reform of the CPC and state leadership system. Deng Xiaoping gave a speech about the subject on August 18, 1980, and declared:

> It is necessary to set up a truly effective work system from the State Council down to the local governments at different levels. From now on, all government work shall be discussed and decided upon, and the relevant document issued, by the State Council and the local government concerned. The party's central and local committees will no longer issue directives or make decisions on such work.

Deng added however:

> The work of the government is, of course, done under the political leadership of the Party. The strengthening of government work means the strengthening of the Party's leadership. (B.R., October 10, 1983: 21)

An outsider in China will ask, where then lies the real power of that great country? Seemingly very often in the hands of great personalities (personal power), whose position in the official hierarchical structure plays a minor role. Mao Zedong changed his own official status during his reign, but kept that of chairman of the party. The strongest man after him, Deng Xiaoping, has not occupied the formally highest positions in the CPC or the government. He rules via his own trusted men, who often occupy the most important positions both in the government and the party.

For example, the premier of the country, Zhao Ziyang, is also a member of the Standing Committee of the Political Bureau of the CPC Central Committee. In his biography, which the *Beijing Review* has published, we are told that Zhao was persecuted during the Cultural Revolution by the counterrevolutionary cliques, and then sent to Inner Mongolia and Guangdong, far away from Beijing.

> In 1975 he was transferred, *at the suggestion of Deng Xiaoping,* to the post of first secretary of the Sichuan provincial Party committee, to

> take charge of the overall work in this populous province which suffered the most during the "cultural revolution." (B.R., January 2, 1984: 8–9; this author's italics)

A strong personality like Deng's is surely not enough to rule a country which has plenty of strong personalities. Some other resources are needed. Probably the most important is the army, which is in a special way linked to the post that the strong man of China in the 1980s occupies. As mentioned earlier, Deng has been elected chairman of the Military Commission of the Central Committee of the CPC.

According to the CPC Constitution, the chairman of the last-mentioned commission must be a member of the powerful Standing Committee of the party's Political Bureau and

> the General Political Department of the Cinese People's Liberation Army is the political work organ of the Military Commission ... The organizational system and organs of the Party in the armed forces will be prescribed by the Military Commission. (Constitution of CPC of 1982, Article 24)

Although the state Constitution in 1982 does not itself mention the Communist Party, it is very clearly stated in the Preamble of the Constitution that the Chinese people of all nationalities are "Under the leadership of the Communist Party of China." In the Constitution it is stated that "The party's leading role in the life of the state ... naturally includes its leadership over the armed forces" (Peng 1982: 94). Thus, the strongest powerlines in China seem to proceed as shown in Fig. 5.5. Of course the influence of the army is not usually "visible", but in any event it is the final basic power unit.

Concerning the relations between different power centers shown in Fig. 5.5, we could say that the army is the wielder of arms power, and its method of influence is coercion and/or the threat of it. The CPC manages through ideological power, and the method of influence is indoctrination and also manipulation. The latter is achieved by efficient use of communication power; censorship. The method of influence of the government organizational units is based on hierarchical power. From Fig. 5.5 we see also that the CPC can control the behavior of government organizational units, not only at the central level, but also at the local level through the large organizational network of the party,, which stretches out all over the country, as we shall see later. But if somebody does not obey the use of ideology or hierarchical power – the orders of a person in a higher hierarchical position – there is always the last possibility to use arms power through police and/or armed forces.

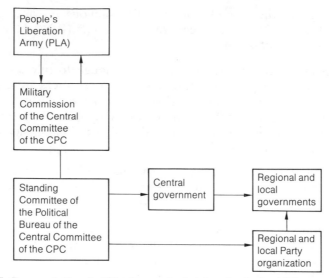

Fig. 5.5. Power relations in China's central administration in the 1980s

The dominant, although more or less invisible role of the army becomes understandable when we remember, on the one hand, that the ruling Communist Party comprises only a small fraction of the population and, on the other hand, that the constitution can be quite easily changed through a majority vote. And, as the basic organizational and decision-making principle is, according to the Constitution, democratic centralism, a group, which can even temporarily receive a majority in the top leading bodies of the CPC and then of the government, can change the Constitutions of both the party and the state as an instrument to rule the country. Thus, as the administrative machinery of the CPC and the government are relatively easily changeable, and therefore also in some circumstances insecure, there has to be in the background a consolidating power, the army. Of course, this power could also become dangerous for the rulers – and take the power in its own hands.

One reason for the unstable state structure of China is no doubt the short tradition of a democratic administrative system. Although the country has long and documented traditions concerning the state administration of the imperial period, the Chinese have relatively little experience of the new democratic administrative system they are aiming for.

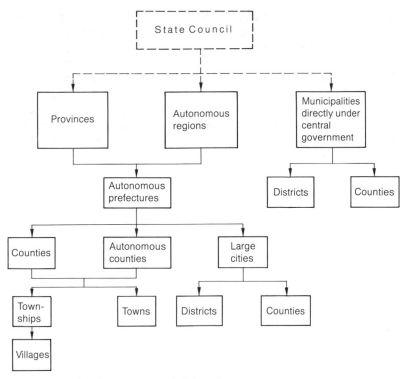

Fig. 5.6. Division of regional government administration

5.2.3 Regional and Local Governments

According to Fig. 5.6 the top echelon of the Chinese regional government structure is divided into provinces, autonomous regions, and municipalities, or large cities such as Beijing, Shanghai, and Tianjin, which are directly under the central government. The autonomous regions are actually like provinces, with the difference that their inhabitants belong for the most part to minority nationalities. The system of prefectures subordinated to provinces represents an ancient tradition in China, as we recall from Fig. 3.1.

The provincial governments have traditionally been the backbone of state administration in China. The administrative structure below the provinces, which in extreme cases includes four levels (Fig. 5.14) is "deep" and hierarchical, but we must remember that we are now studying a country of over 1,000 million inhabitants. If we divide that sum by the number of provinces and autonomous regions, or 27, we obtain an average population for a province of 37 million – a complete fair-sized country in Europe.

The organizational structure of the different levels of regional state administration greatly resembles that of the central government structure; it only becomes less complicated, with a smaller number of specialized units, when we move downward in the hierarchical pyramid. When we study Fig. 5,6, 5.7, and 5.8, we must remember that they represent "enlargement" of different degrees. The first, Fig. 5.6, describes the regional administrative division generally. The following, Fig. 5.7, gives the main features of the province level organizational structure for government administration, while the last, Fig. 5.8 describes in more detail the administrative structure at and below county level.

One of the main organizational differences between the provincial level administration and the level below it is that deputies to the people's congresses, which are formally the highest administrative organs at respective levels, at the province level are elected by the people's congresses at the next lower level. This same principle applies also to large cities divided into

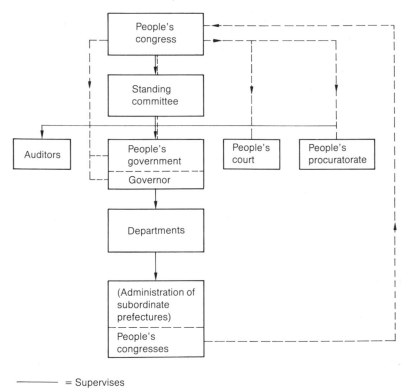

———— = Supervises
– – – – = Elects

Fig. 5.7. Structure of government organization at province level

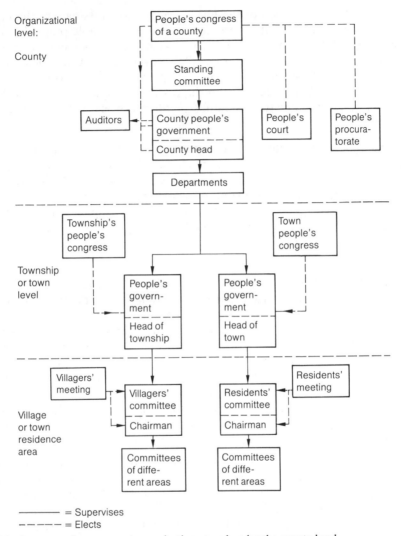

Organizational level:

County

Township or town level

Village or town residence area

——————— = Supervises
– – – – – – = Elects

Fig. 5.8. Structure of government organization at and under the county level

districts (Fig. 5.6). Deputies to the other lower local people's congresses as well as villagers' and residents' committees are elected directly by their constituencies. The other main difference is that the term of office of the people's congresses and of people's governments in provinces, municipalities directly under the central government, and cities divided into districts is five years, but in counties and other lower-level corresponding organs, three years.

The standing committee of the local people's congress has, as the equivalent organ in the central government, quite considerable power because it supervises the work of the people's government, and can annul inappropriate decisions and orders of the people's government at the corresponding level. The standing committee, when the people's congress is not in session, also recalls individual deputies to the people's congress at the next higher level and elects individual deputies to fill vacancies in the people's congress.

Local people's government at every level conduct the administrative work concerning the economy, education, culture, public health, and every other field of activity needed in the locality concerned. For their specialized functions the local governments have departments. In villages and town districts the villagers' and residents' committees (Fig. 5.8) establish committees to take care of public health, security, people's mediation, and other matters in order to manage public affairs and social services in their areas.

The local people's governments at and above county level direct the work of people's governments at lower levels, and have also the power to alter or annul inappropriate decisions of people's governments at lower levels. Thus, the hierarchical order is very strict in Chinese government administration. The power inclines to the top of the central government, because "The state organs of the People's Republic of China apply the principle of democratic centralism" (Constitution of 1982, Article 3). As mentioned earlier this means that the minority is subordinated to the majority. Since the higher-level government organs supervise the lower-level units, the majority, even a very slight one, making up the group at the top, rules the country. This same principle is also applied by the CPC system.

According to the reforms of the 1980s, not only has party management been separated from government administration, but also economic management will be and has already to a great extent been separated from government functions. These measures have brought great changes in the administration systems of rural areas where the majority of Chinese live.

But before we go on to examine the latest changes in rural government organization, we must mention an episode which occurred in commune administration during the Cultural Revolution (1966–1976). During that period so-called revolutionary committees were created for nearly every organization in every field, whether economic, cultural, educational or, e.g., government-administrative. Thus, the Cultural Revolution brought revolutionary committees to the people's communes also. These committees replaced the people's governments as declared in the Constitution of 1975: "The local revolutionary committees at various levels are the permanent organs of the local people's congresses and at the same time the local people's governments at various levels" (Article 22).

The period of the revolutionary committees did not, however, last a long time, because after Mao Zedong's death in 1976 the new rulers abolished these committees and put back the local people's governments to handle the state administration at the local level. The local people's government has, since the establishing of the People's Republic, been to a great extent also responsible for the economic development and management of enterprises in their respective areas.

One of the main distinctions between socialist and capitalist countries is that the enterprise management system in a socialist country forms an integrated entity which begins from the enterprise level and goes through the meso- and macrolevels up to the top of the state (and CPC) hierarchy (Fig. 5.9). In capitalist countries the enterprises are relatively independent, and only some controlling, thin bonds bind them to the government administration.

According to Fig. 5.9, the State Council decides the overall economic strategy of the country and the main economic areas: agriculture, heavy industry, and light industry, as well as the main fields of, e.g., industry. The

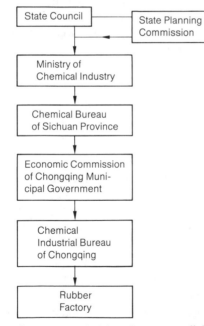

Fig. 5.9. Government administrative structure linked with enterprise management of Chongqing Rubber Factory (2,000 employees in December 1986)

State Planning Commission then prepares the general economic plan. Only a few hundred products, accounting for little over half of the GNP value, are, however, handled directly by the State Planning Commission. It can work out accurate figures only for a few dozen products, and can only make rough estimates for the rest. Especially state enterprises are directly guided by state planning (Xue 1981: 164–165).

Fig. 5.9 shows the linkages between the central government and enterprises; here we take as an example the Chongqing Rubber Factory located in Chongqing City, Sichuan province in Middle China, along the Changjiang (Yangtze) River. The hierarchical line of decision-making goes down from the State Planning Commission and Ministry of Chemical Industry through provincial level government units to the local level, represented by the economic commission of Chongqing municipal government and the chemical industrial bureau of Chongqing.

Thus, the hierarchical ladder, through which all the important decisions have to go, is rather high and contains several time-consuming steps. It is no wonder that the present Chinese leaders have begun to reshape this bureaucratic structure to try to give more independent decision-making power to individual enterprises.

The economic reform, proclaimed, e.g., by premier Zhao in his report at the National People's Congress in May 1984, was designed to separate the state's economic guidance from the enterprises' power to manage their own affairs, so that each could fulfil its responsibilities.

> In state-owned enterprises the system under which a director or manager assumes full responsibility will gradually be instituted. Directors and managers will be entrusted by the state with full responsibility for directing the production, management and operation of their enterprises. (Zhao 1984: 13)

We have earlier mentioned that there have been different kinds of decentralization policies during the People's Republic concerning government administration. We discerned decentralization at the mesolevel, or provincial or local level, and decentralization at the microlevel or directly to production units, enterprises. The latest reform clearly concerns decentralization at the microlevel.

When the basic ideology, how and towards what goals the society should be developed, changed altogether after Mao, the decentralization strategy changed also. The endless class struggle thinking was put aside, and the main terminal goal was to improve the economic performance of the country and the standard of living of its people. In government this meant not only decentralization at the microlevel, but also the separation of government administration from enterprise management as well as from CPC administration.

The government administration has played a dominant role in Chinese society during the Imperial period and also to a certain extent between 1911–1949. In the People's Republic during Mao's time, however, the government came under the shadow of the Communist Party. The new leaders after Mao have criticized both the government and CPC administration. At the end of 1985 vice-premier Tian Jiyun argued that the reform of China's administrative system was not in keeping with the country's economic reforms. He said that China's government administration had the following five drawbacks: (1) redundant organizations, (2) ambiguous departmental responsibility, (3) overstaffing, (4) inefficiency, and (5) lack of strict regulations for evaluating performance, promotion, and retirement (B.R., November 11, 1985). The decision to separate government and CPC administration must also be seen as a measure to improve the efficiency of administration. One may ask, will the government administration regain its former power; and what will happen to the role of the CPC? In the following section we shall examine the development of the role of the party in the People's Republic.

5.3 Management in the Communist Party of China

5.3.1 Significance of the CPC

No revolution can successfully be made without an organization. The organization behind the Chinese Revolution and behind its fruit – the People's Republic of China – is the Communist Party of China. Its role and functioning did not end with the victory of 1949, but have continued up to the present, though with different weighting, all the time since its establishment in 1921.

Although only about 4% of the Chinese population belong to the CPC, the country's regime ensures that the Communist Party represents the organized will of the society, and the interests of the people. According to the CPC's general program stated in its constitution of 1982:

> The Communist Party of China is the vanguard of the Chinese working class, the faithful representative of the interest of the people of all nationalities in China, and the force at the core leading China's cause of socialism. The party's ultimate goal is the creation of a communist social system ... The party must strengthen its leadership over the trade unions, the Communist Youth league, the Women's Federation, and other mass organizations, and give full scope to their roles.

The network of the Communist Party reaches practically everywhere in Chinese society from government to agricultural and industrial organizations. The CPC has its own organizational units at every level of enterprise hierarchy from the grassroots level party groups up to the party committee of the enterprise, which has often been the highest decision-making management body in enterprises.

If one wishes to study enterprise management in socialist countries it would be a mistake to exclude the party from the examination. However, in most socialist management studies and very often also in the publications of "capitalist" scholars, the role of the party has not been included in the study.

In contemporary China there is now a strong tendency to separate the functions of enterprises from the functions of the Communist Party. This idea represents a really crucial change in a socialist country. On what ground will the Communist Party base its power in the future, if the party gives up its economic power bound to economic enterprises? At the same time there is the danger that the CPC will also lose its grip on the millions of people working in enterprises. These tendencies can have a profound effect not only for China, but for all socialist countries in the world. Depending on how it develops it can also have a great impact upon the whole socialist ideology and movement worldwide. To understand how China has come to this interesting stage, it is necessary to examine the development of the role of the Communist Party of China.

5.3.2 Development of the Role of the CPC

The Communist Party of China was established in Shanghai in July 1921 by twelve men. One of them was Mao Zedong, then a young library assistant. As mentioned earlier, at the beginning the CPC had two wings: one leaning upon the Western tradition and thinking that the revolution should be led by the urban proletariat. The other wing argued that peasants formed so powerful group in China that no revolution could succeed without their help; as is well known, Mao Zedong later successfully followed this way of thinking.

The CPC quickly realized that to gain power it had to begin to organize the working class. One of its actions was to establish the Chinese Workers Union. Another action was to spread knowledge about communist ideology. This was done through direct education, and through publications of classic Marxist works in the Chinese language.

The role played by the Communist Party in the development of the People's Republic of China is shown in Table 5.1. The starting point has been

Table 5.1. Development of the role of the CPC

Period	– 1917	1917+	1921+	1931–1949	1949	1949–1976	1978+
	Dissatisfaction and conflicts: landlords – poor peasants; capitalists – workers	Communist ideology began to organize dissatisfaction into the integrated system	Communist Party organized the people under the same ideology (strikes, upheavals, etc.)	PLA became an instrument of CPC and won the civil war	PLA gave power to the CPC to develop the country	CPC and its ideology ruled the country	Economic thinking guides the development of the country

the great drawbacks in old feudal China, which resulted in dissatisfaction among the overwhelming majority of Chinese people especially in rural areas. There were conflicts between landlords and poor peasants in rural areas and between capitalists and workers in urban areas. The ideas of communist ideology channeled this dissatisfaction into a powerful integrated system. The Communist Party took advantage of the growing dissatisfaction, showed its societal rightness (as a power resource), and used organization as an instrument to create strikes and upheavals.

Later the CPC helped to organize the People's Liberation Army (PLA), led it under the ideological umbrella of communism, and won the war against Chaing Kai-shek's troops. After 1949 the PLA was involved not only in military affairs, but played an important role in educating people, helping the peasants in agriculture in rural areas, and taking part in work in economic organization in cities. Since at the same time the CPC and PLA were tightly bound together by common interests and by persons sitting in leading positions both in the CPC and in the PLA, the party could freely rule the country, backed by the military power of the PLA. In the 1980s also the country has de facto been governed by the alliance between the Communist Party and the People's Liberation Army (Fig. 5.5).

Since Mao Zedong's death the role of the Communist Party has gradually changed in Chinese society. This change is connected with the overall change of the development strategy of the country. Goals based on communist ideology formerly dominated, whereas now the economic development of the country has been placed in the foreground. Thus, the CPC, which has been responsible for developing and maintaining the ideological line, has lost its former importance, and organizations responsible for the economic development of the country, the enterprises of different fields, have stepped into the foreground. The changed role of the CPC comes out well when we compare the Constitutions of the party adopted during Mao's time in 1973, and during that of his followers 1982. The 1973 Constitution of the CPC declares:

> State organs, the People's Liberation Army and the militia, labor unions, poor and lower-middle peasant associations, women's federations, the Communist Youth League, the Red Guards and other revolutionary mass organizations must all accept the centralized leadership of the party.

The Party Constitution adopted in 1982 has no such direct statement of party supremacy over other organizations. In its general program, however, it states:

> The focus of the work of the Communist Party of China is to lead the people of all nationalities in accomplishing the socialist modernization

of our economy ... The party members are a minority in the whole population, and they must work in close cooperation with the masses of non-party people in the common effort to make our socialist motherland ever stronger and more prosperous, until the ultimate realization of communism.

Although the old general goals of communist ideology are still mentioned, the spirit of the 1982 CPC Constitution is different from that of the 1970s. The former underlines the endeavor towards economic goals in the society, and the CPC's supporting rather than leading role in this process in relation to other organizations.

5.3.3 Membership and Recruitment of the CPC

It is peculiar that although the CPC actually rules the country its members constitute only a minor part of the population of China, 4% in 1986. The members are carefully selected through special procedures. Sometimes the screening has been more, sometimes less strict, in some periods certain groups, e.g., intellectuals, have been favored, sometimes other groups, e.g., peasants.

According to the 1982 Constitution of the party:

> Any Chinese worker, peasant, member of the armed forces, intellectual or any other revolutionary who has reached the age of eighteen ..., may apply for membership of the Communist Party of China. (Chapter I, Article 1)

> New party members must be admitted through a party branch ... An applicant must be recommended by two full party members. The application must be accepted by a general membership meeting of the party branch concerned and approved by the next higher party organization, and the applicant should undergo observation for a probationary period before being transfered to full membership. (Article 5)

> The probationary period of a probationary member is one year ... Probationary members have the same duties as full members. They enjoy the rights of full members except those of voting, nominating, or standing for election ... (Article 7)

> Every party member, irrespective of position, must be organized into a branch, cell or other specific unit of the party to participate in the regular activities of the party organization. (Article 8)

As the Communist Party actually rules China through its membership-network, which spreads itself all over the country into the smallest villages, it is important that the individual members accept the behavioral principles of the CPC given by its leading organizational unit: the Central Committee (CC). If the policy and at the same time often the leading persons of the Central Committee change, it is important to have a guarantee that the whole CPC organization in every part of the country will follow the new policy. If this is not reached through an informative and educational method, there is no alternative but to change the members of the party: to expel those who will not accept the new line (and perhaps leaders) and recruit new ones, whose attitudes are positive toward the new line.

This kind of change of policy as well as leaders occurred after Mao Zedong's death in the Communist Party of China. The party Central Committee made a special decision on party consolidation in October 1983. The CPC decided on an overall rectification of party style and a consolidation of party organizations over a period of three years beginning in the latter half of 1983.

The tasks for the CPC consolidation were the achievement of ideological unity, the rectification of the party's style of work, the strengthening of discipline, and the purification of the party organization. The strengthening of discipline was to adhere to the party's organizational principle of democratic centralism.

As will be remembered, democratic centralism means that the minority must accept and actively follow the decisions made by the majority. And since individual party members are subordinate to the party organization, lower party organizations are subordinate to the higher party organizations, and all the constituent organizations and members of the CPC are subordinate to the National Congress and the Central Committee of the party, the majority of the Central Committee in practice rules the CPC and through it the whole country.

Thus, the majority decision of the Central Committee of the CPC can change the party ideology and policy, and if needed the whole party organization with its members. Of course, the CPC Central Committee must have sufficient power resources to accomplish this kind of maneuver. This power resource is usually the army, and therefore, as mentioned earlier, the most powerful person in the CPC has usually had a leading position in the People's Liberation Army (PLA). This practice has rather long roots, because already in January 1935 during the Long March the Political Bureau of the Central Committee of the party convened a meeting in Zunyi which established the leading position of Mao Zedong both in the Red Army and the Central Committee of the party (Resolution on CPC History 1981: 6). As has been said, in the 1980s, Deng Xiaoping was elected the chairman of the Military Commission of the party, which controls the PLA.

The latest CPC consolidation in 1983 included purifying party organizations of elements who persist in opposing the party (the decisions of the Central Committee), and expelling them from the party in accordance with the party Constitution, which states:

> Party members must ... execute the party's decisions perseveringly, accept any job and fulfil actively any task assigned them by the party ... uphold the party's solidarity and unity, firmly oppose factionalism and all factional organizations and small-group activities, and oppose double-dealing and scheming of any kind. (Article 3)

To understand the important role of the Central Committee of the party, it should be mentioned that it alone has the power to make decisions on major policies of a nationwide character. Of course the National Congress of the party is nominally the highest organ of the party, but it is convened by the Central Committee, which can always await the most suitable time to call the National Congress of the CPC.

We have dealt in some detail with the procedures of member recruitment and the role of the CC of the party concerning these matters, because these are the basic processes through which the party and hence the whole country is ruled. Now we turn to examine the development of the membership of the CPC.

The Communist Party of China is the largest Communist Party in the world, with 44 million members in 1986 (*China Daily* (Ch.D.), September 27, 1986). The growth of the membership developed rather irregularly after the establishing of the CPC in 1921, but reached 4.5 million in 1949 (see Table 5.2).

One of the main decision areas which the management of an organization will keep in its own hands is personnel matters, especially recruitment policy (IDE, International Research Group 1981a, b). Thus, in examining the development of the membership of the CPC, we see reflections of the

Table 5.2. The growth of membership of the Communist Party of China 1921–1949. (Schurmann 1971: 129)

Year	Members
1921	57
1925	950
1930	122,300
1934	300,000
1940	800,000
1945	1,211,000
1949	4,500,000

applied recruitment policy, and accordingly of management policy of the CPC during different periods of the People's Republic.

Figure 5.10 reveals a slow growth of membership during the first years after 1949. This probably reflects the rehabilitation period of the CPC which we could see also in the economic development of the country. The rise after 1954 is a sign of a new recruitment policy, the aim of which was to build up an efficient membership network covering the whole country. In general the pace of recruitment accelerated during the periods when the party felt especial need for activity in basic-level organizations. Thus, during the Great Leap Forward movement 1959–1960, CPC membership grew by more than 3,000,000.

The occupational composition of the party membership has a great impact upon the power structure of the CPC, because it also determines the composition of the delegates of the National Congress of the party. The latter elects the members of the Central Committee, and makes the final decisions concerning the most important matters of the party and of the whole country. However, the Central Committee is the main wielder of power, because the National Congress has its regular meetings only once in five years.

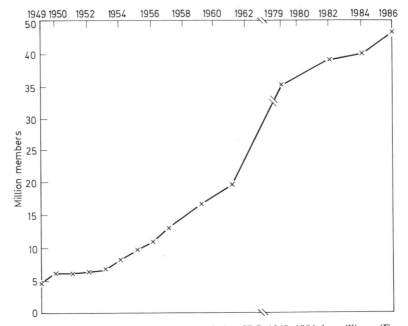

Fig. 5.10. Development of number of members of the CPC 1949–1986 in millions (For 1949–1961, Schurmann 1971:129; for 1979–1984, B.R., July 16, 1984; for 1986, *China Daily*, September 27, 1986)

In 1956 the peasants formed a clear majority of the CPC members. Their share did not, however, quite match their proportion of the whole population, which was more than 80%. It was natural, and also logical according to the power balance, that those who had most helped to realize the revolution also formed the majority in the ruling organization of the country. What stands out in Table 5.3 is the relatively strong proportion of intellectuals, 11.7%. This group is a little vague, but probably both education and occupation have been taken into consideration in it. The rapid increase in the recruitment of intellectuals after 1955 – between 1956 and 1957 their number in the CPC increased by 50% – was the result of the Hundred Flowers Movement, which started in the spring of 1956. The movement encouraged especially freedom of expression among intellectuals. A big new increase in the recruitment of intellectuals occurred at the beginning of the 1980s in connection with the modernization campaign. Among the 6.3 million new members who have been admitted to the CPC between 1981 and 1986, the proportion of "technical professionals" was 1.4 million or 22% (*China Daily*, September 27, 1986).

Table 5.3. Occupational composition of party membership in 1956. (Schurmann 1971: 132)

Occupation	Members	%
Workers	1,503,000	14.0
Peasants	7,417,000	69.1
Intellectuals	1,255,000	11.7
Others	558,000	5.2
Total	10,733,000	100.0

The proportion of industrial workers in CPC membership in 1956 seems quite small, but taking into account the low level of industrialization in China the figure, 14%, corresponds quite well with the proportion of workers in the whole population.

The group "Others" probably mostly refers to the military. Their share in CPC membership seems to have been relatively large, but this is understandable when we remember the decisive role of the PLA in creating the People's Republic, as well as the tight bonds between the party and the PLA described earlier (Schurmann 1971: 128–133).

We finish the examination of CPC membership by comparing the proportion of party members in the whole population in various socialist countries. This is an important relation from the point of view of macromanagement.

The figures in Table 5.4 do not give any clear indication of the relation between on the one hand the ratio of party membership to population and

Table 5.4. Ratio of party membership to population in 1961 and 1984 in various socialist
countries. (Year 1961, Schurmann 1971: 138; year 1984, Staar 1985: 587–591)

Country	1961 (%)	1984 (%)
Albania	3.2	4.2
Bulgaria	6.3	9.2
China	2.5	3.8
Cuba	3.9	4.3
Czechoslovakia	11.6	10.5
German Democratic Republic	9.9	13.2
Hungary	4.8	2.2
Mongolia	4.5	4.1
North Korea	15.5	15.3
Poland	4.3	5.9
Romania	4.7	15.0
USSR	4.2	6.7
Vietnam	3.6	3.0
Yugoslavia	5.4	10.9
Mean	6.0	7.7

on the other hand the general power of the Communist Party in the country. What one could perhaps say is that in countries where the party's
position is strong and where it has itself been mainly involved in creating
the revolution and the socialist system – as in China, Albania, Cuba, North
Vietnam, and the USSR – the share of party members is relatively low;
below the total mean. This can also reflect more strict macromanagement
in the party, and in the country, and thus more careful recruitment of the
new party members.

Table 5.4 shows that on average the ratio of party membership in socialist
countries has grown since 1961 from 6.0% to 7.7% in 1984. In some countries such as Romania, Yugoslavia, and East Germany, there has been a
stronger growth. In Hungary the membership ratio has decreased most –
from 4.8% to 2.2%. The reasons for these changes are different in different
countries, and it is not our purpose here to examine other countries in more
detail.

In China the ratio of CPC membership to population has grown in 23 years
by 52%. In China this means over ten million new members. Since 1979
more than 4.8 million people have joined the Party. Thus, there seems to
have been special activity in recruiting new members to the CPC after the
famous Third Plenum of the 11th Central Committee of the CPC in December 1978. What kind of people was this recruitment campaign directed
towards? Deng's statement back in May 1977 hints at the policy planned.
He said:

> We must create within the party an atmosphere of respect for knowl-
> edge and respect for trained personnel. The erroneous attitude of not
> respecting intellectuals must be opposed. All work, be it mental or
> manual, is labor. Those who engage in mental work are also workers.
> (Deng 1984: 54)

Thus, later especially the institutes of higher learning became the object of
party recruitment activities, and about 10,000 university and college students joined the CPC within a few years before 1984. Also more than
150,000 specialists and technicians joined the CPC during 1980–1983. The
proportion of peasants in CPC membership has dropped considerably;
among the 800,000 new members admitted in 1983 the number of peasants
was 80,000 or 10% (B.R., No. 29, 1984). This is a striking difference when
we recall that the peasants comprised 69% of the total membership of the
CPC in 1956 (Table 5.3). However, because the majority of Chinese live in
rural areas, the majority of CPC members, 22 million, are from the rural
party branches, which number over 1.1 million (B.R., December 30,
1985).

When Deng focused his recruitment policy after 1977 on intellectuals, he
had probably at least four main reasons. First, the economic reforms with
the four modernizations were largely based on advanced knowledge in
various fields. This most required the input of highly educated intellectuals.
Second, as the new reforms with clear steps towards market socialism also
meant a great change in traditional Mao-based political thinking, it was
probably easier to get the young and educated behind the reforms. Third,
the official emphasizing of the importance of intellectuals gave them a
feeling that the new leaders were on their side. Fourth, the intellectuals
were so mistreated during the Cultural Revolution that a taste for revenge
probably played a part in this power game.

Through the CPC consolidation actions already mentioned, Deng and his
supporters have had an opportunity to "clean" the party organization by
removing members who oppose them and their reforms.

All 44 million CPC members had to reapply to the party by the end of 1986.
This maneuver and the new recruitment policy has brought to the CPC new
blood – people who support Deng and his ideas. It is not only the ordinary
party members who have had a blood transfusion; many of the top leaders
of the party have been changed too.

It is clear that a drastically new management policy also requires in a
socialist country great changes in personnel policy, especially in recruitment. The same phenomenon is common in capitalist countries. The leaders of capitalist enterprises often have to go when there are major changes
in management strategy because, e.g., of earlier failures. The difference is,

that the changing of leaders in capitalist systems is normally only at the microlevel, or concern managers of separate individual organizations. A major change in management policy, especially in large enterprises, in socialist countries can first start with a change in the highest top management of the country, or the top leadership of the party. This has been the case in recent years in the two largest socialist countries: China and the Soviet Union.

5.3.4 Managers of the CPC: the Cadres

The concept cadre has had a somewhat ambiguous meaning, especially in discussions of Western scholars and laymen. It has usually been connected with the socialist system and its communist and/or equivalent parties. For them a cadre is a person who holds a formal leadership position in an organization. It follows from the organizational principles of the CPC, that every cadre in China has a specific rank. This rank must be known to every member of the organization, for the CPC hierarchy to function in practice. Thus, there exist tables of cadre rank for every unit of organization. These tables represent similar systems of nomenclature, which can be found in, e.g., the Soviet Union and Poland (Schurmann 1971: 162–163). The nomenclature is actually a management instrument, which hierarchically covers the whole country in a socialist system.

Usually the nomenclature contains all the most important positions and their holders in the country. The nomenclatures are put in hierarchical order; the Central Committee of the party controls the lists and accordingly the filling of the most important vacancies. The CPC committees at different levels are responsible for the nomenclatures – vacancies and persons – in organizations under them. However, very little is actually known about the nomenclature system of China. One thing must, however, be true: the names of persons in Chinese nomenclature tables have been changed since 1976 in the process of changing the leaders of the government, enterprises, and the CPC.

As there were 2.5 million grassroots CPC organizations with 9 million cadres in the country in 1984 (B.R., July 16, 1984) this raises the question: from where has this elite group, which rules a country with over 1 billion people, come? When we consider how many different kinds of changes China has experienced since the establishing of the CPC in 1921, and when we try to find reasons and initiating factors for these changes, we must also seek the reasons for the roles of the cadres and the formation of the elite in the CPC.

The roles and the status of CPC cadres have changed greatly during the history of the CPC. Prior to 1949 the need for self-sacrifice and the risks of death and torture ensured that many party cadres of that time were persons primarily motivated by the goal of revolution. After the communist victory, however, the costs of CPC membership ceased to be high as the party became an establishment. The Communist Party was no longer a band of radical revolutionaries, determined to transform China's social institutions. "Far from being a source of danger, Party membership had become the primary path to personal success" (Kraus 1981: 73).

What kind of career paths are most common for leaders of the CPC? Here we must take into account two important questions: (1) On what level of party hierarchy are we focusing; central, provincial, or local party organizations? (2) What is the time point being examined?

There have been numerous studies concerning elites in the People's Republic. Bullard has done a good review of them. In most of the studies one common background factor seems to be military service, either present or past (Bullard 1979).

Province level elites have been studied by George Sung in the 1960s. He then found eight important background factors: (1) date when party committee was formed, (2) changes in CPC or government leadership, (3) appointments of second secretaries, (4) field army affiliations, (5) insiders vs outsiders, (6) historical power base of field army system, (7) generation differences, and (8) military vs civilian background (Sung 1965: 346–365).

During the 1970s and 1980s party recruitment has drastically changed. The new generation, which is now ready to step in to leading positions, has grown up and been educated in a socialist People's Republic, has learned new values, and has no concrete knowledge of any other kind of societal and ideological system.

Thus, Deng Xiaoping and his colleagues in the leadership group could quite safely change the old veteran party leaders from the time of the Long March and of the Liberation Wars to younger ones, who have received their better education in the higher educational institutions of the People's Republic.

The goals of the CPC cadres have changed: the driving force among the veterans of the Long March and the Liberation Wars was to make the revolution and build a communist society; the main targets of the contemporary young party leaders are probably more materialistic, to modernize and develop their country to the level of industrialized countries, and to use the party's hierarchical ladder for their own careers.

Most of the old CPC veterans from the time of the Long March have left the top leadership positions in the 1980s; however, one, and the most important one, has still continued to act vigorously in the 1980s – Deng

Xiaoping himself. As the main designer of the latest reforms, he also represents the ancient bastion of power in China, the army, as the chairman of
the Military Commission of the party.

5.3.5 Organizational Structure of the CPC

The CPC is strictly hierarchically organized in the shape of a pyramid, the
base of which spreads itself out to every village, government office, and
industrial enterprise. The top of the CPC pyramid is located in the Central
Committee, or more closely in the Standing Committee of its Politburo.

The strict hierarchical management system of the CPC is clearly defined in
its 1982 Constitution, which states:

> Individual party members are subordinate to the party organization,
> the minority is subordinate to the majority, the lower party organiza-
> tions are subordinate to the higher party organizations, and all the
> constituent organizations and members of the party are subordinate to
> the National Congress and the Central Committee of the party. ...
> The highest leading body of the party is the National Congress and the
> Central Committee elected by it. The leading bodies of local party
> organizations are the party congresses at their respective levels and the
> party committees elected by them. Party committees are responsible,
> and report their work to the party congresses at their respective levels.
> (Article 10)

The Chinese divide their Communist Party into three main levels, each of
which has its own subgroupings. The main levels according to Fig. 5.11 are:
(1) Central, (2) regional and local, and (3) primary organizations. We can
call these also (1) macro-, (2) meso-, and (3) microlevel management of
the CPC. In the following subsections we shall examine each of these levels
in more detail.

Central Organization of the CPC:

National Party Congress

According to its Constitution, the officially highest unit in the CPC hierarchy is the National Party Congress (NPC). It elects the Central Committee of the party, examines the reports of the latter, revises the Constitution of the party, and discusses and decides on major questions concerning
the party. In practice the most important tasks of the Party Congress are to
nominate the highest party leaders and to adopt long-term policy lines for
coming periods.

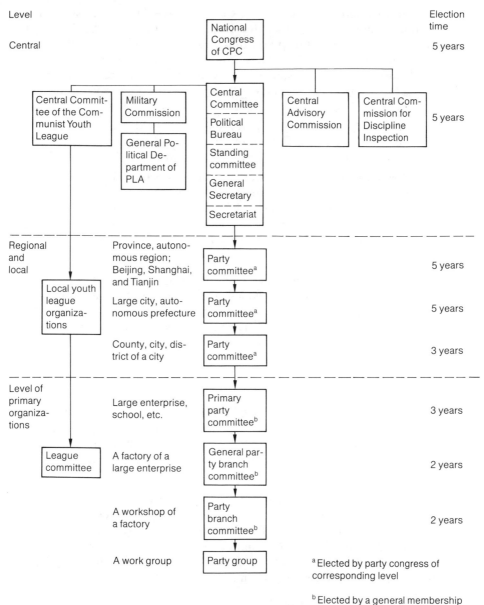

Fig. 5.11. General structure of the Communist Party of China. (Designed according to the decisions of the Twelfth National Congress of the CPC, September 1982)

The Party Congress also elects the Central Advisory Commission and the Central Commission for Discipline Inspection. However, the Central Advisory Commission acts as political assistant and consultant to the Central Committee. It seems to be a kind of honorary unit also, because its members "must have a party standing of forty years or more, have rendered considerable service to the party ..." according to the party's Constitution of 1982.

The National Congress of the party should be held every five years and convened by the Central Committee. Up to 1986 there have been 12 National Party Congresses since the establishment of the CPC in 1921.

It has been noticed that long intervals between National Party Congresses usually reflect the inability of the CPC and its leaders to emerge with an overall party line. Although the main power in day-to-day activities is in the hands of the Central Committee and its subunits, sooner or later, if major changes in CPC policy or among its highest cadres have occurred, the National Party Congress must be convened. In these cases, e.g.,

> The adoption of new policy decisions is always preceded by long reports from the leadership which sum up the existing situation in various sectors of national life and point the way toward the future. Thus, far from being a ritual, the party congresses mark decisive periods in the political development of Communist leadership. (Schurmann 1971: 140)

Central Committee (CC)

As the Party Congress is convened according to the Constitution normally every fifth year, and as the Central Committee carries out its decisions and directs the entire work of the CPC, it is the real power wielder. But this does not apply to the whole Central Committee, because the Committee meets in plenary session

> at least once a year, and such sessions are convened by its Political Bureau. ... When the Central Committee is not in session, the Political Bureau and its Standing Committee exercise the functions and powers of the Central Committee. The Secretariat attends to the day-to-day work of the Central Committee under direction of the Political Bureau and its Standing Committee.

And now comes the key point:

> The General Secretary of the Central Committee is responsible for convening the meetings of the Political Bureau and its Standing Committee and presides over the work of the Secretariat. (Article 20 and 21, CPC Constitution 1982)

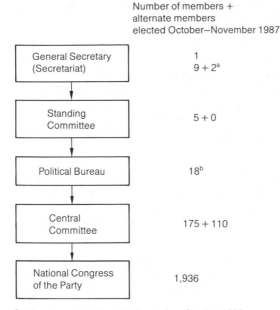

Number of members +
alternate members
elected October–November 1987

General Secretary (Secretariat)	1 9 + 2[a]
Standing Committee	5 + 0
Political Bureau	18[b]
Central Committee	175 + 110
National Congress of the Party	1,936

[a] Figure concerns the situation before October 1987
[b] The number of alternate members not informed in October 1987

Fig. 5.12. Hierarchical structure of the central organizations of the CPC based on the right of convocation. (Thirteenth National Congress of the CPC, October–November 1987)

Thus, if we draw a figure of the power relations of the central organizations of the CPC according to the organs and persons who have the right to convene the different units belonging to the central organization of the party, we obtain a hierarchical order (Fig. 5.12) quite opposite to that presented in Fig. 5.11, which is based on the nominating power.

Thus, the highest power of the CPC and also of the whole country should be in the hands of the General Secretary of the Central Committee. However, everybody in China, and generally also outside it, has known that the key person in Chinese politics since 1978 has been Deng Xiaoping, chairman of the Military Commission of the CC. The earlier Constitution of the CPC adopted by the Tenth National Party Congress in 1973 made no mention of the Military Commission, but the new Constitution of 1982, largely designed by Deng, states:

> The members of the Military Commission of the Central Committee are decided on by the Central Committee. The Chairman of the Military Commission must be a member of the Standing Committee of the Political Bureau. (Article 21)

The role and power of the Military Commission in the People's Liberation Army is clearly stated in Article 23:

> Party organizations in the Chinese People's Liberation Army carry on their work in accordance with the instructions of the Central Committee. The General Political Department of the Chinese People's Liberation Army is the political work organ of the Military Commission; it directs party and political work in the army. The organizational system and organs of the party in the armed forces will be prescribed by the Military Commission.

Normally in socialist countries the most powerful person in the country has the status of the General Secretary of the Communist Party or equivalent. For some special reason, perhaps because of his age, Deng Xiaoping did not want to have the status and tasks of the General Secretary. He chose to rule in the background. How can one do that, though not occupying the officially most important positions?

Deng has gathered behind him so many and such power resources that his influence in important matters is decisive. First, he is backed by the army as the Chairman of the Military Commission. His prominent status came out well during the celebrations of the 35th anniversary of the People's Republic in October 1984. Deng inspected the parading troops, and gave the main speech of the occasion.

Second, Deng has been the main visible architect of the economic and political reform of 1978. Probably many of the top leaders of the 1980s can thank Deng for their position. Third, to be able to plan and to carry out the great reform, Deng has thorough knowledge of the administration of the CPC and of the country after having served for a long time in important positions. In 1966, while Mao Zedong was chairman of the Central Committee, Deng acted as General Secretary (then under Mao) of the Central Committee, and was also a member of the Political Bureau and its Standing Committee.

Fourth, Deng Xiaoping, according to many sources, has a strong and influential personality; the will and power to get through his own ideas. Thus, Deng, without having the highest formal hierarchical position, actually leads the gigantic country with the following power resources in particular: (1) great knowledge resources concerning administration and people, (2) strong personality power, which has been strengthened by a positive exchange balance with many persons in key positions (who often have Deng to thank for their positions), (3) the arms power of the People's Liberation Army, which is available to him through his chairmanship of the Military Commission, thus making it possible to use coercion whenever needed, (4) through being a member of the Standing Committee of the

Political Bureau, Deng always knows what is planned and happening at the top of the power hierarchy and thus has strong communication power.

Regional and Local Organizations of the CPC

Because the CPC's organizational network was mainly formed after 1949, and China had for centuries had quite a developed and solid regional and local state administrative structure before that, the CPC's organizational structure follows the latter. This is also because the party aimed to extend its network everywhere, also to government units, to guide and control the behavior of the society, organizations, and people.

The highest regional organizational level under the central party administration is the province level, which includes the autonomous regions and three cities Beijing, Shanghai, and Tianjin (see Figs. 5.11 and 5.13). The five autonomous regions are actually like provinces, but the designation autonomous region recognizes the autonomous character of the national minorities who mainly live in these regions.

Directly under the CPC's central organization are also the three large cities mentioned above, as well as those big cities which are divided into districts, together with 29 autonomous prefectures. All these – provinces, autonomous regions, large cities, cities divided into districts, and autonomous prefectures – are mentioned in one separate group in the CPC Constitution. They should elect a Party congress every five years.

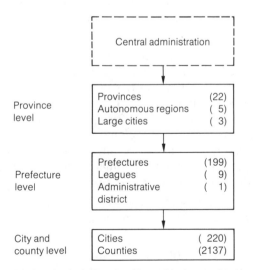

Fig. 5.13. Regional administrative hierarchical organization of China; Number of units in parentheses. (*Administrative Divisions of the People's Republic of China*, 1981)

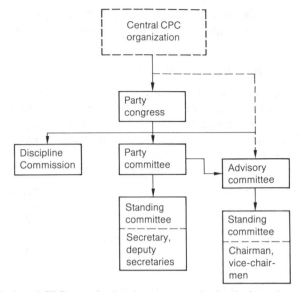

Fig. 5.14. Local CPC organizational structure at the level of province, autonomous region, and large cities directly under the central CPC organization

Within each regional and local level CPC organization, the administrative structure has the same form as in the central organization of the party. In Fig. 5.14, the CPC organization at province and equivalent level is described. The organizational pattern is the same in lower level local CPC organizations with one exception. There is an advisory committee, elected by the party congress only at the province level.

These advisory committees act as controlling links of the Central Committee. Their elections concerning their standing committees as well as their chairman and vice-chairman are not only subject to endorsement by the CPC committee at the corresponding level, but also these elections should be reported to the Central Committee for approval. The members of the advisory committees may attend the plenary sessions of the party committee at the corresponding level as nonvoting participants, and their chairmen and vice-chairmen may attend meetings of the standing committee of the party committee as nonvoting participants.

The local CPC committees should meet in plenary session at least once a year. When they are not in session their standing committees exercise their powers and functions.

The CPC hierarchy forms a very tight organization, which can be effectively guided and controlled from the top; first, because all elections of the standing committees and secretaries as well as deputy secretaries of the local CPC committees at various levels should receive the approval of the higher party committees. Second, as mentioned, according to the main organizational principles of the CPC the lower party organizations are directly subordinate to the higher party organizations.

The strict organizational structure of the CPC goes further down to the primary organizations of the party, which we shall examine in the next section.

Primary CPC Organizations

According to the CPC Constitution of 1982

> Primary party organizations are formed in factories, shops, schools, offices, city neighborhoods, people's communes, cooperatives, farms, townships, towns, companies of the People's Liberation Army, and other basic units, where there are three or more full party members. (Article 30)

The Constitution says further that "The primary party organizations are militant bastions of the party in the basic units of society" (Article 32). These primary party organizations are like heads of nerve-cells in the huge party network (communication power), which sense what is happening in every smallest corner of the society. They also actually carry out the policy of the CPC or its Central Committee. This huge organization with several million full-time party workers, certainly consumes a great quantity of scarce resources in a relatively poor country.

As our main focus in this study is directed to management in economic organizations, we take here as an example a primary CPC organization of an enterprise. According to Fig. 5.15 there are four levels of party organizations in a large enterprise. Following the CPC committee hierarchical line, the highest and the most important unit is the primary CPC committee elected by a membership, or in very large enterprises by a delegate meeting. The CPC committees of some large enterprises have a standing committee which carries out the day-to-day work of the party committee.

The next level, which we can find in, e.g., large factories, is the general CPC branch committee, and under that in workshops there is a party branch committee. The lowest-level unit is a CPC cell, which can be formed in a work group where there are three or more full party members.

A primary CPC committee is elected for a term of three years, while the function time for lower-level party committees is two years. Every party committee has a secretary and usually one to four deputy secretaries, who are in key positions in guiding the party's activity in the corresponding unit.

To control the activities of the CPC organizations and their members every unit which has a primary party committee should have a commission for discipline inspection. A general party branch and a party branch should have a discipline inspection commissioner. To ensure that no unit can deviate from the CPC's ideological line, all the discipline inspection units, both discipline commissions and commissioners, are subordinated not only to party committees at the corresponding level but also to the next higher-level discipline commission (see Fig. 5.15).

The CPC considers it important to ensure the supply of new members and cadres through the training of young people. The organization for this purpose is the Communist Youth League of China, which extends its organization network parallel to that of the CPC everywhere in Chinese society. Thus, in primary party organizations there exists a youth league unit at every level of the hierarchy. A kind of double controlling system exists here also: on the one hand, the youth league committee at every level is subordinated to the party committee of the corresponding level, but on the other hand also to the higher organizations of the league itself.

The members of the youth league normally elect at every main level of organization hierarchy a youth league committee and secretaries for it. Those secretaries of league committees who are party members may attend meetings of party committees at the corresponding levels and of their possible standing committees as nonvoting participants. This system gives them an excellent opportunity for training for future demanding party jobs.

As the CPC extends its network to every corner of the enterprise organization it represents a great power in guiding and controlling the whole Chinese society and its economic organizations. The eternal problem has been, what role the party should play in the economic development of the country. Is the first, most prominent goal the proceeding on the ideological road to socialism and then to communism, or is the goal more pragmatic: first to develop the economic and living standard of the country and its people, and then to proceed in the direction which then seems to be the most purposeful?

The policy of China and its Communist Party has fluctuated considerably between these different goals, largely depending upon the power balance prevailing among the top leaders and groups of the country. Of course environmental circumstances have also played an important role. For example during the years of bad economic results, e.g., because of a poor harvest, the leaders have been forced to leave the pure ideological goals aside and concentrate on getting the economy on its feet again. The fluctuations mentioned have greatly affected industrial enterprises: the influence of the CPC in enterprise management has increased and decreased many times since 1949.

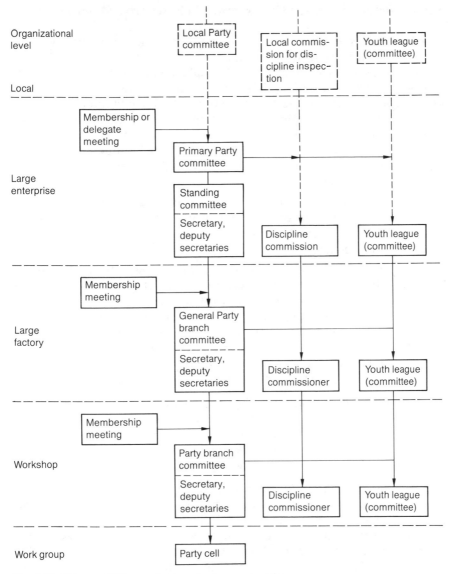

Fig. 5.15. Primary CPC organization of a large enterprise

5.3.6 Fluctuations in the CPC's Power in Enterprise Management

The Communist Party of China was the actual winner of the civil war, which ended in 1949. It was thus natural that the party's influence after the victory was everywhere great. The CPC could not alone rule the country, at least not the economic enterprises, because they did not have the required knowledge resources. Thus, during the period of rehabilitation, 1949–1952, the party had to cooperate with the "capitalist" managers in enterprise management who had remained, and wait for the economy to begin to recover and become ripe for socialization. The CPC's influence during that time was guiding but not overwhelming. Certainly it was decisive in important strategic issues.

With the Soviet aid the Soviet one-man management system came around 1950 to Chinese enterprises. This system gave the greatest power to the general manager of the firm. With this development the party's influence in enterprise management clearly declined.

However, the Chinese soon realized that the borrowed Soviet system did not suit their culture, economic structure, and development stage. Thus, in China the party was again raised to a ruling position in enterprises when they replaced the one-man management system with "collective management by CPC committee" in 1956, and launched the campaign of the Great Leap Forward. The CPC also strengthened its power through a big recruitment program. From 1959 to 1961 the party membership grew by three million (Schurmann 1971: 534).

For various reasons earlier described the Great Leap Forward movement did not succeed and was replaced around 1961 by the so-called "profit and managers' management," where the managers by turn took over the power in enterprises. At the same time the CPC seemed to have lost much of its power to the government and army organizations.

The campaign for the party leadership was intensified in 1964 by the so-called Four Clean Movement, the aim of which was to cleanse the political, economic, and ideological thinking of the cadres. The leaders of this strong movement were said to have been Liu Shao-chi and Deng Xiaoping, who later became the strong man of the 1980s. However, Mao Zedong made a comeback in the winter of 1964–1965, and the struggle that followed within the CPC gradually grew to the launching of the Cultural Revolution in 1966, which lasted until Mao's death in 1976.

However, although the situation in the country was chaotic in some areas during this ten-year period, the CPC at least nominally held the top power, at least in enterprises where the so-called revolutionary committees had been formed to answer for the operational management of enterprises as a sort of collective management. The revolutionary committees were, however, subordinated at every organizational level to the corresponding party committees.

After Mao's death the situation changed quickly. In 1978 the revolutionary committees were abolished in most enterprises and other organizations, and the new economic strategy launched by the Central Committee in 1978 restored the power of professional managers after a 16-year period of CPC power in enterprises. The CPC functions were to be separated from the management of enterprise organizations. This separation was considered so important that it was written into the CPC Constitution of 1982.

If we relate the development of CPC power to other development phenomena in the society, we see first that the power of the party dominated during the periods of favorable economic performance of the national economy and enterprises. One might say that when the societal and organizational environment is stable and developing well, the party can concentrate on developing itself and its power in the society. During times of economic crisis, for example, after the failure of the Great Leap Forward movement, the party has had to make way for professional experts, e.g., in enterprise management to save the situation.

We can see hints of this kind of relation in Fig. 5.16. The beginning of the 1950s was a difficult economic time of rehabilitation, when the CPC had to give way to the one-man management system, which was efficient in a way. When the economy recovered with unexpected speed, the party was free in

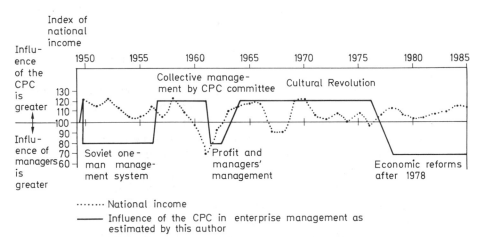

Fig. 5.16. This author's appraisal of the relative influence of the CPC in enterprise management during 1950–1985 compared to the influence of managers, and the fluctuations of national income represented in indexes where the preceding year is 100. (*Statistical Yearbook of China 1985*; *China: a Statistical Survey in 1985*)

1956 – without too overwhelming economic worries – to jump in to exercise guiding power in enterprises. When the Great Leap Forward period ended in an economic disaster around 1960, the Chinese (party and nonparty) leaders had to call the professional managers back to lead the enterprises out of the chaotic situation. When the economy again recovered in 1962 the CPC took the reins in its hands again.

But how and why did the CPC maintain the upper hand in enterprises for 16 years, beginning in 1962 and including the period of the Cultural Revolution? The second reason, in addition to periods of economic prosperity, for the CPC's dominant role in enterprises seems to be the internal struggles within the CPC either concerning the "correct" ideological line or the power campaign between the party leaders, factors which were often closely related. The last long period of CPC domination beginning in 1962 was a period of great internal struggles within the party. All the interest groups tried to strengthen the power of their party group to the utmost degree. On the whole the strength of the party looked, at least to outsiders, relatively strong.

The situation could not last forever, because the economic and cultural (knowledge) development was in stagnation for ten years during the Cultural Revolution. Thus, counterpowers appeared soon after Mao Zedong's death in 1976, and the ideological and economic strategy of the country was changed completely in 1978. How could this change of leaders and of ideological and economic policy happen so quickly and relatively smoothly? The answer is probably that the CPC with its old program had no longer been able to satisfy the needs among the majority of the population which at that time were most urgent.

Thus, in trying to explain the changes in the CPC's power in Chinese society and in its enterprises, we reach the old conclusion concerning the basis of power in organization: The members of an organization are active and involved only so long as the organization can promote personal and/or group interests. If the organization fails to fulfil this basic requirement, the members and/or supporters of the organization leave it or no longer actively support it and its activities. This basic organizational principle is also very suitable for an examination of the development of the power of the Communist Party.

During the civil war the CPC promised to free the majority of the population, the poor peasants, from their oppressors, the landlords and rich peasants. Mao Zedong and his party received the support of the majority of the population, and won the war. The first rise in the CPC's power was in 1949 (see Fig. 5.16). The second rise came in 1956, when the Soviet one-man management system did not satisfy the employees of organizations. The CPC leaders created the collective management by party committee system. The third rise, beginning in 1962, was more or less artificial. The economy was recovering, and the party leaders could safely carry on their struggle for power.

The fight for power and for the right ideology, lasting for many years, did not take into account the basic needs of the population; thus, the people were ripe to accept a new policy and new rulers after the death of Mao Zedong in 1976. The CPC had largely dominated nearly all parts of Chinese society, from the arts and education to government and enterprise management. The "old" ideology of the CPC could no longer satisfy the new needs of the population, especially the younger generation, which had not experienced the miserable past, from which the party had saved the country.

There was no feeling of gratitude among the young generation, but hunger for a higher standard of living after the Japanese and Western model. It was felt that this new hunger could be satisfied with the help of new technology – modernization. Thus, the time was ripe for managers and other experts, knowledge power, to step to the fore.

5.4 Management of Agricultural Organizations

One seldom speaks about management in connection with agricultural production. In a capitalist system this is normally the business of farming families, where the "management" structure is the same as the family, the father being normally the "general manager". Of course the owners of large landed estates, such as landlords in earlier China, had a large number of peasants and hired agricultural laborers under them, who where often managed by a hired manager of the estate. But at any rate the organizational structure was quite simple.

In the People's Republic the organization of agricultural production gradually changed altogether: first to producers' cooperatives and then to people's communes, which were large organizations with tens of thousands of members practicing not only agricultural but also versatile industrial production, handicrafts, and commercial activities. The organizational structure of a people's commune was rather complicated, containing government, CPC, and productive administrative units.

We must also remember that 80% of China's population still lives in rural areas, and is thus "managed" by different kinds of rural, mostly agricultural, organizations. The peasants also formed the core power of China's revolution in 1949. That the rural population still in the 1980s forms the backbone of Chinese society has been shown by the fact that China's contemporary leaders began their economic reforms from agriculture.

In a way we can see here a development circle which is closing: at the beginning of the People's Republic the individual peasant families formed the core units of the economy. These were later joined to large communes, which have now again been taken to pieces, giving to individual peasant families the right to cultivate land independently. But we will start our examination from the beginning of the agricultural circle during the PRC.

5.4.1 Land Reform

As the land reform was one of the main practical targets of China's revolution and as it althogether changed the entire Chinese society, we will describe it here in some detail. To get an idea of the old conditions in agriculture we repeat here some historical facts. Before the communist victory, 70% of the land in rural areas was owned by 8% of the rural population; that is by landlords and rich peasants. The miserable conditions of the more than 90% majority of the rural population who lived on the poverty line, and the promises of a land reform given long ago, had created a great hunger for land.

The new law concerning land reform came into force in 1950. But before that some 170 million peasants had experienced the fruits of the parcelling of land in the areas which had been occupied by the communist troops before October 1949.

Decisive for the accomplishment of the land reform was the defining of what class every household and individual belonged to. This class designation served not only the land reform, but was also a political instrument to control the change away from capitalism and secure the power in the hands of the new rulers. There were altogether more than 60 class designations in China in the early years of the People's Republic, covering all sectors of the society. Below are listed some of the more important class designations concerning the rural population:

- Hired agricultural laborer
- Poor peasant
- Middle peasant
- Old middle peasant
- New middle peasant
- Well-to-do middle peasant
- Rich peasant
- Small land lessor
- Landlord
- Enlightened landlord
- Overseas Chinese landlord

- Landlord who is concurrently an industrialist or merchant
- Sublandlord
- Hidden landlord
- Bankrupt landlord
- Despotic landlord
  (Kraus 1981: 185)

The central government had issued special directives concerning the differentiation of class status in the rural areas.

The law concerning land reform stated that the different rural classes should be treated in the following way:

1. The land, draught animals, farm equipment, surplus stock of grain, and surplus dwelling houses of landlords should be confiscated.
2. The land of rich peasants should be defended from confiscation if they were cultivating the land themselves. The land they had rented out should be confiscated if this land exceeded the area cultivated by the rich peasants themselves or by the labor hired by them.
3. The land of middle peasants should not be confiscated.
4. The poor peasants and the farm workers should receive a fair share of the confiscated land and other confiscated factors of production. An equivalent part should be distributed to the former landlords, so that they could earn their living through their own work and thus change themselves ideologically through work.

To the great surprise of all, including its planners, the land reform proceeded in practice more quickly than originally planned, so that the reform was generally speaking completed by the beginning of 1953. Table 5.5 gives an idea of the development.

Table 5.5. Class structure in rural areas before and after the land reform; percentage of total rural population. (Chao 1960: 101 ff; Chao 1963: 36)

Class	Before land reform (%)	Afer land reform at the beginning of 1955 (%)
Poor peasants	70	20
Middle peasants	20	new 50
		old 20
Rich peasants	5–6	new 2
		old 4.5
Landlords	4–5	3.5
	100%	100%
Rural population	450 million	

With the land reform the peasant family, the household, which had earlier been the basic, although subordinated, production unit in agriculture, became an independent economic unit. In the next subsections we shall examine its gradual change to a subordinated part of a collective.

5.4.2 Team Farming

In the Chinese Communist Party there were different opinions about how to proceed towards socialism in agriculture after the land reform. Some thought, among them Liu Shao-Chi, that China should first strengthen the rich peasant economy, and as the next step begin to mechanize agricultural production. Some others, among them Mao Zedong, thought that there was only one way to avoid capitalistic agriculture, namely a quick change in agriculture towards socialism through a cooperative system. Mao's line won and Chinese agriculture began a careful move towards a cooperative system.

The first step was to develop team farming or groups for mutual help. The system of team farming during the busy time of harvesting had long historical roots, especially among the poor peasants. The CPC very skillfully based its tactics upon this tradition.

In team farming 5 to 15 or even more households each had ownership of their land, agricultural equipment, and livestock, but collaborated in work – sowing, harvesting, irrigation, etc. – with other households.

Peasants who joined the groups of team farming began quite soon to buy new production equipment together, and also gradually to cooperate with other neighboring groups. The next step towards a "lower" type of cooperative system was to cultivate and own the land jointly (Hultcrantz et al. 1974: 57–58).

In October 1950 some 60%–70% of rural households in the "old" areas occupied by Communists had already formed farming teams. In 1952 of all rural households 40% had joined these groups. The road to a rural cooperative system had been opened up (Hsue et al. 1960: 112).

5.4.3 Producers' Cooperatives

The tactics which the CPC applied in agriculture during the changeover were based on voluntariness and mutual interest; mostly through the positive experiences of cooperation in lower forms – and examples of others who had already applied higher forms of cooperation – the peasants should become motivated to proceed on the road towards higher forms of cooperatives. These tactics were in practice even more successful than anticipated. Mutual-aid teams (team farming) were founded at a speed which during the first years always exceeded the plans of 1950.

In the first stage of mutual-aid teams, the peasants worked together in projects which demanded special work efforts and/or during the fall harvest. In the second stage the collective work went on throughout the year, and included side-line production. During this stage common property accumulated because of better division of work and more advanced technology. The third stage already represented the lower form of a cooperative: private ownership still existed, but the production factors were used together.

The process towards collectivization was strongly activated by a report by Mao to a conference of local CPC committees, where the Chairman suggested a target of 1,300,000 cooperatives for October 1956. At the end of the year 96% of rural households were organized in cooperatives, 88% in the higher form (Hsueh 1960: 128–132). Two years earlier only 2% of the rural households belonged to cooperatives. This strong and speedy process towards cooperatives in rural areas also had a great impact upon the changeover process in industry, as we will see later.

In June 1956 the National People's Congress proclaimed "Model Regulations for an Advanced Agricultural Producers' Cooperative." According to these

> Peasants joining the cooperative must turn over their privately owned land, draught animals, large farm implements and other chief means of production to the collective ownership of the cooperative. (Article 13)

In this way the economic resources and corresponding power were transmitted from peasants to collectives among an 80% majority of the population.

> The members' means of livelihood, small holdings of trees, poultry, domestic animals, small farm tools and tools needed for household side-line production shall remain privately owned by the members and not be made common property of the cooperative. (Article 13)

It was also stated in the regulations that "Provided the production of the cooperative is not affected, the cooperative should encourage and suitably help its members engage in household side-line production" (Article 28). Allowing and supporting side-line production on the one hand kept alive an old tradition, and on the other hand gave the peasant households extra, greatly needed income. This side-line production was a seed which later grew to become an important factor in the Chinese economy.

Management and Organization of the Cooperatives

According to the above-mentioned regulations:

> The highest management body of the cooperative is the general meeting of members or the meeting of members' delegates ... The general meeting of members or the meeting of members' delegates elects a management committee to run the affairs of the cooperative, a chairman to direct the daily work of the cooperative and to represent the cooperative in its dealings with other parties, and one or several vice-chairmen to assist the chairman in his work. (Article 55)

The basic unit of the labor organization of the cooperative was the production team, which should assume responsibility for cultivating a definite area allotted to it and be given draught animals and farm implements for its regular use. Each side-line production team should be responsible for a definite side-line trade and be alloted the appropriate tools for its regular use. With regard to the evaluation and payment of the work, the cooperative fixed norms and rates of payment for various jobs so as to put the piece-work system into practice.

The management committee was in the first place responsible for the planning and executing of the economy of the cooperative. It should, at the same time as it made the annual production plan, draw up an annual budget covering income and expenditure, submit it to a general meeting of members for adoption, and then put it into effect.

The producers' cooperatives were, however, not only purely economic production organizations. They also had responsibilities in the area of cultural and welfare services, such as:

1. Organizing members to raise their general educational level and wipe out illiteracy by groups within a few years
2. Promoting cultural, recreational, and sports activities
3. Fostering public health
4. Encouraging division of labor in each family and mutual aid between neighbors
5. Providing material assistance to women members before and after childbirth
6. Helping members improve their housing conditions. ("Model Regulations for an Advanced Agricultural Producers' Cooperative," Article 52)

These tasks and responsibilities greatly exceeded those typical of a purely economic organization, at least according to Western capitalist forms. We can see in these duties traces of traditional Chinese cultural factors in the area of the family and clan system. From cooperatives it was a relatively short step to the next stage of Chinese rural organizational development; namely to the people's communes.

5.4.4 People's Communes

Development of Communes

During a session of the National People's Congress in 1958 Mao Zedong gave a report where he recommended a new political-economic line for reforms in administration, a national plan for 1958, and produced several enthusiastic slogans. Thus, the well-known "Great Leap Forward" was launched; an effort which had bold targets but ended in almost chaotic conditions.

Although the main focus of the development had been in heavy industry, light industry, and especially agriculture had an important role to play. Mao had declared in his speech in April 1956 that

> To develop heavy industries requires an accumulation of capital. Where does capital come from? Heavy industries can accumulate capital; so can light industries and agriculture. However, light industries and agriculture can accumulate more capital and faster. (Ch'en 1969: 65)

One reason for developing agriculture in particular was the fact that it had become the main economic problem of the country. The rapid growth of industry during the first five-year plan had not been matched by agriculture and, by 1957, agricultural insufficiency was an obstacle to further industrialization and economic expansion.

When the enthusiastic slogans of the Great Leap Forward spread over China and demanded that the people rise from the backwardness of agriculture and industrialize the country, the peasants felt that cooperative organizations were too limited to achieve the great goals. Cooperatives were spontaneously united to greater units or they formed associations of cooperatives. Many attempts were made to find an organizational framework best suited for the constantly expanding activities of cooperative associations.

The organizational form which had been developed in 27 earlier cooperatives in Henan province became an example for the people's commune system. With their 9,300 households they united to become an enlarged cooperative. They intended to cultivate the land more effectively, and to create at the same time local small industries, dig irrigation canals, build roads, and take care of child education. The founders of this huge enlarged cooperative thought that they had made an innovation comparable to the first Soviet satellite, and baptized it "Sputnik." The name "people's communes" was born some months later.

The participants of Sputnik prepared preliminary rules for their organized activities. These rules were quickly spread through the mass media to all provinces, and in August 1958 the CPC officially welcomed the communes and gave general instructions for building them. One month later the movement towards people's communes was in full swing and to a great extent accomplished throughout the country. Thus, the number of communes at the end of August 1958 in the whole country was 8,730, but it had grown by the end of the year to 26,578. A people's commune consisted in the late 1960s on average of 2,000 households; the number of communes was then around 70,000.

There were also great problems in building the system of people's communes. The Great Leap Forward was not, however, a success in China for several reasons as mentioned earlier; e.g., during the years 1959–1961 great natural catastrophes hit China.

Some people have said that the people's communes saved China during that difficult time. It was in fact to a great extent the new form of organizational structure which was the decisive factor. Through their large organizational network, covering dozens of villages (production teams) and thousands of households, the commune could organize help in the form of exchange between brigades and communes. The commune could also, being a large organization, act effectively in distributing government catastrophe aid (Hultcrantz et al. 1974: 149–150).

With regard to the task of the people's communes, their aim was different from that of producers' cooperatives; the former had the double task of organizing both the economy and political administration.

To give a picture of a commune, here are some of the features of the Chinese-Cuban Friendship Commune I visited during the Cultural Revolution in June 1973. The commune, established in 1958, was located near Beijing, its area covered 90 km^2, and its cultivated land contained 3,600 hectares. The commune included altogether 39,000 persons in 1973.

The main products of the commune were wheat, rice, corn, and vegetables. The commune also had its own fruit garden, three mule farms, pig farms, and duck farms. In addition there were three stables with 300 horses; altogether there were more than 1,000 horses in the commune. Two years earlier the commune had built a fish pond, which produced 50,000 kilograms of fish for the state in 1972.

The industrial activities were represented by a chemical factory, a flour mill, and a repair shop. To portray the mechanization stage of agriculture, it should be mentioned that there were 30 tractors and 70 small, so-called walking-tractors in the commune.

As I mentioned earlier, the communes also took care of the social services of its members. The educational services were given by 18 primary schools and six secondary schools. The health service included one hospital with eight doctors and 20 nurses. In the whole commune there were 30 medical doctors in six small clinics. In addition there were so-called barefoot doctors in every production team; altogether 160 of them in the whole commune. They had been trained for six months either in the commune's mobile health service groups, or in city hospitals. Normally they took part also in the daily work of the commune.

The commune was thus a societal unit, which took care of the political, economic, educational, cultural, and other social needs of its members. At the same time it was intended to be an independent military unit in case of war.

During the creation of the people's communes and partly as a result of them, another great change in the Chinese rural areas occurred: the status of women changed radically. About 100 million wives of peasants could begin to take part in the productive work of the communes. This was made possible by building 3.4 million homes for small children's daily care; 3.4 million common dining halls, and 150,000 old people's and nursing homes. These institutions freed the wives from their former main tasks (Ten Great Years 1960: 44). This social, political, and economic liberation of women from their traditional subjugated status meant a profound change for the whole Chinese society.

The land reform with more equal distribution of land, the improved status of women, and the organizational reform with the people's communes was one of the greatest societal structural changes in rural areas ever made in the world. It changed the living conditions of hundreds of millions of people.

Management of People's Communes

From the point of view of macromanagement the people's communes functioned as a relay for central, provincial, etc. planning. As the majority of Chinese were living in communes, and received their livelihood through them, and as the communes became deeply involved in industrial production and trade, it is vital to examine also the management and organization of these diversified units during Mao's time.

In the organizational structure of the communes we find that there were five organizational levels:

1. Commune
2. Production brigade
3. Production team
4. Work group
5. Household

Collective ownership was also organized according to these levels (see Fig. 5.17). The commune took care of contacts with the higher state administrative levels concerning planning of production and distribution of commodities.

The people's communes also became important from the point of view of industrial management, since by the end of 1959 some 200,000 small factories had been established in the communes. The bulk of their production value (55%) consisted of commodities for agricultural use. We can only imagine what amount of managerial work must have been needed to run these factories. Since a great number of the employees and also their superiors were illiterate at that time, this must have caused enormous difficulties in running these small plants efficiently. But from them a new managerial body began to grow in China through the principle of self-learning while on the job.

Victor Lippit (1982: 52) wrote that

> The commune is a unique institution, which by combining farming and other productive activities with the activities of local government, integrates the social, political and economic life of the countryside within a single unit.

Thus, the communes had in a way triple management organization: one organization for affairs of local government, one for CPC matters, and one for economic activities. As we have dealt with the government and CPC administration earlier, we concentrate here on management of economic activities.

As can be seen in Fig. 5.17 there were two formal organizational lines which went through the entire commune organization from top to bottom: the CPC management structure and the government management structure. Both these structures were tightly intertwined, in such a way, however, that the CPC management's own special area was party affairs, but it also dealt with all other important matters, though more from the strategic point of view. In economic matters it ensured that, e.g., production followed the principles and goals given by the higher central authorities.

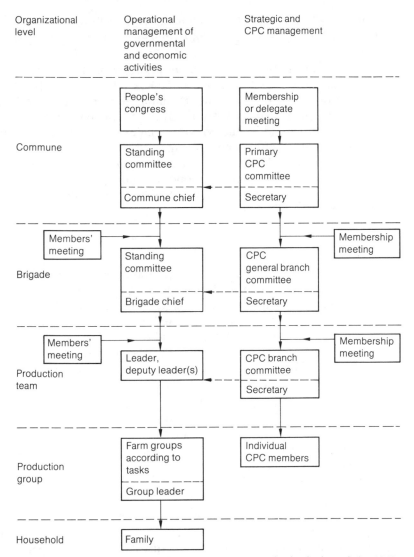

Fig. 5.17. Organizational structure of a people's commune at the beginning of the 1960s before the Cultural Revolution

The other management structure, representing local government organization, was responsible for operational management, ensuring that the planned and necessary activities were really carried out in practice. The CPC organization at different levels of commune organization was superior to the corresponding government unit. Formally this was so, but in practice the CPC and government organizations usually worked hand in hand; or both organizations were "in one hand," because often the party secretary and the chief of the corresponding management committee was the same person.

As Fig. 5.17 reveals, the formally highest government organization unit at the commune level was the people's congress, which elected the standing committee or so-called management committee to take care of the operational management activities, or to oversee the commune's daily functioning. It was chaired by the commune chief. The committee comprised posts for deputy chief(s), and for supervisors of the several recognized sectors of local government, such as a public security supervisor, a cashier, a credit-cooperative member, an economic management member, a political member, and a certain number of lower-ranking clerical and technical positions (Pelzel 1972: 400–401).

Brigade

The next lower level of commune organization was the brigade, which was typically organized around natural villages. An average commune usually had 15 brigades, which in turn averaged about 250 households or a little over 1,000 people. The brigades operated enterprises that were smaller in scale than those of the commune. They also carried out smaller-scale capital construction projects, and took care of smaller-scale educational and health services. For example elementary schools and clinics were normally operated at brigade level (Lippit 1982: 52).

As can be seen from Fig. 5.17, the organizational structure of a brigade considerably resembles that of a commune. Thus, there existed also a standing committee, elected by a members' meeting, which took care of operational management at the brigade level. The standing or management committee of a brigade was chaired by the brigade chief.

Production Team

The production teams were the formal basic units for direct agricultural production, and usually also for income distribution. It has been estimated that an average team in China had 38 households or 160 people (Lippit 1982: 53). As Fig. 5.17 shows, the production team was led by a team-leader and one or several deputy leaders. If there were enough CPC members in the team, they elected a party branch committee, but this was not always the case; so there was no official CPC organizational unit at team-level if there was only one or few party members.

To fulfil their production tasks, the teams were divided into work groups, usually of eight to ten households each, under a deputy team leader or a field management member, whose own household normally belonged to the group. Each work group was given responsibility for certain fields, which it could expect to continue farming for an indefinite period.

It has been said that the different team roles, including managerial ones, became specialized and stabilized in a surprisingly short time. The leader of the team took over most of the work of liaison with the brigade cadres and otherwise confined himself to supervision of his own cadres. Deputy leaders or field management members acted as technical advisors both to the leader and to the farmers. Thus, the managerial work was gradually, but quite quickly, legitimized as one specialized job, which needed the whole time and work effort of its holder (Pelzel 1972: 406–410).

Household

The household did not altogether disappear as a work unit with the collectivization process in Chinese agriculture. There were three important factors which maintained its organizational existence: first, of course family ties, which traditionally have been very strong in Chinese culture. Second, each household had the right to cultivate its own private plots, which accounted for some 5% of the collective lands, sometimes some 65 square meters per family. Third, in most cases household independence and responsibility were retained as a part of the team's work organization, but within a collective framework of supervision and reward. I should like to stress the importance of retaining the relative independence of the household through the periods of the different kinds of collectivization described. This custom of keeping the household and the family as an organizational unit made it possible later on to accomplish successfully and quickly the "Green Revolution" of new economic reforms after 1978. But we shall handle this development later on.

The Cultural Revolution and the Revolutionary Committees

In Section 5.1.4 we described generally the background factors of the Cultural Revolution (1966–1976), and mentioned that among its phenomena were the so-called revolutionary committees, which were installed in all kinds of organizations, also in people's communes. In them the revolutionary committee replaced the standing or management committees at every organizational level (see Fig. 5.18). The CPC structure remained the same. The revolutionary committees were subordinated at every level to the corresponding party committee, and the division of work between the party committee and management committee remained much the same as earlier. However, the structure of the revolutionary committee changed a lot from that of the earlier management committee.

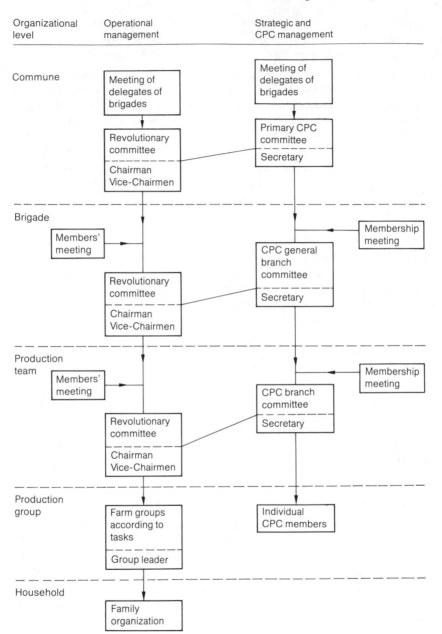

Fig. 5.18. Organizational structure of management during the Cultural Revolution in the Chinese-Cuban friendship commune in 1973

The purpose was probably to accomplish the idea of more participative collective management, and at the same time the new organization gave the supporters of Mao's line the opportunity to change the leaders of the commune. As in the CPC organization, it was also recommended during the Cultural Revolution that in the revolutionary committees a third of the members should represent the elderly, a third the middle-aged, and a third the younger employees. In this way the Chinese tried to bridge generation gaps, which often create serious personnel conflicts. One could argue that behind the idea of securing a position in commune management for younger persons was the belief that the representatives of the younger generation would be more willing to follow the Maoist radical ideas. At the same time it perhaps made it possible to get young, fanatic Red Guards into commune management.

As we will see later, it was a general practice in the revolutionary committees of industrial enterprises for women to be well represented. Thus, through the forming of the revolutionary committees attempts were made to abolish two old Chinese traditions, or at least to lessen their impact; namely the prominent status of men and old people.

The Chinese-Cuban Friendship Commune where I visited in 1973 had 40 members in its commune level revolutionary committee, of whom 20 belonged to cadres and 20 were workers. The composition of the members followed roughly the above-mentioned principle of age distribution: 1/3 elderly, 1/3 middle-aged, and 1/3 younger persons. It is evident that the Chinese tried to extend participation in commune management to many different groups, taking into account the different hierarchical level, different age groups, and both sexes. However, the CPC's dominant role created a problem with respect to the principle of participatory equality, since the most important decisions were in many cases in its hands.

Although there were tendencies to spread the idea of participation during the Cultural Revolution throughout the organizational structure, the practice concerning decision-making did not change much. Changing the formal organizational structure through, e.g., revolutionary committees did not actually change the decision-making hierarchy, as these newly named units did not receive any more decision-making power from the higher authorities than the earlier ones.

We can see that the whole management structure prevailing in people's communes was strictly hierarchical, whether the name of the operational management unit was management committee or revolutionary committee, or whether it had more or less younger and/or female members. One factor which greatly contributed to maintaining the old hierarchical order was the central planning with its guiding and control system. In the prevailing system the central authorities had to decide over the plans and also ensure through macro-, meso-, and microlevel government and CPC agencies that the plans and corresponding activities were carried out. Thus, there was not much freedom of action left for the commune level management. It had to be hierarchical.

This held true both in the CPC and in the operational management structure; in management committees and later on in revolutionary committees. But, as mentioned earlier the CPC always had a dominant position; e.g., over the revolutionary committee, and correspondingly the secretary of the CPC over the chairman of the revolutionary committee, and so on.

One could argue that many conflicts were likely to arise in this kind of double management structure, or between the CPC and operational management represented by the revolutionary (management) committees. Probably there were often severe contradictions, but frequently this was avoided through an interlocking directorate of individuals filling the positions.

In addition to the fact that the Chinese double management organization with separate "lines" for both CPC and operational management could be the origin of many severe contradictions and thus lessened efficiency, this double organization with double manning in most of the positions meant a great waste of human resources. Perhaps for this very reason the economic reforms after Mao included the separation of party, government, and economic management, as we will see in the following section.

5.4.5 The "Green Revolution" and Management of Agricultural Organizations

As was mentioned in Section 5.1.5 the reasons for the "green revolution," which profoundly affected the whole Chinese economy and the great majority of the population, lay to a great extent in the need to strengthen agricultural production.

The reform of China's rural economic system started with the implementation of the contract responsibility system, which links remuneration with output. This change, which actually concerned mostly the individual households, had an impact at every level of the rural organizational system described. In the following we will briefly examine these changes separately for every level.

The people's communes formerly took care of government, CPC, and economic administration within their area. According to the new Constitution, adopted in 1982, "The people's communes will be solely an organizational form of the rural collective economy." The old township organization came back to look after state administration (see Fig. 5.8).

In the contract system the production brigades or production teams make contracts with their members. Contractors can be individuals, households, or groups composed of several households. The scale of a contract depends on the different trades, technical skills, and extent of specialized production involved. The contract, which since 1984 can cover a period of up to 15 years, always includes the amount of land the contractor must till, the output he must produce, what the brigade or team must provide, and how the yield will be distributed.

The contracted household organizes its work on its own. This is a great break from the past, when the brigade and team leaders organized all the work and the peasants were paid by the working day. Thus, the role of the brigade and production team changed from supervisor to supporter or unit giving services to the households. The individual households have again become the relatively independent working units in farming.

The basic idea has at least at the beginning of the contract system been that public ownership of the means of production would not be changed. The peasants had the right to till the land owned by the collective and to use the collective's farm tools and water conservation facilities, but they were forbidden to sell or buy them and transfer them to others. The ownership of "lighter" production means soon became a problem, however, because the peasants wished to increase production, but the required productions means available from the collective were insufficient. Thus, the peasants were gradually allowed to buy tractors for their own use and property. By the end of 1983 the peasants privately owned over two million tractors. Now the farm machines are no longer considered means of production, but commodities freely available on the market. This thinking represents a profound change of philosophy in a socialist country.

The government and the CPC also encouraged the peasants to establish various rural enterprises with their own funds. Soon some of the county governments began to provide obviously skilled peasants with funds, technical know-how, and raw materials to specialize in certain lines of business. These specialized peasants no longer needed to enter into a contract with a production team to work a plot of land, and could gradually disengage themselves altogether from working in the fields. Thus, carpenters, blacksmiths, and tailors could specialize or run side-line businesses, with permission to hire two or three apprentices.

These specialized peasants were also allowed to open shops or run factories, and if they were properly educated or had some technical background, they could begin to run clinics, nurseries, schools, and bookshops individually or jointly, subject to the approval of the authorities concerned.

What was important, and later awakened much discussion both in China and abroad, was the right given also to specialized peasants to buy tractors, horse-drawn carts, or boats to engage in transportation (B.R., November 28, 1983).

The Chinese soon found that especially the specialized households in rural areas actually fell into two categories: (1) contracted households, where the means of production remain part of the collective economy, and (2) self-managing households, where the means of production are owned by themselves. As they also own their own output they are a form of private economy under the socialist system (B.R., April 9, 1984).

As the specialized households were evaluated in different areas with different criteria, the State Statistics Bureau in 1985 defined all rural specialized households in the following way. It should be based on the unit of the individual household. More than 60% of the labor time of the family's labor force must be spent on certain production, and the household must obtain more than 60% of its total income from specialized production. Also more than 80% of specialized products turned out must be for sale.

A survey made in 1984 showed that at the end of that year there were 4.3 million households throughout the country that met the above standard, amounting to 2.3% of all rural households. The annual average income for a specialized household was 4,624 yuan, 81% higher than the average income of the nation's peasants (B.R., December 9, 1985).

As the specialized households were allowed to take two or three apprentices in their labor force, they gradually grew into small private enterprises, whose production value could rise to a quite high level, and correspondingly the income of the household also. Of course, with the growth of personnel and production, leadership and managerial knowledge were needed more and more. However, this need was certainly felt much more by the larger cooperative units, which the peasants began gradually to form, but from a different basis than earlier.

Besides the fact that the rural side-line enterprises provide jobs for the surplus labor force in China's rural areas, their share of the country's total industrial output value has been significant: 13% in 1983 (B.R., April 16, 1984).

The development of the market system has brought the peasants other "new" rights. In order to sell their products they are now permitted to travel to other counties and provinces, or to go into the cities to conduct business, and to transport goods for sale either individually or in a cooperative manner (B.R., August 1, 1983). The possibility to travel more in the country is an important by-product of the economic reforms, which can have more far-reaching consequences than might be imagined at first glance.

5.4.6 Market Socialism and the Return of Cooperatives

The contract system was the first step in the reform of China's rural economic structure which began in 1979. The second step in this reform is resulting in a kind of open market system, which constitutes a market-regulated economic mechanism formed under the guidance of the socialist planning system.

The reforms also covered prices. A major price reform was sweeping across China's nonstaple food market, beginning in June 1985. Uniform price controls on meat, poultry, eggs, and fish were lifted in 35 major cities to make way for prices that fluctuated with market supply and demand. In the meantime, city residents had been issued monthly subsidies to offset possible price hikes.

After the price reform the cost of living began to rise. In May 1985, when price controls on meat and vegetable prices were first lifted, the retail price index rose by 9.3%, which was an all-time high. The free market also opened the door to illegal money-making schemes. Many stores were known to mix fat into lean meat and sell the combination at 100% lean pork prices (B.R., December 9, 1985). These and other problems caused by the price reform stirred up much discontent, and a fair amount of scepticism among consumers about the wisdom of the price reform. It has, however, been said that on the whole the public seemed to favor the changes. In the process, though prices of meat and vegetables went up, other essentials, such as grain, edible oils, cloth, and most consumer goods remained stable.

The reform brought some benefits to all parties. For urban consumers the emergence of market places full of vegetables, many of them fresh with the morning dew, was indeed a dream come true. The farmers again have been delighted to see the prices of their products settle at sensible levels, and have been highly enthused by the sudden flow of cash into their pockets; they have since expanded production to meet the snowballing market demands. Thus, in the first six months of 1985, the volume of business on both the rural and urban markets totalled 3,339 billion yuan, a 65.5% rise over that of the same period in 1984 (B.R., December 9, 1985). However, the increased agricultural production caused imbalance in the economy, since the elasticity of farm product consumption is small. A slight increase in farm products threatens an oversupply in the city. The Chinese think that this problem cannot be solved simply be restricting production; it must be solved by adjusting the economic structure: transferring surplus labor directly from agricultural production to nonagricultural fields.

Township (earlier commune) industries, which have been mushrooming in China during the past few years, have been playing a significant role in the transfer of surplus rural labor and the creation of new job opportunities. In 1984 the total output value of China's township enterprises reached 170 billion yuan. Their composition was agricultural enterprises, 4%; industrial, 71%; transport, 4%; construction, 13%; service trades, 8%.

Most of the industrial enterprises were in the area of machinery (24%), building materials (20%), and textiles (11%). By the end of 1984 the number of employees in these township enterprises had reached over 52 million, including privately run enterprises (Du 1985: 17).

The contract system, which greatly encouraged the peasants' own initiatives in both agricultural and side-line production, demanded a new kind of voluntary cooperation between the peasant households. Often a single family could not buy the production means necessary to develop their production further; cooperation between two or several households was needed. In the same way distribution and selling of products often required more resources than one household could provide. Thus, the peasants began to form different kinds of cooperatives to help themselves.

Other, not purely agricultural cooperatives, were also growing rapidly in rural areas.

> By the end of 1985 there were 480,000 new economic associations formed on a voluntary basis to develop commodity production. They hired 4.2 million employees and netted 13.3 billion yuan. Most of these associations are engaged in industry, construction, and transportation industries and in commerce, catering, and other service trades. (B.R., June 23, 1986)

The rural cooperatives are run under a two-level management system: one is individual household management and the other unified management by the cooperative organization. Table 5.6 indicates clearly how the share of retail sales of collectively owned enterprises as well as of individual firms has increased especially after the economic reforms in 1978. Also the share of peasants' retail sales to nonagricultural residents has grown significantly.

If, to summarize, we examine the organizational development in Chinese rural production units since 1949, we find a one and a half circle movement, as shown in Fig. 5.19. The development began in 1950 with the land reform law, when millions of new independent peasant households were formed. The first step along the way to socialism was the strengthening of the team-farming system. This was only a transitional stage in a careful move towards

Table 5.6. Total value of retail sales by form of ownership in 1952–1985; percentages. (*China: A Statistical Survey in 1986:89*)

Year	Publicly owned (%)	Collectively owned (%)	Jointly owned (%)	Individual (%)	Peasants' sales[a] (%)	Total (%)	Yuan (100 million)
1952	34.4		0.4	60.9	4.3	100.0	276.8
1957	62.1	16.4	16.0	2.7	2.8	100.0	474.2
1965	83.3	12.9		1.9	1.9	100.0	670.3
1978	90.5	7.4		0.1	2.0	100.0	1,558.6
1979	88.3	8.9		0.2	2.6	100.0	1,800.0
1980	84.0	12.1		0.7	3.2	100.0	2,140.0
1981	80.0	14.5	0.1	1.6	3.8	100.0	2,350.0
1982	76.6	16.1	0.1	2.9	4.3	100.0	2,570.0
1983	72.1	16.6	0.1	6.5	4.7	100.0	2,849.4
1984	45.6	39.6	0.2	9.6	5.0	100.0	3,376.4
1985	40.4	37.2	0.3	15.3	6.8	100.0	4,305.0

Note: The 1984 retail sales of collectively owned units include those of supply and marketing cooperatives, which were covered in those of the publicly owned units previously. Before 1956, the jointly owned enterprises were those under joint state-private ownership. Since 1981 they include various forms of jointly owned enterprises and joint Chinese-foreign enterprises. In 1952 and 1957 the individual enterprises include private enterprises.

[a] Value of retail sales of peasants' goods to nonagricultural rural residents.

a cooperative system, about which the CPC had made a decision in 1953. The cooperativization process went on very quickly, and in June 1956 92% of all peasant households were already part of cooperatives. Peasants joining the cooperative had to turn over their privately owned land and chief means of production to the collective ownership. In this way the economic resources and corresponding power were transmitted from peasants to collectives among the 80% majority of the population. From cooperatives it was not a long step to people's communes, which began to grow during the Great Leap Forward in 1958. In the commune system the Chinese united the economic, government, and CPC management.

The core of the "Green Revolution," which began in 1979, was the establishment of the contract system. This system made the individual peasant households again the basic production units in the rural areas. Thus, the development had gone full circle according to Fig. 5.19, and began to make a second round as the independent peasants started to form their own cooperatives to foster their own production, service, and distribution activities. That the whole development circle in rural areas, beginning in 1950, has gone relatively smoothly depends on the fact, that all the time, during this period of team, cooperative, and commune organization, the

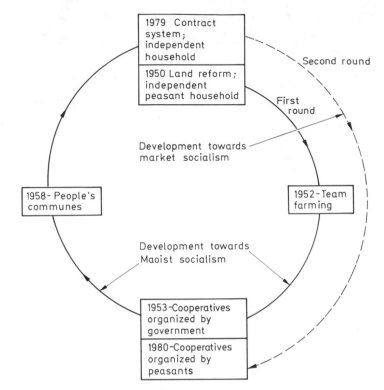

Fig. 5.19. Development of agricultural organizational units during the People's Republic of
China

household, the individual family, has remained the basic working unit of
other superior organizations.

The development of the rural organizations in the People's Republic represents a unique phenomenon, which can be seen in the eyes of an organizational researcher to have contained varying, interesting experiments in real
environments. One could interpret many of the developments with the help
of the ideas of the contingency theory, however, taking into account the
fact that Chinese culture itself has all the time had great influence.

I have examined the structure and management of China's rural organizations quite extensively, on the one hand, because 80% of the Chinese work
and live in these organizations and, on the other hand, because these
organizations have not only been ordinary "rural organizations" in the
Western sense, but special systems, where economic, state, and CPC management have been experimented with both together in the same units and
separately.

5.5 Management in Industry and Commerce Under Mao

I believe that contemporary Chinese enterprise management can be examined and understood best with the help of an historical analysis, by studying how the management and structure of organizations have developed. As we have already looked at the development before 1949, we concentrate in the following four subsections on the period before the Cultural Revolution.

5.5.1 Socializing Industry

As was the case in agriculture, the CPC applied a carefully planned step-by-step strategy in industry during the period of rehabilitation. This strategy was based on a careful analysis of the class structure, that is, the ownership relations prevailing in industry before the revolution of 1949.

The Guomindang government (GMD) had quite early taken under its control much of the heavy industry, and after the Liberation War against the Japanese, Chiang Kai-shek's government took over all Japanese, German, and Italian enterprises in China. Thus, in 1948 two-thirds of all industrial capital was controlled by (GMD) bureaucrat-capitalists in the areas occupied by their troops. In October 1949, 60% of all banking capital was in the hands of GMD supporters. Thus, at the time of the communists' victory the bureaucrat-capitalists dominated banking, the largest industrial enterprises, all the existing heavy industry, and even the bulk of light industry (Hsueh et al. 1960: 26 ff.).

The national-capitalists, or private entrepreneurs, were first of all active in light industry and commerce. Their enterprises were mostly small. It has been estimated that in 1949 there were over 123,000 industrial enterprises with 1,640,000 employees managed by national-capitalists. The number of commercial enterprises in 1950 was some 4 million, employing 6.6 million persons, of whom a little under one million were paid laborers (Kuan 1960: 24).

As briefly mentioned before, the tactics applied by the CPC in changing industry and commerce towards a socialist system were the following: to confiscate as quickly as possible the enterprises controlled by bureaucrat-capitalists and foreigners, but, during the period of changeover, to let the national-capitalists develop their enterprises for the sake of rebuilding the country. Step by step the activities of the national-capitalists would be controlled more and more and would be integrated with the socialist sector (Hultcrantz et al. 1974: 63).

The confiscation of the bureaucrat-capitalist enterprises (former GMD-controlled) proceeded quickly. At the end of 1949 the CPC had nationalized 2,858 enterprises with a total number of 750,000 workers. These confiscated enterprises became the trunk of the industries in the socialist sector, which by the end of 1949 accounted for 35% of the total value of industrial production, handicrafts excluded (Ten Great Years 1960: 38).

The functioning of the remaining foreign enterprises was made more and more difficult through heavy taxation and other discriminatory measures. Thus, many of them decided voluntarily to cease functioning or "gave" their firms to the state. In December 1950 all the remaining US enterprises were confiscated, and during 1952 all the British and French.

The national-capitalist (Chinese) enterprises could at first continue with the same management as before. They also had some opportunities for expansion. Unification of these firms with the social sector took place gradually under the leadership of the latter. Jointly owned state-private enterprises were formed, where the state took formal ownership, while the former capitalist received annual interest on the capital he had given to the state; in most cases he could also go on acting as part of the management of the firm (Hultcrantz et al. 1974: 63–64). From Table 5.7 it can be seen with what speed this movement towards socialism proceeded in China during the period of rehabilitation.

Table 5.7. Change of national-capitalist industry towards socialism during the period of rehabilitation; percentage of production value of total industry excluding handicrafts. (*Ten Great Years* 1960:38)

Year	Socialist industry	State-capitalist jointly owned industry	Of this state-private commonly owned industry	Private industry producing for the state	National-capitalist industry which produces and sells by itself
1949	34.7	9.5	2.0	7.5	55.8
1950	45.3	17.8	2.9	14.9	36.9
1951	45.9	25.4	4.0	21.4	28.7
1952	56.0	26.9	5.0	21.9	17.1

In 1956 the CPC thought the time was ripe to move more quickly towards joint ownership in industry. Now whole fields of industry, and not only individual enterprises, were included in the new system of joint ownership. The take-over proceeded quickly:

> By the end of 1956, more than 60,000 factories and 280,000 shops had been taken into joint state-private ownership. The remaining 20,000

small private factories and 2 million small private shops were reorganized as cooperatives. (Xu et al. 1982: 7–8)

5.5.2 Towards Handicraft Producers' Cooperatives

Handicrafts also became a target for socialist change during the period of rehabilitation (1949–1952). The privately owned and managed handicraft enterprises were encouraged to unite with other similar firms, and form handicraft groups organizing purchases and sales together in cooperation with the state trading companies and trade cooperative. The next step was that several of these handicraft groups formed producers' cooperatives, which at first themselves owned their production equipment, but later ownership was joint. By the beginning of 1952, these wholly socialist producers' cooperatives had become the most common type; they could grow quite large and mechanize their production. By the end of 1956, over six million handicraftsmen (92% of the total) had joined together to form over 100,000 handicraft producers' cooperatives (Xu et al. 1982: 7). The final step in the process of socializing the artisans was taken at the end of the 1950s by "including" them in common ownership, i.e., they became state socialist enterprises (Hsueh et al. 1960: 138–).

5.5.3 Socializing Trade

Before 1949, the wholesale business as well as the larger retail dealers had to a great extent been in the hands of Guomindang capital, which had taken several enterprises from the Japanese in the mid-1940s. These enterprises were quickly confiscated by the central administration of the People's Republic. State trading corporations and state offices for wholesale trade under the control of the ministry of trade were formed from them. By the end of 1951 60% of wholesale business and 18% of retail business was controlled by these state organs. The number of sales and purchasing places increased from 8,000 to over 500,000 by the same point in time (Prybyla 1970: 62–).

The rapid expansion of state control over trade had a great impact on the step-by-step socialist integration of private industry. This happened through greater and greater control both of acquisition of raw materials and sales of commodities of the capitalist enterprises (Kuan 1960: 65).

The retail trade had previously been mostly in the hands of small private shopkeepers in rural areas. During the rehabilitation period rural retail trade was gradually taken over by so-called trading cooperatives. This kind of cooperative had already been established earlier in the areas occupied by the communists during the Yan'an period in northern and northwestern China. At the beginning of the 1950s about 90% of the members of the cooperatives were peasants; often every household had at least one member. In 1954 a national federation for all the trading cooperatives of the country was established, with a membership of 150–160 million.

The trading cooperatives were involved both in the purchase of products of handicrafts, etc. as a result of the side-line production which existed in rural areas, and in the selling of essential goods: consumer goods and farm implements, artificial fertilizer, and other commodities for agriculture. In 1950 there were altogether 44,000 purchase/sales places organized by trading cooperatives. This number grew to 113,000 in 1952, and they then employed over 700,000 persons (Prybyla 1970: 63). We can imagine that the whole new organization of trading cooperatives from the central national federation down to the more than 100,000 local distribution points required a great number of new managers at different levels.

5.5.4 Soviet Influence

The Russian revolution in 1917 had a great impact on the Chinese, and especially on the development of the communist movement in the country long before 1949. The ties to the Soviet Union were strengthened during the civil war, when the Americans placed themselves on the side of Guomindang (Chiang Kai-shek) and with their navy blocked the coast-line of China against the communists. This obliged the Chinese to develop their own production and find economic and military help from the Soviet Union. Thus, in 1950 China and the Soviet Union made an agreement for 30 years of "friendship, alliance and mutual assistance."

The most direct effects of Soviet influence stemmed from the presence of large numbers of Soviet teachers, and technical advisers, and the training of many Chinese students in the Soviet Union. It has been estimated that at least 10,000, perhaps as many as 20,000, Soviet experts and industrial advisers worked in China during the 1950s, primarily in construction and planning. But this was not all: at least 80,000 Chinese engineers, technicians, and advanced research personel were trained in the USSR. Together these two groups, sophisticated theoretically, and formally educated, were an important segment of industry (Richman 1969: 406).

After the breaking off of relations between China and the Soviet Union in 1960, the number of foreign teachers in China declined sharply, so that by 1960 fewer than 100 foreign professors and teachers, chiefly in engineering and advanced physics, remained in China. The number of Chinese going to the Soviet Union for education also declined sharply during the 1960s. All the remaining Chinese students in the Soviet Union were sent home in October 1966.

How relatively great was Soviet aid to China? We can get some idea of this by comparing it internationally. For example US economic aid to India in the late 1950s and early 1960s was more than four times the Soviet economic help to China, and US economic aid to Yugoslavia was somewhat more than Soviet help to China (Richman 1969: 405–407).

The Soviet aid ended abruptly in 1960, and the Russian technicians and experts were withdrawn from China. This pull-out worsened Chinese economic development at that time very much. The Soviets chose an extremely critical moment to withdraw – a severe economic crisis was already emerging because of the ideological fanaticism of the Great Leap and also because of poor crops. For a long time there were clear and rather depressing signs of the effects on Chinese industry of the sudden Soviet pull-out (Richman 1969: 407).

What were the reasons for the abrupt Soviet withdrawal? Probably there were several factors: political, ideological, power-related, even personal. One major contributing cause was the mentioned ideological fanaticism. China's extreme emphasis on self-sufficiency and disdain of foreign methods during this period meant that the advice, opinions, suggestions, and decisions of the Soviet industrial experts were often ignored and scorned. Many of the Soviet experts were exposed to hostility and abuse.

After the conflict with the Soviet Union, China turned sharply to the West and Japan in its foreign trade. Also a substantial number of complete factories were being constructed in China by companies and consortiums from several West European countries and Japan. In the 1960s there was also a growing Western and Japanese influence in the cultural area; there were student and faculty exchanges, borrowing of educational and technical books and materials, and the teaching of foreign languages. Chinese students and a limited number of Chinese professors and specialists were sent to England, France, Japan, and other noncommunist countries for education, training, and the exchange of ideas and information (Richman 1969: 409). After this relatively short opening up to the West, China again changed its policy and closed its boundaries to foreign countries for ten years during the Cultural Revolution, 1966–1976.

If we turn back to the period of Soviet aid and influence, 1950–1960, we note that one of the most important impacts that period had for China concerned Soviet influence upon Chinese management systems at the macro- and microlevels. Now we will begin to examine the development of Chinese micromanagement in enterprise organizations.

5.5.5 Development of Enterprise Management under Mao

After their victory in 1949, the communists were faced with a difficult problem: how to begin to manage the thousands of industrial enterprises which should guarantee both the economic progress of the country and the political and economic power in the hands of the winners, and help the country's progress towards a socialist system. Two options for organizing the management in factories soon emerged. One option was the idea of taking advantage of the small patriotic group of Chinese workers and Communist Party members who had experience in administration generally and/or in industry. The management system, which developed from this option was called the "Shanghai system." The second option was the idea of following the experiences of the socialist Soviet Union, and was based on the so-called one-man management system (Andors 1977: 50).

Shanghai or Committee Management

After October 1949 the winners had to establish their new political authority, and in many cases to replace enterprise owners and managers who had fled or otherwise disappeared. Thus, military leaders and trustworthy workers were sent all over the country during the first months of the People's Republic. In East China there developed in factories a system of collective leadership, which was exercised by a committee. The factory manager was responsible for carrying out and organizing the production operations.

The committees, which were typical of this management system, could take many forms. Sometimes they were made up of technicians and owners who cooperated with the communists. Sometimes they were made up of military leaders and former underground CPC workers. In many cases they consisted of large numbers of workers, especially in cases where workers had taken over plants when the former owners or manager had fled. Also women workers were active, especially in the textile mills.

The management committees were responsible for getting production going in the plant. They made decisions regarding plans, personnel, organization, and welfare. In the early years, the management committees worked hard to create mass organizations in the plant and to mobilize workers for production as well as for political purposes. Trade union and youth league groups became important in the administration of the factories.

The committee management was not confined only to East China and the coastal cities like Shanghai, but it was dominant in most of the country when after 1953 the Soviet system of one-man management became official national policy with the formal beginning of the first five-year plan. The committee management embodied significant worker participation because of its relationship to the old decentralized operational autonomy of the gang-boss system, which the communists had earlier attacked and reformed but could not eliminate. The committee management was also characterized by a certain equality and unity between the new managers and the workers, especially where the system of incentives was reinforced by mass campaigns to undermine values and priviledges of the urban bourgeoisie.

Why did the committee management system vanish after some years although it had evolved in areas where Chinese capitalism had had its greatest independence and development? One reason is that this system developed only within individual workplaces. It was not applied to the problems of economic coordination. When the Chinese economy began to recover from decades of war the problems of planning and coordination became more central in development towards a socialist economy. Thus, the Shanghai management system was not suitable for solving these new problems at that time. On the other hand, the Soviet management system, which had been developed in a socialist country, and had been applied in the northeast, seemed to promise not only efficient production within the factories and enterprises, but also a method for centralized economic planning and coordination (Andors 1977: 52–53).

Soviet One-Man Management

The spreading of the Soviet management system in China was the result of a series of agreements in 1949 and 1950 which culminated in the Sino-Soviet Treaty signed in February 1950. Already before the first five-year plan began in 1953, major Soviet aid was present in the industrial centers, particularly in the northeastern provinces. Later the Soviet aid projects were scattered in other parts of the country, especially in heavy industry. This Soviet aid had an important effect upon production during the first five-year plan. By 1956 over 200 complete industrial units were planned or already under construction. These projects were planned down to the smallest operational detail under the close supervision and advice of the Soviet experts. Along with technology and operational blueprints, they now also gave advice on how to manage the industrial enterprises. By the end of 1953 the Soviet management model had gained general, though only tentative, acceptance.

The typical features of the Soviet management system were:

1. A close connection between the so-called scientific management system of each industrial enterprise, and the tight central planning system within the total industrial system. These two systems were intergrated. "Scientific management involved detailed work plans for each phase of production

and administration. These plans were standardized, based on exact measurements of mechanical, technological, and human performances, and, once formulated as targets, were to be followed precisely." (Andors 1977: 54)

2. The Soviet model was organized according to a production-territorial principle. In every plant there were three basic levels of organization: the factory, the workshop and the work team. The factory level was responsible for coordinating and controlling all activity within the plant, and it contained sections dealing with the functional matters of personnel, wages, quality control, supplies, storage, and communications with planning authorities and other plants.

3. The Soviet responsibility system, called the one-man management system, was related to the described production-territorial organization of the plant above. The system usually functioned in the following way: There was normally a control team in the plant, made up of high-level management. This team was responsible for ensuring that production leaders and individual workers were carrying out their responsibilities, "most of which were outlined and standardized in enormous detail by the measurements of scientific management. Daily production logs were kept by management for each worker, recording output for the day, rate of production (output per unit of time), and rate of material consumption" (Andors 1977: 53–54).

The name "one-man management system" comes from the principle that one person, the factory director, was in complete control of the factory. One individual was also responsible for and had power over each production unit, down to the work team or section. Thus, a strict hierarchy prevailed. At the factory and shop level an adequate system of staff sections was established with defined tasks and responsibilities (Schurmann 1971: 251). Coordination between staff sections and administrative and production leaders was handled by the leader of each functional section and production unit.

The one-man management system was not restricted to individual factories, but was applied also in the planning apparatus. Thus, at every level of the planning hierarchy, beginning from the central ministries, one person was responsible for getting accurate and comprehensive information upon which to formulate targets for his section and for reaching these targets.

The Soviet management system also contained a corresponding incentive system to motivate the employees, and the Chinese gradually "inherited" the same kind of incentive system. The "scientifically" determined output and consumption quotas computed by high-level managers and experts in the staff sections of the factory became the basis for a complex system of individual sanctions: bonuses and rewards were paid in addition to wages and salaries, while these calculations were also the basis for fines and other punishments. The control requirements of this kind of management also fitted in well with piece-rate wages in those industries where the production process lent itself to piece-rate wage calculations.

The piece-rate system grew rapidly in China. By the end of 1952 slightly over one-third of all industrial workers were paid according to this system, and by 1956 about 42% of all industrial workers belonged to the piece-rate incentive system. Very quickly also bonus payments became common throughout industry, including industrial personnel of all types: managers, technicians, and party cadres (Richman 1969: 314).

By the mid-1950s the average wage for a worker was about 65 yuan per month. Middle-level managers and key specialists frequently earned two to three times more than workers. A top-paid chief engineer could earn around 280 yuan, and directors and vice-directors as much as 263 yuan, with a minimum of about 132 (Richman 1969: 231).

For a person from a capitalist industrialized country, it is surprising to note that the general director can earn less than for example his chief engineer. When I was interviewing in Chinese enterprises for the first time in 1973, I remember that repeatedly in answer to my question concerning who had the highest salary in the enterprise the reply was: "Chief engineer." But this becomes understandable when we think that in a centrally planned socialist economy the managers more or less blindly follow the directives of the central economic planning, without having much to say concerning these orders coming from higher authorities. The chief engineer, on the other hand, has to find the ways of fulfilling the plan using the available equipment, machines, and material. He actually has much more concrete responsibility than the general manager.

Problems the Soviet Management Model Met in China

Cultural factors play a crucial role when attempts are made to plant new foreign management methods in a country whose culture differs considerably from the country where the methods have been formed. This was exactly the case when the Chinese tried to adopt the Soviet one-man management system at the beginning of the 1950s.

Because the Soviet one-man management system has played a very important role in the economic and management development of the People's Republic, we examine here the clashes between the Soviet system and Chinese traditional culture:

1. It was difficult, often impossible, to get adequate hard data in China for planning and judging the performance of individuals by which rewards and

punishments were allocated. Therefore planning and production within the factory system became difficult, and accordingly planning and coordination at the provincial and central ministry levels could be severely hampered.

2. The Soviet system required larger economic entities, and thus amalgamation of many small and scattered shops and factories in the cities, in order to unify their operations and rationalize their structures. This very often required physical relocation of people and equipment and a merging of technical and managerial manpower from different plants into one new factory. There was also the great conflicting problem: which managers, owners, and technical personnel from which of the old plants would have what responsibility and powers in the new set-up.

3. The Soviet management model required a large number of people educated in skills that were not abundant in China, compared to skills that were already available. The Soviet system favored management and leadership methods that were typical among the engineers and technicians, many of whom were of bourgeois origin. It was natural that many members of Chinese cadres rebelled against a system which was clearly threatening their own authority and status, but they also felt sure that such developments were a threat to the cooperative, egalitarian ideals of the revolution and socialism.

4. There was in addition a quite opposite group which was dissatisfied with the ideology of the Soviet system; namely Chinese capitalists and bourgeois technical personnel, who were still influenced by traditional Confucian ethics, ideas about authority, obedience, and discipline which came from inner morality rather than from external rule-bound constraints (Andors 1977: 56; Schurmann 1971: 253–254).

5. Another value-laden source of conflict stemmed from the fact that a number of Chinese engineers, designers, and technicians of industrial machinery and building had been trained in the United States or Britain and were either anti-Soviet or wedded to American or British ways.

6. The Soviet incentive system also brought many problems when planted in Chinese institutions. It was felt that the management-worker split grew wider from the control system and the realities of decision-making, and was exacerbated by the system of incentives based on quotas and differential bonuses. The competition for rewards and promotion among cadres led to a paralyzing factionalism, but this was only part of the problem with the Soviet-type incentive system. It was quite soon realized that the system was not only detrimental to the production process but also to the planning process.

The new system led many factory directors and also planners to set low targets which could be easily met and preferably also exceeded. The system also led to concealing one's own mistakes or to covering up mistakes of others if they might reflect on oneself. Some Chinese also "learned" quickly to report achievements that did not exist or to listen to only good news in order to be able to report it to higher authorities in order to gain rewards or promotion.

This kind of malpractice spread quickly to every level of the societal structure. It occurred not only at the factory level, but also at the municipal level CPC committees, which had to supervise the work of economic planning. The same kind of phenomena were seen in the local administrative branches of central ministries which were responsible for planning. They were clearly unacceptable to those Chinese planners who were ideally oriented to building a new, better society. These phenomena were an uncomfortable reminder of the behavior of that group of administrative bureaucrats that had dominated China earlier for thousands of years (Andors 1977: 58).

7. The introduction of the Soviet management model also caused unhealthy competition, and serious conflicts between the CPC system and managers in enterprises, especially in firms which had earlier adopted the Shanghai system of management. In this system the CPC committees had gained much influence, and this more or less collective type of management collided with the principle of the one-man management system; who had the right to make what kinds of decisions? As rewards, honors, and promotions were tightly bound with the reaching of production targets, an unhealthy competition to get recognition in these matters within the CPC and management as well as between them arose. This competition was often very damaging for the effective functioning of the enterprise (Andors 1977: 57).

To secure their decision-making power and to be able to manage the enterprise effectively, the managers of firms often tried to occupy important positions in the CPC committee of the enterprise, or vice versa. Later in 1973 when I was interviewing the representatives of Chinese enterprises in different parts of the country I could recognize that the general manager was very often the first or second secretary of the CPC committee or at least a member of it. Thus, they united the power of the party and line management, and in this way secured the functioning of the one-man management system in practice.

Collective Management by CPC Committee

The problems which the one-man management system caused in Chinese society and its enterprises, led to a situation where the Chinese had officially to change the management practice. This was done at the Eighth Party Congress in 1956. The new system then announced attempted to combine CPC collective leadership with individual responsibility, and was officially called "factory-manager responsibility under the leadership of the Party Committee" (Schurmann 1971: 285).

The new system was largely based on an umbrella-concept of mass line, which meant in practice, that when adjusting the enterprise economic plan to the state plan, management must first take the initiative in drawing up a draft plan. According to the mass-line principle this draft plan must be discussed among the mass organizations of the enterprise. After that the actual plan could be drawn up (Schurman 1971: 286).

However, in the shadow of the frequently mentioned mass-line system, two developments emerged which were of great importance to the development of Chinese management in the following years. These were: first, the growing CPC domination, and, second, the decentralization of planning and decision-making.

Actually behind the discussions of the new management model there were crucial problems about the relationships between politics and economics, and between the state, the enterprises, and the CPC. These relationships were again closely connected with other important and difficult problems concerning the relations between the practical daily management process in enterprises and the overall planning process, the problems of motivation and incentives, distribution of income, and keeping up reliable statistical work. It has been argued that the Chinese did not actually know at the beginning of 1957 how management at the enterprise level and planning at the macro- (societal) level should be adequatedly related.

One of the main phenomena in the new administrative system was the growing power of the CPC in planning and decision-making in enterprises. The party committee of the enterprise was responsible for integrating the individual enterprise into the national plan, or the party committee ensured that the enterprise reached the targets set for it according to the central plan. The party committee was responsible also for the political leadership in the enterprise, and ensured that the employees followed the "correct" political line (Andors 1977: 60–61).

It seems that the relations between operational management and the CPC must have been confusing in many enterprises. The party committee had the power to make the most important decisions, but the factory director was responsible for the behavior of the employees as well as the effective functioning of the production process. Perhaps for this reason the manager tried to wear two hats in the enterprise: to be a member of management as well as also to occupy an important position in the CPC committee (Laaksonen 1984a: 17).

The CPC was not only heavily involved within the enterprise as a major policy-making body and often as a body determining appropriate labor norms and production quotas, it also became involved in coordination matters at the level above the enterprise. This development proceeded from two directions: First, the enterprise's party organization had actively to make contacts outwards, as it was mainly responsible for the functioning of the firm. Second, with the decentralization of planning, the provincial and municipal level party committees gained much more power and responsibility. Thus, both the micro- (enterprise-) and the meso- (provincial and communal) levels of the party organization gained more power and responsibility.

The decentralization of planning had other effects also. As there were no detailed plans given by the central authorities, and thus no accurate information on which to base the plans, the party committee members at the municipal and provincial level had to leave their offices much more often than previously to make contacts in the enterprises on the spot. According to the practice of the time, these CPC authorities had to take part in labor within the factories in order (1) to follow the principle of cadres taking part in manual labor, which I call participation down the line, (2) to get really accurate information for their planning and guidance, and (3) to lessen bureaucracy in the form of paper work and reports (Andors 1977: 93–94).

During the enthusiastic time at the beginning of the Great Leap Forward the Chinese tried several different management methods to solve their problems. There emerged two main systems of management. One was the "factory manager responsibility under the leadership of the party committee." The second, partly new and revolutionary system was called "two participations, one reform, and triple combination" (Andors 1977: 95).

The main feature of this period was the growing power of the CPC at micro-, meso-, and macrolevels of management. However, the management systems applied during the period of the Great Leap Forward also included several kinds of participation methods, which were later crucial for Chinese management.

The management system of "two participations, one reform, and triple combination" was actually an idea of participation in three dimensions: (1) participation of workers in management, representing participation "up the line," (2) participation of cadres in labor, representing participation "down the line". These were the "two participations." (3) The idea of "triple combination" was based on technical mutual-aid groups to solve, e.g., technical problems. These groups consisted of engineers, technicians, administrators, and workers, and thus also represented horizontal participation, e.g., between engineers and administrators. The slogan of "triple combination" referred to: the combination of (1) leadership with the masses, (2) labor with technique, and (3) technical theory with production practice.

The words "one reform" in this management slogan mean the reform of rules and regulations that inhibited the two participations and effective management. Before the Great Leap Forward there were numerous written orders and regulations (norm power), designed by the central government or authorities above the enterprise level, which slowed down, e.g., technological change and development: "Elaborate procedures were required before a screw could be requisitioned and changed or a pipe altered." The technical management's time was largely spent in constant filling out of reports, orders, requisitions, etc. which again had to be approved at the appropriate level before any action could be taken (Andors 1977: 83).

In spite of the great enthusiasm and the many experiments made in the area of management, the Great Leap Forward turned out, for many other reasons, to be an economic failure; this raised heated discussion in China about the economic policy applied.

From Party Management to Profit Management

Because of the setbacks of the Great Leap Forward, soon two different lines of thinking appeared: First that represented by Mao Zedong and his followers, who had activated the policy applied during the Great Leap Forward, and, second, a line which was represented by a group of people headed by Liu Shao-chi, one of the vice-chairmen of the Central Committee of the CPC. These contradictions became openly apparent during the plenary session of the Eighth Congress of the Party in January 1961.

According to Liu Shao-chi's line, it was decided to activate the economy as follows: First, to enlarge the size of the private pieces of land which the peasants could cultivate for their own needs; second, gradually to open up free markets for agricultural areas; third, to encourage the forming and developing of small and middle-sized enterprises in the countryside. These should function on their own responsibility concerning profits and losses, and their production targets should be set according to the needs of the individual households. The fourth and most significant characteristic of Liu Shao-chi's economic line was to replace the quantitative production targets with a profit target for every enterprise. Closely related with this principle were new administrative principles in enterprises. These gave the director of the enterprise, middle managers, experts, and technicians all decisive power over the enterprise and its management. Both the CPC and trade unions lost much of their former power (Wheelwright and McFarlane 1970: 66–76). The effects of the new policy seemed promising; production undoubtedly rose sharply in the country after 1961, as we could see from Fig. 5.1.

Concerning the power relations of this period we can say that at the micro-level the managers and other professionals of enterprise management had won, and the power of the party committees had declined, but at the macrolevel the struggle over the "right" political line went on between Mao Zedong and Liu Shao-chi. Actually a definite solution had not yet been reached in the battle at the microlevel either; the siege of the Liu Chao-chi group was more or less temporary, and the final battle was still ahead and was fought during the Cultural Revolution.

Contradiction Between Democracy and Centralism

The clash between Mao and Liu in the 1960s concerned also a contradiction between two ideological currents: (1) that concerning Mao's concept of democracy, and (2) that of centralism identified by Liu Shao-chi. Though both persons and their corresponding groups accepted "the notions of de-mocracy and centralism as crucial to proper organizational functioning," Mao stressed the primacy of democracy and Liu the primacy of centralism. For Mao, democracy meant a populist upsurge of the masses, a spiritual liberation unleashing their creative energies. For Liu, centralism meant the rule of organization, specifically that of the party (Schurmann 1971: 518–519).

The two different concepts of democracy and centralism had actually been traced from Lenin's well-known concept of democratic centralism, which the Chinese – and Liu Shao-chi already at the beginning of 1940s – had split into two nominal entities.

> The Chinese Communists understand *"democracy"* essentially as *im-pulses coming from below,* in contrast to *"centralism,"* which means *impulses coming from above.* . . . Therefore, Liu, in effect, maintained that here is a necessary contradiction between these two types of impulses. . . . Liu made clear. . . that the juxtaposition of leaders and followers always gives rise to contradictions. (Schurmann 1971: 54; this author's italics)

As the differences between the concepts of "democracy" and "centralism" in China have not been only theoretical and philosophical, but also practi-cal, especially from the viewpoint of management, we examine these con-cepts here more closely. According to the Chinese,

> Impulses are related to policy, since every policy can be said to be based on an impulse leading to a decision. The Chinese Communists distinguish between various kinds of policy, ranging from the general to the specific. Centralism implies a system where both general and specific policy impulses originate from the center. Democracy, on the

other hand, implies a system where policy impulses originate from a level below the center. The Chinese Communists have never advocated instituting democracy at the full expense of centralism, but rather a system which combined the two in a unity of true opposites. During the Great Leap Forward, this took the form of centralization of general policy impulses and decentralization of specific policy impulses.... In other words, Peking laid down the general policy guidelines, but the regions were allowed to develop specific policies to make sure to "do the best according to local conditions." (Schurman 1971: 86–87)

Going through the research literature on the forming of the organizational structure – like centralization or decentralization – Leena Ylä-Anttila (1983: 151) came to the conclusion that the most important factors were the principles of (1) efficiency, and (2) power structure. Very often, especially in socialist countries, where a one-party system prevails, the power factor overshadows efficiency, at least in the background. Officially this is often stated more or less directly in the constitutions of the Communist Parties. For example, the CPC Constitution states:

Party members must fulfil the following duties: ...To adhere to the principle that the interest of the party and the people stand above everything, subordinate their personal interests to the interests of the party and the people, ... (Twelfth National Congress of the CPC, September 1982: 99)

It should be noted that the party here comes before "the people."

These matters refer more to the concept of centralism, which means that impulses come from above. The other key concept "democracy" refers to impulses coming from below. This is closely related to the concepts of industrial democracy and participation, which are of vital importance for management of enterprises. In the following chapter we examine the different participative systems which have emerged in Chinese enterprises, especially after 1949.

5.5.6 Participation in Chinese Enterprises Before the Cultural Revolution

By "participation" we mean that persons or groups working in certain tasks or organizational units take part in decision-making or work mainly belonging to the area of other persons or organizational units.

Participation can occur in three different main dimensions as mentioned briefly earlier:

1. Participation up the line, which generally means that people in lower organizational levels take part in decision-making and/or work which "belongs" normally to the higher organizational levels

2. Participation down the line, which represents the opposite direction. In this the persons at higher organizational levels participate in work and decision-making of lower hierarchical levels; for example, superiors take part in the work of their subordinates

3. Horizontal participation, which means that persons or groups take part in decision-making and/or work of other persons or groups or organizational units at the same hierarchical level; for example, technicians of one department discuss matters and make decisions with technicians of another department at the same organizational level

Participation up the Line

Workers' Congresses

The idea of workers' congresses can be traced back to the 1920s when the Communist Party of China as well as the Red Army were established. The communists' doctrine included the idea of democratic management for industrial enterprises. According to this idea, a workers' congress would provide an opportunity for rank and file workers to influence to a limited degree the decision-making of enterprise management or the enterprise director, the party's branch secretary, and the union chairman. The workers' congresses became official organizational units in 1950, when a law was passed "requiring each industrial enterprise with more than 200 employees to establish a workers' congress." A new law was passed in 1961 according to which the workers' congress should "become involved in the discussion and resolution of central problems of enterprise management relevant to workers' interests" (Lansbury et al. 1984: 59).

The power of worker's congresses has often changed back and forth since 1950, depending both on the power structure and balance in enterprises and in society as a whole, and on the possibility for workers and other lower-level employees to use other participation channels, such as the "two participations, one reform, and triple combination" system during the Great Leap Forward. However, in no period during the 1950s and 1960s has the power of workers' congresses in decision-making concerning important matters in enterprises been great. For example, the minister of labor wrote in 1964 that the two-participation, triple-combination system and workers' congresses were management tools "for smoothing over human conflict and making communications more efficient" (Andors 1977:

136). Thus, the workers' congresses represented a more or less manipulative device in the hands of the managers and CPC committees to guide and motivate the workers.

CPC Committees

When we speak about industrial democracy and participation in enterprises, we usually mean that all those working at the lower levels of the organization have an equal opportunity to influence decision-making in the organization. This rule does not actually apply to the party, because only a small proportion, usually 10%–13% of the employees of an enterprise belong to the CPC. However, as according to its constitution "The Communist Party of China is the political party of the proletariat" (Tenth National Congress of CPC 1973: 61), and has the greatest political power in management at all levels, the Party gives some persons working at lower levels in the enterprise hierarchy the opportunity to take part in important decision-making procedures in enterprises.

Actually in many cases the most powerful person in the enterprise, the first secretary of the CPC committee, has been a worker or a former worker. Although this person has been elected from among a selected group of people – members of the CPC – he has belonged personally to a lower hierarchical level and thus has represented participation up the line.

The importance of up-the-line participation in an organization depends upon both the power of the organizational unit in which the decision-making occurs and the degree to which the actors can influence the decision-making and the matters concerned. Often these aspects are closely related.

With regard to the power of the CPC committee, it extended not only to managerial and ideological matters, but also to union activities. The labor unions were mostly under the complete control of the party committee. For example, the CPC usually selected the candidates for union elections concerning trade union chairmen in enterprises (Richman 1969: 268).

Although the power of the CPC changed often and very much during Mao Zedong's regime it never diminished so much as to become altogether insignificant. The CPC, with its wide organizational network, has kept the whole socialist state system together. The strongest power, backed by the army, has always been in the hands of the central bodies of the party, and they could quickly change the power balance in the enterprises in favor of the party committees. The managers of the enterprises have been well aware of this, and, as has already been pointed out, have ensured their own power by wearing two hats: the manager's and the secretary of the CPC committee's.

Group and Self-Criticism

I would here like to mention separately one participation up the line device: the Chinese system of criticism, because one can see in it a link between direct and indirect participation – a control mechanism exercised by the electorate. Through the criticism system the electorate, subordinates, were in principle able to carry out constant direct evaluation of the leadership of their representatives and/or superiors and get immediate feedback. Leader accountability is an important dimension of participation and democracy. The criticism system can also be looked at as functioning as an instrument reducing resistance among subordinates by regulating the conflicts through "uploading" of tensions (Laaksonen 1984b).

During the periods of rapid changes, which were connected with certain development processes, the Chinese often officially underlined the importance of self-criticism and criticism of superiors. These criticism campaigns occurred especially during the Great Leap Forward both concerning operational management as well as CPC organization. In the latter criticism was normally kept inside the party, because it was not desirable to shake the authority of the party, which formed the base of the socialist system. Another "boom period" of criticism occurred during the Cultural Revolution; this we will describe later.

When speaking of participation up the line, we must recall the system created during the Great Leap Forward: "the two participations, one reform, and triple combination." The two participations meant, first, participation of workers in management, i.e., participation up the line, which we have dealt with here, and, second, the participation of cadres in labor, which represented participation down the line, to be described in the next chapter.

Participation Down the Line

Participation up the line generally means that subordinates take part in higher-level decision-making, an activity traditionally reserved for their superiors. We more rarely conceive of participation in other directions, especially downward. The latter was generally ignored in the main literature until the Chinese Cultural Revolution. However, in these connections the concept of participation was rarely mentioned. The peculiar phenomenon was simply understood as a system where managers took part in the work of their subordinates from time to time, often on the shop floor. This system has generally been related to the throes of the Cultural Revolution. However, the Chinese Communists "officially" created this system long before, during the Yan'an period, under hard environmental circumstances.

As participation down the line represents a phenomenon which is especially connected to Chinese management during Mao Zedong's period, it is proper that we examine this system more closely here. I see, moreover, another reason why it is important to go into this phenomenon in more detail. Participation down the line can represent in the future a noteworthy option for widening the concept of industrial democracy. It is surprising that workers demanding equality in working life have not claimed equality from above downward. Why have they demanded only the sharing of "good things" such as managerial decision-making and the opportunity to sit on the board of directors? Why have they not demanded the sharing of the "bad things," such as heavy and monotonous work?

Development of Participation Down the Line

The participation down-the-line system can be traced back to the Yan'an period. As we have seen, Yan'an was the area where the communists formed their base after the Long March. Especially after 1940 the conditions in Yan'an were difficult. The area was very poor and the communists were constantly under military pressure on the one hand from the Japanese, and on the other from the Guomindang (Chiang Kai-shek's) troops. The population was very poor and the conditions grew still poorer because of the extra economic burden the communist "newcomers" brought.

We must remember that the communists were altogether dependent, as guerilla troops, on the support of the local population, first of all the peasants. Thus, to help the local production processes with both their knowledge and physical resources, the cadres had to take part in manual labor. The communists also had to win psychologically the support of the local population. This they tried to do by behaving differently from the earlier feudal landlords, who had exploited the peasants and treated them almost as slaves. In addition, the mass-line principle presumed participation down the line. When communist soldiers and cadres worked side by side with the poor peasants in Yan'an, this was something very new and positive, because the local people had, over hundreds of years, learned to fear and hate both military personnel and administrative officials. In Fig. 5.20 the Yan'an origin of the development described above is summarized.

During the period of the Soviet "one-man management system" (1950–1956) there was not much discussion or practical application of participation down the line. However, along with the criticism directed towards the Soviet management system, the demand that the gap between managers and workers should be reduced also grew. There was also considerable criticism concerning the bureaucratization of organizations. Thus, in May 1957 the Central Committee of the CPC gave a directive stressing the

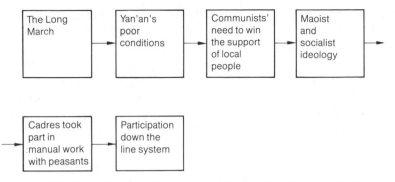

Fig. 5.20. Impact of Yan'an period upon the development of participation down the line

importance of all administrative, managerial, and technical cadres participating in manual labor.

This organizational development action became public in the Chinese mass media at the beginning of 1958. In the discussion that followed, three arguments were mentioned for the participation of cadres in manual labor: First, the more and more clear division of personnel in enterprises between brain labor and brawn labor was leading to a separation of workers and administrators, as earlier mentioned. Second, as Chinese traditional values did not appreciate manual labor, the cadres looked down on workers and were often not willing to participate in manual labor. It was also mentioned that cadres did not appreciate and often care for workers' suggestions and questions.

The third argument was the fight against bureaucracy. It was argued that the workers were unable to supervise and criticize cadres because of a lack of knowledge and/or confidence. If the cadres participated in workers' tasks, the workers could be "closer" to the cadres and would be better able to supervise or criticize them, e.g., in workers' congresses (Andors 1977: 70–71).

Dimensions of Participation Down the Line

We defined participation down the line as a system where persons or groups belonging to higher organizational levels take part in work and decision-making of lower hierarchical levels. We can distinguish different dimensions in this participation:

1. The depth of participation down the line. Does it cross one or more levels of the organization's hierarchy? For example, does a department head take part in his foreman's work (one level), or the work of a shop-floor worker (two levels)?

2. The direction of participation down the line. Does it happen in a straight line or diagonally, e.g., that the head of a marketing department takes part in work on the production line?

3. The regularity of the system. Does participation down the line occur regularly according to some specified rules or is it more or less occasional, irregular, e.g., according to when it suits the person concerned?

4. The breadth of the system. Does it concern all superiors from the general managers to the foremen, or is it limited to certain persons, groups, and/or positions?

5. The duration of participation down the line: (a) How long does it last at a time? (b) How often does it happen, e.g., one day a week or one month a year? (c) Does it mean a permanent, complete change of tasks?

6. The scope of participation down the line concerning the tasks one has to do. For example, should the general manager who is taking part in the work of a storeman do every part of the storeman's work or only a part of it, e.g., storage-bookkeeping?

7. The basic idea behind the system; is the purpose, e.g., to level out class differences, to improve communication, to make the organization more efficient, or to train management?

It should be noted that the same kind of dimensions can also be found in participation up the line.

Advantages of Participation Down the Line

Some of the Chinese soon noticed that the system they had to a great extent created to level out class differences also produced certain purely organizational advantages. I will deal here with both the positive practical experiences of the Chinese, and with the advantages which participation down the line could theoretically provide to firms.

1. Communication upward is improved. The inadequate upward flow of information in organizations is frequently regarded as one of the most serious problems of communication and efficiency. The Chinese discovered that the system opened up new direct channels for the upward flow of information.

2. Management learns in practice about the really important problems (personnel and other) of the lower levels of the hierarchy. Walter Korpi has shown in Sweden that more than one-half of all strikes are caused by shop-floor grievances (Korpi 1974).

3. The managers have a unique opportunity to examine their own working routines from "outside."

4. Better hierarchical cohesion throughout the organization could develop. Numerous studies show that personal contact reduces preconceptions and conflicts, and increases positive attitudes (e.g., Etzioni 1961).

5. The managers of organizations are often quite old and have lost the energy and innovativeness they had when they were younger. Often they have become a burden for their organization. An approved system for moving "down" to less demanding tasks could be a relief both to a manager and his firm.

6. Many studies concerning the managers' actual use of their time show that a very small part of their working time is devoted to important managerial tasks like strategic planning, etc. (e.g., Stewart 1967). The managers waste a great deal of their time on routine tasks of secondary importance for the efficiency of the enterprise. One can argue that the time a manager would invest in participation down the line could cause a many-sided positive return for the enterprise and its employees.

We have to remember that the continual rise in prominence of the senior managers or at least the permanence of their positions is mainly the creation of the historically relatively young industrial society. In earlier agricultural and other societies, older people shifted gradually with age and decreasing efficiency to less-demanding tasks. As we shall see later there are many developments also in contemporary highly industrialized societies that seem to support participation down the line or at least recommend a serious study of it.

Horizontal Participation

So far we have examined in some detail various up- and down-the-line participation systems, but we must remember that the Chinese quite clearly saw the problems which would arise if there was not enough horizontal participation in enterprises, e.g., between technical and administrative departments and people.

One solution to this kind of problem was the development of so-called technical mutual-aid groups for the making of technical decisions. Experienced technicians first consulted in these groups with skilled workers. Quite soon the Chinese probably realized that in cases of technical change administrative matters, e.g., new wage systems, were important. Thus, these groups soon consisted of engineers, technicians, administrators, and workers. As earlier mentioned, this combination of leadership with the masses, labor with technology, and technical theory with production practice, was introduced under the slogan: "triple combination."

According to the communist ideology the vertical participations, up and down the line (labor with technology and leadership with the masses), were especially emphasized, and the horizontal participation, e.g., between administration and production engineering, was in the background, at least in slogans. In practice, however, I submit that the cooperation between administrative and technical personnel was as important in China as the problems of cooperation between production and marketing departments have been in capitalist enterprises. The last-mentioned problems were not so acute in socialist China, because in a centralized planning economy there were no independent marketing or corresponding departments in Chinese enterprises until the latest economic reforms after 1978.

What was, and still is, a great problem of coordination and thus participation, is between enterprise management and the CPC, or between economics and politics. These relations have been difficult and complicated in all socialist countries, but they have especially come to the foreground in China, a country which has made abrupt great changes in the power relations between the party and practical management, or between the power of party committee and managers of enterprises. As mentioned earlier, the managers have often solved this problem, in order to guarantee the continuing efficiency of the firm, by occupying leading positions also in the party committee.

As the managers have usually belonged to the CPC and often been members of the enterprise party committee also, this has usually implemented horizontal participation between enterprise and party management in enterprises in practice.

5.5.7 Cultural Revolution and the Management of Industrial Enterprises

We will study the period of the Cultural Revolution quite thoroughly, because it forms the base from which the new leaders after Mao had to start their reforms.

Mao's Antiurban Strategy

In Section 5.1.4 we examined the reasons for the Cultural Revolution, and in Section 5.4.4 we studied its impacts upon the management of rural organizations, especially of people's communes. Before we begin to examine the impact of the Cultural Revolution upon industrial and mostly urban organizations, we must remind ourselves that this campaign was especially focused on Chinese cities to purge them of bureaucrats and specialists. Mao was afraid that they would form a new upper class, and therefore they had to be brought into contact with the masses again. As has been said, Mao was also worried that the younger generation would not grow up in a "correct" ideological and societal environment, especially in cities. Mao's antiurban strategy concentrated especially on the following three points:

1. The sending of urban youth to the countryside was the most visible phenomenon of this strategy. Most urban high school graduates had to go to the rural villages to do farm work for at least a short period.

2. Outside China perhaps the best-known measure during the Cultural Revolution was to send bureaucrats, specialists, and teachers – even university professors – to rural villages to be reeducated through physical labor.

When in 1973 I visited Beijing University, and Sun Yat-sen University in Guangzhou (Canton), I realized that the departments were empty of professors. In 1980, 1984, and 1986 I met several professors in various universities, but they were seemingly unwilling to speak about their experiences during the Cultural Revolution to a foreigner; most of them had, however, been in the countryside during that period.

3. Decentralization of industry from large cities in order to relocate urban factories and offices in outlying areas was an important part of Mao's antiurban strategy. This was actually not a new measure for Mao's administration, because campaigns to decentralize administration and to limit the growth of the cities had occurred before. But now this happened on a larger scale.

The relocation of industry was often explained as making China less vulnerable to possible military attack. During my interviews in 1973 I often heard that the Chinese were trying to build thousands of independent fortresses, which could defend themselves and also be self-sufficient. Every larger enterprise which I visited during the Cultural Revolution had its own military department. People's communes were good examples of self-sufficient units which produced nearly everything necessary, from grain to iron. If needed they were excellent bases for guerilla war strategy. One should also remember that the creation of people's communes occurred at the same time as the relations between China and the Soviet Union broke down at the end of the 1950s.

The relocation of industry and the shifting of investment objects away from the cities to rural small-scale industry worsened the capacity of urban industrial enterprises, which anyway formed the core of Chinese industry, to function. This again had a great impact upon the opportunities for action by the enterprise managers.

Goals and Planning in Enterprises

During my visit to Chinese enterprises in 1973 I several times heard quotations from the "Constitution" of the Anshan Iron and Steel Company. This "Constitution" stressed the importance of politics and the strengthening of CPC leadership as well as the extending of the mobilization of the masses. It stressed also participation both up and down the line and the importance of developing technology.

During my interviews in 1973 chairmen and vice-chairmen of revolutionary committees stressed the importance of the following functional goals for their organizations:

1. Willingness to change; the Chinese stressed the importance of continuing change in industrial enterprises as elsewhere

2. Innovativeness; every employee had the obligation to try to better his own and his units' production technology

3. Antibureaucracy

4. The organization should have as few rigid rules and regulations as possible

5. The organization should enable participation; workers in management and managers in productive labor.

Concerning planning, the Chinese industrial enterprises were strictly under centralized control during the Cultural Revolution. The center of the planning process was in a five-year plan around which all the other plans gravitated. It included annual growth rates for major sectors. An essential part of the management of the economy were annual plans. The sharing of responsibilities in this planning was sharply defined. First, the individual provincial governments drafted initial annual plans for the people's communes and for the bulk of the enterprises located within their respective territories. Then the provincial governments submitted their production plans to the sundry sectorial ministries, which had meanwhile also issued their own annual forecasts. After that the regional sectorial plans were analyzed by the National Planning Commission, which was responsible for seeing to it that the main strategic targets were achieved.

The production units, which thus far had been consulted only with respect to the achievement of the plan currently in progress, were issued extremely detailed plans for the following year, covering quantities to be produced, quality, manufacturing costs, productivity, manpower requirements, and profits. In any given factory, the plan was first discussed by the revolutionary committee (explained later) and then by workers as a body in the light of certain considerations, i.e., can the plan be achieved? Could more be accomplished with the same production means (du Rivaux 1974: 20)?

Revolutionary Committees in Industrial Enterprises

The CPC organization structure, which was responsible for the party and strategic management of enterprises, generally remained the same before and during the Cultural Revolution. However, the management structure, which was responsible for the operational management, was greatly changed. The revolutionary committees were introduced in industry as representing collective management. The first one was established in the management of the City of Shanghai. Gradually they were diffused to other cities and then also to industrial enterprises. Later they received the stamp of officialdom for nearly every kind of state, communal, military, educational, industrial, and agricultural organization. As we remember, revolutionary committees were also formed in people's communes.

I learned from my interviews in 1973 in Shanghai area that the first revolutionary committees were established there more or less improvisationally by workers and cadres. The core group of the first committees included the reformist members – following Mao's line – of the old party committees. At the same time the old party committees ceased to function, and the core group at first took care of the tasks of the party committee. Perhaps it was no coincidence that the first revolutionary committees were established in Shanghai. I would like to argue that the revolutionary committees were successors of the management committees of the Shanghai management system, which was created after the communist victory (1949) especially in East China to get the industrial enterprises on their feet again after the chaos of the Civil War. These management committees also represented a form of collective management, in which technicians, (former) owners, military leaders, and workers were represented. When the revolutionary committees were created "to save the country from falling back on the capitalist road," Mao perhaps remembered as an old man those former enthusiastic times 20 years earlier.

Figure 5.21 gives as an example the management structure of the Shanghai Watch Factory in 1973, which then had 3,600 employees. There were several revolutionary committees at different levels of enterprise organization, and the party organization followed the same principle. However, the revolutionary committees were always subordinate to the CPC units of and above the corresponding hierarchical level.

The revolutionary committee of the enterprise was responsible for the operational management of the firm. Its subordinates were on the one hand the administrative departments and on the other hand the line processing organization, which often contained several subordinate revolutionary committees; every larger workshop had usually one revolutionary committee. In workshops there was a workshop leader and in large workshops –

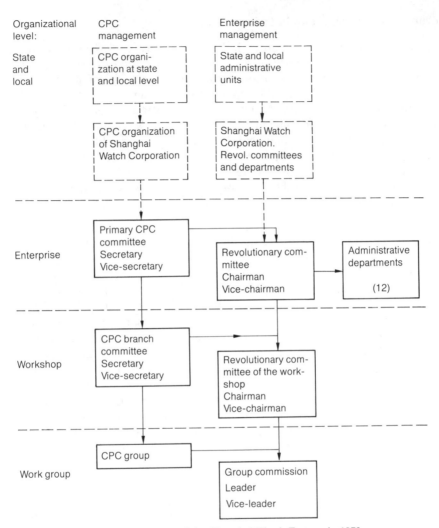

Fig. 5.21. Organization structure of the Shanghai Watch Factory in 1973

as in the Shanghai Heavy Machine Plant – there were also leaders of production sections. For example in a 1,000-employee workshop of the Shanghai Heavy Machine Plant there were four production sections and corresponding leaders. In the same way work groups also had a leader, like a foreman, who was usually vice-leader of the group commission. It was peculiar that, for example, in the Shanghai Watch Factory the leader of the group commission was responsible for the ideological and political education of the work group and the vice-leader acted as foreman.

The revolutionary committee of the enterprise consisted of 20–50 members depending on the size of the firm. The members did not all need to belong to the CPC, but certainly the chairman and vice-chairman did. I realized that the chairman of the revolutionary committee was very often either the secretary or the vice-secretary of the party committee of the organization.

If the enterprise had several workshops, their employees proposed persons to be elected as members of the revolutionary committee. These proposals were combined into one list of candidates, which was bowled back and forth between the party and revolutionary committees until a final list was achieved. The candidates were then voted on. The composition of the revolutionary committee was not yet clear after this process; it had to get the approval of the party and revolutionary committee hierarchically above it.

In the case of large and/or strategically important enterprises the nomination of the chairmen and vice-chairmen of the revolutionary committees of the enterprise – as well as also the corresponding party unit – was made or approved by the local or state administrative units.

Usually the leaders of the largest and most important organizational units – such as workshops and administrative departments – belonged to the revolutionary committee of the firm. As in the party organization, it was also recommended in the revolutionary committees that

- ⅓ of the members should represent the old
- ⅓ the middle-aged
- ⅓ the younger employees

In the case of large and/or strategically important enterprises there were also standing members in the revolutionary committees as in party committees. If we take the Shanghai Steel and Iron No. 3 as an example, of the 44 members of the revolutionary committee 16 were standing: 12 merited veteran workers and four persons represented the People's Liberation Army. One of the army men, who was the secretary of the party committee, was also the chairman of the revolutionary committee of the factory.

Despite the above-mentioned collective organizational units of the Chinese organizations, I got the impression that the daily line routine work was managed in quite the same way as in enterprises in the Western market economy.

As is probably clear from the above text, a change of top leaders of the enterprises also occurred when the revolutionary committees were introduced. In some cases very young persons were nominated to important positions. In most of the enterprises I visited in 1973 the managers were changed. Many times the new managers were probably more ideologically suitable than purposefully trained and experienced persons. For example, I learned that the newly appointed head of the important office of the revolutionary committee of a large metal factory was a 30-year-old worker. Most problematic for the whole economy were of course the rapid changes of managerial personnel, which created among other things a feeling of insecurity.

Staff Organization During the Cultural Revolution

In order to be able to operate efficiently, staff units were created in even slightly larger Chinese enterprises to support line organization. These units functioned directly under the party committees and the revolutionary committees. Their tasks were more or less the same as in Western enterprises, but certain distinct differences can be distinguished, arising from China's unique political and military system.

To continue with our earlier example, the Shanghai Watch Factory had in 1973 the following 12 staff departments:

1. The planning department (7 persons), whose task was to plan and supervise the division of labor, the wages of personnel, and matters concerned with efficiency
2. The social department (7 persons) mainly responsible for the planning and coordination of the firm's social activities
3. The organization department (6 persons), responsible for supervising party and other personnel matters
4. The political propaganda department (6 persons), in charge of political training of personnel
5. The military department (7 persons), responsible for the military training of personnel and planning of the factory unit's defence
6. The office of the revolutionary committee (7 persons), through which the factory's revolutionary committee worked directly, supervising office routines
7. The financing department (7 persons), in charge of the financing of the enterprise. Resources were allocated according to centralized planning
8. The marketing department (6 persons), looking after the marketing of products
9. The technical department (9 persons), responsible for product development and the maintaining of a high degree of innovation
10. The quality control department (7 persons), responsible for supervising the quality of the enterprise's products

11. The construction and repairs department (8 persons), responsible for new building and repairs

12. The machinery and equipment department (8 persons), seeing to the acquisition of machinery, equipment, etc.

Activities differing from those in Western enterprises included the strenuous political training, under the supervision of both the political propaganda department and to some extent the organization department. A department responsible for military defence could be found in the staff organization of practically all even slightly larger enterprises in China.

In the strategically important Shanghai Heavy Machine Plant there was one staff department responsible for the People's Militia Armed Forces. Among the tasks were the military training of the employees and building of bomb shelters. In the plant there was also another security department defending the factory against internal "enemies."

As is well-known, Chinese enterprises are also largely responsible for the social care of their employees. For example, concerning health care, in the Shanghai Watch Factory there was a total of 30 persons working in the health service in 1973. Of these 10 were fully trained medical doctors and 20 "barefoot" doctors and nurses.

Depending on the quality of the production technology, the different enterprises had often developed quite comprehensive vocational training systems for their employees. For example, in the Shanghai Watch Factory in 1973 there was a technical school where the students, elected by workers, studied for one year.

In addition to the vocational training, in practically every enterprise I visited there was comprehensive compulsory political training. In the Shanghai Watch Factory this included an hour and a half of political studies twice a week after working hours. In the Beijing Department Store all the managers had to take part in ideological training for a total of 12 hours a week, six hours during working time and six hours (2 × 3 hours) after work. The other employees had political training six hours a week: two hours during working time and four hours after it. This training included studying the thoughts of Mao, discussions, group criticism, and self-criticism. Participation in ideological training was intensified by the fact that among the main criteria applied in questions of promotion and wages was ideological developedness, "purity."

5.5.8 Participation During the Cultural Revolution

We have argued before that many of the management measures applied during the Cultural Revolution were actually not quite new; they had been experienced before, often temporarily, and for shorter periods. While the Cultural Revolution was also a struggle of power between different persons and groups for the inheritance of Mao's position of power, the measures applied were not all purely "democratic," but carefully selected to guarantee that the power was maintained in the hands of Mao, and especially of his closest group of supporters. Thus, some participation measures applied earlier, like workers' congresses, were not especially strengthened during the Cultural Revolution. There was the danger that, e.g., elections of persons to managerial positions through workers' congresses could mean that power would slip out of the hands of its wielders, and persons representing an opposite political line could gain power in enterprises.

In the following we will briefly examine the different kinds of participation – up the line, down the line, and horizontal – especially applied during the Cultural Revolution.

Participation Up the Line

The revolutionary committees should be mentioned first. It is evident that the Chinese tried to extend participation through these committees to many different groups. They tried to take into account the different hierarchical levels, different age groups, and both sexes. Thus, e.g., the shop-floor workers were usually well represented in the committees, as were women. As mentioned earlier it was also recommended that one-third of the members should represent the elderly, one third the middle-aged, and one-third the younger employees. In this way the Chinese tried to overcome generation gaps, which often create serious personnel conflicts.

Three-factor project groups were devices through which the Chinese attempted to reduce hierarchy and to increase participation and innovational ability during the Cultural Revolution. These project groups were created to solve various technical and other problems. In principle these groups included: administrators, technical experts, and shop-floor workers. It was clear that the Chinese tried to avoid emphasizing the status of, for example, technicians and other experts. The political motive was to avoid creating a new elite or social class, but there was also a motivational reason. Highlighting expert groups would have destroyed the spirit of initiative among ordinary workers in enterprises, "the participation of the masses," on whose contribution the Maoist model had greatly relied.

However, the "three-factor project groups" were not a new invention in China either. They had been introduced especially during the Great Leap Forward under the label of "triple combination", which referred to the combination of leadership with the masses, labor with technology, and technical theory with production practice.

Group and self-criticism was greatly intensified during the Cultural Revolution, but this system was not experienced for the first time then in Chinese enterprises either. Great criticism campaigns often occurred in China during the periods of rapid change, e.g., during the Great Leap Forward.

Party committees represent one kind of limited participation up the line, where, e.g., workers who belonged to the CPC had the possibility to take part in important decision-making in enterprises. The CPC's dominant role during the Cultural Revolution created a problem with respect to the principle of participatory equality, since the most important decisions were made by the party committee of the enterprise or of units above the firm.

Horizontal Participation

It is a matter of taste where to include the "three-factor project groups," in up the line or horizontal participation. In so far as they included growing cooperation between technicians and administrators at the same hierarchical level, these groups represented horizontal participation.

Unofficial workers' social groupings represented horizontal participation at the lowest hierarchical level. Special efforts were made to ensure the participation of shop-floor workers by trying to activate those in subordinate positions through unofficial social groupings. These were based on the work groups and discussion groups formed for ideological training and discussion etc. These groups, which usually consisted of six to a dozen members, chose their own officials and arranged leisure-time activities, held political study meetings outside working hours, and engaged in self-criticism and group criticism.

Participation Down the Line

The participation down the line, where managers work part of their time at shop-floor tasks with workers, has outside China been considered a peculiar phenomenon of the Cultural Revolution. However, as we mentioned earlier, the Chinese practiced this system back in the late 1930s in the hard conditions of Yan'an. That this system became in a way one of the landmarks of the Cultural Revolution was because participation down the line was especially intensified during this period, perhaps mostly for the purpose of levelling out class differences, and establishing contact between the cadres and the masses.

In the industrial and commercial enterprises where my interviews took place in 1973, the rule was that cadres – managers, experts, other office workers, and officials – did physical work one day a week. At the Shanghai Steel and Iron Factory No. 3 in addition to this weekly physical work, the cadres did one month work in the factory during the warmest period of the year, "so as not to lose touch with the masses." The custom of the Cultural Revolution of sending the urban cadres, students and teachers, to rural areas to do physical work represented the same kind of participation down the line. These were, however, generally more long-standing changes in work, and included punitive aspects.

One kind of participation down the line represented also the practice during the Cultural Revolution of removing symbols indicating hierarchical status. Thus, e.g., marks of rank were abolished in the army – as in Yan'an in the late 1930s – and generally people at all levels had to dress in the same way. Even women and men had the same kind of clothes. However, when I asked several persons in China in 1973 whether they could distinguish between office and shop-floor workers, they said they could do this at a glance, and in fact they often proved this in practice by their very different behavior towards persons between whom a Westerner could not distinguish any clear external differences.

Effects of Applied Participation Systems

To summarize the applied participation systems during the Cultural Revolution, we could say that perhaps never have so many different systems – up the line, horizontal, and down the line – been experienced in the same period. These could have resulted, as seemingly was also intended, in high motivation and efficient performance among employees of enterprises. What then went wrong?

First, the many-sided participation system was to a great extent a sham because enterprises had in practice very little effective decision-making power of their own; they had to follow plans and orders from the top of the hierarchical pyramid of the society. A small group of CPC officials at different levels in fact made the really important decisions. Thus, the participation system did not activate positive power but probably rather covert negative power, i.e., workers' resistance, in the form of low performance. Second, if the official ideology and decisions were not followed, resistance was often overcome by coercion, which usually creates fear, alienation, and covert resistance in the form of decreasing motivation and efficiency (Etzioni 1961).

Some of the measures taken during the Cultural Revolution were enthusiastic but counter-productive, and were often applied in the wrong place and at the wrong time in relation to the development phase of Chinese society and enterprises. For example, the sudden substitution of CPC ideology and corresponding more or less apparent participation systems for

economic rewards (bonus systems) could not succeed in a developing country with a low standard of living, where the majority of the people had to
fight hard for their daily bread.

5.5.9 Use of Different Powers During the Cultural Revolution

Resource Powers

Economic and Ideological Power

Perhaps the greatest change which occurred during the Cultural Revolution
in guiding enterprises was the move from the use of economic rewards
(economic power) to the appliance of ideological rewards (power; Table
5.8). This was created by abolishing, e.g., the bonus systems in enterprises;
the normally received bonuses were included in the basic salary. In the
same way the enterprises began to be guided by quantitative production
targets set by central authorities, instead of profit targets.

In Western capitalist countries it is traditionally assumed that reducing the
mutual dependence between work efficiency and reward leads to poorer
work performance. The Chinese leaders seemed to have thought during the
Cultural Revolution much like Amital Etzioni: the weakening of this relation provides a greater opportunity for preventing calculated commitment
to the organization and the consequent lack of initiative (Etzioni 1961).

The chief criteria determining personal wages in China during the Cultural
Revolution were:

1. Level of technical knowledge and skill of the individual relative to his
   effective work performance
2. Years spent on the job
3. Ideological "purity" and activism

As mentioned before, several measures were taken during the Cultural
Revolution to strengthen the ideological commitment of employees. The
basic factors of ideological power in China were communism, or rather,
Maoist ideology, and a strong feeling of patriotism. The latter was greatly
strengthened by reminding the Chinese continuously of the threat from the
Soviet Union; it was the old, often-used measure to strengthen the internal
conditions of the country by external threat.

Personal Power

Although Mao was considered to be the very visible figurehead of the
Communist Party and the state, the Chinese system did not officially favor

Table 5.8. Use of different powers in different administrative systems and levels of management during the Cultural Revolution (this author's evaluation)

Administrative system/ levels of management	Resource powers					Instrumental powers		
	Economic power	Ideological power	Personal power	Knowledge power	Arms power	Hierarchical power	Norm power	Communication power
CPC System Central and province level (macro- and meso-)management	−	+++	+	−	++	+++	+++	+++
Organizational (micro-) level	−	+++	−	−	+	+++	+++	++
Economic system Macro- and meso-management	−	+++	+	−	+	+	+	+
Enterprise-(micro-) management	−	+++	−	−	+	−	−	+

+ + + = Very much used
+ + = Much used
+ = Some use
− = Little, or no use indicating a negative general attitude towards the use of the power concerned

individual power, at least according to the bureaucratic model of administration. Maoist ideology did not support a formalistic impersonality either. The Chinese did, however, want their organizations to be "impersonal" in the sense that individual ties of friendship and rivalry should not be allowed to affect operations and decisions.

The ideal was seen as a working comradeship in which each person showed individual interest in and concern for his neighbor. People should not treat each other only as players of a narrow working role, but as individual entities, whose every problem and private life affected organizational behavior. There was no side of human life that was not regarded as affecting the organizational behavior of the individual. Thus, unofficial contacts within the enterprise, leisure time with workmates, family life, and many other corresponding factors outside work were considered to strongly affect the working behavior of the individual (White 1983). From this point of view, the enterprise was considered to be an extremely open working system, thus differing somewhat from the way of thinking in Western countries, where the workers' behavior is analyzed, often narrowly, within the framework of the organization.

Efforts were made to prevent personal power from becoming too strong by the many-sided system of criticism. Besides heeding the constant obligation of self-criticism, when necessary one had to criticize fellow-workers and everyone who deviated from the official line. The men on the job also had the right to criticize managers and office personnel, the cadres.

Knowledge Power

It was surprising for me to note in 1973 that although the bottlenecks in Chinese economic development were caused especially by lack of experts in various fields, the Chinese tried, nevertheless, to avoid emphasizing the importance of expertise. As mentioned before, thousands of students, professors, and other teachers were sent to rural areas to do physical work, and not a single new instructor was appointed to many universities between 1967 and 1973.

The Chinese did not then altogether ignore training, knowledge, and skill, but they stressed the importance of political "purity." Thus, when they considered placing workers in various tasks, the Chinese preferred the politically pure all-around person to the nonpolitical technical expert.

In Western countries, the expediency of such principles might be questioned, especially from the standpoint of keeping organizations constantly developing. Maoists believed, however, that there was not only political but also good economic justification for their principles. According to the Chinese, great emphasis on technical expertise would produce a specialist elite or class that would embrace China's otherwise limited number of experts. A development such as this would destroy the spirit of initiative of the ordinary workers in enterprises, "the participation of the masses" on whose contribution the Maoist model was strongly based.

When the Chinese have criticized the policies of the Cultural Revolution after Mao's death, the most severe criticism has been focused upon the education and training policy. It was a great irony that during a movement labeled as the Great Cultural Revolution its worst effects hit the cultural development of the country; one entire young generation was left without adequate education and training. It has been said that China will suffer for this negligence for decades.

Arms Power

In China the People's Liberation Army (PLA) has been looked upon as being a strong arm of the CPC. It is difficult to judge the real role of the army in China during the ambiguous changing circumstances of the Cultural Revolution. But it seems quite clear that the Chinese top leaders had to call on the help of the PLA when the turmoil was beginning to get out of control and becoming dangerous.

To ensure a stable development, PLA representatives were placed in the newly formed revolutionary committees of strategically important enterprises. As mentioned earlier, in Shanghai Steel and Iron No. 3 among the 44 members of the revolutionary committee four persons represented the People's Liberation Army, and one of them was both secretary of the party committee of the enterprise and chairman of the revolutionary committee of the enterprise.

Bringing military leaders into the management of enterprises was also in a way copying the policies applied after 1949 especially in eastern China, when PLA officers were brought into the management committees of enterprises.

Ordinarily the military forces have been kept more or less invisible. They have guided, or help to guide, the management of the country from the distant background. During the Cultural Revolution in a crisis situation arms power played a direct role in micromanagement also.

Use of Instrumental Powers

Hierarchical Power

As mentioned in the Appendix, we mean by hierarchical power on the one hand the place where different kinds of decision-making occurs in the organizational structure, taking into account central, provincial and organizational levels, and on the other hand the degree of rigidity in the hierarchical order. In forming organizational structures the leaders are striving after efficiency and/or power. These were the targets of Mao and his supporters during the Cultural Revolution, but the attempts to achieve both the targets in the turbulent circumstances of the period became contradictory in many ways, and correspondingly the structural solutions caused much confusion and in many cases inefficiency.

Throughout his political career, Mao had severely criticized bureaucracy and bureaucrats, rigid hierarchy, and rigid following of the hierarchical rules. During the Cultural Revolution it was particularly stated that the main struggle was then between two trends, a bureaucratic trend of development and the Maoist nonbureaucratic development model. During 1966–1976 the Chinese tried in many ways to reduce hierarchical differences in enterprises. We dealt with most of the measures applied earlier when we described the different participation systems of the period.

However, the levelling out of hierarchical differences often became ostensible during the Cultural Revolution. Although there were many efforts to reach more equality within the enterprise organizations, the other aspect of the hierarchical structure, to keep the power in the hands of Mao and his supporters, required measures which were in opposition to the democratization tendencies. The whole country was actually ruled – after the few months of the chaotic beginning – through a very hierarchically and rigidly formed CPC structure, where all the important decisions were made at the macro-, meso-, and microlevels of the society.

Though Liu Shao-chi and his supporters had been proclaimed to be supporters of centralization, their profit management line gave quite a lot of real decision-making power to the enterprise managers during the early 1960s, and the economic results were positive. This actually represented microdecentralization. Fearing that profit management and a developed partial market economy would bring China back to the capitalist road, and also fearing loss of power, Mao and his supporters centralized anew the planning und guiding system of the economy. Thus, centralized hierarchical power was actually activated during the Cultural Revolution both through the centralized government planning system and the party system. The participation and corresponding democratization processes in the enterprises remained in the shadow of the CPC structure.

Norm Power

With regard to the use of norm power, the Chinese enterprises were dual during the Cultural Revolution; the party and the national economic system were directed by means of strict norms, whereas in the enterprises efforts were made to keep the system that kept production rolling free from norm bureaucracy. For example, special "shake-up" campaigns were arranged in the enterprises from time to time, with the purpose of cleaning out "dusty corners" and doing away with unnecessary instructions, orders, and poor methods. This kind of airing and openness was directed during the Cultural Revolution primarily at the enterprise's administrative and production systems.

In the political area, however, norm power prevailed. Divergences from the ideological norms set by the central administration of the CPC were prevented by political training, self-criticism, and group criticism meetings, as well as by standard written instructions approved by the central administration of the party. Thus, there were great and confusing contradictions in the usage of norm power between the overall party system and the enterprise operational management.

Communication Power

Communication power differs from knowledge power in that those who wield it can prevent, filter, and guide the flow of information (knowledge) through different channels, e.g., mass media.

Communication power has been used effectively in China. In this respect, the whole country has formed a closed system into which only screened information has been allowed as "input." There have been natural barriers that have helped this isolation: the geographical distances from the borders to the center of the country are so great that for example foreign TV programs cannot be seen in the central areas. Also very few households had TV sets in the 1960s and 1970s. The same was to a great extent also true of foreign radio programs. Another effective communication barrier is the language: relatively few foreigners know Chinese, and vice versa.

During the Cultural Revolution a duality could be observed in the use of communication power inside the country. On the one hand, the flow of information regarding the political system and the administrative apparatus connected with it was severely regulated in the CPC system from the top to the bottom of society, right down to small party groups in the enterprises. On the other hand, efforts were made in the enterprises' production and administration system to make communication as open and lively as possible, both horizontally and vertically. The duality mentioned created great confusion because everyone knew that the ultimate power – including control of communication – was in the hands of the CPC anyway (Laaksonen 1984a: 8–9).

Before we move to examine Chinese management after Mao I would like to point out that the Cultural Revolution has remained in the minds of the outside world a mysterious period during which many "new" incomprehensible phenomena occurred, also in the area of enterprise management. This is also what I thought in 1973, when I was visiting Chinese enterprises for the first time. Gradually, after more study of the history of China, I realized that most of the striking features of the Cultural Revolution were policies already experienced before 1949 only perhaps in a more separate and modest way.

One could argue that during the Cultural Revolution the Great Helmsman tried with his diminishing strength to emphasize greatly all those special features of his administration which represented his ideas of equality, continuous class struggle, and ever-repeating revolution. Probably Mao tried also to ensure, as he felt that his time was ending, that his ideological inheritance would be passed on to the following generation in as pure a form as possible. But in trying to do this Mao had to use coercion, and displace strong personalities such as Deng Xiaoping, who thus remained on the side lines, waiting for his departure to radically change the course of the great nation.

5.6 Management of Industrial Enterprises After Mao

5.6.1 Changing the Managers

There were two main reasons for changing the managers of enterprises in connection with the economic reforms after Mao. First, the new leaders of the party and government had to be sure that their new political and economic line would be correctly followed in the primary organizations around the country. As the reform was to a large extent economic, it was of profound importance that the enterprises would carry out orders correctly, otherwise there would have been the danger that there would have been no actual reform and corresponding development, and the top leaders would have faced serious criticism, and perhaps would even have lost their positions. Thus, changing the policy presupposed changing the leaders, not only in the top echelons of the party and government, which had been accomplished first, but also in grassroots organizations. It was also part of the overall power game, because power is always in the final analysis mediated through people.

Second, the economic reforms gave the enterprise managers quite new qualitative demands, e.g., in the following areas:

1. Strategic management
2. More independent planning than earlier
3. Marketing in altogether new forms and areas
4. Organization of production and personnel according to changing demands
5. Requisition of raw materials and semifinished goods from the "open" market
6. Personnel management, especially in the areas of hiring and dismissal procedures, training, performances appraisal, wage determination, and promotion
7. Accounting and budgeting
8. Innovation management
9. Interorganizational relations
10. International relations according to the open door policy

As we have noted, the changing of leaders had begun in high CPC and government posts, especially after the meeting of the Political Bureau of the Central Committee of the CPC in August 1980. Deng Xiaoping then summarized that the main maladies concerning leadership and the cadre system of the party and state were bureaucracy, the patriarchal way of doing things, life-long tenure of leading posts, various kinds of privileges, and over-centralization of power.

To reform the cadre system, the 12th National Congress of the CPC decided in September 1982 to abolish the de facto life-long tenure for leading cadres. The reform was expected to increase the educational level and professional competence, and to lower the average age of cadres. The Central Committee presumed in 1984 that the change of leading cadres, especially in key enterprises, would be completed before the end of 1985. In addition it was required that plans should be made to train quickly a great number of general managers, who would be able to succesfully organize and lead the production and other activities of the enterprises.

The head of the organization department of the Central Committee of the CPC, Qiao, said in 1984 that most of the directors and CPC committee secretaries in the country's more than 3,000 major state-owned enterprises should have a college-level education. Two-thirds of the deputy leaders should also have a college-level education. Qiao added that the leaders should be younger than 55 during their tenure of office. According to the above requirements, 40% of the directors and 70% of Party Committee secretaries should be replaced.

Beginning in 1985, a fixed tenure for factory directors was to have been instituted in these 3,000 state-owned enterprises. Their term of office would be four years. But directors would be able to continue in their posts longer if endorsed by the workers' congress of their factory. Directors might also submit their resignation when proved incompetent, or they might be removed from office (B.R., September 17, 1984).

As a result of the above-mentioned policy changes, there seem to have been two waves of changing managers in Chinese enterprises after Mao. The first wave was directly connected with the changing of top leaders of the country and with the economic reforms of 1978. Of the nine industrial and commercial enterprises I visited in 1980 six had received a new general manager after 1978; four in 1978, and two in 1979.

The second wave came seemingly in 1982 in connection with the 12th National Congress of the CPC. Of the eight enterprises I visited in October 1984, four had received a new general manager during 1982–1984, three after 1978, and only one had a manager who had been appointed before 1976. Of the four enterprises I had visited both in 1980 and 1984 all had received a new general manager during the period between my interviews.

Thus, it seems that, if we go back in time some 20 years until the beginning of the Cultural Revolution (1966), there have been during this period three big waves of changing enterprise managers. The first one was after the beginning of the Cultural Revolution and the creation of revolutionary committees, when new collective management was established in enterprises. The second wave came in 1978 in connection with the economic reforms. The third and last wave came in 1982, and was perhaps the most complete one. Most of the "old" managers had to go, although they had often not been in their position long enough to learn their job properly.

It is difficult to evaluate how much harm these changes of enterprise managers have caused the Chinese economy. Probably, however, they were necessary for the new top leaders of the country. One can look on the waves both after 1966 and after 1978 as a securing the new political lines and new power structures at the macro- and microlevels. The wave after 1982 was probably more based on criteria of managerial competence and effectiveness, and was therefore also a more profound one. It is easier to recognize incompetent managers than persons whose political ideas differ from those of the top leaders; the latter differences are easier to hide.

It has been a kind of miracle that the Chinese economy has anyway developed relatively well during the past 20 years, although there have been so many profound changes during this period. Perhaps, taken as a whole, the changes have after all only rubbed the surface structures of Chinese society, and the basic structure, leaning upon the old culture, has not been destroyed too much. In the first place, the foundations of China are still in agriculture in the rural areas, where 800 million persons live. The Cultural Revolution mostly hit the cities, leaving the rural areas quite untouched.

The "Green Revolution" with the contract responsibility system was well-timed for the developmental phase of agriculture at the end of 1970. Also the personnel changes in industrial enterprises mostly concerned superiors; the great majority of employees at lower hierarchical levels remained in their positions, accepted the reforms, and saw the changes in top management as inevitable consequences of the reforms.

5.6.2 Reforms in Enterprise Management

In Section 5.1.5 "Reforms after Mao" we described the main phases of the reforms after 1976. All the phases had their special impact upon the management of Chinese industrial enterprises. The slogan of the four modernizations: (1) industry, (2) agriculture, (3) defence, and (4) science and technology, contained the ideological frame for the new line. The actual breakthrough of the reforms occurred at the famous Third Plenum of the 11th Central Committee of the CPC in December 1978. This meeting decided "to correct the shortcoming of over-concentration of power in economic management and give local authorities and enterprises more control" (Tian 1982: 93).

Breakthrough of the Reforms

Sichuan Experiments

Chinese economic reforms concerning industrial enterprises did not take place overnight, but gradually and carefully. They began in Sichuan province, which was then led by the later premier of China, Zhao Ziyang. He, with his colleagues, had noticed that some industrial urban enterprises in the province that were collectively owned and had not been incorporated in the state plan were relatively flexible and responsive in adapting themselves to market demand. It usually took them at most six months to change their line of production, which was in those circumstances fast, and demonstrated to Zhao and his colleagues their vitality.

They thus decided to introduce reforms that would grant the enterprises the necessary authority to run their business on their own and be held responsible. These reforms would give scope to market regulation under the guidance of state planning. How was it possible to begin this kind of exceptional reform in one province? One reason was probably the fact that Zhao has for a long time had close relations with the factual leader of China of that time, Deng Xiaoping; perhaps Deng more than just approved the experiments.

Although the managers were generally willing to accomplish the reforms, they were at first hesitant, because they were afraid of the probable resistance this kind of great change would provoke; but anyway they felt that the change would be necessary. Similar hesitant thoughts were especially in the minds of those at the Ningjiang Machine Tool Plant in October 1978. However, later at an emergency meeting of the factory party committee, all welcomed the idea of loosening their bonds by asking for enlarged decision-making power. The provincial authorities welcomed this initiative, which they had awaited, and they immediately agreed. In October 1978, six enterprises, including Ningjiang, became the first firms in the country to be granted extended autonomy on an experimental basis. Later the provinces of Yunnan and Anhui also selected some enterprises for experimentation (Tian 1982: 91–93).

In July 1979 the State Council decided to enlarge the experimentation to 4,000 enterprises throughout the country.

> This number rose to over 6,000 in 1980, comprising 16 percent of the nation's state-owned enterprises. Their output values and profits accounted for 60 and 70 percent respectively of the total from state-owned enterprises. Among the 6,000 experimental enterprises, 191 operated according to a new policy of delivering to the state only income tax, industrial and commercial taxes and tax on fixed assets, while keeping all the remaining profits and assuming sole responsibility for profit or losses. (Tian 1982: 93)

The experiments encouraged the Chinese because the output values and profits of the trial enterprises increased more than those in firms where no extended autonomy was granted. Not only did the output figures grow in 1980 over those of 1979, but the total volume of profits they delivered to the state also increased by 7.4% (Tian 1982: 93).

There were eight special rights granted to enterprises taking part in the experiment in Sichuan. Because they became the base for later further experiments we mention them here:

1. Right to reserve part of the profits. After fulfilment of the main economic and technical targets set in the state plan the enterprises could reserve 3%–5% of the profits they had made according to plan. In addition, they could keep, depending on their industry, 15%–25% of the extra profits made outside the state plan. The profit kept by the enterprises went in developing production, improving workers' welfare, and paying bonuses to the workers.

2. Right to expand production with funds they themselves had accumulated and to keep the profits derived from it for themselves in the first two years.

3. Right to retain 60% of the depreciation fund for fixed assets as against 40% in the past.

4. Right to engage in production outside the state plan, such as processing for other factories and turning out more products needed on the market; this might be done only when the state plan had been met.

5. Right to market the part of their products which the commercial and materials departments did not purchase at a trade fair.

6. Right to apply to export their products and to reserve part of the foreign exchange earnings for the import of new technology, raw and other materials, and key equipment.

7. Right to issue bonuses at the enterprise's own discretion, that is, in the light of its specific conditions within the range as approved by the state (generally not more than two month's average wages of the workers and staff).

8. Right to penalize those who had incurred heavy losses to the state, including workers, party secretaries, and factory directors, due to negligence in work or other subjective reasons. The most serious would be expelled from the factory (Tian 1982: 94–95).

China's main strategy with the reforms was to bring about intensive rather than extensive growth in the economy. The Chinese had felt that their problem had been poor use of available resources; thus, the important target was to use resources (e.g., labor, capital, and energy) more efficiently rather than use more of them. The aim of the reforms was to stimulate technical innovation both in products and processes, and especially to improve the motivation to work both among workers and cadres in existing enterprises, rather than to rely upon building new factories, which would quickly eat up China's scarce resources (Lockett and Littler 1983: 686–689).

The results of the experiments were good, as can be seen in Table 5.9.

Table 5.9. Results of enterprise autonomy experiments in Sichuan 1979–1980 (Lockett and Littler 1983: 686)

	1979	1980
Output value	+14.9% (+ 3.2%)	+9.7% (+ 6.8%)*
Total profit	+33.2% (+6.9%)	+7.9% (..)
Profit remitted to state	+20.2% +14.2%	−0.7% (..)
No. of enterprises	100 (6000)	417 (5600)

Note: Figures in brackets are for enterprises not in the experiment, except * which denotes all enterprises
.. = Information not available

One must bear in mind that the price system used had a great impact upon the results of enterprises. Thus, the figures of 1980 did not look so good because of various price adjustments in fuel and other important commodities. These drawbacks provided a lever for those who wished to criticize the reforms. One must also remember that the enterprises for the experiment were not selected randomly, but because they were expected to be especially suitable for reform by those favoring the planned change. Therefore, it was natural that expansion of the reforms to more enterprises which were at the starting point less suitable, inevitably meant poorer average results. There were also other problems:

First, we should mention the old rigid price system. This price structure was really irrational if the profitability of enterprises should be the base in evaluating performance and distributing funds. As previously fixed prices were usually maintained, it meant that enterprises seeking to maximize profits would gain more by changing their product-mix to more profitable lines than by actually trying to increase efficiency.

Second, prices were closely associated with inflation. Between 1950 and 1979 the Chinese had experienced an average inflation rate of under 1% a year. In 1980 the prices went up quickly, so that estimated according to the retail prices inflation was 6%. This was high in Chinese eyes, and created much dissatisfaction, especially among those who had not received large bonuses which would cover the inflation.

Third, the bonus system of enterprises also caused problems, because the bonuses were often paid in an inappropriate way without being linked to productivity. Thus, the State Council had to issue special national regulations limiting the amount that enterprises could use for bonuses in 1981. This again produced new problems, because, e.g., when the incentives for workers in successful experimental enterprises were reduced this caused dissatisfaction.

Fourth, the reforms required of the enterprises much more skill and experience in auditing and accounting than earlier. The problems in these areas created opportunities for corruption and/or the development of "gray" areas where economic advantages were gained from breaking the spirit – if not the letter – of economic policies linked with the reforms.

Fifth, the reforms required a new kind of relationship between the state and enterprises. There was a great lack of legislation and other formal norms which would have set the boundaries between the enterprises and state administration at different levels. "As a result, managers experienced ad hoc changes of production targets as well as the administrative transfer of machinery, equipment, and staff disregarding the formal rights of the enterprise" (Lockett and Littler 1983: 687).

Sixth, the reforms required not only a new kind of relationship between the enterprises and the government administration, but also between the firms and the party. The CPC had kept in its hands the main decision-making power, especially in strategically important matters. The autonomy of enterprises struck hard against this old socialist principle. Something had to be done if the Chinese leaders wanted to go on with their reforms.

Separation of Government and CPC Administration

Perhaps the most far-reaching decision taken in a socialist country was the separation of party and government administration from each other. In practice this had profound implications upon enterprise management, because it was the government bodies at different levels which officially guided and controlled the enterprises under their administrative area, and these government units were always subordinated to the corresponding party committees at the same level.

As a practical result of separating the CPC and the state administration, gradually the party and enterprise management in enterprises became separated. Thus, as we will see later, the same persons no longer in 1984, as in 1980, wore two hats, those of general manager of the firm and of first secretary of the firm's party committee.

Economic Responsibility System for Industrial Enterprises

The Chinese leaders soon realized that an economy of a country cannot be changed quickly, that one can only reform a part of it at a time. Everything affects everything else. For example, the reforms had their special impact upon the state budget. At the end of the 1970s half of the state revenue had come from its share of enterprise profits. Between 1978 and 1980 the revenue from the profits of state enterprises had dropped by almost one-quarter.

Actually the reformers thought at the end of 1980 that the experimental enterprises were only a first step towards reforming the whole economic system. The important decision affecting enterprise management was that made in 1981 concerning the introduction of the so-called economic responsibility system in industrial urban enterprises. The same kind of system – at least by name – had been adopted earlier in agriculture, as we have mentioned earlier.

The system has in practice centered on industrial enterprises around contracts stipulating the enterprise's responsibility for its profit and loss in the inter-enterprise field and for payment systems within enterprises.

These contracts have typically been profit-sharing ones, with enterprises "contracting" with the state to provide a certain volume of profits. If this target is exceeded, the above-quota amounts are divided in fixed proportions between the state and enterprise funds. If there is a shortfall, the enterprise must compensate for at least a proportion of this by giving from its own funds to the state (Lockett and Littler 1983: 689).

Time for Consolidation

Great changes nearly always bring with them unintended consequences. Thus it was with China's economic reforms at the beginning of the 1980s. Especially corruption and other forms of financial crime grew rapidly, partly because needed legislation and other forms of regulations (norm power) were not created. Also the accounting systems of enterprises were old-fashioned and not suited to the new circumstances. Thus, many kinds of interlocking options for corruption were opened up. China's leaders realized the possible development in this direction quite quickly, indeed, they had to some extent foreseen it. Thus, they began in 1981 to focus on the internal consolidation of industrial enterprises, especially of their management. The main lines were summarized by Lockett and Littler (1983: 690) as follows:

1. Reorganize enterprises' top management bodies
2. Strengthen economic responsibility systems, especially those within enterprises, rather than concentrating on profit-sharing
3. Consolidate basic management work, practising overall economic accounting and quality management (the latter being a priority in experimental enterprises)
4. Strengthen political and ideological work, especially directed at the widespread phenomenon of slack labor discipline existing in enterprises and "consolidating factory regulations"
5. Strengthen democratic management
6. Consolidate financial and economic discipline, in order to tackle such problems as corruption and dubious deals by enterprises

To supervise the consolidation program, special teams were sent to enterprises to see how the enterprises were organized and to check their performance. These teams were composed of officials from both government and party organizations at the provincial and local level. The purpose of the consolidation process was also to make the management more effective by replacing less competent with more competent and usually younger managers (Lockett and Littler 1983: 690). That the Chinese really believed in their policy decision to replace incompetent managers came out clearly during my interviews in 1984 as described in Section 5.1.

Although the economic reforms had, as had been anticipated, unintended consequences such as corruption and financial crimes, these were of minor importance compared with the rapid economic development as a result of the reforms. Thus, after a short time of consolidation the Chinese leaders decided to go on with the reforms concerning enterprise management.

Ten Rights Given to Enterprises in 1984

To help the enterprises to solve problems arising from the economic reforms and to strengthen the motivation of managers and employees, in May 1984 the State Council promulgated the "Provisional Regulations on Further Extending the Decision-Making Power of the State Industrial Enterprises," giving such enterprises due power in the following ten aspects:

1. *Production.* Businesses have the right to produce whatever is needed or is in short supply, after fulfilling their state plans and orders.

2. *Sales.* With certain exceptions, firms have the right to sell products they retain for themselves, products in excess of state quotas, their own trial-produced or overstocked items, and those refused by state purchasing agencies. They must keep special accounts for the products they sell themselves and pay tax according to regulations.

3. *Pricing.* For the means of industrial production which they sell themselves and the products exceeding state quotas, businesses have the right to set prices within a 20% range of the state price, or to negotiate the prices with buyers. They must abide by the state prices for the means of livelihood and the means of farm production.

4. *Purchase of materials.* Businesses have the right to choose their suppliers when they order state-distributed raw materials. Businesses may also obtain raw materials directly from producers without going through state monopoly suppliers.

5. *Use of funds.* Enterprises have the right to decide whether their share of profits goes into expanding production, trial production of new products, a reserve fund, the workers' welfare fund, or bonuses. They also have the right to use other funds for the first three items, together with funds for depreciation and large-scale renovation and repair.

6. *Handling of assets.* Businesses have the right to lease or transfer with compensation unneeded machinery or other fixed assets, but the income must be used to upgrade or renew their own facilities.

7. *Structural establishment*. Businesses have the right to decide on the setting up of organizations and to assign their staff according to their needs as long as they stay within their authorized size.

8. *Personnel and labor*. The factory director or manager has the right to appoint or dismiss cadres under him. His deputies, however, are subject to approval from above. The director or manager and the party secretary are to be appointed by the higher competent departments concerned. The factory director has the right to reward and punish his workers and staff, with promotions, wage hikes, or even disciplinary dismissal. Directors have the right to employ workers on the basis of examinations under the guidance of the state labor-recruiting agencies. They also have the right to reject forced assignment from higher agencies or individuals.

9. *Wages and bonuses*. Businesses have the right to adopt any wage system, in line with state standards. Factory directors may promote 3% of their workers each year, with the increased wages counted as a cost of production.

10. *Interunit operations*. Enterprises have the right to enter into joint projects which cut across official divisions, as long as they maintain their present system of ownership, finances, and subordinate relationships. (B. R., June 11 and 18, 1984)

Since the 1950s a system had prevailed in most Chinese enterprises under which the director of a factory assumes full responsibility under the collective leadership of the party committee. At the Sixth National People's Congress, Premier Zhao stated on May 15, 1984 that this system would be gradually replaced by another, under which the factory director or manager alone assumes full responsibility for directing the production, management, and operation of his enterprise.

It was also planned then that under the leadership of the enterprise director, each firm would set up a management committee composed of the director, the CPC committee secretary, the trade union chairman, engineering and technical personnel, and workers' representatives. The committee would make major production and operational decisions, leaving the director responsible for the organization and implementation of the decisions, the day-to-day production.

The director of the enterprise has, under the unified state leadership, the power to decide on the production and sales of products, the purchase of raw and semifinished materials and the technical transformation of the enterprise, and to control appointments, transfers, rewards, and penalties among the workers and staff.

After the director of the enterprise assumes full responsibility in his enterprise, the party committee can free itself from day-to-day production and administrative affairs, and concentrate its efforts on the party's work, and the political and ideological work of the enterprise.

The enterprise director can be appointed by higher department, or he can be chosen by the authorities through the election of the workers' congress (B. R., June 18, 1984: 4–5.). Thus, we can see that the higher authorities wished to control the nomination of the top managers of enterprises.

Zhao Ziyang in his speech on May 15, 1984 dealt with participation in enterprises, saying:

> It is also necessary, at the same time, to adopt a series of measures for ensuring effective participation by workers and staff in the democratic running of enterprises, improving the system of workers' and staff congresses and giving full play to its important role in such matters as examining and deciding on major measures to be taken by the enterprises and protecting the rights and interests of workers and staff, so that they function as the true masters of the enterprises. (B. R., June 11, 1984)

The year 1985 became "the first year of overall reform," as Premier Zhao said in January 1986. He added that

> the steps we took turned out to be bigger than we had expected, and so were the effects... the whole economy is, as it may be said, turning from tension to ease.... The major goals for 1986 were to consolidate, digest, supplement, and improve on last year's reforms, and, at the same time, make preparations for larger steps in reforms over the next two years. (B. R., February 3, 1986)

Figure 5.22 is a kind of summary of how the economic reforms since Mao have affected Chinese industry in terms of output value according to different forms of ownership. The most significant changes concern, first, the decline of the share of state-owned enterprises, which sank from 83% in 1975 to 74% in 1984. Second, a contrary development can be seen in the growth of collective ownership, from 17% to 25% during the same period. From 1982 on there are also signs of the initial growth of individually owned industries (0.2% in 1984). "The other economic forms" probably represent mostly Chinese-foreign joint ventures, which have been growing relatively strongly after the opening up of the Special Economic Zones (SEZ) in 1980, from 0.6% to 1.2% in 1984.

If we examine the development trends during the whole period since 1949, we see, first, the great growth of state-owned industry between 1949 and 1965, and the corresponding decline in privately and individually owned

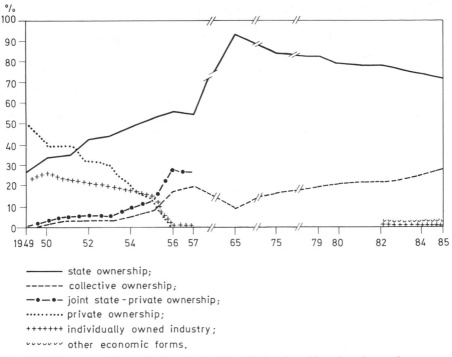

Fig. 5.22. Percentage changes in the output value of industries with various forms of ownership, 1949–1985. (*Statistical Yearbook of China 1985*; *China: A Statistical Survey in
1986*: 50)

industries. After 1965 collectively owned industry takes the place of individually and privately owned enterprises. The latter, will, however, begin
to live again, because the Chinese can now buy shares in enterprises.

If we further take into account agriculture, where the individual peasant
families cultivate their contracted land independently, actually like private
entrepreneurs, we see that the changes in economic and production relations since Mao in China have been really profound.

In the following subsection we will, however, go back to the enterprise
level and examine how the economic reforms appear in the management of
human resources in firms.

5.6.3 Management of Human Resources

To examine the changes in the Chinese systems of human resources management, we start with a general model of a human resources planning and implementation system (Fig. 5.23). With the giving of more autonomy and decision-making power to enterprises, and with their being required to make their own active adaptation to the demands of the environment or to move towards market socialism, the enterprises are facing quite new demands in the area of human resources management.

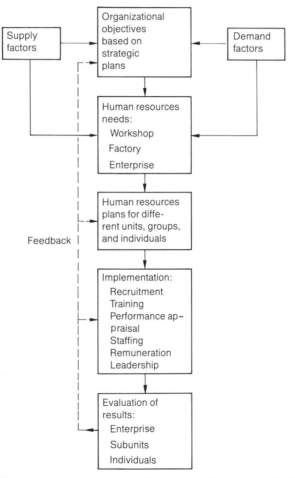

Fig. 5.23. Human resources planning and implementation system. (Partly based on French 1978: 201)

The main general change concerns the formulating of organizational objectives. During Mao's time the enterprises received through the process of centralized planning exact objectives for production, distribution, use of manpower, etc. Now the central plan gives only rough directions and the enterprise has to adapt itself to the changes in demand and supply. Because of these changes the whole implementation of different parts of personnel administration has had to be altered with regard to: (1) job policy and recruitment, (2) training and development, (3) performance appraisal and staffing, (4) remuneration and reward, and (5) leadership (Fig. 5.23).

Implementation of Personnel Administration

Job Policy and Recruitment

China has three kinds of economies, which have different personnel administration systems especially regarding recruitment and rewards policy. The sectors are: (1) the state-owned economy, which occupies the dominant position in China's economy; (2) the socialist collective economy; and (3), the individual economy. As earlier described the collective and individual economies have developed rapidly in the past few years, and have thereby absorbed a large number of workers. In 1984 the workers employed by the collectively owned enterprises accounted for 50% of total new employment, compared with 43% in 1980. The privately owned enterprises made up 11% in 1984, compared with 6% in 1980. By the end of June 1985, there were 4.1 million people working in the private sector, 27 times more than in 1978 (B. R., November 11, 1985).

During the past few years China has begun to discard its long-time practice of the state being responsible for finding jobs for all its eligible urban workers. Instead the country introduced a three-pronged policy of job finding. The options in the new plan are: (1) The government finds positions for the unemployed based on recommendations from area labour bureaus; (2) unemployed persons can opt to join together in small groups to start up their own businesses; and (3) people can operate on an individual basis, selling vegetables, repairing bicycles, etc. (B. R., November 11, 1985).

Also a new cadre system has been proposed. According to it, China would introduce a two-track system for the country's offices and cadres. The persons belonging to the first category would work in the CPC, government, and army institutions, as well as economic, cultural, and social organizations directly administered by the state. According to the proposal the number of such offices should be limited and their structure streamlined.

The state cadres, with the exception of a few leading cadres appointed by higher authorities, should be tested before they are hired. Thus, China seems to be returning to her earlier long tradition of entrance examinations for civil servants, which was abolished in 1906 (see Chapter 3.1.3). There should also be strict rules for their appointments and dismissal. The other cadre section would be the personnel employed in nonstate organs. These units would be eventually required to provide their own funds and assume sole responsibility for their earnings. At the same thing these units would have the power to decide their own wage scales and retirement plans including age limits and offerings.

It is interesting to notice that as many state organs as possible that fulfil the requirements should be encouraged to adopt nonstate status, or a status where a more flexible personnel policy is possible, e.g., in recruitment, appointment, and dismissal. The target is the gradual destruction of the principle of the "iron rice bowl," or equal treatment of everybody (B. R., February 3, 1986).

One of the ten rights given to enterprises in 1984 mentioned above was the right to employ workers on the basis of examinations. The factory manager was also given the right to appoint or dismiss cadres under him. As the state cadres should also be tested before they are hired, one can expect that a great variety of new recruitment techniques will probably appear as every organization becomes more or less responsible for its results. Competition for capable workers and cadres will probably grow, and the recruitment procedures will correspondingly become more and more developed.

The State Council gave new regulations implementing the reform of the labor system, which went into effect in state-owned enterprises in October 1986. There were four sets of regulations: (1) on implementation of a contract system, (2) on the dismissal of workers for violating work rules, (3) on recruiting workers, and (4) on labor insurance for the unemployed.

According to the first-mentioned regulations, workers will be offered contracts that set out both their responsibilities and their rights. A new pension system is also an important measure to ensure implementation of the contract labor system. Money for pensions will be largely derived from enterprises at a rate of 15% of their total wage bill. Contract workers will also pay into the fund 3% of their monthly wages.

Unemployment insurance will be available to help four kinds of people: (1) workers of bankrupt enterprises, (2) workers let go by enterprises on the verge of bankruptcy or ordered to reorganize to improve their productivity, (3) workers dismissed for violating work rules, and (4) contractual workers, whose contracts have expired (Ch. D., September 3, 1986). We see here clearly how reform in one area requires regulating reforms, i.e., norms, in other connecting areas.

Education and Training

The Chinese emphasize that in the long run the success of the country's modernization program is largely hinged on how well it can employ its abundant human resources. In China there will not only be over one billion mouths to feed, but also there will be an enormous source of potential talent. However, the prerequisite for development is a level of education and training corresponding to the requirements of modern technology and management practice. The enterprises are again totally dependent upon the knowledge and experience of the basic labor force; and therein lies one of China's main problems. There are still 230 million illiterates or semi-literates in the country, though mostly in the countryside and the backward regions of the country.

> Nearly 80 percent of the labor force in the industrial sector have only junior middle school (9-year) education or less. The educational re-form, whose aim it is to change this state of affairs, seeks to broaden and strengthen the base with universal primary education, enrich sec-ondary education by giving more attention to technical and vocational training, and improve college education. (Lin Wusun, B. R., January 6, 1986)

As education and training of the present and future workforce are key factors affecting China's economic development and management, we ex-amine in the following the country's educational system in more detail. Table 5.10 shows that since the Cultural Revolution (1966) the Chinese have invested especially first in education in secondary schools, and second in university education, the total enrollment of which has doubled between 1965 and 1984 *(China: A Statistical Survey in 1985)*. Table 5.11 reveals the fields of higher learning that have grown most according to number of graduates. However, the growth rate has been different during different

Table 5.10. Student enrollment by level of schools 1949–1985 per 10,000 population. (*Statisti-cal Yearbook of China 1985: 487; China: A Statistical Survey in 1986:* 114)

Year	University students	Secondary school pupils	Primary school pupils
1949	2.2	23	450
1952	3.3	55	889
1962	12.3	124	1,029
1965	9.3	197	1,602
1978	8.9	693	1,526
1980	11.6	578	1,489
1984	13.5	472	1,316
1985	16.4	489	1,284

Table 5.11. Graduates of institutions of higher learning by field of study 1949–1984 (persons) and growth 1965–1984 (times). (*Statistical Yearbook of China 1985:* 591)

Field of study	1949	1955	1965	1975	1984	Growth 1965–1984 (times)
Engineering	4,752	18,614	80,294	48,240	97,546	1.2
Agriculture	1,718	2,614	15,665	6,490	15,551	1.0
Forestry	92	370	3,237	810	2,965	0.9
Medicine	1,314	6,840	22,027	20,760	31,899	1.4
Pedagogy	1,890	12,133	28,966	20,516	84,821	2.9
Liberal arts	2,521	4,679	8,252	11,298	14,414	1.7
Natural science	1,584	2,015	20,668	8,167	17,907	0.9
Economics and finance	3,137	4,699	2,079	905	14,976	7.2
Politics and law	4,015	962	857	160	3,103	3.6
Physical culture	80	783	1,876	618	2,421	1.3
Art	250	757	1,600	991	1,334	0.8
Total	21,353	54,466	185,521	118,955	286,937	1.5

periods. Since 1955 the most rapid growth has been in the natural sciences, forestry, agriculture, pedagogy, and engineering.

Since 1965, on the threshold of the Cultural Revolution, the growth has been fastest in economics and finance, in which the number of graduates steadily lessened between 1955 and 1975. The reason of course was that in a centrally planned economy without any real private sector there was no great demand in higher education in this field. However, since the economic reforms, with their greater enterprise autonomy, greater demand for knowledge in marketing, accounting, finance, personnel management, etc., a large number of students have found their way into faculties and schools of higher learning in economics and finance. As education is one of the greatest problem areas in China, it is natural that graduates in pedagogy have greatly increased in number. The more liberal thinking and atmosphere in the country since 1976 affected studies in the liberal arts, in which graduates have more than doubled in number.

The Chinese targets to quadruple the total industrial and agricultural output value in 1980 by the end of this century makes a great demand on human resources, especially in education. Thus, the CPC Central Committee in May 1985 made a decision concerning the reform of the educational system, one major goal of which is to train millions of skilled workers for all trades and professions (B. R., June 10, 1985). The educational reform consisted of the following main points:

1. Entrusting local governments with the responsibility for developing elementary education and gradually introducing a 9-year compulsory education schedule.

2. Readjusting the structure of secondary school education and devoting great effort especially to the further development of vocational and technical training.

3. Changing the plan of enrollment and the job assignment system of the institutes of higher learning. China will restructure its higher education and enlarge administrative powers for its universities and colleges.

Thus, China will abolish the old practice of enrolling all students according to state quotas, and state job assignment for all university and college graduates. Instead, the following options will be introduced: (a) Students can be enrolled according to the state plan. Under the guidance of the state plan, the students will be assigned, upon graduation, with due consideration to their wishes, the schools' recommendations, and the employers' preferences. (b) Schools are entrusted by other units with the training of students. According to contracts, the units will pay a certain amount of the training fees, and the students will work in these units after graduation. (c) The third option is to admit, outside the state plan, some students who meet their own expenses, or have to pay for their tuition fees and other expenses. After graduation these students may ask the schools to recommend them for jobs or seek jobs on their own.

An important point is that all students have to pass entrance examinations before admission to colleges and universities (Wang Yibing, B. R., December 23, 1985). In 1984, for example, the entrance examinations took place in early July at the same time all over the country, covering altogether 1.6 million applicants. Of these, one million were trying for science and engineering colleges, 415,000 for liberal arts colleges, 88,000 for foreign language institutes and schools, and 15,000 for sports universities and schools (B. R., July 30, 1984).

In 1981 China also renewed her academic degree system, which now is very similar to the Western system; China then instituted bachelor's, master's and doctoral degrees in the main academic fields. As China's higher education was practically stopped during the Cultural Revolution, the country now has a great shortage of younger capable teachers and researchers in universities. The professors are generally rather old. For example, the average age of the 134 full professors of Beijing University in 1983 was nearly 70 (B. R., January 24, 1983).

One thing which struck me when I was visiting some Chinese universities in 1980 was the relatively low number of students, although the teaching facilities were quite large. The reason was often the old traditional custom that all students have to live in the student dormitories of the university. Thus, in the Jiao Tong University in Shanghai there were 5,000 undergraduates, all living in the student dormitories. No students lived in the large neighboring city of Shanghai. The professor who acted as my guide there told me that the university would have probably been able to take more students, but the dormitories were the bottleneck.

As external education and training cannot fulfil the great training needs for the permanent work force in enterprises, the Chinese have, often with the help of state and communes, established large-scale internal training programs in enterprises. Both the workers and cadres are probably now better motivated to take part in these programs as their own income, according to the contract responsibility system, will greatly depend upon their own individual work performance, but also upon the performance of the work group and the entire enterprise.

Table 5.12, which contains material collected by Malcolm Warner, indicates that the resources invested in training varied quite a lot. It is understandable that the investments were high in the watch industry, which is technically demanding. Warner found in 1984 that the Watch and Clock Corporation, situated in Sichuan province, with 6,200 employees, had a "staff and workers' college," a technical school, and a spare-time school for workers. "In 1984, over 130 went to the College, over 150 young employees were sent to the technical school, and over 250 attended the spare-time studies school" (Warner 1985: 7, 14).

Who decides which workers can take part in the training course during working hours? This decision seems to be quite centralized in Chinese enterprises according to my interviews in 1980 and 1984. In most cases the

Table 5.12. Enterprise size, type of industry and industrial training. (Warner 1985: 11)

Organizational variables	Type of industry					
	Steel	Glass	Watch	Textile	Handi-craft	Machine-tool
Plants (n)	32	20	14	30	50	100
Employees (n)	110,000	10,000	6,240	10,000	10,000	30,000
Cadres (%)	11	10.5	11	10	16	6
No./training department	21	8	6	5	10	30
Budget for train-ing (%)	2	4	8	2	2	1.5

top management itself made these decisions, and the middle management, workshop directors, and department heads, had relatively little to say in these matters.

The Chinese also use apprenticeship training in industrial enterprises. After passing the entrance examination a new employee can enter into apprenticeship training for one year; if he or she wishes to become a technician, the time is three years. The salary for the apprenticeship time is usually on average about one-third of that of an older employee.

Management Education

The Chinese have realized that one of the greatest hindrances to their economic development is the low quality of their higher enterprise managers. Very few of them are aware of modern management methods concerning, e.g., strategic management, marketing, international business, finance, and human resources management. One reason for the relatively low quality of Chinese enterprise managers is the repeated changes of managers during the time of the People's Republic as described in Section 5.1. Few managers had enough time to train themselves in their new managerial top positions before they were dismissed.

The Chinese themselves seem to be well aware of the inadequate professional quality of many of their enterprise managers. The premier of the country dealt with this problem in his "government report" to the National People's Congress in May 1984. Zhao Ziyang said: "The state will organize uniform examinations (plus assessment of professional performance) for factory directors and managers. Those who fail must not be allowed to remain at their posts."

At the end of 1984, China actually organized a state examination for the first group of factory directors and managers to test their understanding of the basic principles and policies concerning China's economic structure, and their general knowledge of business management. Altogether 9,000 directors and managers from industry, commerce, foreign trade, building, post and telecommunications, transportation, and communications took part in the examinations (B. R., October 22, 1984). Since 99% passed the examinations in the subject of principles and policies, and 94% in business knowledge, the examinations must have contained very general questions and/or only those managers took part in them who already had good knowledge in the subjects. Of course it is risky to take part in an examination in which failure means losing a high job position.

China is now concentrating great resources on the field of management education. As mentioned before, in higher educational institutions the number of graduates in economics and finance has increased most between 1965 and 1983, by over six times (Table 5.11).

In 1979 the China Enterprise Management Association (CEMA) was established. One of its main tasks is to develop management training especially for top and middle level managers. CEMA has local branches all over the country, which organize different kinds of courses for managers. When I visited the city of Chongqing in central China in 1980, I was asked by the local CEMA organization to give a lecture about enterprise management in Western capitalist countries. When I came to a great lecture hall there were to my surprise more than 400 local managers, who were especially interested in marketing and marketing research. The discussion was free, open, and lively. One could really feel that new winds were blowing strongly.

CEMA has also invited a great number of foreign scholars to give lectures to Chinese managers and future teachers and consultants in management. Because international trade is becoming more and more important, CEMA also organizes foreign language training programs in English, Japanese, French, and German. A number of senior executives, managers, management instructors, and researchers have also been sent to training programs abroad.

Performance Appraisal and Staffing

Chinese enterprises have experienced great changes during the People's Republic in task assignment and performance appraisal, staffing, and promotion. The first great changes occurred when the Soviet one-man management model was introduced at the beginning of the 1950s. This model followed the rules of so-called scientific management, where detailed work plans were assigned for each phase of production and administration. These plans were highly standardized, based on exact measurement of human and other performances. As the performance was matched against the targets of the plans, the managers and also planners aimed at low targets which could be easily met and exceeded.

As human performance under the one-man management model had been measured against the planned targets, in the profit management system of the early 1960s the performance was matched against profit making; how the individual workers helped to create profitable results. This seemed to suit the Chinese society then, because the production went up sharply after 1961. However, the overall strategy did not please Mao Zedong, who saw in the development too many capitalistic features. Thus, the result, also affected by the power struggle of Mao's inheritance, led to the Cultural Revolution. This again, as we have learned earlier, altogether changed the attitude towards performance appraisal and promotion. The goal was then to keep differences between persons small and to reduce them, and one of the main criteria for performance appraisal was ideological "purity" and activeness (Laaksonen 1975: 14).

After Mao and the economic reforms in 1978, the bases of performance appraisal changed altogether. The idea was to overcome step by step the prevailing defect of "everybody eating from the same big pot": the enterprises "eating" from the pot of the state, and the individuals eating from the common pot of the enterprise. Egalitarian thinking should be done away with, and the principle of "to each according to his work" should be upheld.

In the rural peasant household with their contract responsibility system it is easier to apply the principle "to each according to his work" because the production unit, the individual household, is small, and in it one can better evaluate one's performance and be remunerated. In large urban enterprises with thousands of employees the slogan is much more difficult to put into practice. In a large industrial firm everything is dependent upon everything else, not only within the organization, but also concerning relations with the environment. One of the most difficult things is the traditional rigid price mechanism, which greatly determines the economic result of an enterprise, and thus also the performance appraisal of the firm, as well as of the workers.

The Chinese are just now developing their system of performance appraisal, which now greatly varies between enterprises. The main principles are fairly clear, but the methods and techniques have not yet been satisfactorily developed. There is great haste to solve these problems, because such important matters as remuneration and rewards should be based on adequate performance appraisal systems.

Remuneration of Employees

In a country with a relatively low living standard like China material rewards play an important role in motivating workers and cadres to better working efforts. However, during the Cultural Revolution great importance was put on ideology and egalitarian wage policy. Mao and his supporters thought that relying on ideological rewards would create better results than using material ones.

The principle of Deng and his supporters of "to each according to his work" changed the wage policy altogether. First, the bonus system was retracted, and the income of Chinese workers was made up of their basic wages plus bonuses (Table 5.5). Basic wages were defined according to their jobs and set wage grades. There were altogether eight grades, and the worker could be promoted according to his educational level, skill, and work performance to a higher rung of the wage ladder which also corresponded to special status (or positions). Generally, workers are paid monthly, and their pay is fixed. A bonus which is added to the basic wage is a reward for a worker's additional efforts in a given period (Jin, B. R., July 1, 1985). The application of the different components of economic reforms is a delicate matter and requires continuous guidance and control of different measures and their consequences. Thus, it very often naturally occurs that one special order from the top leaders is soon followed by another, partly contradictory order, which is meant to control the unintended consequences (see Fig. A.3) of strong application of the first order. This kind of zig-zag, with suggestions and counter-suggestions, has occurred with the development of the new remuneration system.

The CPC Central Committee announced on October 20, 1984, that the differences between wages paid in enterprises should be increased by fully applying the principle of rewarding the hard-working and good employees and punishing the lazy and bad workers. The wage system should clearly take into account the amount of work done as well as differences between intellectual and physical work, complicated and simple tasks, between work which requires special skills and unskilled work, and between heavy and light work.

When the bonus system was recreated after the Cultural Revolution it led quickly to a situation where nearly every employee received a high bonus, which then actually became a solid part of his basic wage. Thus, in the organizations where I interviewed at the end of 1980, the average bonus was 25% of the basic wages – ranging from 7%–50%. The mean monthly basic wage was 59 yuan (US$ 29.70). The highest salary was 280 yuan (US$ 141.10) and the lowest 32 yuan (US$ 16.10) in enterprises (Laaksonen (1984a: 5).

As a consequence of the "wild" bonus system, the government ordered that the bonuses paid in state enterprises should not exceed a worker's two months' basic wages. In May 1985 this limiting of bonuses was abolished, and a new system, where the state began to collect bonus tax from enterprises, was created. This tax is to be collected from enterprises whose yearly bonus awards exceed a sum equal to the workers' average two and half months' wages.

> A 30 percent tax will be imposed on bonuses equal to the workers' average two and a half months to four months' wages; a 100 percent tax will be imposed on bonuses between the workers' average 4–6 months' wages, and 300 percent tax on bonuses exceeding the workers' average six months wages. The government also stipulated that

bonus awards and taxes must be taken from an enterprise's awards funds, and should not be included in the production costs to reduce their tax payment. This will help to control the growth of consumption funds. (Jin Qi, B. R., July 1, 1985).

In connection with the economic reforms and in trying to motivate the employees after the turmoil of the Cultural Revolution, the Chinese created many different wage systems in enterprises. In examining them it is expedient to divide the wage systems into the following main categories:

1. Time rate wage system, which was largely used during the Cultural Revolution when the bonuses had been abolished. A system of time wages plus bonuses was carried out before and after the Cultural Revolution. The bonuses were often divided equally among workers and staff members, and the principle of reward according to work was often not followed. The Chinese stressed after 1978 that if it was not possible to apply a piece-rate wage system, then they should adopt a system of recording points for awarding bonuses (Ma 1983: 107).

The bonuses have often been based also on the profits of the enterprise. There have been systems of "profit sharing" and "profit taking." Under the "profit taking" system the workers could take a certain proportion of profit as award incentives if the enterprise could reach a certain level of profit laid down by the state. In principle, it was "more profit, more taking; less profit, less taking; no profit, no taking." The amount of profit taken by the principle of reward according to work was often not followed. The Chinese stressed after 1978 that if it was not possible to apply a piece-rate wage system, then they should adopt a system of recording points for awarding bonuses (Ma 1983: 107).

In the "profit-sharing" system the enterprise, in addition to a certain proportion of profit taken on a monthly basis in the form of awards, at the end of the financial year took a certain amount of the annual net profit, left after "profit taking," for the development of the welfare of the workers and the development of the enterprise. In these cases the profit was shared between the state and the enterprise in a ratio of something like six to four. The profit shared was, e.g., for building workers' quarters, developing the workers' welfare system, giving workers an annual bonus, developing the production system, and adding more production facilities for the enterprise (Chen 1984: 190).

2. Incentive wage system. (a) There is a direct piece-rate wage system in which the wage is based directly on the result of work. This system has gradually spread in China. It was 0.8% of the total wage bill of state-owned units in 1978, but 9.5% in 1984 (Table 5.13). (b) Subcontract wage system. In this the total wage always contains a basic wage and in addition a piece-

Table 5.13. Composition of total wages of state-owned enterprises 1978–1985; Percentages. (*China: A Statistical Survey in 1986*)

Item	1978	1980	1981	1982	1983	1984	1985
Time wages	85.0	69.8	67.2	64.4	63.5	58.5	59.5
Piece wages	0.8	3.2	5.5	7.6	8.5	9.5	9.9
Of which							
overfulfilment wages	0.1	0.6	1.1	1.6	1.8	2.1	2.2
Various bonuses	2.3	9.1	10.2	10.9	11.1	14.4	12.9
Various allowances	6.5	14.1	14.0	14.1	14.1	14.5	15.2
Overtime payments	2.0	1.6	1.6	1.5	1.3	1.5	1.6
Other	3.4	2.2	1.5	1.5	1.5	1.6	0.9
Total wages	100	100	100	100	100	100	100

rate wage depending upon the result of work. However, carrying out any kind of a piece-rate wage system requires of the enterprise the fulfillment of certain necessary conditions. In Chinese conditions there should be relatively accurate production targets for working hours and quotas for raw material consumption. A strict quality control must be implemented, and the supply of both raw materials and electricity should be quaranteed. There must also be a market for the products. In addition, it should be possible to perform accounting of output on a per capita, per machine, or per group basis. The quota stipulated should be attainable by a majority of the workers if they work hard. In general in this wage system the enterprise needs a strong and capable management (Ma 1983: 108).

At the beginning of 1986 most Chinese industrial enterprises still used a pay system combining basic wages with bonuses. The total bonuses increased in 1985 in these enterprises from the equivalent of two and a half months' basic wages to four months'. This increase was caused by new stipulations that require firms to pay bonus taxes only when their bonuses are more than four months' basic wages. As a result of this most of the workers' incomes increased after 1984.

Because of the very complicated existing wage systems, the Chinese government made an overall wage reform in the second half of 1985 for its organizations and undertakings. This is called the position wage system; it includes first the administrative position wage system, and second the technical position wage system. The latter is more complicated and has had a poorer foundation to work on. It requires meticulous study and a well-organized effort to work out a practical wage reform program (from a speech of vice-premier Tian Jiyan, January 6, 1986, B. R., February 10, 1986).

The Chinese realize that there are complications in operating a performance-based wage system in the country because of China's irrational price system, the varying conditions of enterprises, the lack of coordination of their reform measures, and the striking difference in the economic benefits between trades and between enterprises. "Without scientific and rational measures, it would be impossible to solve the problems in the original wage system; moreover, new problems would arise" (Tian Jiyan, B. R., February 10, 1986).

Who has the power to decide about the wages? As we remember, those enterprises which belonged to the Sichuan experiments back in 1978 had the right to issue bonuses at the enterprise's own discretion within the range approved by the state; however, generally not more than two months average wages of the workers and staff. Later in 1984 when the State Council announced the ten rights given to the state industrial enterprises, one of the rights was that enterprises could adopt any wage system in line with state standards. Factory directors could then promote 3% of their workers each year.

From my interviews in Chinese enterprises in 1980 and 1984 it seemed that decision-making concerning wages was centralized at the top of the enterprise. The middle managers and foremen had very little to say in these matters.

How are the economic reforms reflected in the overall development of wages in China? Figure 5.24 shows that in 1952 the wages in industry were clearly higher than in the other main branches of the economy. The average annual wages in agriculture, commerce, government service, and in educational institutions were about the same. At the end of the 1950s wages began to be differentiated, and generally fell during the bad economic years of 1959–1961. The wages and salaries for government officials dropped least. While the Chinese society was in great turmoil during the Cultural Revolution, the income of government employees rose on average even higher than those of industry. When the new Chinese leaders introduced their economic reforms in 1978, industry was in a key position, and regained its lead in the "wage competition." However, after 1982 the salaries of government employees again rose over those in industry. The reason was perhaps that the completion of the reforms required reliable, competent, and motivated government officials; and that must be paid for. From the curves of Fig. 5.24 we can also see the rise of the importance of education and science.

Thus, the wage policy has been determined by two criteria: First, political and power aspects. According to this criterion, the incomes of government employees were kept relatively high during the periods of political change, when the government structure was the instrument of creating change as well as the instrument of wielding power; it thus represented instrumental hierarchical power. Typical periods of this kind have been the years of the

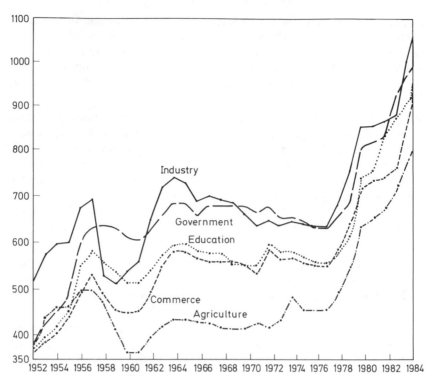

Fig. 5.24. Average annual wage of staff and workers in state-owned units in (1.) industry, (2.) agriculture, forestry and water conservancy, (3.) commercial catering and service trades, (4.) education, science, culture, and public health, and (5.) government agencies 1952–1984; Yuans. (*Statistical Yearbook of China 1985*)

Cultural Revolution and the years of economic reform after Mao. The government structure has acted as an agent of change.

The second important aspect determining wages is, of course, the economic one – to motivate people and organizations to better performance in areas which are looked upon as critical for development. Those areas were in fact education and science during the economic reforms. Table 5.14 shows that the wage curves since 1976 reflect rather well the slogan of the four modernizations of: (1) industry, (2) agriculture (real incomes of peasants), (3) defense (government), and (4) science and education. Thus, Deng and his supporters have efficiently used a flexible wage policy in supporting their economic reforms.

The curve in Fig. 5.24 describing the development of wages in agriculture does not tell the whole truth. The curve describes the average wages of staff and workers in state-owned units in agriculture, i.e., staff and workers in

Table 5.14. Rewards structure according to hierarchical levels and industry in China in 1984; salary in yuan per month (Warner 1985: 23)

	Steel	Glass	Watch	Textile	Handi-crafts	Machine-tool
Hierarchical level	Salary in yuan per month					
Corporate director	150–290	150–160	130–	100	130	100
Factory director	100–150	80– 90	70	100	100	100
Workshop director	100	70	60	60–70	90	80
Group leader	100	60	55	50–60	70–80	50
Factory worker	65	50	58	55	65	50
Plants (n)	32	20	14	30	50	100

earlier communes and later state administrative units of townships. The incomes of those peasant households working independently under the contract responsibility system are not included. Their incomes have often increased so much that they create great problems for Chinese leaders, because earlier poor peasants are now earning enviably large sums, and the whole Chinese socialist, egalitarian wage, and income system is in "danger."

There has been much discussion and rumor in China about households whose annual income is 10,000 yuan (US$ 3,125) or more. A survey conducted in 1984 in Beijing, Hebei, Shandong, Liaoning, Jiangsu, Shaanxi, and Heilongjian revealed that there were 150,000 households earning at least 10,000 yuan a year in the six provinces and one municipality, making such households 0.3% of all peasant households (Wang Dacheng, B. R., November 18, 1985).

In November 1986 I visited an industrial cooperative near Tianjin. Before 1979 there were 700 peasants living in the village, and in 1986 there were 800 families, most of them working in a large printing house and industrial plant producing electrical transformers run by the cooperative. There were 34 peasants left who took care of the 39 hectares of farm land with highly mechanized equipment provided by the cooperative. I was informed that the peasants' monthly income could be 2,500 yuan (US$ 674), but they had to pay 30% tax. The average monthly income of an industrial worker was 450 yuan (US$ 121) and the highest was 1,600 yuan (US$ 431) in 1986. The general manager's salary was 2,000 yuan (US$ 539) and represented, without doubt, an extreme case.

It is noteworthy that also workers can themselves now act as independent "entrepreneurs" under the contract system. Workers can sign contracts with firms after consultation on the duties, rights, and interests of both sides. Contracts may be extended if both sides wish, but workers remain free to look for new jobs, and businesses to hire new people. It was estimated that China had 3.5 million contract workers in 1986 (B. R., August 4, 1986).

Thinking about the future development of wages in China in various fields, it is important to realize that they are all dependent on each other. Earlier people from rural areas tried to move to the cities hoping to get better pay in urban industries and services. After 1978, in connection with the agricultural contract system, peasants' incomes grew very much and rapidly. Many of the peasant families are now among the well-to-do people in China. There has been much discussion in China about income gaps between people of various social strata, and the source of this discussion has been mainly in the rural areas. This is not only because people in rural areas have earned better than city people, but also because of discrepancies in the incomes in rural areas themselves between grain growers and the rural families specializing in industry, side-line production, and commerce.

However, the wages in different industries are not at the same level either as we see in Table 5.14. We may also observe notable differences between the same hierarchical groups in these industries. It looks as if the employees in the steel industry are better paid at all hierarchical levels. It is interesting but, I think, also logical that workers in the handicraft industry are as well paid as in the steel industry, while persons in various superior positions in handicrafts earn less than their counterparts in the steel industry. The handicraft enterprises greatly depend upon the skilled "handwork" of their workers.

Table 5.15 shows the average, lowest, and highest wages paid to workers in those enterprises I visited in 1980 and 1984. Because the composition of the enterprises is not quite the same at both time points, we cannot reliably compare the wages of 1980 and 1984. But what is interesting is the great difference in wages paid in the Special Economic Zone (SEZ) of Shenzhen

Table 5.15. Average, lowest, and highest wages of workers in enterprises visited in 1980 and at the end of 1984, and separately the same wage figures for two enterprises in Shenzhen Special Economic Zone (SEZ) in 1984; Yuan

Workers' wages	1980	1984	
		Interior China	SEZ
Average wage	59	68	210
Lowest wage	32	47	165
Highest wage		140	250
Enterprises	9	6	2

near Hong Kong compared with the wages in (interior) China. We must, however, remember that the costs of living are much higher in Special Economic Zones, but even so these areas represent an Eldorado for the Chinese.

With regard to bonuses, I discovered that at the end of 1984 the mean bonus for average wages in the firms interviewed was 16.6 yuan or 24% in interior China, whereas it was 22.5 yuan in the two enterprises of the SEZ area, or 11% of the average wage of their workers.

Economic rewards such as bonuses are among the most important measures of Chinese management in trying to motivate the employees of enterprises to work more efficiently. However, it has been reported from several sources that Chinese managers "voted" better housing as the best incentive system for themselves, "meaning a two-room apartment for their family. The pay came next, and some choice in job selection was also mentioned" (Olve 1984: 8). I can very well understand this preference, thinking of the often very crowded apartments, where Chinese managers as well as others have to live. And there is the problem that deficiencies in housing are not solved overnight in a country like China with over a billion inhabitants and a great lack of capital. Now Chinese enterprises have, with their greater freedom in decision-making, the opportunity to invest surplus profit (after taxes) in better housing conditions, but there are also many other competing investment objectives, and perhaps bonuses are anyway the safest way to divide "extra profit" fairly.

Leadership, Participation, and Industrial Democracy after Mao

During the Cultural Revolution China experimented with a kind of collective management in enterprises when the operational decision-making was concentrated in the revolutionary committees, where different personnel groups were represented. Also many other participation systems – up the line, horizontal, and down the line – were tried out. However, as mentioned in Section 5.6.8, these formal, many-sided participation systems did not work in practice; they did not give decision-making power to the participating groups because the CPC system at the level of the enterprise and above it made the really important decisions.

Thus, striving towards the four modernizations and trying to fulfill the economic reforms after Mao, the Chinese leaders had to discover new and more efficient ways of managing industrial enterprises and motivating their employees. It seems that the Chinese tried to find a balance between two leadership styles in enterprises: between a participative, democratic style and a quite autocratic, one-man management style. Since the Chinese had tried out many participation systems during the Cultural Revolution, and stressed the democratic way of management in political propaganda, it was difficult for the leaders of a socialist country to jump directly to another extreme. Perhaps they thought that a participative system, although an indirect one with representative bodies of workers and staff in enterprises, would be well suited to fulfil the demands of the economic reforms.

Reestablishment of Workers' Congresses

Speaking "On the Reform of the System of Party and State Leadership" in 1980, Deng Xiaoping said:

> Congresses or representative conferences of workers and staff members should be introduced in all enterprises and institutions. This was decided on long ago. The question now is how to popularize and perfect this system. The congresses or representative conferences of workers and staff members have the right to discuss and make decisions on major issues concerning their own units, to propose to the higher organizations the recall of incompetent administrative leaders of their units, and to gradually introduce the practice of electing their leaders within an appropriate scope. (B. R., October 10, 1983)

Actually Deng Xiaoping stressed already in 1978, when speaking at a national conference of trade unions, that the system of workers' congresses should be established in all enterprises. In 1982 about 90% of the large and medium-sized enterprises in Beijing, Shanghai, Tianjin, and other major cities had established workers' congresses. The provisional regulations concerning workers' congresses given in 1981 stated that the congresses have the following main functions and powers:

1. To discuss and examine the director's work reports, the plans for production and construction, the budgets and final accounts

2. To discuss and decide on the use of the enterprise's funds for labor protection, welfare of the workers and staff members, and bonuses

3. To discuss and adopt reforms of the system of organization, plans for wage adjustments, plans for training workers and staff members, and important rules and regulations governing the whole enterprise

4. To supervise leading cadres and working personnel at the various levels of the enterprise; to propose to the higher authorities the criticizing, punishing, or dismissing of those cadres who have neglected their duties and caused losses

5. To elect leading administrative personnel of the enterprise in accordance with the arrangements of the higher organ of the enterprise; democratically elected cadres should be submitted to the related higher organs for examination and appointment according to their respective jurisdictions.

Representatives of the workers' congress are directly elected by workers and staff members with work groups, work sections, or workshops as the electoral units. Representatives are elected for a term of two years and may be reelected. Workers' congresses are composed of representatives of workers, scientific and technical personnel, administrative personnel, leading cadres, and other personnel. Workers account for no less than 60% of the total number of representatives. Appropriate representation should be guaranteed to other groups mentioned above as well as to young and female employees.

The workers' congress meets at least once every six months. When the congress is in session, a presidium is elected to preside over it. Workers are the majority in the presidium. At the grassroots level the working organs of the workers' congresses are the trade union committees. They also take care of the day-to-day organizational work of the congresses while they are in recess (Su 1982: 193-202).

When Deng Xiaoping launched the idea of reestablishing the workers' congresses in 1978, there seems to have been great enthusiasm in certain circles about their planned functions and powers. For example, when I was interviewing the managers of different industrial enterprises during the fall of 1980, I heard many times that in the future the workers and other employees would elect the enterprise managers and other leading persons of the enterprises. I was informed that this had already happened in many enterprises. Gradually the Chinese top leaders became more and more careful about how much power it was wise to give to the workers' congresses so as not to lose too much control and to avoid a jump into an unknown future concerning enterprise management.

Therefore, when the above-mentioned provisional regulations were published in 1981, the rights given to workers' congresses were much less than anticipated. It was several times stressed in the regulations that the workers' congresses should function under the leadership of the party committees.

According to the general picture I got at the end of 1984 of the role and functioning of the workers' congresses, they functioned generally according to the regulations mentioned. However, the real power actually given to them seemed to be as small as possible in the frame of the official norms. In no firm that I visited was there a regular system that the employees should elect, e.g., the workshop director.

In the Third Knitting Mill in Beijing they had once experimented in one workshop with the workers electing its head; he then appointed the shift leaders, who again appointed the group leaders, but this remained only a brief trial. They did not follow this procedure any longer.

Thus, in the Knitting Company, to which the Third Knitting Mill belongs, the company director had been nominated by the economic commission of the Beijing Municipality, and the director of the factory (Third Knitting Mill) was appointed by the company director after the approval of the party committee. The heads of the workshops were nominated by the factory director after the approval of the party committee and so on downwards in the hierarchy.

In the Knitting Company there were workers' congresses only at the factory level. At company level the trade union took care of the corresponding tasks. In the workers' congresses of the factories 7% of the workers were represented. The congress held meetings twice a year, just as the regulations stipulated.

Depending especially upon the manager of the enterprise, the role of the workers' congresses seemed to vary very much. In one factory in Chongqing in central China, the manager said that the workers congress "can organize entertainment activities." There 20% of employees belonged to the congress, or 270 persons. However, the manager added that in the future, in the second stage of the development program, they would perhaps move to a system where the workers could elect the managing director of the firm also. But this would depend upon experience with the present system.

If we follow the development of different reforms beginning from Deng's demand concerning workers' congresses in 1978, we notice an interesting and quite complicated sequence of decisions and proposals, which have affected the powers of workers' congresses, party committees, and general managers in enterprises. A second event we must remember is Deng's article in August 1980, where he announced that government and CPC administration should be separated. Third were the regulations concerning workers' congresses. Fourth, we must recall the increased decision-making power given to enterprises and especially to their managers in the ten rights of 1984 (Section 5.6.2). For example, according to point 8, the factory director has the right to appoint or dismiss cadres under him. These "rights" were further enlarged and confirmed through new regulations on reforming China's labor system given by the State Council in September 1986. These regulations also contained new directions concerning the so-called labor contract system. We can demonstrate the development, which has led to the increased decision-making power of enterprises and their managers, in the way shown in Fig. 5.25.

It is difficult to say whether the Chinese top leaders planned in an integrative way the sequences of the many different decisions which led to more autonomous enterprise management and the decreasing power of the CPC in enterprise decision-making. This can clearly be seen in my interviews at

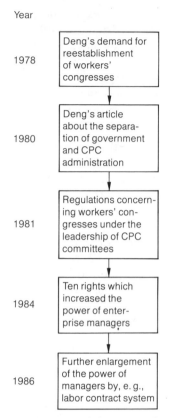

Fig. 5.25. Development of the power of workers' congresses, CPC committees, and enterprise managers after 1978

the end of 1984, which we will examine in more detail later in Chapter 6. These observations were further confirmed in my new interviews in Chinese enterprises in November 1986.

Probably the Chinese leaders had realized quite early that the double or triple organization structure of enterprises, consisting of party committees, government agencies (above the firm), and operational management, had been inefficient and a great waste of resources. The same was also true of government administration at the societal, provincial, and local levels.

If we compare the influence upon decision-making in enterprises between the CPC committee und the workers' congress, we notice that their "total" influence concerning 16 different investigated matters for decision was about the same, but when examining the different decisions separately one notices that the workers' congresses had more to say in decisions concerning working conditions, assignment of tasks to workers and changes concerning wages. The CPC committees again had more influence in the appointment of superiors, e.g., department heads, changes concerning organization structure, and employees' training. However, in all the mentioned decision areas the influence of both party committee and workers' congress was much less than that of the general manager.

I noticed during my interviews at the end of 1984 that workers' congresses were established in all those enterprises I visited, but their influence in decision-making in enterprises was quite modest, depending considerably upon the general leadership style of the top manager of the enterprise.

Although the workers' congresses were regular organizational units in all larger enterprises in interior China, this was not the case in Special Economic Zones (SEZ) on the Pacific coast, at least not in enterprises in which foreigners owned a majority of the shares. Thus, in those two enterprises in Shenzhen SEZ near Hong Kong, one of which was a joint venture with a Hong Kong firm and the other with a Japanese multinational company, there were no workers' congresses. This shows that the Chinese authorities really followed the regulations given for firms located in the zones that foreign-owned firms have the right to manage themselves independently, and that the governments of the Special Economic Zones do not interfere in the administration of the enterprises.

Although the workers' congresses were reestablished in China with a certain enthusiasm after 1978, their role in the decision-making of enterprises has been quite modest. For example, if we compare the influence of Chinese workers' congresses to that of the corresponding units of twelve European countries at the end of the 1970s, we see that on average the Chinese workers' congresses had less influence in all the 16 decision matters examined, as we will learn in Chapter 6 (Industrial Democracy in Europe (IDE) 1981a, b).

Towards a One-man Management System

In trying to find out the "right" way to activate Chinese economic life after the Cultural Revolution, the Chinese proceeded carefully but decisively. In enterprise management they began cautiously with the Sichuan experiments, giving more autonomy to the firms. In internal guidance and control of enterprises they reintroduced the workers' congresses, apparently with the idea of giving them relatively large influence; e.g., the right to elect the managers and other superiors of enterprises.

This bold jump probably did not succeed well, either from the point of view of effectiveness or from that of the power game. At any rate, the idea of electing managers by workers' congresses was withdrawn, and the higher authorities in the CPC and government decided upon the appointment of new general managers and their deputies in enterprises. The difference from earlier practice during the Cultural Revolution and previously was that pure political ideology was no longer the decisive criteria for selecting managers, but knowledge, education, and demonstrated managerial capability. "Correct" economic thinking in accordance with the economic reforms was more important than ideological enthusiasm. The Chinese thus moved towards a professional one-man management system, with the general manager of the enterprise as the core of the power coalition of the enterprise management. The CPC committee was left outside this coalition as we shall see later in Chapter 6.

One can now ask, are the Chinese returning in the 1980s back to the Soviet one-man management model practiced during the 1950s? I should say that the new Chinese model differs from the Soviet one especially concerning the responsibility of the top management. In the Soviet model he or she is mainly responsible for carrying out the directions of the central plan. Chinese managers are according to the reforms responsible for the firm's whole behavior in a (limited) free-market environment. Chinese managers should, in other words, concentrate on strategic planning in order to adapt the firm's behavior to a rapidly changing environment.

The trend towards a "capitalistic" one-man management system and still more independence for enterprises, almost totally free from the control of the CPC system, is strongly represented in the Special Economic Zones, which we will examine in the next chapter.

5.6.4 Opening the Doors and Management

We examined generally in Section 5.1.5 the reasons for the establishment of the Special Economic Zones (SEZ) and coastal open cities, which now cover almost the entire eastern coastline of China, embracing some 200 million Chinese.

However, the opening up to the West and Japan was not a new phenomenon in the history of the People's Republic. After the conflict with the Soviet Union, at the beginning of the 1960s China turned sharply towards the West and Japan in its foreign trade (Fig. 5.26). Also a substantial number of complete factories were being constructed in China by companies and consortiums from several West European countries and Japan. In the 1960s there was also growing Western and Japanese influence in the cultural area; there were student and faculty exchanges, borrowing of educational and technical books and materials, and the teaching of foreign languages. Chinese students and a limited number of Chinese professors

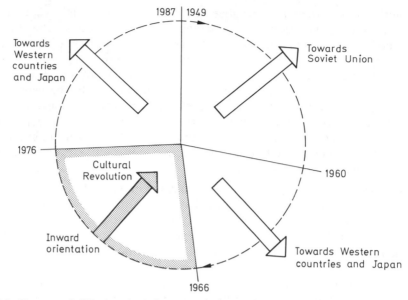

Fig. 5.26. Changes of China's orientation towards international environments during the People's Republic

and specialists were sent to England, France, Japan, and other non-communist countries for education, training, and the exchange of ideas and information (Richman 1969: 409). After this relatively short opening up to the West, China again changed its policy and closed its boundaries towards foreign countries for ten years during the period of the Cultural Revolution, 1966–1976. It is of special interest that the strong man of China in the 1980s, Deng Xiaoping, was one of the top leaders of the country in the 1960s, and was probably one of the architects of the opening of the doors to the West then as well as 20 years later. It thus seems that strong personalities in their own way carry history forward.

The Special Economic Zones were opened carefully and gradually in the 1980s, beginning with four limited zones of which three were around Hong Kong, the idea being to spread their impact stepwise throughout China. The Chinese saw many advantages in the establishment of the zones, such as: (1) through preferential policies these zones can use large amounts of foreign investments in a better way and import foreign advanced technology; (2) by dealing regularly with foreign capital and businessmen, the Chinese are able to observe and understand the development and changes in the modern capitalist world, and keep abreast of the changes on the international markets and in science and technology; (3) through cooperation with foreigners the Chinese thought that they could learn modern urban construction; and (4) what is important from our point of view, they especially thought that they could learn modern management methods and train their own management professionals (B. R., January 23, 1984).

The managerial systems, policies, and measures actually began to develop quite differently in the SEZ areas from those in the rest of China:

1. Enterprises run exclusively by foreign or overseas Chinese capital are given more rights to manage themselves independently, provided of course that they observe Chinese laws and regulations.

2. Joint ventures and cooperative enterprises are managed by their own boards of directors. In general, the governments of the special economic zones do not interfere in the administration of the enterprises. For example, I learned during my interviews in Shenzhen Goodyear Printing Co. Ltd, a joint venture with the Hong Kong Goodyear Printing Co., that the managing director was a native of Hong Kong and lived in Hong Kong, while the deputy managing director taking care of the operative management in the plant was a Chinese from the People's Republic. In another enterprise in the Shenzhen Special Economic Zone, the "Huaqiang Sanyo Electronics Co. Ltd," a joint venture with the Hong Kong Sanyo Company, the general managing director was a Japanse and the deputy managing director of the plant was a Chinese. The important strategic decisions of both these firms were made by their board of directors, situated in Hong Kong. Probably the most important decisions for the firm belonging to the great Japanese Sanyo concern came from Japan.

The management structure and measures in these Shenzhen firms deviated considerably from those in other parts of China. There were, for example, no workers' congresses in these firms, and the proportion of CPC members in the whole personnel was lower than in other parts of China; e.g., in the Shenzhen Goodyear Printing Co. it was 7.7%, compared to 13.2% in the interviewed enterprises in other parts of China.

3. An important right given quite early to the enterprises in the SEZ was the possibility to use the labor contract system in recruiting personnel, and to elect qualified workers through exams. When a person is being accepted both the enterprise and the employee sign a contract.

4. Enterprises are also allowed to pay floating wages and salaries or to pay by the piece. The income level for workers developed quite differently from that of other parts of China. In the two enterprises I visited in the Shenzhen SEZ, for example, the mean of the lowest wage paid to a worker was 165 yuan (US$ 42), the mean of the highest 250, and the average worker's wage 210. The corresponding wages for six enterprises in other parts of China were: lowest 47 yuan (US$ 13), highest 140 yuan (US$ 36), while the average worker's wage was 68 yuan (US$ 17; see Fig. 5.15). Thus,

it was no wonder that access to the Special Economic Zones, those El-dorados in the eyes of the Chinese, was strictly restricted and required special passports from the Chinese. Otherwise there would have been a huge "gold rush" which would have disturbed the whole idea of the SEZ.

5. A largely market-regulated system of prices has been established, on condition that prices remain relatively stable (B. R., January 23, 1984).

As mentioned, the Chinese government has given the SEZ many rights which greatly encourage foreign trade and investments in these areas. At the same time these zones form an excellent training field for Chinese managers concerning much more versatile business in a very changing environment than has been the case in the earlier, from the management point of view quite safe, centrally guided planned economy, where the manager has only to follow the plans and orders from above. In the independent SEZ enterprises the Chinese manager has alone to decide matters, e.g., concerning marketing, acquisition, prices, export and import, and personnel policies. Quite a challenging situation, especially for managers whose earlier formal education and practical training have hardly at all dealt with this kind of "new" problem.

Against this background we see that Chinese leaders have intentionally or unintentionally gradually created an integrated national development system, which began with the first four SEZ in 1980. During the same period more autonomy and decision-making power was given to enterprises in "main interior China," which pointed in the same direction as the enterprise autonomy in the SEZ. When this development was somewhat consolidated, the Chinese continued to advance on three fronts: First, in 1984 by giving 14 more coastal cities and later on almost the whole Chinese coastal area privileges concerned with doing international business. Second, after the consolidation period described, the State Council confirmed the earlier experimental rights, the so-called ten rights, to cover all state industrial enterprises in the country. Third, China's leaders gave seven great industrial cities (Chongqing, Dalian, Guangzhou, Harbin, Shenyang, Wuhan, and Xian) the special powers of a province concerning planning. Their economic and social development plans are separate in the state plan. Their enterprises, formerly under the administration of 22 ministries and their own provinces, are now under the management of the city.

The provincial level decision-making powers of these cities include foreign trade. For example, Chongqing has set up its own customs and a commodities inspection house. It has the right to conduct trade talks, bid for prices, sign contracts, and close accounts in foreign currencies, all independently. In 1983 Chongqing had already developed trade with 38 countries and regions in less than a year (B. R., November 12, 1984).

Thus, there has been considerable decentralization of decision-making at both the local and enterprise level. In Chapter 6 we will examine in more detail how this decentralization to enterprise level has appeared in practice in the distribution of influence among different interest groups of enterprises. At the same time we will get a more concrete picture, based on empirical material, of the management of Chinese industrial enterprises, and will compare the situation with that in Europe and Japan.

5.7 Summary and Conclusions

Chapter 5 is the largest and main chapter of this book. In the following summary we concentrate mainly upon the period after the Cultural Revolution for the following reasons: First, we have already earlier in Section 5.5.9 given a kind of summary concerning the developments during the Cultural Revolution. Second, in the last main Chapter 7 we shall try to give an integrated summary of the development of Chinese management, and the main content of that chapter will be composed of the elements presented in Chapter 5. In limiting our focus here we try to avoid too frequent repetition.

The period of economic reforms after Mao has often been called China's new revolution, so profound have the changes been, especially compared to the period of the Cultural Revolution. Successful revolution nearly always means that new men take power. Thus, the new period after 1976 began first with the change in macromanagement, the top leaders of the country. Gradually the changing of managers proceeded to the provincial and local level, and soon also reached the microlevel; the majority of company and factory directors were changed, especially in large enterprises. The abolition of life-long tenure greatly helped this changing of wielders of hierarchical and often also personal power.

The reforms in enterprise management began cautiously in the province of Sichuan in 1978. Eight special rights were then granted to experimental enterprises. As the experiments proved to be successful, the State Council decided to extend them in 1979 throughout the country in state-owned enterprises. In 1984 the so-called ten rights were given to enterprises, giving more decision-making power to managers of the firms. It was also decided that the CPC committees, which earlier were the most powerful units in the enterprises, should concentrate on party affairs and not interfere in the day-to-day production and administrative affairs. Thus, the hierarchical power in the firms was removed from party managers and given to enterprise managers.

The new rights given to enterprise managers also greatly changed the management of human resources. Factory directors were given the right to appoint and dismiss cadres under them, and workers could be employed on the basis of examinations. The bonus system was retracted and the income of Chinese workers was made up of their basic wages and bonuses. Thus, the Chinese moved from using ideological rewards (power), which were typical under the Cultural Revolution, to economic rewards (power). The "new" wage system should clearly take into account the amount and quality of work done as well as its knowledge requirements.

At the same time the education of both workers and managers was greatly intensified. The government created special state examinations for enterprise managers. Knowledge resources (power) were extensively emphasized not only in enterprises, but in the whole country. Higher education was greatly intensified and students began to study especially subjects, such as economics and finance which had been greatly neglected during the Cultural Revolution, but which were important for carrying on the economic reforms at the central, provincial, local, and enterprise levels.

At the beginning of the economic reforms it was enthusiastically planned that the reestablished workers' congresses would get much power and, e.g., would elect the managers of the enterprises. After some, probably not very successful experiments, the last mentioned decision-making power was withdrawn from workers' congresses, and their possibility to influence important decision-making in enterprises became in practice quite modest. This development was also caused by a movement towards a new kind of one-man management system, where the top manager of the enterprise and factory had much influence in decision-making in firms.

The open-door policy was begun in 1980 by creating the first four Special Economic Zones, which in 1984 were extended to 14 more coastal cities. Later on almost the whole Chinese coastal area received privileges in doing international business. Although the main target of creating the SEZ was to encourage foreign trade and investments in these areas as well as the transfer modern technology to the country, it was also planned that these zones would form a training field for Chinese managers.

Perhaps the most far-reaching decision made in connection with the economic and political reforms after Mao was to separate CPC administration from the management of enterprises and government organizations. This will not only affect enterprise management as mentioned earlier, but will also have great impact upon the Chinese macrolevel power structure, and can with time, if extensively implemented, have profound effects upon other socialist countries and gradually upon the whole global power balance between capitalist and socialist blocs in the world.

The economic reforms have also changed the ownership-structure of the Chinese economy. The share of the state-owned enterprises has declined significantly and that of firms under collective ownership has grown correspondingly. Also there are signs of the initial growth of individually owned industries. The dislocation of ownership of enterprises or economic resources means also changes in the entire power structure of the country.

In Table 5.16 we try to summarize the changes in power structure of enterprises after the Cultural Revolution. The main change concerning resource powers (see Appendix) is the move from the use of ideological power in guiding organizations and their employees to the applying of economic power to motivate both managers and other personnel groups. The use of personal power has not changed much; only the macrolevel wielder of this power has changed from Mao to Deng Xiaoping in the 1980s. However, the new one-man management system gives an opportunity to use more personal power than before.

The visible use of arms power to calm down the extreme phenomena of the Cultural Revolution has perhaps declined, although Deng in a way showed during the 35th Anniversary celebration of the PRC in Beijing on October 1, 1984, that he had the army backing him, when he alone inspected the parading troops on that day at the Tian'an Men square in sight of hundreds of millions of TV viewers around the world.

The use of knowledge resources has undergone profound changes since the Cultural Revolution, when China was a strictly closed system trying to rely only upon her own knowledge resources. One main reason for the open-door policy in the 1980s was to attract modern technology and also modern management know-how to the country.

Concerning the use of instrumental powers we notice that in applying hierarchical power the Chinese have heavily decentralized the decision-making at the micro- or enterprise level. The use of norm power has probably increased also at the enterprise level, because much new legislation and many new directions (norms) are needed at the micro-, meso-, and macrolevels to guide enterprises. As will be recalled, the use of norm power was in a way dual during the Cultural Revolution: the CPC system was directed by means of strict norms, whereas in the enterprises efforts were made to keep production rolling free from norm bureaucracy.

In the use of communication power, a duality could also be observed during the Cultural Revolution. The flow of information regarding the political or CPC system was severely regulated, whereas efforts were made in the enterprises' production and administration system to make communication as open and lively as possible both horizontally and vertically. After the economic reforms we could notice a great opening of the doors also for communication. The slogan of modernization requires new information

Table 5.16. Changes in the power structure of Chinese enterprises after the Cultural Revolution (this author's subjective judgement)

Period	Resource powers			Knowledge power	Arms power	Instrumental powers		
	Economic power	Ideological power	Personal power			Hierarchical power	Norm power	Communication power
During the Cultural Revolution	–	+++	+	–	++	–	+	++
After the economic reforms	+++	+	+	+++	+	+	++	+

+++ = Used very much
++ = Used much
+ = Some use
– = No or little use (indicating a negative attitude toward the use of the power concerned)

flows into enterprises from the outside world, especially concerning new production techniques and management systems. On the other hand, the free flow of information is still limited to certain areas, and the flow of political and ideological communication is to a great extent still regulated within certain frameworks. Therefore the sign "+" appears in Table 5.16 in the column of "communication power."

How were the methods of influence changed with the economic reforms? I would argue that the main ways management influenced other actors during the Cultural Revolution were indoctrination with ideological power, and manipulation using communication power (Fig. A. 3). These forms of influence were backed by coercion when needed. After economic reforms the main method of influence has been socioeconomic exchange in using, e.g., bonuses under the slogan "to reward everybody according to his/her work performance." Some manipulation through communication power is still being used as is indoctrination, but to a lesser degree than previously. For example, in the university where I was teaching in Beijing during the fall of 1986, every Friday afternoon two hours are spent on political education given by the CPC secretary of the faculty in question.

However, we can conclude that the general organizational climate has profoundly changed in China compared to the time of the Cultural Revolution. This has been achieved mainly by great changes in the use of both different resource and instrumental powers, as well as changes in the methods of influence.

6. Chinese Management in Cross-National Context: Comparison with Europe and Japan

6.1 Purpose of the Analysis

We have examined in some detail management in the government, CPC, and enterprises. As management in these three systems in the People's Republic has been closely linked, and as this linkage has changed during the 1980s, we now examine how these developments appear in decision-making in enterprises. First, we study the influence of different interest groups upon decision-making in Chinese enterprises, and how this influence has changed, comparing our data from interviews in 1980 and 1984. Second, we compare the influence structure of Chinese enterprises with European and Japanese firms.

In a way this empirical study is like a summary concerning Chinese enterprise management compared with management in other countries. Thus, the analysis is enlarged to cross-country and in a sense cross-cultural analysis as we come closer to the end of our study.

6.2 Data and Method of Comparisons

The Chinese enterprises included in this analysis are described earlier in Chapter 1.2, according to size and type of industry. To obtain a comparative picture of the influence of personnel and other interest groups in the decision-making process in enterprises, I used the same measure as was used by the Industrial Democracy in Europe (IDE) International Research Group in a study involving 11 European countries plus Israel. Following this method I interviewed expert informants in Chinese enterprises selected from among managers, the CPC, and sometimes also union representatives, about the influence which organizational and other interest groups have in 16 specified decisions.

In the analysis the decisions were grouped according to their main content and time perspective into: (1) working conditions (short-term), (2) policy decisions (medium-term), and (3) strategic decisions (long-term). The decisions appear in Table 6.2, and are the same as in the international IDE study. The influence measure used was a mixture of the so-called reputational approach and the decision-making approach for measuring influence (Bachrach and Baratz 1970; Tannenbaum 1968).

In the "reputational approach" the respondents are asked how much influence they and others generally have in an organization. This approach has been criticized, e.g., because not all respondents know the "real" influence structure of the organization, and different respondents connect the evaluated influence with different matters and different decision areas. To avoid these problems in the IDE and this study, on the one hand the persons interviewed were selected from among those experts in the enterprises who should know the influence of different interest groups. On the other hand, the respondents were not asked generally about the influence of different groups, but specifically, how much influence they considered different groups had concerning the 16 specified decision matters.

The last-mentioned "decision-making approach" contains the problem that some important decision matters have perhaps been omitted. From a comparative point of view it helps if the evaluated matters are specified. In cross-national comparisons this of course requires that the decisions used are relevant and meaningful in the enterprises of all countries concerned. According to experience from the 12-country IDE study (Industrial Democracy in Europe (IDE) International Research Group 1981a, b), and from my studies in China (Laaksonen 1984a) the measure used has proved to be relevant and sufficiently meaningful.

We must remember that the whole concept "influence" is a very complicated one, and there arise problems of validity in using it. Though theoretically one can examine the concept as multidimensional, we have considered it as unidimensional through our operational definition, in which the word "influence" is used without further explanation. In our semistructured interview we asked the expert respondents: "How much influence do the different groups have over this decision?" Rus argues that some respondents may understand the word influence positively, some negatively, and some in both ways (Rus 1980). There is also the possibility that some respondents have understood the word to mean only behaviorally exercised attempts to influence, and that others have understood it as a more latent relationship (power) based on control over resources (IDE 1981a: 146).

Thus, it is possible that our data could reflect different kinds of influence: that which is defined as a dependence relationship, that defined as a resource-based relationship, and that based on the involvement of employees (IDE 1981a: 147). However, because I myself conducted all the interviews in China both in 1980 and 1984, and I stressed the involvement aspect of the concept of influence, or how the different personnel and other interest groups are really involved in the decisions asked about, I hope that some consistency was achieved. When one tries to make international comparisons and thus use the same measures which have to be translated into different languages, one has, of course, to face semantic problems arising, e.g., from translation.

The gathering of the data from China in 1980 and 1984 differed from the European IDE study in that in the latter the interviews of both managers and union representatives were made separately, whereas in China the interviews were made in a group situation, where representatives of managers, the CPC, and often the union were present. While unions do not have the same importance and influence in China as in European capitalist countries, the Chinese managers interviewed especially in 1980 were usually also officials or members of the enterprise CPC committee, so they should have had an overall view, from their particular vantage point, of the influence of different interest groups in their organizations.

When there was more than one person present at the interviews in China, I had the feeling that the other persons were not checking the answers of the managers interviewed, but were specialists giving detailed information on questions concerning wages, fringe benefits, etc. The measure of influence was written both in English and Chinese. One person in every organization (the manager or similarly appropriate person) filled in the Chinese form by putting a cross (sign) in the relevant place, representing his/her evaluation of influence of each interest group for each of the 16 questions asked. This was done under my guidance without any direct interpreting or other mediating procedures. Only at first, before the filling out of the forms, the interpreter went briefly through the forms to explain what, e.g., was meant by different interest groups – workers, foremen, middle management, top management, etc. Concerning the reliability and validity of the data, it must be said once more – this applies also to the European as well as the Japanese study – that as usual in this kind of research venture, it was not possible to use conventional research sampling procedures in selecting the enterprises studied or persons interviewed. As mentioned earlier, they were selected by the Chinese hosts according to my expressed wishes concerning the field and size of the firms.

It was a pity that I could not, for practical reasons not dependent on myself, study all the same firms in 1980 and 1984. As mentioned in Chapter 1.2, four of the interviewed enterprises were the same in 1980 and 1984, but only two of these represented industry and could thus be included in the following comparative analysis concerning the influence structure of enterprises. I have, however, separately analyzed these two firms and found, when comparing their results to the results of the enterprises included in the analysis, that the results were largely the same with regard to both the values of means, and their differences. In this connection it should be mentioned that many of the figures for 1980 are taken from my article in Organization Studies, 5/1, 1984.

When comparing organizations in different cultures, one of the key problems is the validity of measures. Did the 16 questions and the different personnel groups mean the same things to Chinese and European interviewees? And, as mentioned earlier, one must consider the problem of translation. It would need a separate study to examine this thoroughly, but, contrary to my assumptions, the Chinese interviewees quite quickly understood the relevance of the structured interview questions and form in Chinese. Moreover, since most of them were in contact with this type of study for the first time, it would certainly have been very difficult for them to manipulate the results through their answers, because they could not "see" how the results were constructed from 16 different questions (decisions) each concerning eight different interest groups on a five-point scale.

The best way to judge the results is to compare them internally, e.g., the influence of different hierarchical groups, and relate them to the qualitatively analyzed power structure of Chinese enterprises described in other chapters, and then to use the comparison with results of other similar studies such as IDE as a "compass reading" for their assessment. Looked at in these terms, I find the results sufficiently valid. I must add once more that in the interview situations there were no restrictions on my questions at any time. However, I would like to point out further that the empirical Chinese material used is relatively limited, and does not give statistical evidence for the results presented. One may ask, why present the results of this kind of limited material? I venture to say that I have succeeded in collecting – thanks to the helpfulness of the Chinese counterparts – unique empirical material from China during a very interesting period, when the entire society was changing rapidly. If we examine the material with sufficient care, relating the empirical quantitative results to other collected qualitative material, and to the announced changes in applied policy and norms, we can, I think, achieve reasonably reliable results.

6.3 Shift of Influence Structure After Mao

In this and the following subsections we shall examine how the influence of various interests groups in decision-making in Chinese enterprises has changed since Mao between 1980 and 1984. This examination gives us a picture of how the new economic reforms have affected the influence structure of enterprises. At the same time we get an idea of the decision-making processes in Chinese enterprises. We speak here about influence rather than power, because in interview situations the respondents were asked their evaluation of the "real" influence of the various interest groups in decision-making, not the potential influence of the groups, which would have referred more to the concept of power according to our definition.

From Table 6.1 we see how the distribution of influence changed between 1980 and 1984, when the economic reforms had already begun to have an impact upon enterprises. In this table the 16 decisions are grouped in three different types according to the contents or time perspective. We call the decision types here according to their contents decisions concerning working conditions (short-term), policy decisions (medium-term), and strategic decisions (long-term). The decision types are aggregate variables formed (containing questions), as shown in Table 6.2, where the means of all 16 questions are presented according to different interest groups.

There were eight industrial enterprises in China from which I collected complete material regarding the influence of different groups in decision-making. However, two of these were enterprises situated in the Special Economic Zone of Shenzhen. They were both joint ventures with large foreign enterprises. The management and influence structure of these enterprises differed greatly from those situated in interior China, because enterprises in the special economic zones (SEZ) have their special privileges concerning the management of enterprises, and because the foreign ownership also considerably affected their management. Therefore I have left them out of the main analysis, and the Chinese material thus contains six enterprises in the following tables. Later we shall compare the two SEZ enterprises with firms located in interior China.

Because the enterprises studied in 1980 and 1984 are not all the same, as explained earlier, we cannot make a very exact comparison between 1980 and 1984, but certainly from the results we can see some of the main changes.

The main change according to Table 6.1 concerns the influence of the party committee of the enterprise, which has lessened most of all the interest groups studied in every decision type. The decrease has been greatest in important strategic decisions, from the mean of 2.5 in 1980 to 1.3 in 1984. This development probably shows the results of the economic reforms, which included the principle that enterprise, CPC, and government administration should be separated. Concerning the CPC, this certainly seems to have happened, but the influence of the government body – usually a local industrial bureau – has not decreased so much, though a little in every decision type. Thus, it seems that the main idea was in the first instance to separate the CPC from the management of enterprises. Earlier the CPC's

Table 6.1. Distribution of influence across levels and decision types in industrial enterprises in China (C) in 1980[a] and 1984[b], in means[c]; and differences between means of groups D (top Management) and A (workers)

Decision type	A Workers		B Foremen		C Middle managers		D Top management		E CPC commitee		F Labor union		G[d] Government body		H[e] Workers congress	Differences D-A	
	1980	1984	1980	1984	1980	1984	1980	1984	1980	1984	1980	1984	1980	1984	1984	1980	1984
Working conditions[f]	1.4	1.2	2.3	2.2	3.1	2.8	3.8	3.7	2.1	1.4	1.4	1.4	1.9	1.7	1.6	2.4	2.5
Policy decisions[g]	1.8	1.5	1.8	1.4	2.4	1.7	3.9	3.9	2.7	2.0	1.3	1.5	2.5	2.0	1.9	2.1	2.4
Strategic decisions[h]	1.2	1.1	1.3	1.2	2.1	1.5	4.2	3.9	2.5	1.3	1.3	1.1	3.8	3.5	1.5	3.0	2.8
All 16 decisions	1.6	1.3	2.0	1.7	2.6	2.2	3.9	3.8	2.4	1.6	1.4	1.4	2.4	2.1	1.7	2.3	2.5

Source: This author's interviews in Chinese enterprises in 1980 and 1984

[a] Nine industrial enterprises
[b] Six industrial enterprises
[c] Scale: 1 = no influence; 2 = little influence; 3 = moderate influence; 4 = much influence; 5 = very much influence
[d] Government body immediately above the enterprise, e. g., local industrial bureau
[e] Question not asked in 1980
[f] Working conditions = decisions nos. 1, 4, 5, 10, 12, and 16 in Table 6.2
[g] Policy decisions = decisions nos. 2, 3, 8, 9, 11, 13, and 14
[h] Strategic decisions = decisions nos. 6 and 7

involvement in the management of firms undoubtedly caused a lot of duplicated work and inefficiency.

Where then has the earlier influence of the party been transferred; to the hands of enterprise managers? If we look at the means of top management we see that there are minor changes in their influence, and the changes are downwards. I come here to the following interpretation: Probably the influence of the top management has in practice increased according to their position as managers, but as they were usually also first or second secretaries of the powerful CPC committee earlier, they have, in the evaluation of the experts interviewed, lost the CPC part of their earlier influence in a way.

This interpretation is confirmed by the figures in Table 6.3, which show the differences of means between top management (D) and other interest groups in 1980 and 1984. According to this the influence position of top managers in relation to their subordinated personnel groups in enterprises has not changed essentially. As mentioned earlier, the main change appears in relation to the CPC committee, especially concerning strategic decisions. The difference of the influence between top management and CPC committee rose in strategic decisions from 1.7 to 2.6 between 1980 and 1984. This difference does not, however, mean that the top managers had relatively so much less influence in enterprises in 1980. We must remember that earlier, to ensure their influence in often changing circumstances, the general managers of the firms were usually also first or second secretaries of the CPC committee.

The CPC committee of the enterprise was earlier the most powerful unit in the firm. If the general manager of the firm was at the same time the first secretary ("chairman") of the enterprise CPC committee (1 in Table 6.4) he had concentrated influence very much in his hands. Table 6.4 confirms this; if we look at the means of all 16 decisions we see that they all show less influence for 1 than for 2 (the general manager is vice-secretary or only a member of the CPC committee) except for top management (usually general manager in the Chinese one-man management system) and labor unions. The same is also true concerning nearly all different decision types except decisions on working conditions made by a government body, and strategic decisions made by a labor union. However, these exceptional differences are only 0.1 and 0.2. It is noticeable that in both groups (1 and 2) and all decision types the influence of the labor union is not even "little" according to the scale. However, we must stress that the numbers of enterprises in the two groups are only three and six, so the results are merely suggestive.

What they suggest is that when the general manager was also the first secretary (1) of the CPC committee, decision-making power over working

Table 6.2. Distribution of influence across levels and decisions in China in 1980[a] and 1984[b] (in means); for details see Table 6.1.

Decisions No.	A Workers		B Foremen		C Middle managers		D Top management		E CPC committee		F Labor union		G Government body		H Workers' congress
	1980	1984	1980	1984	1980	1984	1980	1984	1980	1984	1980	1984	1980	1984	1984
1. Improvements in working conditions of a work group	2.0	1.7	2.2	2.2	3.2	3.0	4.8	4.5	3.0	1.2	2.1	2.2	3.9	4.0	3.3
2. Appointment of a new department head	1.6	1.2	1.7	1.0	2.2	1.0	4.4	4.8	3.7	2.7	1.1	1.3	2.9	1.0	1.7
3. Establishment of criteria and procedures for hiring and selection of new employees	1.1	1.0	1.1	1.0	1.2	1.0	3.6	3.5	2.7	1.2	1.0	1.2	4.6	4.3	1.2
4. Whether workers can follow a vocational training course (during work hours)	1.2	1.2	2.1	1.7	3.1	3.0	4.2	4.8	3.7	2.5	2.0	2.0	3.1	1.5	1.5
5. Permanent transfer of workers to other jobs within the plant	1.3	1.0	1.4	1.3	3.7	2.8	4.2	4.8	2.6	1.8	1.2	1.0	1.4	1.0	1.0
6. Major capital investment, e.g., an additional production line, a new plant, etc.	1.1	1.0	1.3	1.0	2.0	1.0	4.2	3.0	2.6	1.5	1.3	1.2	4.6	4.8	1.7
7. Whether the company should make a completely new product	1.5	1.2	1.5	1.3	2.5	2.0	4.6	4.8	2.9	1.0	1.3	1.0	3.4	2.2	1.3

Decision															
8. To establish who will be one's immediate superior	2.2	3.0	1.7	1.8	1.5	1.8	2.0	1.0	2.3	1.3	2.1	1.3	2.0	2.2	3.6
9. Changes in how much a certain grade (wage group) shall earn	1.0	1.0	3.2	1.0	1.0	1.0	3.9	3.8	4.3	2.3	2.8	1.5	2.1	1.2	2.1
10. Replacement of personal equipment (hand tools) of the workers	1.7	1.2	1.2	1.5	1.1	3.0	1.0	1.0	3.2	3.2	3.8	3.2	2.9	1.4	1.9
11. Change in the way one or more departments are organized	1.0	1.0	2.2	1.0	1.0	1.0	2.9	4.8	4.6	1.7	1.8	1.2	1.1	1.2	1.1
12. Assignment of tasks to workers	3.2	1.8	1.2	2.0	1.8	2.2	1.7	1.6	2.4	3.3	3.2	3.5	3.6	1.0	1.3
13. Dismissal of one of the workers	1.7	1.0	2.8	1.3	1.3	1.0	3.3	4.0	4.3	2.2	2.7	1.6	1.7	1.2	1.6
14. Whether or not work study technique is to be used	1.0	1.0	1.6	1.0	1.6	1.0	1.6	4.8	3.4	2.8	3.9	2.2	2.8	2.2	1.4
15. From when to when one can go on a holiday	1.7	1.7	1.0	1.0	1.1	1.0	1.0	3.8	3.1	3.5	2.8	2.7	2.8	1.7	1.2
16. From when to when are the working hours	1.7	1.2	1.2	1.0	1.0	1.0	1.6	4.8	4.7	1.4	1.8	1.2	1.2	1.0	1.1
All 16 decisions	1.7	2.1	2.4	1.4	1.4	1.6	2.4	3.8	3.9	2.2	2.6	1.7	2.0	1.3	1.6

a Nine enterprises
b Six enterprises (firms located in Special Economic Zones (SEZ) not included)

Table 6.3. Differences of means of working conditions and strategic decisions between top management and other interest groups in 1980 and 1984

Top management (D) Minus:		Working conditions decisions		Strategic decisions	
		1980	1984	1980	1984
Middle managers	(D–C)	0.7	0.9	2.1	2.4
Foremen	(D–B)	1.5	1.5	2.9	2.7
Workers	(D–A)	2.4	2.5	3.0	2.8
CPC committee	(D–E)	1.7	2.3	1.7	2.6
Labor union	(D–F)	2.4	2.3	2.9	2.8
Government body	(D–G)	1.9	2.0	0.4	0.4
Workers' congress	(D–H)		2.1		2.4

Table 6.4. Distribution of influence across levels above foreman, by decision type, in Chinese enterprises where the general manager was either first secretary (1[a]) or second secretary, or only a Member (2[b]) of the CPC committee of the firm in means relative to 1980 data

Decision type	Middle managers		Top man-agement		CPC committee		Labor union		Govern-ment body	
	1	2	1	2	1	2	1	2	1	2
Working conditions	2.9	3.2	4.0	3.7	1.7	2.2	1.7	1.4	1.9	1.8
Policy decisions	2.1	2.4	4.1	3.7	2.6	2.8	1.9	1.2	2.5	2.6
Strategic decisions	1.8	2.2	4.7	3.9	2.0	2.8	1.2	1.4	3.0	4.2
All decisions	2.4	2.7	4.1	3.7	2.1	2.5	1.7	1.2	2.3	3.4

[a] Three enterprises
[b] Six enterprises

conditions and policy decisions was concentrated in him and he was able to hold all the strings. When the general manager was also the highest CPC boss in the enterprise, middle managers did not dare to make decisions independently, but waited for the decisions from him, and thus the work had to wait also, which could cause great inefficiency. Perhaps this was one of the main reasons why the CPC and enterprise administration was separated later on.

The differences of means between top management and the personnel groups subordinated to it can also be seen in Table 6.3 as presenting a degree of delegation. The smaller the differences, the greater the grade of delegation in decision-making and vice versa. We notice that there are not great changes in this matter in relation to workers and foremen between

1980 and 1984. In the case of middle managers there is a slightly increased difference in strategic decisions from 2.1 in 1980 to 2.4 in 1984, which means decreased delegation from top management to middle managers. Although the difference is not especially remarkable, it may contain a sign of a changed leadership process: First, the general managers had become more independent of CPC control and, second, they were now more personally responsible for the profits and losses of their enterprises; thus, they began to control more tightly the level directly under them, middle management.

Although the Chinese firms and their managers have been freed from the tight control of the CPC, the other controlling "line," the state administration, has more or less remained at the level shown by the figures in Table 6.3. The influence differences concerning strategic decisions are the same and quite small both in 1980 and 1984, namely 0.4. According to the principles of the economic reforms, enterprises and so also their managers were to become more autonomous in their relations to government bodies. The idea was that enterprises ought to be managed inside the relatively loose frames of central guidance. Probably this tendency towards greater independence from government control has not yet – at least by the end of 1984 – proceeded very far.

Though in all 16 decisions the influence of top management changed hardly at all between 1980 and 1984 (means of 3.9 and 3.8 in Table 6.1), there were changes in some of the decisions within these overall means.

If we consider these individual decisions in which the influence of factory managers increased most, 0.4 or more, between 1980 and 1984, we see from Table 6.5 that all these decisions concern personnel matters. There are at least the following reasons for this development: (1) Human resources are in a key position when developing the efficiency and profitability of the firm, for which the managers are, according to the economic reforms, more responsible than earlier; (2) those who have power over the personnel also have power over the enterprise; (3) top management has in a way inherited the power of the CPC committee in these personnel decisions because these were the ones in which the CPC committee had the highest influence in 1980.

The idea that he who would like to change the organization has first to change the persons in key positions is not new. Thus, the new wielders of power after Mao first changed the leading cadres in government and the CPC at the macrolevel. Then, when the reforms proceeded down to microlevels, it was time to change the enterprise managers, as we have described earlier.

From the point of view mentioned, the appointment of new persons to superior positions plays a key role. We see from Table 6.5 that when top

Table 6.5. Decisions where the influence of top management has increased most between 1980 and 1984 (means)

Decision No.	Top management		CPC committee		Government body		Middle managers		Workers	
	1980	1984	1980	1984	1980	1984	1980	1984	1980	1984
2 Appointment of new department	4.4	4.8	3.7	2.7	2.9	1.0	2.2	1.0	1.6	1.2
4 Whether the workers can follow a training course during working hours	4.2	4.8	3.7	2.5	3.1	1.5	3.1	3.0	1.2	1.2
5 Transfers to another job	4.2	4.8	2.6	1.8	1.4	1.0	3.7	2.8	1.3	1.0
14 Whether work study technique is to be used	3.4	4.8	1.6	1.0	1.6	1.0	3.9	2.8	1.4	2.2
15 When one can go on holiday	3.1	3.8	1.0	1.0	1.0	1.0	2.8	3.5	1.2	1.7
All 16 decisions	3.9	3.8	2.4	1.6	2.4	2.1	2.6	2.2	1.6	1.3

management has gained more influence in deciding on "Appointment of new department head," all the other groups appearing in the table have lost very much decision-making power; not only the CPC committee, but especially the government body above the enterprise. The influence of the latter had fallen from 2.9 in 1980 to 1.0 in 1984, which means "no influence." The decrease in influence in this decision has also been great among middle managers, who were mostly workshop heads.

Figure 6.1 shows that the one-man management system appears clearly in the Chinese appointing system of enterprises. Thus, the manager of the factory nominates the director of the workshop, who again appoints the foremen or group leaders. I took as an example the Chongqing Rubber Factory because I visited it also in 1980, and interviewed the same person. Then it was clearly mentioned that the appointment of for directors for the workshops was made both by the manager of the factory and the CPC committee. In 1984 the CPC committee was not mentioned.

In 1980 the group leaders were elected by the workers, and the election was approved by the director of the workshop. This early experiment, which was according to the principles of the system of workers' congresses was, however, scrapped in the Rubber Factory as well as in many other enterprises interviewed after some, probably not very successful, experience.

My interviews in all enterprises showed that the Chinese have adopted a clear one-man management system – Chinese style. This is understandable because the manager is now mainly responsible for the profits and losses of the enterprise; great responsibility requires great authority.

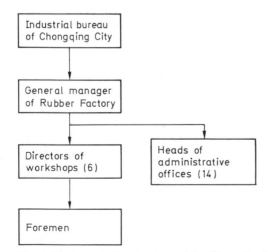

Fig. 6.1. Hierarchical appointing structure of the Chongqing Rubber Factory (1900 employees) in October 1984

6.3.1 Changes in Influence Coalitions After Mao

We have shown that to hold sufficient influence in his hands to guide the enterprise, the top manager often used to hold two important positions: that of the manager and that of the first or second secretary of the CPC committee. Thus, a strong influence coalition between the CPC and the operational management of the enterprise was concentrated in the manager's person; however, within the tight frame of central planning and control. Thus, the third center of influence in 1980, in addition to the CPC and the manager, was the government body above the enterprise, normally the local industrial bureau.

In Table 6.6 it can be seen, from the values of the interlevel correlations, that in 1980, when the reforms had not yet been effectively applied in firms, two influence coalitions could be found in Chinese enterprises: the first at the bottom of the organizational hierarchy: between workers, foremen, and middle managers. Corresponding correlations were in the same order: 0.58 and 0.31. We call this the internal lower influence coalition (Mintzberg 1983: 116 ff.). The second coalition was at the top of the hierarchy between top management and the CPC committee ($r = 0.59$). We call this the mixed higher coalition, where both internal (top management) and external (CPC through CPC committee) were represented. The CPC committee can be looked upon as being half an external influencer, because it largely carried out CPC orders given from "above" the enterprise (Fig. 6.2).

If we consider the creation of these two coalitions, we could argue that the second one, including top management and the CPC committee, was more or less consciously formed, probably at the initiative of top management; whereas the internal lower coalition between workers, foremen, and middle managers was not consciously formed, but was merely a result of the coalition at the top – as a counter power – and simply represented a picture of decision-making processes at levels under top management.

At the end of 1984 the influence structure looked quite different. The earlier mixed higher coalition between top management and CPC committee had altogether disappeared and changed to a field of opposite powers. Correlations in 1980 were positive (0.59), but in 1984 negative (-0.59). In the latter year there seems to have been one great internal influence coalition between top management, middle management, foremen, and workers (Fig. 6.2). The correlations between top management and the other three were in the order mentioned: 0.41, 0.72, and 0.65 (Table 6.6), and the same values as the chain: top management – middle managers (0.41) – foremen (0.48) – workers (0.54). This coalition is backed by the workers' congress and labor union. In both of these the workers are strongly represented.

Table 6.6. Interlevel correlation of influence for all decisions in Chinese industrial enterprises in 1980 and 1984 (Product moment correlations, which have been constructed from the means of ratings of 16 decisions concerning separately eight interest groups (A–H) in nine (1980) and six (1984) enterprises.)

		A 1980	A 1984	B 1980	B 1984	C 1980	C 1984	D 1980	D 1984	E 1980	E 1984	F 1980	F 1984	G 1980	G 1984
Workers	A														
Foremen	B	0.58	0.54												
Middle management	C	0.20	-0.04	0.31	0.48										
Top management	D	0.23	0.65	0.17	0.72	-0.11	0.41								
CPC committee	E	0.37	-0.41	0.06	-0.41	-0.07	-0.39	0.59	-0.59						
Labor union	F	0.09	0.39	-0.28	0.68	0.17	0.69	0.14	0.41	-0.07	-0.00				
Government body	G	0.18	-0.60	-0.24	-0.70	-0.28	-0.58	0.13	-0.84	0.18	0.23	0.06	-0.79		
Workers' congress	H		0.65		0.68		-0.25		0.43		0.09		0.36		-0.44

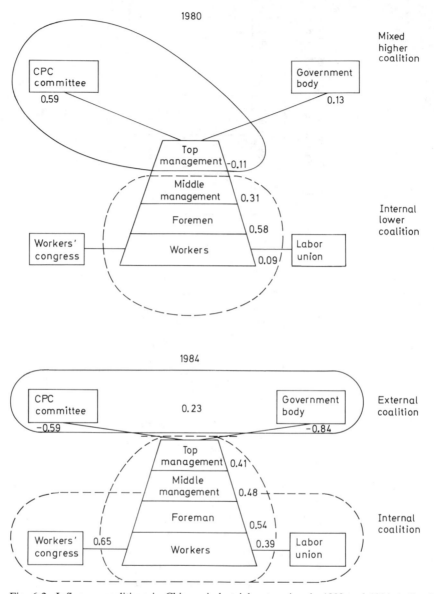

Fig. 6.2. Influence coalitions in Chinese industrial enterprises in 1980 and 1984; indicating correlation coefficients as 'binding' or 'separating' units of different coalitions

The only negative correlation in this group is between workers' congress and middle managers (-0.25). This is difficult to interpret, but it can be a weak sign of a power struggle between the workers' congress and workshop directors; perhaps the former limits the liberty of action of the workshop directors, who are also under tight control by top management, or factory directors.

In 1984 there was another, although weaker external coalition between the CPC committee and the government body above the enterprise (Fig. 6.2). The correlation between these was not especially high (0.23), but if we look at the correlations of these two organs with the "members" of the internal coalition, the values were without exception negative and relatively high. These two "great" coalitions in Chinese enterprises seemed to play the zero-sum game with each other, where the power of one came at the expense of the other. It appears in the clearest way in relations between top management and the CPC committee of the enterprise (-0.59) on the one hand and the government body above the firm ($r = -0.84$), on the other.

Thus, it can be quite clearly seen from the correlations that at the same time as the top management had become – according to the principles of the reforms – more autonomous in its decision-making, the other two, and especially the CPC committee, had lost their earlier influence. This came out clearly before, for example from Tables 6.1 and 6.2. The means of Table 6.1 showed that the CPC committee had lost its former influence equally in both working conditions and policy decisions (-0.7), but mostly in strategic decisions (-1.2). The government body again had more or less lost its influence equally in all decision types, but still had between "moderate" and "much" influence (mean 3.5) in strategic decisions.

If we examine the individual decisions in Table 6.2, we observe that in 1984 the government body had greatest influence in the decision concerning "Major capital investment, e.g., an additional production line, a new plant, etc." Its mean in this decision (4.8) corresponds closely to "Very much influence" (5). Since the corresponding mean for top management was 3.0 ("moderate influence") we realize that at the end of 1984 the government was especially controlling economic resources, or had great economic power. We must, however, remember that at the time of these interviews – at the end of 1984 – the new economic reforms concerning the autonomy of enterprises and their ability to decide themselves about investments from their own funds had been in force only a short time. If enterprises can for a longer period accumulate their own investment funds through profitable results, the opportunities for strategic decision-making by top management can become greater.

We must, however, here give a word of warning regarding the reliability of the data, because the number of enterprises both in 1980 and 1984 was small, nine and six. We have nevertheless presented the results here, first, because they greatly confirm what we have learned from interviews otherwise from the same enterprises, and also from enterprises from other fields, e.g., trade, and, second, and what is important, the results correspond well with the measures of the Chinese economic reforms. One of the main targets of the reforms was to change management practice. The data strongly hint that the present Chinese top leaders have succeeded in implementing their plans in practice.

6.3.2 Decision-Making in SEZ Enterprises

What we have learned about the more independent status of enterprise management in interior China, holds still more true in the firms of the Special Economic Zones (SEZ). As earlier described, one of the important reasons for establishing the SEZ was to learn modern management methods and train China's own management professionals. The argument was that if the management experience obtained from the SEZ proved successful, those systems would be quickly extended from the "open areas" over the whole country.

As I also conducted interviews at the end of 1984 in two industrial enterprises in the SEZ of Shenzhen, it is interesting to examine the data collected from these enterprises and compare the results to the corresponding data from firms of interior China. I make the comparison, although there were only two SEZ enterprises, because the results correspond well with the policy of economic reforms, and especially of that in the SEZ.

First, a short description of these two enterprises. As already mentioned, one of the firms, the Shenzhen Goodyear Printing Co. Ltd., was a joint venture with the Hong Kong Goodyear Printing Co. The firm was producing chromolithographs as advertising material, and paper boxes for packaging. It had three workshops in Shenzhen, and the total number of employees was 260, of whom 40% were female. The firm had a board of directors which, along with the managing director, functioned in Hong Kong. The enterprise was established in 1980.

The other SEZ firm studied was the Huaqiang Sanyo Electronics Co. Ltd., which was also a joint venture, but with a Japanese firm: the Hong Kong Sanyo Co. The main products were color television sets and tape recorders. The company had two factories in Shenzhen: one producing television sets and the other tape recorders. The total number of employees was 850, of whom 40% were female. This firm also had a board of directors working in Hong Kong. The board nominated the factory directors and heads of workshops and staff departments. The foremen were appointed by the factory director.

Table 6.7 shows an influence structure that seems quite different in the two SEZ firms compared to enterprises in interior China. First, in the SEZ joint venture enterprises the middle managers have much more decision-making power than their counterparts in interior China. This especially concerns working conditions and policy decisions. If we study the individual decisions, the middle managers had "much" or "very much" influence in decisions on "hiring new employees" (mean 4.5), "dismissals" (4.5), "transfers" (5.0), "whether work study technique should be used" (4.5), "assignment of tasks" (5.0), and "replacement of personal equipment" (5.0). Thus, the top management in the SEZ had delegated much more decision-making power to middle managers than their counterparts had in interior China. This delegation also concerned many decisions on personnel mat-

Table 6.7. Distribution of influence across levels and decision type in industrial enterprises in interior China (IC[a]) and in the Special Economic Zone (SEZ) of Shenzhen[b] (means); and differences between means of groups D (top management) and A (workers); and between D and C (middle managers)

Decision type	A Workers		B Foremen		C Middle		D Top Manager	
	IC	SEZ	IC	SEZ	IC	SEZ	IC	SEZ
1. Working conditions	1.2	1.3	2.2	2.1	2.8	3.8	3.7	2.8
2. Policy decisions	1.5	1.0	1.4	1.2	1.7	2.6	3.9	4.1
3. Strategic decisions	1.1	1.0	1.2	1.0	1.5	2.0	3.9	4.0
4. All 16 decisions	1.3	1.1	1.7	1.6	2.2	3.1	3.8	3.5

	E CPC committee		F Labor union		G Government body		H Workers' congress		Differences D–A		D–C	
	IC	SEZ	IC	SEZ	IC	SEZ	IC	SEZ	IC	SEZ	IC	SEZ
1.	1.4	1.3	1.4	1.2	1.7	1.4	1.6	–	2.5	1.5	0.9	−1.0
2.	2.0	1.1	1.5	1.0	2.2	1.5	1.9	–	2.4	3.1	2.2	1.5
3.	1.3	1.0	1.1	1.0	3.5	1.0	1.5	–	2.8	3.0	2.4	2.0
4.	1.6	1.1	1.4	1.1	2.1	1.4	1.7	–	2.5	2.4	1.6	0.4

[a] Six enterprises
[b] Two enterprises

ters as described above. But in the most important personnel decisions such as "appointment of a new department head," "changes in how much a certain grade (wage group) shall earn," and "change in the way one or more departments are organized," top management seemed to keep the main strings in their hands, because in all these decisions the mean of top management was 5.0. This is very reminiscent of the practice of European capitalist organizations, as we will see later in the next section. This is understandable, because the SEZ firms studied were joint ventures with capitalistic enterprises from Hong Kong, and one of these was, from its roots, Japanese.

The degree of delegation by top management appears in the last two columns of Table 6.7, where differences between the means of top management (D) and of workers (A) and middle managers (C) are shown. As will be remembered, the smaller the difference the greater the grade of delegation. Concerning the middle managers the "amount" of delegation seems to be in all decision types greater in the SEZ than in interior China, but concerning workers the same holds true only regarding decisions on working conditions. This could be interpreted that in SEZ enterprises the delegation is more differentiated according to the substance of the decision matter, and thus reflects a clearer division of work and authority between different hierarchical groups related to decision matters. In interior China the top managers seem to be bosses in all matters, perhaps reflecting the traditional Chinese authoritative culture.

Above we examined the differences between top managers' influence related to personnel groups directly under them. The second great difference between the SEZ enterprises and firms in interior China lay in the relations of top management on the one hand and the CPC committee, labor union, and workers' congress, and the government body above the enterprise, on the other hand. With regard to the workers' congress, neither of the two enterprises had one. In one enterprise they answered that "They did not yet have a workers' congress," and in the other they said that "They have a trade union," meaning that this body took care of corresponding matters as necessary. The power of labor unions in decision-making was small. Considering the individual 16 decisions separately, the labor union had in all other decisions "no influence" (1.0), except in the decisions concerning improvements in working conditions, where it had "little influence" (2.0).

It was interesting to learn that the CPC committee of the enterprise also mostly had "no influence" – in 12 decisions out of the 16. Only in the decision "Whether workers can follow a vocational training course (during working hours)" did the CPC committee have "little influence" (2.0).

The only body outside the internal hierarchy of the enterprise which seemed to have some influence in decision-making in the SEZ enterprises was the government body above the enterprise, or the local industrial bureau. Its "total influence" concerning all 16 decisions was, however, clearly lower in SEZ enterprises than in firms of interior China. In examining the individual decisions separately, we learned that the government body had "moderate influence" only in decisions involving personnel matters. The highest mean (3.5) was in the decision concerning the hiring of new employees. This is understandable, because, on the one hand, the Chinese tie foreign enterprises to the Special Economic Zones by cheap labor, and, on the other hand, the Chinese authorities have to exercise strict control over the labor trying to come to the SEZ areas from interior China, because there would be millions of workers seeking to benefit from these Chinese Eldorados.

It is remarkable that the Chinese authorities in the SEZ do not seem to control the capital investment of joint-venture firms. The mean of this decision was 1.0 or "no influence." In interior China it was this decision concerning major capital investments which the government body controlled most strictly; the mean was 4.8, indicating "very much influence."

We have examined the influence structure of SEZ enterprises here in some detail, although the interview material included only two enterprises. The reason is that these Special Economic Zones have interested foreigners very much, and there have often been questions about whether the Chinese promises will really hold concerning the special status and great autonomy of the wholly or partly foreign-owned enterprises in these areas. My own experience suggested that the Chinese really had given foreign and joint-venture enterprises in the SEZ plenty of elbow room in decision-making, as they had promised.

6.4 Comparison of Influence Structures Between China, Europe, and Japan

Is there a special Chinese style of dividing decision-making in enterprises between different interest groups? Can we find cultural differences between East and West in this matter? We try to answer these questions by comparing results of empirical studies made in 12 European countries and Japan with the same measures.

6.4.1 Comparative Material

The following countries were included in the European study: Belgium, Denmark, Finland, France, Israel, Italy, the Netherlands, Norway, Sweden, the United Kingdom, West Germany, and Yugoslavia. The material was collected in every country from a minimum of nine enterprises, 70% metal and engineering companies and 30% services (banks and insurance), including small, medium-sized, and large units. The total number of enterprises was 134, and the number of "experts" interviewed was 997 (IDE 1981a, b). This author was the leader of the Finnish IDE research group.

The Japanese material included six enterprises, all of which represented the metal and engineering industry. Two of the enterprises were small, having under 100 employees, two were medium-sized, 200–500 employees, and two were large, over 500 employees. The Japanese material was collected by Professor Akihiro Ishikawa, Chuo University, Tokyo.

Of the eight Chinese industrial enterprises studied, four of the six firms from interior China and one of the two firms located in the Special Economic Zone represented the metal and engineering industry. However, the system of production technology in the three Chinese nonmetal enterprises did not differ so much from the metal industry firms as to have made an essential difference. The enterprises in the countries compared differed somewhat according to size; the Chinese establishments were on average larger than their European and Japanese counterparts. In the European and Japanese study about half of the enterprises had between 200 and 500 employees, whereas only one of the eight Chinese enterprises came into this bracket.

Because there are some differences in the material between the countries compared, we must be careful in drawing conclusions concerning the comparisons. However, the same kind of difficulties beset nearly all cross-country and cross-cultural comparisons. The results are not exact, but indicative, and we have to examine their reliability by comparing them to other possible similar studies, of which there are, at least concerning China, very few, and to qualitative material collected from interviews. Also one checkpoint is how the empirical results coincide with the stated strategy and policy in the countries concerned, especially China.

6.4.2 Chinese Influence Structure Differs from Europe and Japan

Practically all the Chinese interest groups studied seemed to have less influence in decision-making when compared both to European and Japanese enterprises, as seen in Table 6.8 where the influence is examined across decision types. The Japanese pattern of influence structure seems to follow the European quite closely, although Japanese cultural values are probably much closer to Chinese than to European values. The similarity between

Table 6.8. Distribution of influence across levels and decision type in China (C)[a], European countries (E)[b], and Japan (J)[c]; means[d]

Decision type	A Workers			B Foremen			C Middle managers			D Top management			G Level above plant			H Representative bodies		
	C	E	J	C	E	J	C	E	J	C	E	J	C	E	J	C	E	J
Working conditions	1.2	2.5	2.3	2.2	3.2	3.8	2.8	3.5	3.8	3.7	3.6	3.9	1.7	1.8	3.2	1.6	2.5	2.8
Policy decisions	1.5	1.6	1.6	1.4	2.2	2.3	1.7	3.0	3.3	3.9	4.1	4.1	2.0	2.5	4.2	1.9	2.4	2.6
Strategic decisions	1.1	1.3	1.7	1.2	1.8	2.1	1.5	2.7	3.0	3.9	4.3	4.3	3.5	4.2	4.9	1.5	1.9	2.6
All 16 decisions	1.3	2.0	2.0	1.7	2.6	2.7	2.2	3.2	3.5	3.8	3.8	3.9	2.1	2.4	3.8	1.7	2.4	2.6

[a] Six enterprises, material collected in 1984 (this author's interviews)
[b] 134 enterprises, material collected in 1976–1978 (IDE 1981a)
[c] Six enterprises, material collected in 1981 by Akihiro Ishikawa, Chuo University, Tokyo
[d] Values are means of means: means of appraisers → enterprise means → national means (China and Japan) → means of 12 countries (Europe)
Scale: 1 = no influence; 2 = little influence; 3 = moderate influence; 4 = much influence; and 5 = very much influence

Japan and Europe probably comes from the similarity in production technology – more automated and"modern," and from Japanese close contacts after World War II with Western culture.

Influence of Top Management

If we look at the means of the internal "hierarchical" personnel groups in Table 6.8, we see that the influence of top managers is closest to each other in all the three "countries" compared. But the hierarchical groups under top management in all decision types have less influence in China than in Europe and Japan. The phenomenon that in China top management seems to keep nearly all the decision-making strings in its hands comes out clearly in Table 6.9, which shows the differences of means between top management and representatives of lower hierarchical levels in enterprises. Most of the differences are greater in China, thus reflecting the greater centralization of power in the hands of top management of enterprises. This phenomenon is illustrated also in Fig. 6.3, where the great power distance between top and middle management in China comes out clearly. The hierarchical pyramid looks much the same in Europe as in Japan, although in Japan the power distance between top and middle management is somewhat smaller and between foremen and middle management somewhat

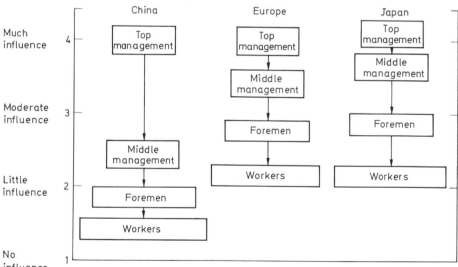

Fig. 6.3. The influence structure and power distance between different personnel groups in Chinese, European, and Japanese Enterprises. Means of all 16 decisions. The lower edges of the »boxes« correspond to the mean of the personnel groups concerned. (For sources see Table 7.8)

larger. According to Table 6.9 the differences of "differences" are especially high in China concerning working conditions decisions in all personnel groups. However, the differences are quite even concerning workers and policy and strategic decisions; in no country do the workers have much to say in these matters.

The generally smaller influence of Chinese personnel groups can be a sign of traditional authoritarian and patriarchal Chinese culture. It can also reflect the whole structure of Chinese socialist society, where the most important plans and decisions are made centrally by "higher authorities."

At least earlier, before the economic reforms, Chinese top management did not need to bother much about strategic decision-making, which is looked upon as being the main task of top management in capitalist organizations. Thus, the main attention of Chinese top managers was directed towards internal matters, supervising the behavior of subordinates, whereas the main attention of enterprises in free-market economies is towards the environment of the enterprise, especially the evaluation of the development of the firm's competitive situation in different markets.

If we examine the different decision types, we notice that the greatest differences between, on the one hand, Chinese and, on the other hand, European and Japanese top management are to be found in strategic decisions: the mean for China is 3.9 and for Europe and Japan 4.3. If we look closer at the individual decisions in Table 6.10 we see that the difference arises from decision no. 6 "major capital investment" (China 3.0; Europe 4.3, and Japan 4.1). The reason is that in China the government body above the enterprise decides these matters. The mean for China is 4.8, but it is also high for Japan, 4.9. The deciding organs are, however, different: in China the decision is made through the local industrial bureau, whereas

Table 6.9. Differences of means of influence between top management (D), workers, foremen, and middle managers in China (C), Europe (E) and Japan (J), according to decision types

Decision type	Top management – workers			Top management – foreman			Top management – middle managers		
	C	E	J	C	E	J	C	E	J
Working conditions	2.5	1.1	1.6	1.5	0.4	0.7	0.9	0.1	0.1
Policy decisions	2.4	2.5	2.5	2.5	1.9	1.8	2.2	1.1	0.8
Strategic decisions	2.8	3.0	2.6	2.7	2.5	2.2	2.4	1.6	1.3
All 16 decisions	2.5	1.8	1.9	2.1	1.2	1.2	1.6	0.6	0.4

Table 6.10. Distribution of influence across levels and decisions in China (C), Europe (E) and Japan (J)

Decisions	A Workers			B Foremen			C Middle managers			D Top managers			G Level above plant			H Worker's congress/council		
	C	E	J	C	E	J	C	E	J	C	E	J	C	E	J	C	E	J
1. Working conditions	1.7	2.7	2.9	2.2	3.1	3.6	3.0	3.5	3.9	4.5	4.1	4.5	4.0	2.5	4.0	3.3	3.4	4.2
4. Training courses	1.2	2.2	1.7	1.7	2.7	3.0	3.0	3.5	3.7	4.8	3.9	4.2	1.5	1.8	3.7	1.5	2.3	2.2
5. Transfers	1.0	2.5	1.9	1.3	3.1	3.0	2.8	3.7	4.0	4.8	3.7	4.5	1.0	1.6	3.3	1.0	2.5	2.6
10. Personal equipment	1.4	2.8	3.5	3.2	3.5	4.2	3.2	3.6	3.7	1.0	3.2	3.1	1.0	1.7	1.9	1.0	2.0	2.0
12. Task assignment	1.0	2.2	1.8	3.5	3.9	3.9	3.3	3.6	4.1	1.6	2.7	3.6	1.0	1.4	2.5	1.0	1.7	1.9
16. Working hours	1.0	2.8	2.1	1.2	2.4	2.5	1.4	2.7	3.0	4.8	3.8	3.3	1.7	2.0	3.8	1.7	3.2	3.7
All working Conditions	1.2	2.5	2.3	2.2	3.2	3.2	2.8	3.5	3.8	3.7	3.6	3.9	1.7	1.8	3.2	1.6	2.5	2.8
2. New department head	1.2	1.2	1.1	1.0	1.6	1.7	1.0	2.5	3.7	4.8	4.5	4.3	1.0	2.8	4.8	1.7	1.9	1.8
3. Hiring procedures	1.0	1.4	1.2	1.0	2.5	1.5	1.0	3.3	2.5	3.5	4.0	3.5	4.3	2.2	4.6	1.2	2.3	2.2
8. Appointment own superior	2.2	1.3	1.6	1.3	1.5	2.8	1.3	2.0	4.0	1.0	3.6	4.6	–	2.8	4.1	–	2.0	2.0
9. Pay levels	1.2	2.0	1.9	1.5	2.4	2.1	2.3	3.1	2.8	3.8	4.2	3.7	3.0	2.7	4.6	2.2	2.9	4.2
11. Reorganization	1.2	1.7	1.2	1.2	2.4	1.8	1.7	3.4	3.0	4.8	4.4	4.5	1.2	2.8	4.7	1.7	2.4	2.4
13. Dismissals	1.2	1.7	2.1	1.6	2.9	2.6	2.2	3.4	3.5	4.0	4.1	4.3	1.8	2.0	4.4	3.2	3.2	3.4
14. Work study	2.2	2.0	2.0	2.2	2.8	3.3	2.8	3.5	3.9	4.8	3.9	3.7	1.0	2.1	2.3	1.7	2.7	2.1

All Policy decisions	1.5	1.6	1.6	1.4	2.2	2.3	1.7	3.0	3.3	3.9	4.1	4.1	2.0	2.5	4.2	1.9	2.4	2.6
6. Investment	1.0	1.3	2.0	1.0	1.8	2.0	1.0	2.7	2.7	3.0	4.3	4.1	4.8	4.4	4.9	1.7	2.0	2.7
7. New product	1.2	1.3	1.4	1.3	1.7	2.1	2.0	2.8	3.3	4.8	4.3	4.5	2.2	3.8	4.8	1.3	1.9	2.4
All strategic decisions	1.1	1.3	1.7	1.2	1.8	2.1	1.5	2.7	3.0	3.9	4.3	4.3	3.5	4.2	4.9	1.5	1.9	2.6
15. Holidays	1.7	3.2	3.3	2.7	2.9	3.5	3.5	3.1	3.5	3.8	3.1	2.9	1.0	1.6	2.4	1.0	2.2	2.5
All 16 decisions	1.3	2.0	2.0	1.7	2.6	2.7	2.2	3.2	3.5	3.8	3.8	3.9	2.1	2.4	3.8	1.7	2.4	2.6

C = 6 enterprises
E = 12 countries, 134 enterprises
J = 6 enterprises

in Japan "the level above the plant" is usually a supervisory board, of the same kind as in Europe.

If we pick out those individual decisions from Table 6.10 where the means of Chinese top managers are higher than those of European and Japanese managers, we see from Table 6.11 that the decisions concern either (a) personnel matters directly, e.g., "appointment of new department head" (2), "permanent transfer of workers" (5), or (b) organization of work of the whole enterprise, e.g., "reorganization" (11), and "work study" (14).

We earlier noted that an area which top management likes to control strictly is the recruitment, development, and organization of personnel resources. This seems to hold true both in Europe and in the East. The only exception in the decisions of this area is "Establishment of criteria and procedures for hiring and selection of new employees" (no. 3). Here the mean for European firms is 4.0 and for both Chinese and Japanese 3.5. However, if we study Table 6.10 we see that this decision is not underestimated in the last-mentioned countries; on the contrary these decisions are considered so important there that they are concentrated at the higher hierarchical level, i.e., the level above the plant. The corresponding means are for China 4.3, for Japan still higher 4.6, but for Europe only 2.2. These differences also reflect of course differences in organizational structures in the countries, but in any case they show the key position of personnel matters in decision-making in enterprises.

Influence of Middle Managers

The middle managers were defined in the Chinese structured interview form for measuring influence as "workshop leaders or technical experts." In the Chinese enterprises interviewed the workshops had between 100 and 400 employees; for example in the large Capital Iron and Steel Company in

Table 6.11. Individual decisions in which the mean of Chinese top management (C) is higher than European (E) and Japanese top management (J)

Decision (Number)	Means		
	C	E	J
New department head (2)	4.8	4.5	4.3
Transfers (5)	4.8	3.7	4.5
Reorganization (11)	4.8	4.4	4.5
Work study (14)	4.8	3.9	3.7
Training courses (4)	4.8	3.9	4.2
Working conditions (1)	4.5	4.1	4.5
Working hours (16)	4.8	3.8	3.3
All 16 decisions	3.8	3.8	3.9

Beijing the number of employees of the workshops averaged 200. Normally the middle management level is defined as a hierarchical position between foremen and top management, including heads of the large staff departments. I believe that the hierarchical position of middle managers in China, Europe, and Japan was more or less equivalent.

The influence of Chinese middle managers in decision-making seems to be clearly smaller in different decision types compared to their European and Japanese counterparts, as can be seen in Table 6.8. The difference seems to be greatest in policy and strategic decisions, in which the Chinese middle managers have not even "little influence" according to the means. Also the Chinese middle managers have not even "some influence" in working conditions decisions where the mean for, e.g., Japanese middle managers is 3.8, i.e., close to "much influence." The small influence of Chinese middle managers in decision-making comes out clearly in Table 6.9, where we see the influence differences between top and middle managers. These differences are overwhelmingly greatest in China in all decision types compared to Europe and Japan.

Although the Chinese top managers seem not to have delegated much decision-making power downward in the hierarchy, the situation may change in the future when enterprises become more autonomous and have to take responsibility for their profits and losses. Then the top managers will probably be much more occupied with activities directed towards the environments of the enterprises, or they must concentrate more and more upon strategic decision-making as do their counterparts in Europe and Japan. In this case the Chinese managers will simply no longer have enough time to supervise all the doings of their subordinates. Thus, they will probably have to delegate more and more decision-making power to middle managers in order to make their enterprises more effective and profitable.

If we examine the individual decisions in Table 6.10, we see that the means of Chinese middle managers are in every single decision lower than their European and Japanese counterparts. This can reflect the different organizational structure of the Chinese enterprises and thus the status of the middle managers, and/or the actual smaller decision-making power of Chinese middle managers, which can be a sign of traditional Chinese authoritarian culture and the centralized decision-making system of a socialist society. All the factors mentioned act together to lessen the decision-making power of Chinese middle managers.

Influence of Foremen

The concept of a foreman in China is somewhat different from that in, e.g., Europe. The main difference lies in the fact that a Chinese foreman, or rather production group leader, engages himself in production, whereas in Europe the foreman supervises the work and seldom takes part in the work itself, perhaps only exceptionally when advising a worker how to perform a certain task.

The hierarchical level of a work group is below that of the workshop. The work groups are organized on the one hand according to what is produced, e.g., a work group can be established for the production of a particular component, and on the other hand according to the type of technology used, e.g., some production groups are engaged in lathe work, some in drilling, milling, etc.

It is noteworthy that a work group in China is also financial accounting unit of an industrial enterprise. According to the Chinese

> The system of economic accounting at the work group level enables the factory and the workshop to have a better understanding of the situation regarding the actual fulfillment of production, technical, and economic targets so that corrective action can be promptly taken to resolve problems and ensure that all targets will be met. (Lingnan University Research Institute 1982: 32)

The Chinese system of supervision of workers at shop-floor level may be an inheritance from the time before the 1949 revolution, when the system of "gang bosses" was created. Then the owners of industrial enterprises hired "professional" managers or administrators to run the factories. These administrators again delegated the authority for operations to skilled, experienced workers, who thus became so-called gang bosses, as described earlier.

In Table 6.8, we saw that the Chinese foreman or work-group leaders seemed to have less influence in decision-making in all decision types than their European and Japanese colleagues. As the degree of influence of top management is very similar in China, Europe, and Japan, we can use this as a point of comparison, and look at the differences of influence between top management and foremen in the three countries according to decision types (see Table 6.9). We notice that the "differences of differences" between China and other compared countries are greatest in working conditions decisions; Chinese top management will decide matters which typically should belong to the responsibility area of foremen. The only individual decisions where the Chinese foremen, or work group leaders, have more than "moderate influence" (mean over 3), are: "replacement of personal equipment of workers" (no. 10) and "assignment of tasks to workers" (12; Table 6.10).

The fact that Chinese top management seems to desire to decide matters which in other, more developed countries are delegated to lower hierarchical levels, can be one reason for the inefficiency of Chinese enterprises, something for which the Chinese leaders after Mao are seeking different kinds of solutions. One efficient solution could be: more delegation of decision-making power to lower hierarchical levels, also to foremen. The top managers would then have more time to concentrate on tasks which, since the economic reforms, they must do to an increasing extent; namely those involving strategic planning and decision-making.

Influence of Workers

The influence, or I would like to use here the word power, of workers in decision-making seems to be markedly slight in China compared to Europe and Japan. This appears clearly in Table 6.8, where the Chinese workers have almost "no influence" (mean 1.2) in matters closest to them at the work place, i.e., working conditions decisions. Table 6.9, which shows the difference of influence means between top management and workers, supports this observations. Top management prefer to control these matters in China.

There are no very great differences between the countries compared in the case of policy decisions, where the mean for China is 1.5 and for both Europe and Japan 1.6 (Table 6.8). If we study the individual decisions in Table 6.10, we notice that among these policy decisions there are only two in which Chinese workers have more influence than their European and Japanese counterparts, no. 8, "To establish who will be one's immediate superior," and no. 14, "Whether or not work study technique is to be used." Both of these decisions are in the area where the workers' congress of the enterprise has its say. This occurs, however, more or less indirectly, because according to the regulations mentioned in Chapter 5.3.4, the workers' congress has the power "To elect leading administrative personnel of the enterprise in accordance with the arrangements of the higher organ of the enterprise."

As we mentioned earlier, the original enthusiastic idea after Deng Xiaoping's speech in 1978 was that the workers' congresses should elect the top managers of the enterprises directly. This indeed occurred in some parts of the country, but it probably did not work well, because the system was quickly mostly abandoned, and the workers' congresses did not become the kind of powerful guiding unit in enterprises that was originally intended.

The bigger influence of European and Japanese workers, and especially of the former, is largely due to the labor union system, which especially in European countries, together with workers' councils and corresponding representative units, is in the background, giving workers some kind of indirect power especially in decisions concerning working conditions and strategic matters. This came out clearly from the European and Japanese means concerning these decision types, as seen in Table 6.8.

The different attitude towards workers' influence in China and, e.g., Finland was apparent in the interview situations also, when I asked about the influence of workers in the 16 decisions. The attitudes of the Chinese interviewees were certain and clear; in most decisions the workers just had no influence at all. But in Finland, where I conducted many of the interviews myself personally, the attitudes of the experts interviewed were much more "uncertain." They seemed to think that the workers do not have as much influence as individuals, but there were often outspoken opinions that through their interest organizations – labor unions – the workers actually have much more influence, especially in matters concerning working conditions, than their hierarchically low position would suggest.

Herein lies, as is widely known, one of the main differences in management between capitalist and socialist countries; in the latter the labor union system does not function, at least openly, as a counter-power to enterprise management. But in capitalist organizations the purpose of the labor union is to defend the interests of the workers against managers and owners of firms. For example in Finland the labor union movement is very powerful and is, when necessary, a strong negative power against the employer. Especially in North European countries, the labor unions exercise their influence on behalf of the workers and on enterprises indirectly through the macrolevel labor market or industrial relations system, which to a large extent decides on wages, and norms concerning, e.g., working conditions in enterprises. The indirect influence of the labor union is significant also because, for example in Finland, more than 90% of the industrial workers are unionized.

In a way the Chinese workers were in a secure position before the reforms, because they had life-long tenure in their job and position; children often "inherited" their job after their parents' retirement. This life-long tenure became evident during my interviews in Chinese enterprises especially in connection with the decision question: "Dismissal of one of the workers." The interviewed person often said: "That does not happen here." However, the new labor reform will gradually change the situation.

It will be interesting to see how the economic reforms applied in China after Mao will affect the status and power of Chinese labor unions. One can imagine that when decision-making concerning, e.g., wages is more and more delegated from the central government authorities to the enterprises, and this decision-making has thus come closer to the workers, and when in addition it is also partly under their control through the workers' congresses, that the workers may make big wage demands. It would be no surprise if Chinese labor unions changed their role from passive supporter of management to active defender of workers' interests in, e.g., getting their share of the available "wage cake." Signs of a coming change in the role and status of Chinese trade unions can already be seen, because, for example, a new trade union law is under discussion and will probably be approved and implemented in 1987 or of the latest in 1988 (Ch. D., November 19, 1986).

6.4.3 Comparison with Scandinavian Enterprises

In 1982 the Finnish and Swedish IDE research groups performed a replication study with the same measures as were used by the 12-country IDE International Research Group in 1978. Professor Bengt Stymne from the Stockholm School of Economics was the leader of the Swedish research group. Because the extensive IDE study which has been referred to above was done six years earlier than my Chinese study of 1984, and because Finland and Sweden were both included in the 12-country IDE study of 1978, I wanted to ensure that the European results had not changed significantly during this period. Of course it was also interesting to compare the Chinese and Scandinavian influence structures, but as the Scandinavian results greatly resemble those of the larger European study, and the latter represents 12 countries, we have mainly used the extensive, although older European IDE study in the comparisons.

Table 6.12 indicates that generally the means of Finnish and Swedish enterprises to a great extent follow those of the European means (See Table 6.8). Top management seems in "Continental" Europe and in Scandinavia to have about the same degree of influence in strategic decisions (corresponding means, 4.3 and 4.5), whereas Chinese general managers have less (mean, 3.9; Table 6.12). As mentioned earlier, the latter have lost their influence in strategic decisions upwards, often to the local industrial bureau, whereas Scandinavian top management has often delegated it downwards to middle management without losing its own influence.

The great concentration of influence in Chinese top management appears clearly in Fig. 6.4. The Chinese workers, foremen, and middle managers have almost nothing to say in policy and strategic decisions. However, it is interesting that in policy decisions – probably thanks to workers' congresses – Chinese workers have more influence than their foremen; but neither group has even "little influence." From the figure it also is clearly apparent how influential Finnish middle managers are. Top management in Finland has effectively delegated decision-making power to middle managers, and they in turn to foremen. Figure 6.4 also shows how Japanese management has become westernized in decision-making. The means between Japan

Table 6.12. Distribution of influence across levels and decision type in industrial enterprises in China (C)[a] 1984, and in Finland and Sweden (F+S)[b] in 1982; and differences between means of Groups D (top management) and A (workers); in means[c]

Decision type	A Workers		B Foremen		C Middle managers		D Top management		Differences D–A	
	C	F+S	C	F+S	C	F+S	C	F+S	C	F+S
Working conditions	1.2	2.6	2.2	3.4	2.8	3.7	3.7	3.2	2.5	0.6
Policy decisions	1.5	1.6	1.4	2.3	1.7	3.2	3.9	3.9	2.1	2.3
Strategic decisions	1.1	1.3	1.2	1.8	1.5	3.4	3.9	4.5	2.8	3.2
All 16 decisions	1.3	2.0	1.7	2.7	2.2	3.4	3.8	3.8	2.5	1.8

Sources: This author's interviews in China 1984, and interviews made by Finnish and Swedish IDE research groups, the latter under the leadership of Bengt Stymne, Stockholm School of Economics
[a] Six enterprises
[b] Eighteen enterprises
[c] Values are means of means: means of appraisers → enterprise means → national means (China) → means of 2 countries
Scale: 1 = no influence; 2 = little influence; 3 = moderate influence; 4 = much influence; and 5 = very much influence

and Finland are almost the same in all personnel groups concerning policy decisions, and also in other decision types Japan is closer to Finland than China, to which culturally it is certainly closer. Here technological and societal (Japan and Finland are both capitalist countries) factors probably play a greater role than geographical and old cultural proximity.

6.4.4 Influence Coalitions in Chinese and European Enterprises

Theories derived from Marx's ideas on class antagonisms suggest that a zero sum game of power exists in capitalist organizations especially between those organizational levels representing the interests of labor and capital, or workers and top management (IDE 1981a: 157–158). The inter-level correlations in Table 6.13, seem to strengthen this hypothesis. In capitalist European countries the correlation of the influence of top management and workers is negative (−0.32) – the more influence top management has the less workers have and vice versa – whereas in socialist China the correlation is strongly positive (0.65).

If we recall how the interlevel correlations changed in China between 1980 and 1984, and examine Table 6.6 again we see that the correlation has

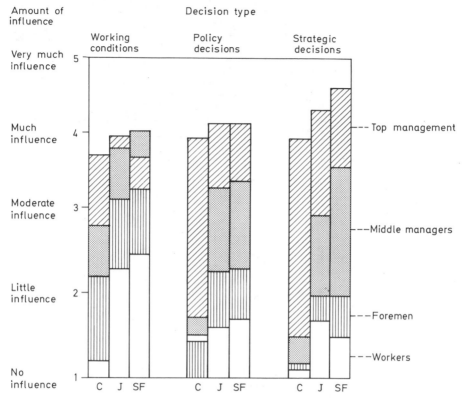

Fig. 6.4. Distribution of influence across levels and decision type in industrial enterprises in China (C), Japan (J), and Finland (SF); means. (Sources: This author's interviews in six Chinese enterprises in 1984, Japanese material collected by Professor Ishikawa's research group in six firms in 1981, Finnish material collected from nine enterprises in 1982 by my research group)

risen, from 0.23 in 1980 to 0.65 in 1984. This may seem at first sight a little confusing, because the Chinese economy should have become more market oriented since 1978, and thus moved in a more "capitalist" direction. However, I think that this is not a difference between capitalism and socialism, but between those who control the economic resources – capital – and those who control other, especially human resources. At bottom the core question is the same: In China, after the economic reforms, the government body above (and "outside") the enterprise and also the CPC still largely guide the allocation of economic resources which the enterprises and thus also their management greatly need.

We see this tension in the correlation between Chinese top management and the level above the plant, in China usually the local (government)

Table 6.13. Interlevel correlations of influence for all decisions in six Chinese industrial enterprises in 1984 (C) and in European countries (E); product moment correlation; more detailed explanation in Table 6.6., page 291. (Industrial Democracy in Europe (IDE) 1981a: 159)

		A		B		C		D		E		F		G	
		C	E	C	E	C	E	C	E	C	E	C	E	C	E
Workers	A														
Foreman	B	0.54	0.44												
Middle management	C	−0.04	0.17	0.48	0.37										
Top management	D	0.65	−0.32	0.72	−0.02	0.41	0.02								
CPC committee	E	−0.41		−0.41		−0.39		−0.59							
Labor union	F	0.39		0.68		0.69		0.41		−0.00					
Level above plant	G	−0.60	0.07	−0.70	−0.04	−0.58	−0.01	−0.84	0.18	0.23		−0.79			
Workers' congress/council	H	0.65	0.37	0.68	0.08	−0.25	−0.08	0.43	−0.05	0.09		0.36		−0.44	0.26

industrial bureau; the correlation is high and negative (−0.84). The same kind of negative correlation (−0.59) is to be found also between top management and the CPC committee of the enterprise, which earlier largely decided capital allocation in enterprises.

Thus, the "conflict" between economic resources (power) and human resources seems to go on in a socialist system also. However, control of these resources resides with different groups. The economic resources are, or at least have been, mostly in the hands of government units, and indirectly in the hands of the CPC committee as mentioned earlier. In a capitalist system economic resources (power) are largely in the hands of owners, who are represented at "the level above plant" – usually the supervisory board. This came out clearly in Table 6.10, where the mean for the decision concerning "major capital investment" for Japan was 4.9 (very much influence), for Europe 4.4, and for China also high, 4.8. In China the deciding body was usually "the local industrial bureau," a government organization. Thus, both in socialist China and in capitalist countries the professional enterprise managers have to fight for economic resources (power); in China against the government bodies and the party, and in capitalist Japan and European countries, against the owners or their representatives on the supervisory boards.

The influence coalitions to be found through these correlations can thus be thought to represent a "fight" over resources, especially economic ones. In European countries we find one coalition at the bottom of the organization where alliances between workers and foremen are more or less supported by middle management, the internal lower coalition (Fig. 6.5). Another coalition is above the organization between the level above the plant, usually the supervisory board and external groups (IDE 1981a: 159), the external influence coalition. Top management lies between these two influence coalitions, partly isolated, partly in opposition to them. (IDE 1981a: 158; Mintzberg 1983: 125). As mentioned in Section 6.3.1, there were two main power coalitions in China also in 1984: the first between top management, middle management, foremen, and workers (Table 6.6, page 396), which was backed by the workers' congress and the labor union, the internal coalition. This could be said to represent the knowledge and human resources of enterprises through the skill of professional managers and workers. The second, the weaker external coalition was formed in 1984 between the government body above the enterprise and the CPC committee.

In the above-mentioned coalitions in a socialist system and in a capitalist system, top management played a special, but different role according to its position in the power fields of both societal systems. In a capitalist system professional top management lies between the external coalition, which represents the owners, and the internal lower coalition, which represents

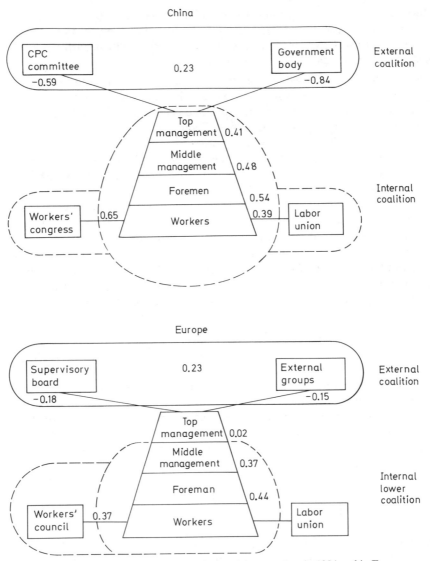

Fig. 6.5. Influence coalitions in Chinese industrial enterprises in 1984 and in European enterprises, showing the correlation coefficients 'binding' or 'separating' the units of
different coalitions. (IDE 1981a: 159)

the demands of employees from the employers. However, although capitalists top management can be looked upon as being the first representative of employers, it is not always the direct representative of the owners of the enterprise. The owners are, as mentioned before, usually represented by the supervisory board, which also normally nominates the general manager of the enterprise. Thus, the top management in a capitalist enterprise is really between two fires: between the workers and other employees strongly backed by their labor unions, and the owners, who have the power to dismiss the top manager if he does not achieve satisfactory results, i.e., profit.

In China again, top management represents, or at least it is intended to do after the economic reforms, the whole enterprise, with its entire body of employees at different hierarchical levels, vis-à-vis the external influence coalition, demanding more autonomy and decision-making power concerning especially economic resources. This situation in China is peculiar and interesting. Will the internal influence coalitions of Chinese enterprises now split into parts so that Chinese top management in the future must balance between demands from the lower hierarchical levels of the enterprise concerning the division of the economic cake, and demands concerning more efficiency and better financial results from the higher authorities? The threats to top management from above the enterprise after the economic reforms are the same in China as in capitalist countries: if no profit is shown, dismissal can be expected.

Thus, as the objectives of enterprises are the same – efficiency and profit-making – and the technological industrial environments of the firms are beginning more and more to resemble each other in different countries, so too the requirements faced by managers seem to be converging all over the world, both in capitalist and socialist societies.

6.5 Summary and Conclusions

Chapter 6 with its empirical study is a summary of Chinese management after Mao, and its relation to management in Europe and Japan. We must point out, however, that the empirical Chinese material used is relatively limited, and does not give statistically significant evidence for the results presented. If we relate the empirical quantitative results to other collected qualitative material, however, we should achieve a reasonably reliable picture of the changes in Chinese management since the beginning of the economic reforms.

Probably the most important change in influence relations of Chinese enterprises has been the declining power of the CPC committees of the firms. Such committees earlier played a dominant role. The results of this empirical study, comparing the situation between 1980 and 1984, clearly show that the Chinese have accomplished in practice the goal of separating enterprise and CPC management. This separation also appears clearly from the inter-level correlations of influence. In 1980 there was a high positive correlation between top management and CPC committees of the enterprise, but four years later the same correlation was strongly negative.

The correlation matrices showed also that the influence coalitions changed profoundly after 1980. The earlier strong coalition between CPC committee and top management faded, and in 1984 we found a strong internal influence coalition comprising all the internal personnel groups of the enterprises backed by workers' congresses and labor unions. The CPC committee and government body above the enterprise formed a weaker coalition, but in an opposite position to the large internal coalition.

In comparing the Chinese, European, and Japanese influence structures, we notice that Chinese top management holds nearly all the strings of decision-making in its hands, and allows very little power to lower levels. Thus, although the influence of top management was fairly equal in the three "countries" compared, the Chinese middle managers, foremen, and workers all had much less influence in decision-making than their European and Japanese counterparts.

The influence structures of European and Japanese enterprises were quite similar, though differing somewhat concerning the position of middle management in the enterprise hierarchy. The power distance between Japanese top and middle management was "shorter" than that in Europe, where the power distance seemed to be quite even between all the internal personnel groups of the enterprises.

The influence coalitions derived from the correlation matrices differed between China and Europe especially as to the position of top management. In Europe the top management lies isolated between an external coalition, formed by supervisory board and external groups, and an internal lower coalition of the enterprise. In China, as mentioned, the top management heads a strong internal influence coalition comprising all the personnel groups of the firm.

In conclusion, first, China seems to have succeeded in separating in practice the CPC and enterprise management, a development which has certainly aroused considerable astonishment and suspicion both inside and outside China, especially in other socialist countries. Second, the great power Chinese top management has in decision-making seems to strengthen the significance of traditional culture in management.

Third, the comparison between the Chinese, European, and Japanese enterprises still seems to strengthen the importance of the "cultural approach" in management, as the power distance between Chinese top management and the lower-level personnel groups was clearly larger in China than in Europe and Japan, thus manifesting the existence and impact of the traditional Chinese patriarchal values.

Japanese cultural values are in many ways similar to those of the Chinese, yet the Japanese influence structure seems quite close to the European. Thus, it will be interesting to see whether the influence structure of Chinese enterprises will converge towards that of the technologically more developed Japan and Western countries. Or will technology come to dominate culture?

7 Final Summary and Conclusions

This final chapter has been divided into three parts:

1. In section 7.1 we summarize those developments during China's history which we believe have had greatest impact upon the management practice of the next historical period and upon contemporary Chinese management. We focus here especially upon the management of enterprises.
2. In section 7.2 we examine the Chinese power struggle of the late 1980s with the help of our theoretical frame presented in Appendix.
3. In section 7.3 we try to point out those characteristics in Chinese management which we feel need more research and elaboration in the future.

7.1 Historical Developments of Chinese Management

In this section we summarize chronologically the developments of management in China beginning from the time of the Emperors.

7.1.1 Heritage of the Emperors

The cultural unity of China was created during the Shang dynasty ca. 16th–11th century B.C. The time of the next Zhou dynasties (ca. 11th century B.C. to 221 B.C.) created many administrative characteristics for Chinese society, traces of which can still be seen today.

During this period the society changed gradually from a slave-owning to a feudal society, which gave birth to the concept of the family, i.e. the household, as a productive unit. Already during that time women were in a subordinate position to men. A strong centralized governmental system was also created during the Zhou dynasties. These also became fertile soil for lively management thinking. The so-called One Hundred Schools of Thought flourished, of which especially Confucianism and Legalism became important from the point of view of management. The ideas of Confucius have had the longest-lasting effects upon administrative thinking in China. In a way he legitimated the strong hierarchical order (power) which dominated in the family and in the entire society of this time and later on until our time.

The Legalist school also had a strong impact upon earlier management. The Legalists considered it important to use together norm power (laws), hierarchical power, and the personal power of the ruler, the emperor. The principles of the Legalist school were effectively applied in practice especially in Qin province, which succeeded in unifying the country in 221 B.C.

During the Qin and following Han dynasties (221 B.C.–220 A.D.) the seed was sown for the 1949 revolution, because especially then the peasants became oppressed and exploited under the feudal rule.

From the point of view of management thinking and practice we must still mention the hierarchical clan system, the centralized government administrative structure, and the educational system of government officials from the time of the emperors.

From the point of view of education of managers, or government officials, the Hanlin Academy became important from the time of the Ming dynasty (1368–1644). During the time of the emperors, management thinking and experience largely came from public administration, but the clan system with large estates and professional managers also gave management a more economic, "modern" flavor. The European invasion of China, which was actually begun in the sixteenth century, did not speed up Chinese industrialization until the nineteenth century. Despite the gradually growing industrialization, the main part of the country remained largely in feudal circumstances, which had prevailed for hundreds of years during imperial times.

If we try to summarize the factors that guided Chinese society and organization during those times, we can use our theoretical frame (Fig. A. 3) and examine first the main cultural value systems consisting of:
• Worship of ancestors
• Hierarchically organized family and other personal relations
• Strong central administration with one person, the emperor, at the top
• High respect for the old and men in interpersonal relations

These value orientations had great impact upon how resources (power) were used in administration (see Fig. A. 3).

The most-used resource powers during the period of the emperors were economic and arms power, which were in the hands of the emperor, government officials, and landlords. Quite strong personal power was connected to the emperor's person. The knowledge resources were mostly in the hands of educated government officials and also among the family members of landlords and gentry.

The ideas of the philosophers, especially of Confucius, gave strength to the use of different instrumental powers in guiding society and its organizations. The most typical instrumental power was hierarchical, which controlled organizational behavior from family and clan systems to the organizations of the government and of course the army. The Legalists had established the strong use of norm power first in the powerful Qin province and it was later needed to guide the expanding imperial China in a uniform pattern.

During the time of the Emperors the form of influence directed towards peasants and other lower social classes was mainly coercion, with the help of which the oppressed peasants and hired agricultural workers were forced to an uneven economic exchange with the land-owning classes. Because the lower classes were also kept uneducated, the use of manipulation was strong; the manipulated poor people could not see any other options for their life than complete obedience to the higher classes.

7.1.2 Period of the Republic: The Labor Pains of New China

Under the pressure of foreign invaders, and dissatisfied with the bad internal and foreign policies of incompetent and crude rulers, China gradually became ripe for revolution, which after many attempts to overthrow the imperial regime at last succeeded in 1911 under the intellectual leadership of Sun Yat-sen.

Soon the development began which gradually first led to the establishment and strenthening of the Communist Party of China (CPC), and then to the 1949 revolution. We can discern the following important events for the Republic:

1. The Russian October Revolution in 1917, which brought the ideas of Marxism-Leninism concretely to China
2. The Movement of May Fourth (1919), which showed the great power of mass movements
3. The establishment of the Communist Party of China in July 1921
4. At the gates of Shanghai, Chiang Kai-shek allied in 1927 with the capitalists, and Mao Zedong established the first units of the peasants' and workers' army, revolutionary base areas in the mountains, and formed a central government for these areas
5. The Long March, and the Yan'an period in the late 1930s, created and/or strengthened the following administrative practices, which had a profound effect upon Chinese management:
   - A more egalitarian and cooperative society and organizations were established;
   - The economy, production, education, and the military became interrelated in the same organizational units;
   - Production units became self-reliant economically;

- Different kinds of participation systems, e.g., down the line, were created;
- Mao's mass line principle was created;
- The status of women was radically changed – they were given a more egalitarian role in society

The time of the Republic was filled with wars so that at the end of the period China was badly damaged materially and psychologically. This in a way helped the creation of the new China, because the communists could begin to build it from the ashes; very few opposing forces were left in mainland China, but instead there was fertile ground for the building of a new administrative system.

7.1.3 Management Under Mao

We shall summarize the development of Chinese society and management during Mao's time by dividing the period into the following developmental stages: (1) Period of economic rehabilitation (1949–1952), (2) socialist transformation (1953–1956), (3) readjustment (1957–1965), and (4) Cultural Revolution (1966–1976).

Economic Rehabilitation (1949–1952)

China's economy as well as its administrative machinery was in chaos after the communist victory in 1949. Mao's strategy for rehabilitation was to utilize all the factors of urban and rural capitalism that were beneficial to the national economy.

The tactics applied in changing industry and commerce towards a socialist system were to confiscate as quickly as possible the enterprises controlled by the bureaucrat-capitalists and foreigners, but during a time of change, to let the national-capitalists develop their enterprises for the sake of rebuilding the country.

The enterprise management developed immediately after the CPC victory in two different directions. In east China a system of collective leadership developed in factories, exercised by a committee. It was called Shanghai or committee management. The other direction was the Soviet so-called one-man management system, which by the end of 1953 gained general, though only tentative, acceptance.

Socialist Transformation (1953–1956)

In agriculture, collectivization developed through several stages. The stage after first forming the mutual-aid teams was to organize cooperatives. The socialization process also proceeded step by step both in industry and commerce. It has been estimated that the output value of socialist state industry during the period accounted for 67.5% of the gross industrial output value; the share of joint state-private industry was 32.5%.

In management the great problems which the Soviet one-man management system had caused in Chinese enterprises led to a situation where the Chinese had officially to change the management practice. The new system announced in 1956 was officially called "factory-manager responsibility under the leadership of the CPC committee."

The whole process of socialist transformation was a huge undertaking, which brought with it many unintended consequences, causing serious problems for the entire society. A period of readjustment was needed.

Readjustment (1957–1965)

The period of readjustment contained in some areas, e.g., in agriculture, a clear organizational process towards more advanced socialization, but in some areas the period can be characterized by a kind of double readjustment, where contradictory forces were marching back and forth. Of the last-mentioned we must note the Hundred Flowers Movement, during which the status of the intellectuals was greatly improved as well as the opportunities for free speech. This changing use of communication power did not, however, last long. The following period of the Great Leap Forward included a nationwide, strong antiintellectual campaign.

The idea of the Great Leap Forward was based upon a kind of overoptimism, which the successful first five-year plan (1953–1957) had created. In this optimistic atmosphere Mao Zedong "required" a doubling of output within one year. However, several drawbacks soon appeared, suddenly halting the favorable economic development. This aroused critical discussion about the economic policy practiced, ending in a temporary victory for the so-called Liu Shao-chi line. In the following we shall summarize the developments in agriculture and industry.

In agriculture the most important organizational development of the period was the creation of the people's communes. First, cooperatives were united with greater units, and soon in 1958 the first people's communes were born. The aim of the people's communes was different from that of the producers' cooperatives; the former had the tasks of organizing the economy, educational, and social welfare activities, as well as political administration. To revive the Chinese economy after the great setbacks of 1959 and 1960, new motivational measures were needed. These included in agriculture the enlarging of the size of private plots of land which the peasants could cultivate for their own needs, and the creation of free markets in rural areas.

In industry during the beginning of the Great Leap Forward campaign the Chinese tried two main management methods to solve their problems: (1) factory manager responsibility under the leadership of the CPC committee, and (2) the system of "two participations, one reform, and triple combination."

However, the setbacks of the Great Leap Forward which were aggravated by the sudden withdrawal of Soviet aid and experts in 1960, ended these "experiments" in management, and new measures to motivate industry were created. The most significant characteristic of the so-called Liu Shao-chi economic line was to replace the quantitative production targets with a profit target for every enterprise and give the managers of the firm all decisive power. Both the CPC and trade unions lost much of their former power. The effects of the new policy seemed promising: production rose sharply after 1961.

However, when the economy of the country was put on its feet, the ideological campaign between Mao Zedong's and Liu Shao-chi's line started up again and the final battle was fought during the Cultural Revolution. One leading person who supported Liu Shao-chi's line, or free markets and microdecentralization, was Deng Xiaoping, who finally after Mao's death had the opportunity to apply the 20-year-old ideas.

Cultural Revolution (1966–1976)

There are two main reasons for the "Great Cultural Revolution":

1. Ideological. Mao Zedong and his supporters were afraid that China was sliding back to the capitalist road with Liu Shao-chi's economic strategy.
2. Power-related. Perhaps the strongest factor in the background was the fight over inheritance of the power of old Chairman Mao Zedong.

The economic performance of the country fell quite sharply during the first chaotic years of the Cultural Revolution, but the production figures began to rise in 1969 and 1970. The turmoil of the Cultural Revolution did not hit agriculture as badly as the urban areas. However, this period also brought to the agricultural organizations, or people's communes, new management ideas and structures. The most noticeable phenomenon was the introduction of the so-called revolutionary committees to the administration of the communes.

The Cultural Revolution was especially focused on Chinese cities to purge them of the bureaucrats and specialists so that these groups could not form a new upper class. They had to be brought into contact with the masses again. In this sense urban youth and intellectuals were sent to rural villages to be reeducated through physical labor. Another measure of Mao's antiurban strategy was the decentralization of industry from large cities in outlying areas.

The management structure of industrial enterprises, which was responsible for operational management, was greatly changed. The revolutionary committees were introduced as representing collective management at all levels of enterprises. However, the CPC committees were always superordinate to the revolutionary committees at the same organizational level. Through the revolutionary committees the Chinese tried to give different personnel groups the opportunity to take part in the management of an enterprise and its subunits. For example, different age-groups and hierarchical levels from workers to managers as well as both sexes had to be represented on the committees.

The period of the Cultural Revolution has especially become known for its many-sided experiments in participation. Particularly the different measures connected with participation down the line have awakened special interest outside China. This practice, where superiors work part of their time at the tasks of lower-hierarchical levels, was, however, not an innovation of the Cultural Revolution. The system had, under the force of hard environmental factors, already been widely applied in the late 1930s in the poor conditions of Yan'an.

The many-sided participation systems of the Cultural Revolution were, however, to a great extent a sham, because the enterprises had in practice very little effective decision-making power of their own; they had to follow plans and orders from the CPC and/or from the top of the hierarchical pyramid of the society.

The period of the Cultural Revolution ended the Mao era of the history of the People's Republic of China. As it was greatly dominated by the ideas of Mao Zedong, we notice that the Old Helmsman tried with his last energies to apply those management measures during the Cultural Revolution which had proved victorious during the creation of the People's Republic back in the 1930s. However, the circumstances had greatly changed from those times, and were no longer suitable for the different China of the 1960s and 1970s.

In the following we summarize the use of different forms of power during the Cultural Revolution which also in a way culminated in Mao's general management practice.

The greatest change which occurred during the Cultural Revolution in guiding enterprises was the move from the use of economic power (rewards) to the application of ideological power (rewards). Personal power largely connected with Mao's personality was widely used at the macrolevel in the entire society.

The use of knowledge power during the "Great Cultural Revolution" has caused most severe criticism from the Chinese themselves. One whole young generation was left without adequate education; it has been said that China will suffer for this negligence for decades.

In the young developing People's Republic, arms power played an important role, sometimes behind the curtains, sometimes visibly on the stage. The latter happened during the Cultural Revolution, when the turmoil was beginning to get out of control and becoming dangerous. In connection with these operations, PLA representative were placed in the newly formed revolutionary committees of strategically important enterprises.

The use of different instrumental powers usually has two aims: striving after power and after efficiency. These two different targets often lead to the applying of conflicting measures. Thus, especially in the use of hierarchical power during the Cultural Revolution when the Chinese tried in many ways to reduce hierarchical differences in enterprises, e.g., using different kinds of participation systems. However, these measures often became ostensible during the period, because the power aspect of the hierarchical structure required measures which were in opposition to the democratization tendencies. The whole country was actually ruled through a very hierarchical party structure.

In the use of norm power the Chinese enterprises were also dual during the Cultural Revolution; the CPC and the macroeconomic system were directed by means of strict norms, whereas in the enterprises efforts were made to keep the system that kept production rolling free from norm bureaucracy.

In the use of communication power also two different goals conflicted: that of greater efficiency and that of keeping power in the hands of the rulers. From the latter point of view, the flow of information regarding the political (CPC) system was severely regulated from the top to the bottom of the society. From the efficiency point of view efforts were made in the enterprises' production and management system to make communication as open and lively as possible, both horizontally and vertically. This duality also created great confusion because everybody knew that the ultimate power – including control of communication – was in the hands of the CPC anyway.

The form of influence in the use of different powers was changed during the Cultural Revolution in the following way: The move from the use of economic power (rewards) to ideological power (rewards) corresponded to the change from applying socioeconomic exchange to the use of manipulation and (ideological) indoctrination.

The violence of the beginning of the Cultural Revolution represented coercion as such, and when Mao had to call in the PLA to calm down the Red Guards, a kind of counter-coercion was used.

On the whole we can say that the forms of influence typical of the period of the Cultural Revolution were ideological indoctrination, manipulation caused by effective use of communication power, and coercion created by arms power, the PLA, and police forces. The change was sudden and great compared to the period before the Cultural Revolution, but the wheel of history turned around in ten years and China in the 1980s was in a situation where the main force activating the economy was again socioeconomic exchange.

7.1.4 Management After Mao

To radically change the strategy and politics of a country or enterprises nearly always also requires a change of the leaders who should accomplish the new strategy. After the death of the Great Helmsman, Chairman Mao Zedong on September 9, 1976, and after the arrest of the "Gang of Four," Deng Xiaoping, the strong man of the late 1970s and 1980s, immediately began to fill the top positions of macromanagement of the CPC and government with his "own" men. However, this was not enough; a total CPC consolidation followed which included a reregistration of all party members later on.

The Third Plenum of the Eleventh Central Committee in December 1978 became the actual turning point of China's economic and political strategy. It discarded the old slogan "Make class struggle the key link" and made the strategic decision to shift the focus of work to the four modernizations of: (1) industry, (2) agriculture, (3) national defence, and (4) science and technology.

In agriculture an economic reform called the "green revolution," contained first the contract responsibility system in which the peasant households became relatively independent commodity producers. A second step of the rural reform was a kind of open-market system formed under the guidance of the socialist planning system. The reforms gradually covered prices also.

The organizational structure and tasks of the people's communes were changed. They became solely an organizational form of rural collective economy. The old township organization came back to look after state administration. At the same time the revolutionary committees were abolished from rural as well as from urban organizations.

The ownership of the main means of agricultural production, namely land, was not changed. However, gradually the peasants were allowed to buy tractors and trucks for their own use and property. This thinking, that farm machines are no longer considered means of production, represents a profound change in socialist philosophy.

The government and the CPC encouraged the peasants to establish various rural enterprises with their own funds. The quickly developed side-line industry, which soon absorbed a great deal of affluent rural labor, played an important role in China's industrial production. Different kinds of voluntary cooperatives were also created. Thus, the wheel of development seemed to repeat the rotation of the mid-1950s, when the earlier cooperatives were formed, then however subject to the force and the strict regulations of the government.

The next important decision concerning enterprise management was made in 1981 when the so-called economic responsibility system was introduced also in urban industrial enterprises. In 1986 this management system was set up in some 23,000 of the 54,000 state-owned industrial enterprises. The regulations given in January 1987, which are still on a trial basis, officially stipulate that the factory director, and not the secretary of the firm's CPC committee, is the sole director of the enterprise, and has the responsibility for the production and management of the enterprise (*Far Eastern Economic Review*, March 19, 1987: 65).

The economic reforms set the enterprise managers quite new qualitative demands in many new areas. These made it necessary to change the managers, not only at the macrolevel, but also in enterprises. In the background was of course also the overall power game, because power is always in the final stage mediated through people.

To reform the cadre system, the CPC decided in 1982 to abolish the de facto life-long tenure for leading cadres. In 1984 it was announced by the CPC that most of the directors and CPC committee secretaries in the more than 3,000 major state-owned enterprises should have a college-level education. Beginning in 1985, a fixed tenure for factory directors was to have been instituted in these 3,000 enterprises. Their term of office was to be four years.

As a result of these policy changes, there seem to have been two waves of changing managers in Chinese enterprises after Mao; in 1978 and 1982. It seems a miracle that China's economy and enterprises have survived so well despite these frequent changes in top management.

Perhaps the most far-reaching idea in a socialist country connected in China's economic reforms was the separation of party and government administration. A practical result of this was that gradually also the CPC and management in enterprises became separated. This separation was "confirmed" during my interviews in Chinese enterprises in 1984 and 1986.

The most striking feature of China's "new revolution" for people outside China has perhaps been the so-called open-door policy, which began in 1980 with the creation of the first four Special Economic Zones and later on other "open areas." Although the main target of creating these "open areas" was to encourage foreign trade and investments, especially in high technology, it was also planned that these zones would form a training field for Chinese managers in modern management methods.

Many of the above-mentioned features of Chinese management after Mao are "confirmed" in Chapter 6 through the empirical study in which we examined the influence relations between different interest groups in enterprises. The results, comparing the situation in 1980 and 1984, showed that the Chinese had accomplished the goal of separating enterprise and CPC management in the firms studied. However, the state administration had more or less kept its influence, especially in strategic decisions.

The empirical results also "confirmed" that the Chinese have moved towards a one-man management system – according to the economic responsibility system – where the managers especially took care of decisions concerning personnel matters. At the same time the importance of the many earlier participation systems had declined and, e.g., the influence of the workers' congresses was slight or almost nonexistent in 1984.

When comparing the influence coalition in Chinese enterprises between 1980 and 1984 we found that the earlier strong coalition between CPC committee and top management faded, and in 1984 we found a strong internal influence coalition comprising all the internal personnel groups of the enterprises headed by the top management. However, we are aware that this, at least for Western countries rare coalition, can in the future break down because of the fight of different personnel groups over the growing economic cake – profit – of the enterprise.

When comparing the Chinese, European, and Japanese influence structures it seemed that Chinese enterprises differed most from the others. In China top management seemed to hold nearly all the decision-making strings in its hands. Chinese middle managers, foremen, and workers all had much less influence in decision-making than their European and Japanese counterparts.

The influence structures in Europe and Japan were quite similar, differing greatly from that of the Chinese, who should, however, have the same kind of cultural value-heritage as the Japanese. This raises the question, will the influence structure of Chinese enterprises converge in the future towards that of the technologically more advanced Western countries and Japan; or will technology come to dominate culture?

7.1.5 Main Roots of Contemporary Chinese Management

Figure 7.1 shows from a historical perspective those factors which we think have most affected management in China.

1. The hierarchically organized family system should be mentioned first. This dates from the earliest dynasties and it still affects behavior in families, enterprise, government, and CPC organizations.

2. Closely connected to the family system is the fact that the household has been for centuries the basic economic unit, not only in agriculture, but also in trade and small industry.

3. That man (father) is the head of the organization has also long historical roots. The Chinese are masculine-oriented according to Hofstede's cultural dimensions. However, since the 1949 revolution, the "status-distance" between men and women has declined, but not disappeared.

4. The one-man management system is closely connected to the hierarchical family and old clan system. It has been wiped out and brought back again several times during the PRC. In new China it was introduced during the Soviet influence in the beginning of the 1950s, replaced in 1956 by the collective management by CPC committee, and changed in 1960 to "one-man profit management" with the help of Liu Shao-chi and Deng Xiaoping. This was replaced again during the Cultural Revolution (1966–1976) by the revolutionary committees, and when these were abolished in 1978 Deng brought the one-man management system in Chinese form back again.

5. Respect for the old and ancestors was already part of traditional Chinese values during the imperial dynasties. This tradition is still strong, and is reflected especially in the old-age structure of Chinese top management both in government and the CPC.

6. One of the greatest changes which the 1949 revolution brought China was the raising of women from their subjugated status, where they had been from the beginning of China's known history. The coming of hundreds of millions of women to the labor market has had a great impact upon the economy at the microlevels. The share of females in high leading management positions is still small, but growing.

Emperor's period   Period of the Republic People's Republic

Shang Qing   Mao's rule Deng's rule
dynasty dynasty

1600 200 200   1000 1800 1910 1920 1930 1940 1950 1960 1970 1980 1988
B.C. B.C. A.D.

Hierarchical family
organization

Household as a basic
economic unit

Man, father, as
head of the
organization

One-man management
system

Respect for ances-
tors and old

Status of women

Importance of inter-
personal relations

Importance of »face«

Centralized
government system

Confucius' thoughts

Hierarchical structure
of the CPC

Large-scale changing
of managers
during PRC (*)   *   * *   * *

Meaning of the
symbols: ⊏⊐ Factor had   – – – Factor had
                    strong effect   little effect
                                            or has been
                 —— Factor had   in the
                    some effect   background

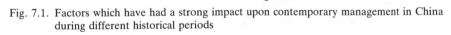

Fig. 7.1. Factors which have had a strong impact upon contemporary management in China
during different historical periods

7. The importance of interpersonal relations, which is closely connected to the family system, cannot be overestimated in China. Through these networks the Chinese themselves can overcome the hindrances of hierarchical bureaucracy, which often seems for a Westerner an insuperable barrier in business and other contacts with the Chinese.

8. Closely connected to interpersonal relations is the importance of "saving face". It is tightly linked to the family system, where everybody knows his or her place and behaves accordingly.

9. The centralized hierarchical government system stems from the earliest Chinese dynasties. There was a visible break in this structure during the turbulent times of the 1930s and 1940s, but the government organization is much the same in the People's Republic at the central, provincial, and local levels as it was hundreds of years ago.

10. Although Confucius' thoughts do not play the same official role in contemporary China as during many early dynasties, we cannot omit them from our list, because Confucius' philosophy strengthened most of the above-mentioned factors, which largely guide contemporary Chinese management behavior at the macro-, meso- and microlevels.

11. The Communist Party of China (CPC), although its historical roots are relatively short, has often criticized Confucius' thoughts. However, it is organized and managed in such a way that it in fact represents a most typical traditional Chinese organization, with a strict hierarchical organization structure. The party has a one-management system, usually with an old person, who is a man, sitting at the very top of the pyramid.

12. When we examine the management in the People's Republic we cannot forget one factor which has not perhaps long traditional roots, but which even so has greatly affected Chinese management during recent decades, and that is the frequent changes of managers in enterprises. These have been a reflection of changes of either the persons or of the political line of the top macromanagement. There have been "clear" changes of enterprise managers, first, after the revolution of 1949, second, after the rejection of the Soviet management model in 1960, third, with the beginning of the Cultural Revolution, fourth, in connection with the economic reforms launched in 1978, and, fifth, with the change of managers after the 12th National Congress of the CPC in 1982. The new managers should be elected according to the criteria of managerial competence and effectiveness.

If we "simplify" Fig. 7.1 and pick out those main factors which mostly guide Chinese management behavior, we end up with Fig. 7.2. The main historical roots of contemporary management originate from the hierarchical family (household) system, where the father, the man, was the head. Because

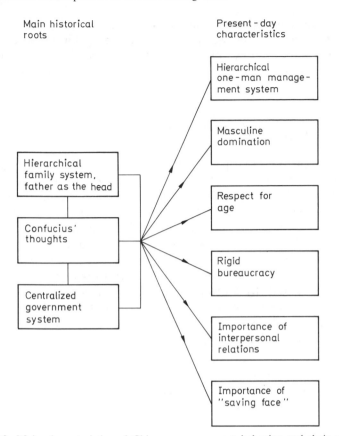

Fig. 7.2. Main characteristics of Chinese management behavior and their main historical roots

of the fights between the numerous early kingdoms, a strong central government was needed. Both these systems – hierarchical family and centralized government – were greatly strengthened by Confucius' thoughts.

From these main roots the characteristics of contemporary Chinese management have grown, i.e., (1) a hierarchical one-man management system, (2) masculine domination, (3) respect for age, (4) rigid bureaucracy, (5) special interpersonal relations systems, and (6) importance of "saving face" in personal relations.

During the period of the People's Republic, the Chinese have made "experiments" with many different management methods, some of which have been strongly against Chinese traditional values. The countercultural experiments have usually failed, as e.g., the participation down-the-line system, where superiors from time to time take part in the work of their subordinates. This developed as a necessity during the hard circumstances of Yan'an at the end of 1930s, was tried again by force during the Cultural Revolution, but after Mao was quickly abolished. It seems that traditional cultural values have played an important role also in the People's Republic.

7.2 Power Struggle of the Late 1980s

As the results of the power struggle, which became more visible in China in the late 1980s, are having a great impact upon the whole of China and its management, we try to analyse them here with the help of our theoretical frame, which we have presented in the Appendix. This frame described relations between managers and subordinates. When we study the power relations in the late 1980s in China, we have to focus – not on managers and subordinates in enterprises, but – on different political groups, which have different terminal values. The core question concerns what the society and its organizations should strive towards: Should the main target be (1) efficiency reached by economic reforms, or (2) maintaining first the old "right" political line, stressing the primacy of Marxism-Leninism and Mao Zedong thought (Fig. 7.3, box 1.)?

An ideology must have some visible personalities as standardbearers, and the human resources which follow them. Power can be converted into influence only through people. Thus, here we have the contradiction between (1) Deng and other reformers and (2) the conservatives. We have

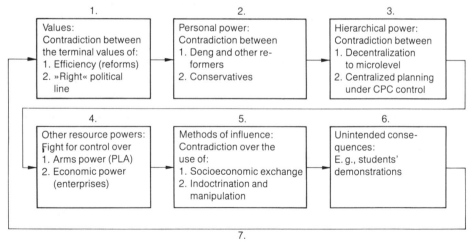

Fig. 7.3. The power struggle of the late 1980s examined with the help of our theoretical frame

included in personal power other people, i.e., human resources, necessary to implement the power (box 2 in Fig. 7.2).

The contradiction between the two political lines is closely connected to hierarchical power in two ways. First, in the form of organizational structure, which is preferred. Deng and his reformers would like to decentralize the decision-making power to the microlevel under the economic responsibility system, whereas the conservatives prefer centralized control and planning (box 3 in Fig. 7.3). Second, there is a struggle about who controls the hierarchical organization structure. Here lies one of the big differences between socialist and capitalist systems. In a socialist Chinese system the person or group that receives under the democratic centralism a majority in the (20 + 2)-member politbureau of the CPC or in the five-member standing committee of it can get power over the entire hierarchical structure of the CPC, government, and economic organizations, and thus over the whole country. The main trunk-echelon of this power is the party organization. Deng and his reformers have tried to separate party, government, and enterprise organization, and thus to lessen the power of the CPC in the country – and so also the power of the conservatives.

In socialist China the other resource power, which in addition to ideological (values) and personal power is important, is arms power. In the background of the power fight of the late 1980s in China arms power, in the figure of the PLA, is probably playing a decisive role. Deng Xiaoping has in a way anticipated this, as he has placed himself as chairman of the Military Commission of the CPC (box 4 in Fig. 7.3).

As to the method of influence, there also lies a contradiction between reformers and conservatives in China. The reformers require that the economy should be based on relatively independent enterprises, which exchange commodities "freely" in the frame of a market socialism so that the result of different exchange processes should be profit from which the enterprises pay taxes to the government. At the individual level the exchange of labor and economic rewards is based on the principle of "to everybody according to his/her performance."

As the conservatives have to defend the "old" political ideology, their methods of influence are largely indoctrination: to plant the political ideology as deeply as possible in the minds of people by enforced propaganda and political education. At the same time it is necessary to use manipulation; to prevent harmful political options – knowledge and information from, e.g., the West, reaching people and especially youth (box 5 in Fig. 7.3).

Different political, economic, and other especially new activities often produce unintended consequences. The student demonstrations at the end of 1986 were probably surprising unintended consequences (box 6 in Fig. 7.3). The feedback of these demonstrations actually turned out to be a kind of second-order unintended consequence, against the purpose of the demonstrators who belonged to the reformers. The students through their behavior put a weapon into the hands of the conservatives, and made the power fight at the same time overt, visible for the whole world. Although the extent of the demonstrations was quite modest in a country of one billion people – a few thousand students in some ten cities – they had special meaning because they were connected in the minds of people and of the top rulers of the country to the famous student Movement of May the Fourth in 1919, the which movement then spread quickly over the whole country among most social groups, and had great long-lasting consequences.

China's surprising historical events, long and many-sided cultural inheritance, and a special kind of socialism, as well as rapid economic, political, and social changes during the People's Republic, have made the country seem an unsolvable mystery. To make China less "mysterious," new many-sided research is needed. In the following last subsection we propose some research topics which we think would further increase knowledge about management in China.

7.3 Prospects for Future Research

We began this book with a statement that "China during recent decades has been like a huge management laboratory where different kinds of management applications have been 'tested' in huge natural environments." We have tried to describe and analyse some of these "experiments" in this book, but many interesting research problems still await their investigators, and probably new exciting topics will arise in the future, e.g., in connection with the impacts of the economic reforms after Mao. During my writing of this study, especially the following interesting and in my opinion important research areas and problems have arisen in my mind:

1. Further investigation of the development of Chinese management in the future as a longitudinal study. As China is a very large country where circumstances differ between different regions, a large research project would be needed, to cover different parts of the country – perhaps as separate projects – and also organizations from different lines of activities. As research methods, both large surveys and deep-reaching case studies would be desirable.

2. The impact of China's traditional culture upon contemporary management needs further investigation. Especially it would be interesting to follow how modern technology will affect the behavior of Chinese management; e.g., upon decision-making compared to Western countries. The core question is: will technology conceal the traditional Chinese culture altogether, or will the Chinese create a new management behavior of their own, which will assimilate Chinese values with modern technology?

3. Closely connected to the last-mentioned problem would be research, examining the diffusion (channels, barriers, and speed) of modern technology in China from, e.g., the Special Economic Zones to other parts of the country.

4. An exciting research topic would be a study of the old Chinese management thoughts during the time of the dynasties and especially around Confucius' time. There seems to be plenty of valuable and interesting material directly or indirectly concerning management, about which the world outside China has very little knowledge.

5. One of the most important research problems, at least for a Westerner, is the functioning of the mysterious Chinese interpersonal relations, which open doors through the seemingly insurmountable barriers of bureaucracy, and which contemporary Chinese often call "back-door policy."

6. When the Chinese and foreigners study Chinese management, e.g., in industrial enterprises, one important and at least earlier most decisive factor has usually been altogether left unexamined; that is the Communist Party of China (CPC), which extends its network everywhere in Chinese society. As the role of the party has undergone great changes during the 1980s, it would be interesting and important to study the real role of the party in different decision-making processes in China at the micro-, meso- and macrolevels.

This book has been a broad survey of contemporary Chinese management and its historical roots. In the future more differentiated, specified studies will be needed to throw light on the many exciting phenomena of Chinese management.

Appendix
Concepts and Instruments of Analysis

To be able to analyze adequately how the management of organizations and people has changed during different periods of the history of China, we need to define the concepts we use and describe the 'instruments' we shall apply in our analysis especially for those readers who are not acquainted with the terminology and theoretical concepts of organizational behavior. We have placed this chapter in the appendix firstly because many of the readers know well enough the concepts used and secondly we feel that a theoretical chapter at the beginning of the book would break up the presentation. In places in the text where we have used more of the concepts of our theoretical frame, we have refered to this appendix.

When choosing a theoretical frame and concepts we have many different options. In this selection task we have been guided on the one hand by the special central matter, management, which we are studying, and on the other hand by the environment, Chinese socialist society, in which the management process functions. Naturally, some of the methodological and conceptual solutions have also been guided by the fact that we have also compared – mostly in the latter part of the book – Chinese management with European and Japanese management.

Management and its Levels

First we shall define management as striving towards a special goal by using overt and/or covert power through different kinds of systems, resources and instruments. The 'systems' can be institutions, organizations, groups, individuals etc. When individuals or human groups are managed directly, we call this leadership; when we speak of guiding whole large systems like countries, institutions or organizations we call it management. When studying the management of a large socialist country like China it is useful to distinguish between three main levels of management:

1. Macro-management, or societal management, represents the management of an entire country, national economy or the country's Party system.

2. Meso-management represents an intermediate level of guidance, which functions between the macro- and micro-levels in regional and local systems such as provinces, prefectures, cities and other communes. As there are different levels of meso-management, we can call them also, according to their level, provincial and local management. By the latter we mean management of larger and smaller cities, rural communes, townships etc.

3. Micro-management refers to the guidance of individual organizations such as industrial enterprises on the lower operating level of the society (Richman 1969: 30). Although the main focus of our study is on industrial enterprises, we examine also other kinds of organizations such as rural organizations, where the majority of Chinese work, and government and party organizations at micro-level.

Table A.1. The administrative systems and three levels of management

Level of management	Administrative systems		
	State system	Party system	Economic system
Macro-management	Central government (e. g. State council)	Central administrative of Party (e. g. Central committee of Party)	(State Planning Commission)
Meso-management	Provincial and municipal governments	Provincial and local party organizations	Corporation
Micro-management	(State enterprises)	Party organization at enterprise level	Enterprises

When studying a socialist country, one must remember that there are three different hierarchical administrative systems, all of which also have different levels of management:

1. The economic system, where the basic units are enterprises.

2. The party system, which is highly hierarchical and extends its network everywhere in the society, also in industrial enterprises.

3. The state or government system, which extends its guiding structures from the central government down to local level (Fig. A. 1).

Methods of Management When Striving Towards Goals

We defined management as the striving towards a special goal by using overt and/or covert power through different kinds of systems, resources and instruments. We must also examine how the activity (or non-activity) in order to reach the determined goals can be brought about. We see here the following main possibilities: 1. exchange, 2. manipulation, 3. indoctrination and 4. coercion. In the following we shall examine these a little more closely.

1. Socio-economic exchange, where the influencing actor offers material and/or immaterial commodities which the influenced actor needs or wants, in exchange for the behavior desired by the influencing actor. Because in the exchange processes initiated by management both material and immaterial, social, commodities are used, and because we focus especially on economic organization, where economic rewards are common, we call these exchange processes socio-economic exchange.

2. Manipulation means that the influencing actor manipulates knowledge and/or other resources so that it prevents the influenced actor(s) from seeing other options for their behavior than that suggested by the influencing actor.

3. Indoctrination represents "a process of transfer of values, norms, or interests shaped by the power holder to those persons, groups, or subsystems which are the object of this power; indoctrination is an internalization of the subject's values on the part of the object." (Rus 1980: 12). The difference between manipulation by knowledge and indoctrination is that a manipulated actor has been prevented from seeing any options for his activity other than that suggested by the influencing actor, whereas an indoctrinated actor has been so forcefully served with special values and knowledge that he sees the behavior suggested by the influencing actor as the only right behavior. Both influenced actors see the one behavior suggested as right or necessary, but for different reasons.

4. One actor can influence other actors also by coercion, often by physical force. This corresponds to coercive power (e.g. Etzioni 1961), and is most clearly applied in prisons, mental hospitals and in the army. It is often linked to political activity.

As socio-economic exchange is a very typical phenomenon between contemporary societies, organizations and individuals, we examine it some more in the following.

Actors can make both positive and negative exchange. They exchange both rewards and penalties. For example the role of 'face' is very important in

Oriental cultures, and thus also among the Chinese. Helping or not helping to preserve face are strongly felt as positive or negative sanctions, exchange commodities.

The three men who have perhaps most developed the so-called social exchange theory are Claude Lévi-Strauss (1949), George Caspar Homans (1961) and Peter M. Blau (1964). Lévi-Strauss developed a collectivist theory of social exchange, while Homans represented an individualist orientation in social exchange theory. Peter Blau followed and further developed the theory along the lines of Homans. Blau linked the social exchange process especially in producing power-relations between individuals and organizations.

Closely linked to exchange behavior is Olson's theory of collective action, where he makes a distinction between collective rewards and private rewards. Collective rewards are given to all participants in an organization, whereas private rewards can be given to only one participant (Olson 1965).

Exchange, Power and Influence

When we now examine management in a socialist country, we must remember that it differs from that in a capitalist country especially in the ownership of means (resources) of production. In a socialist country it is said that the people own the means, resources, of production through the state or collective ownership. In capitalist countries again private ownership dominates. Thus, when we compare socialist and capitalist organizations, we feel it appropriate to use the so-called control of resources approach in examining power (French and Raven 1959). This approach seeks to define and measure the power of an actor in terms of the socially scarce resources the actor controls. The greater the control an agent has of such resources, the greater is his power. Here the difference between different competing actors concerning their possibility to control resources is especially important (More recently e.g. Laaksonen (1977) and Mintzberg (1983) have studied the power relations in organizations). Blau defines power as the result (if it is a result; we call it here influence) of an exchange process. Actor A acquires a power relation towards actor B when A can offer (or prevent B from obtaining) material or social commodities which the other desires or needs. The greater the value of the commodities which A can offer to B in relation to the rewards B can get from elsewhere, the greater the power of A. According to this, individuals, organizations or states can become more independent of the power of another actor simply by receiving fewer rewards from the other. In practice in a work place, for example, this is difficult to carry out because a worker cannot just walk out suddenly from his workplace and forfeit the wage he gets when offering his labor to the employer in their exchange process (Blau 1964: 118–119).

We make the following distinction between power and influence: power represents the ability – potential power – to influence other actors, whereas influence represents the actual activity created by power. One can have plenty of power (resources), but the power wielder does not activate it towards a special goal. Influence means that power resources has been used to create activity towards certain goals.

We try to avoid the "bottomless swamp" when using the power concept (Dahl 1957: 201) firstly by using the concept of influence, secondly by focusing our examination upon special defined resources which we have found especially relevant when studying managemet in socialist China, thirdly by making more general interpretations and conclusions, and fourthly by using the collected empirical material of influence-structures to 'support' the interpretations.

Thus, when studying the management in socialist China, it seems appropriate to focus especially on the following five resources and call the corresponding powers, potentiality to create influence, resource powers:

1. Economic power, representing the control of economic resources using remunerative and punitive sanctions.

2. Knowledge power, taking effect through the special knowledge or expertise that an individual or another system has.

3. Personal power, resting on the personal power (influence) of an individual. For example, Mao Zedong's personal power has greatly affected the whole People's Republic of China, and has also had a broad effect outside the country.

4. Arms power, guidance with the help of military and/or police forces, is used more or less invisibly. But it is always present, backing the dominant administrative system. The People's Liberation Army kept the Cultural Revolution within tolerable limits, and the special power of Deng Xiaoping probably largely has rested on the fact that he has been the chairman of the Military Commission of the Party.

5. Ideological power, having its foundation in the value system that an individual, group, society, or another system shares strongly. Thus ideological power is based on common values, but means at the same time that this value-system does not act passively, helping actors to choose suitable options in exchange-processes, but that it is so forcefully rooted in the minds of individuals that it becomes an active force, resource, in exchange processes. Examples are certain political and religious values, e.g. the birth of the Islamic revolution in Iran. There, this

ideological power helped decisively to conquer the strongest military force in the Arabic Middle East.

As values, especially in the form of communist ideology, have played a very outstanding role in the birth and growth of the People's Republic of China and at the same time in Chinese management, we must examine this concept more closely here.

According to Rokeach: "A value is an enduring belief that a specific mode of conduct or end state of existence is personally preferable to an opposite or converse mode of conduct or end state of existence". When examining values, exchange processes and the use of power (influence) distinction should be made between two types of values:

1. terminal values, which guide and control to what ends exchange operations are conducted and scarce power resources used, and

2. instrumental values, which indicate how different power resources are used to reach the goals (Rokeach 1973: 5–7).

When the object of management's use of power resources are the members of the organization, the instrumental values of managers and other supervisors can be closely connected to their leadership style. On the other hand values also determine to a great extent what individuals in a subordinate position regard as acceptable goals and forms of operation; how motivated they are to use effectively their own resource, their working labor, in exchange processes at work. The so-called acceptance theory of authority puts special emphasis on the significance of this acceptance (Simon 1957: 126), i.e. the area of manageability in regard to effective managing. If some order or directive does not fit into this area (exchange process and situation) it will not be effective; in other words, the subordinates will not behave – take part in the exchange process – in the way desired by their superior.

In Figure A.1 we try to describe the process of using ideological resources (power) in management. E.g. in China one of the basic values have been represented by the communist ideology, or as it was written in China's Constitution adopted in 1975, "Marxism-Leninism-Mao Tsetung Thought is the theoretical basis guiding the thinking of our nation." (Article 2). The ideology contains an idea of an abstract, ideal target state of affairs toward which individuals, organizations and nation have to strive. The proceeding to this ideal target goes through several intermediate, more concrete objectives, which are interpreted and defined by the leaders of the country (and of the party), managers of enterprises and so on. The employees get a general direction and principles for their work behavior from the ideology, which is being operationalized to become work goals by their superiors in organizations.

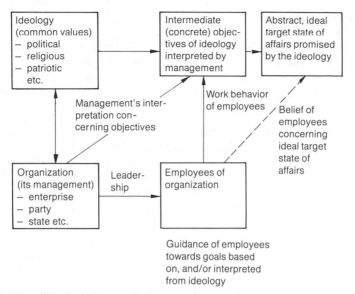

Fig. A.1. Use of ideological power in management

If the individuals do not believe in the official ideology, or there exist strong competing values, the guidance of individuals according to the official ideology becomes difficult if not impossible. These difficulties can appear as poor work motivation and morale etc. During the last few years there have been great changes in the content of the 'official' Chinese ideology also concerning how to manage enterprises. Therefore the study of ideology and corresponding power and influence is especially important in our study.

Values are closely connected with culture, which again according to contemporary research greatly affects the behavior of managers and other employees in organizations. In Europe there exist whole research groups focusing upon 'organizational culture'. As China has a long and rich cultural inheritance, we must take this especially into account when examining management in China. Therefore we have also devoted quite a lot of space to study the background of Chinese management, or how the contemporary Chinese value system emerged during the time before the People's Republic.

Instrumental Powers

As there exists a situation of scarcity of available exchange commodities, both regarding the society, organization, its subunits and members, the ongoing and planned exchange processes should be guided and controlled in order that the society, organization and its subsystems could satisfy their needs, reach their goals and function properly (Burns 1977).

The regulating apparatus should be able to take care that the means of production are properly used, that the production is effective, and that the results of productions are divided among the citizens with the maximum possible justice. In the contemporary world there exist two main regulatory systems. As we know, one is capitalism, which is based on price mechanism, and the other is socialism, which is characterized by central planning and management. However, there is scarcely any entirely socialist or capitalist country; they are all somewhere in between with more or less flavor from the other system. The main differences between these two economic and societal systems lie firstly in the ownership of means, resources, of production, secondly in the regulatory system, which guides the economic and also social behavior of individuals, managers and organizations.

To express this once more we have here chosen, just because of the two differences mentioned, to examine on the one hand how and where the resources, power, are allocated, and on the other hand what kind of regulating and controlling systems, instruments, exist in society and organizations which affect the behavior of members of organizations.

In practice there exist innumerable different, more or less influential guiding and controlling systems in society. As we cannot examine all of them, we have to choose those most appropriate for this study. We have chosen here the following guiding instruments, which, in our opinion, help especially in the study of the fluctuations of the Chinese management system during the period of the People's Republic. These instruments are: 1. Organizational hierarchy, 2. Applied norms, and 3. Control of communication networks. When we examined the different resources which caused power in society and organization, we called these resource powers; we now examine the above-mentioned instruments for controlling and guiding the society and organizations as instruments capable of transforming power resources into real influence. Therefore we call these measures 'instrumental powers'.

1. Hierarchical power. Hierarchy as an organizational phenomenon has changed greatly and often in China as a device of macro-, meso-, and micro-management. We see hierarchy as a dimension of organizational

structure. According to Child the purpose of the structure is to help the organization to reach its objectives in three different ways: a) It helps the realization of plans by allocating human and other resources and by giving mechanisms for their coordination. b) The structure shows the members of the organization what kind of demands are addressed to them by the different structural mechanisms in the form of standing orders, operating procedures etc. c) The structure indicates the different mechanisms used in decision-making and thus helps in accomplishing these processes (Child 1977).

Here we focus especially on the decision-making aspect of organizational structure: where different kinds of decision-making occur in the organizational pyramid consisting of several levels, how this decision-making has changed concerning e.g. the centralization of the decision-making power sometimes more to the macro-level, sometimes decentralization to the meso-, or to the micro-level. The rigidity of the hierarchical order will also be taken into consideration, i.e. how much deviation is tolerated from the formal organizational hierarchical structure.

According to different researchers the main factors which explain the forming of organizational structures are the striving after efficiency and power (Ylä-Anttila 1983: 151). These strivings have especially characterized organizational behavior in the People's Republic of China.

When examining the use of hierarchical power in this study, we look at it from two different angles: firstly where the main (decision-making) power or influence is located in the hierarchical structure; e.g. in central government (party organization), at provincial level, or enterprise level. Secondly, who has the power to decide where the different kind of (decision making) power is located in the hierarchical structure; or to decide over delegation – where and how much; or non-delegation.

2. Norm power. Norms, the rules of the game, also form one main group of instruments for guiding the behavior of individuals and organizations. We mean here especially written norms, which on the one hand are prescribed at a level above the organization, such as parliament or its equivalent, which prescribes the constitution and general laws, or the party, which in China through its norms regulates to a great extent the behavior of individuals and organizations in the whole country. In China many guiding, written norms are also given at the meso-management level by provincial and local governments.

On the other hand organizations themselves, e.g. enterprises, use norms (work rules, principles of personnel policy, organization handbooks etc.) to guide and control the work behavior of their employees.

The so-called Aston Research Group came to the result that the main dimensions of organizational structure are the specialization of activities, standardization and centralization. The norm power refers here to the standardization dimension of organizational structure, and the hierarchical power largely covers the dimension of centralization – decentralization, but also refers to the degree of specialization.

3. Communication power. The control of communication flows at the macro-, meso- and micro-levels forms an effective guiding instrument in all societies, but especially in socialist countries where the societal system is relatively new, and is still searching its 'correct' form. It is often the purpose of the leaders of socialist countries to protect their system and ideology against strange influences by strictly controlling the communication network, and to let in only such information as is accepted, strengthens and does not harm the official ideology and the way of thinking of the citizens. This communication power is close to knowledge power, and can sometimes eliminate the effect of the latter, e.g. when the holder of the knowledge resources cannot communicate his or her knowledge – activate it to influence people – being manipulated out of the communication network e.g. of the mass media. In practice this is called censorship, and happens more directly or indirectly both in capitalist and socialist countries.

Co- and Counter-Influence

As we have mentioned, the most common means management uses to create activity among other actors towards a certain goal is exchange.

When the management of an organization needs labor and the workers need money to buy the commodities they want, there develops an exchange situation containing a situation of mutual dependence. Long ago George C. Homans wrote: "Influence over others is purchased at the price of allowing one's self to be influenced by others." (Homans 1961: 286).

John Kotter especially has studied the behavior of management on the one hand as an activity to obtain power and on the other hand as an activity to administer the dependence of managers on other actors, especially of subordinates (Kotter 1979).

During the last few decades the dependence of the different interest groups of organizations has greatly increased because of the new information technology and expanding trade all over the world, and because of the more and more complex organization structures. Especially in capitalist countries the workers' and other unions have grown very powerful and possess great economic resources. For example in Finland the employers have for many years collected the fees of workers' and other employees' unions. Since the agreement which made this possible, the economic situation of these unions has grown much stronger. They have resources through which they can exercise counter-influence, resistance, towards management.

Some researchers quite early defined power as the inevitable contradiction between induction and resistance. E.g. Max Weber defined power as "the probability that an actor within a social relationship will be in a position to carry out his own will despite resistance." (Weber 1947: 152). Rus defines induction as positive power, as an ability to initiate activity, and resistance as negative power, as an ability to stop some activity (Rus 1980: 3).

Because there always exist greater or smaller differences between the goals and interests of organizations and their members, there also exist contradictions between two groups: managers, who define the goals of the organizations, and members of the organization, who because of their own interest at least partly resist the goals of the organization, and accordingly, exercise counter-influence on the influence, induction, of managers. To overcome this counter-influence, resistance, is of vital importance for managers. Rus says: "The fundamental problem faced by the management is: how to use power so as to overcome more resistance than this very use of power will generate ... it is clear that such uses of induction, which generates more resistance than it overcomes, lead to a vicious circle, therefore, to nonefficient management." (Rus 1980: 8).

We can distinguish many different ways used in different societies to overcome resistance from those who have been the objects of influence (power):

1. The most radical solution is the elimination of resistance through privatization, indoctrination or coercion.
2. Avoidance of resistance by removed or indirect control. This is a less radical solution, which is widely used in contemporary societies.
3. Localization of resistance to a certain part of the organization, which is being carried out through a vertical (hierarchical) and horizontal division of organization (Rus 1980: 8–10.)

Overt and Covert Power

We defined management earlier as the striving towards a special goal by using overt and/or covert power. In most definitions power means the capability of one actor to overcome resistance in achieving a desired result (Pfeffer 1981: 2). It is often stated that power cannot be exercised unless conflict is present. However, especially European scholars have demonstrated that power is also used to prevent conflict from a rising.

Some argue that power is most effective and insidious in its consequences when issues do not arise at all, when actors remain unaware of their claims, i.e. power is most effective when it is unnecessary. This can be achieved according to Lukes by affecting the other actors' values, preferences, cognitions and perceptions so that grievances and issues do not arise at all (Lukes 1974).

According to Lukes we can see in the use of power two distinct categories: 1) to defeat opposition and 2) to prevent opposition. The former we can call overt power, which "refers to the ability to secure preferred outcomes in the face of competition and conflict among declared opponents" (Hardy 1985: 388; Lukes 1974). The second type we can call covert power, which can again fall into two categories as viewed by the objects of power: a) conscious covert power, where the power wielder uses his or her resources to exclude certain issues and/or actors from the decision-making process, and b) unconscious covert power, called unobstructive power by Hardy, which refers to the ability to secure preferred outcomes by preventing conflict from arising (Hardy 1985: 389).

Unconscious covert power is used by manipulating symbols and language in order to produce certain sentiments among the objects of power. Hardy says that it "is thus founded on the ability to define reality, not only for oneself, but also for others." (Hardy 1985: 390). Very often the ability or 'right' to define reality in a country is restricted solely to dominant classes or party, which use it to support their domination, thus preventing challenges to their position. The power mainly used is then ideological. We can, however, say that the same kind of power resources and/or instrument can be used to apply overt and covert power. Especially important is also the ability of the power holders to control information flows through communication channels.

By way of summarizing this subchapter we could enlarge the definition of power to include also the ability to restructure situations and/or perceptions of these situations in such a way as to get the objects of power to act as the power holder desires in order to achieve special goals (see Hardy 1985: 396–397). The discussion above, concerning the use of overt and covert power in management, and their outcomes, is put in a nutshell in Figure A.2.

Unintended Consequences of Influence Processes

When actors influence or counter-influence 'other' actors, unintended consequences of these activities often appear, despite more or less careful planning of these acts. In general human beings are not capable of or interested in taking into account in their planning consequences which are

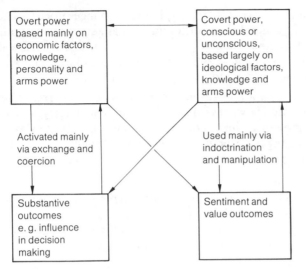

Fig. A.2. Use of overt and covert power and their outcomes (developed from Hardy 1985: 396)

remote, in time or in space. As we mentioned earlier, a manager can influence other actors in different ways, but mainly through exchange. In the following we examine some of the main unintended consequences of exchange processes:

1. Unintended results of planned exchanged events. Exchange processes often contain so many different participants and relations between them that the results of the whole process are quite impossible to cope with for a human being.

2. Unintended exchange processes (or non-exchange), often created as by-products of planned exchange.

3. Emergence of unintended, often new systems (structures) which guide and control the exchange process and again produce unintended results. A powerful actor A in pursuit of his objectives, for instance increased domination of B and C, may also create counter-processes from B and C which change the earlier and planned exchange relations. "The genesis of working class consciousness and organzation hinged on the heightened density and interaction of workers brought together into the factory context" (Burns 1977: 220). The Islamic revolution and government in Iran gives a contemporary example of unintended new exchange systems.

In economic organizations new technology can demand new structures for guiding and controlling exchange processes as mentioned earlier.

4. Emergence of new actors, participants, in the exchange process. There is always an unlimited number of different exchange processes going on outside the control limit of actor A. These can suddenly have deep-going, unintended consequences upon A. Iran and its religious leader Ayatollah Khomeni are a good example here too.

5. Unintended new allocation of resources, rewards, used in exchange processes often alter the (power) relations between exchanging and potential actors. Technological innovation can create entirely new products which radically change the power of actors in exchange relations, and often cause unpredicted consequences for all parties concerned (Burns 1977).

With contemporary management thinking stressing the idea of participative management, we must point out that the participative and democratic decision systems, at the organization and societal level, where sometimes hundreds of "equal" participants are involved, make the results of influence processes often rather unpredictable.

Summary

As a summary we present in a nutshell in Figure A.3 the frame formed of the instruments used in our analysis. We see that managers mainly create activity, influence, toward special goals through socio-economic exchange, manipulation, indoctrination and/or coercion (point 1 in Fig. A.3). To be able to exchange, one needs resources, which become the bases of potential influence, power (point 2a = managers' resources, 2b = subordinates' resources).

One of the main factors affecting the use of resources in exchange and other influence processes and corresponding decision making are the values of both managers (point 3a) and subordinates (point 3b). In societies of uniform culture, the common values representing this culture have a profound effect upon management.

Because on the one hand there exists scarcity of available resources and on the other hand they should be directed towards certain goals without causing harmful effects, the use of resources should be guided through special instruments (point 4).

Through their values, resources, and taking into account the guiding and controlling instruments, managers try to influence their subordinate individuals and other systems towards special goals (point 5a). Depending on the degree to which the subordinates accept the goals of the managers and

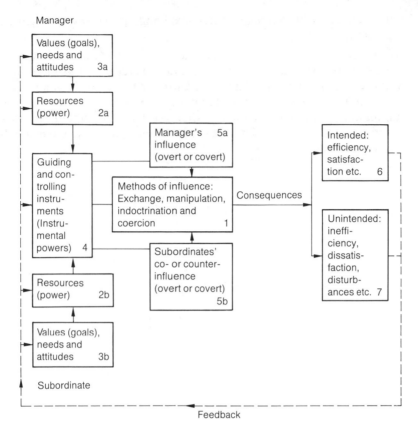

Fig. A.3. Frame formed by main instruments of analysis

depending on their own interests, subordinates activate their resources either according to the wishes of the managers, co-influence, or more or less against them, counter-influence (resistance) (point 5b).

Only after the process mentioned do we reach the final exchange, behavior, of both managers and subordinates. Concerning the managers, this can appear e.g. in their leadership behavior towards subordinate individuals, or in how they reward or punish their subordinates. Concerning the subordinates, the corresponding exchange behavior can appear in different work behavior which is the main exchange commodity of the employees.

Human beings are not capable of planning very far into the future, and/or of taking into account the innumerable factors involved in the steadily ongoing exchange processes. Thus, there appear besides intended consequences (point 6) also unintended consequences (point 7), which again can have profound effects (feedback) upon the future values, resource allocation, controlling structures and new exchange processes, behavior, in organizations.

At the end of this chapter we must once more stress that we have not used the concepts mentioned here throughout the study, as this might have led to difficulties in understanding, especially for those not familiar with these kinds of behavioral concepts. However, we have tried to use them in summaries of the main chapters, when we have attempted an integrated description, analysis and interpretation of what has happened in Chinese management and why.

References

Administrative Division of the People's Republic of China (1981) Beijing: Cartographic Publishing House

Agriculture in New China (1953) Beijing: Foreign Languages Press

Allardt, E. (1983) Sosiologia I. Porvoo: Werner Söderström Osakeyhtiö

Andors, S. (1977) China's Industrial Revolution. New York: Pantheon Books/ Random House

Asia 1987 Yearbook (1986) Hong Kong: Far Eastern Economic Review

Bachrach, P. and M. S. Baratz (1970): Power and Poverty: Theory and Practice. New York: Oxford University Press

Bagozzi, R. P. (1978) "Marketing as Exchange." American Behavioral Scientist 21 (4), March/April

Bai, S. (Ed.) (1982) An Outline History of China. Beijing: Foreign Languages Press

Benson, J. K. (1975) "The Interorganizational Network as a Political Economy." Administrative Science Quarterly 20, June

Blau, P. M. (1964) Exchange and Power in Social Life. New York: John Wiley

Bullard, M. R. (1979) "People's Republic of China Elite Studies: A Review of the Literature." Asian Survey 8, August

Burns, T. R. (1977) "Unequal Exchange and Uneven Development in Social Life: Continuities in a Structural Theory of Social Exchange." Acta Sociologica 20 (3)

Burt, R. S. (1977) "Power in Social Typology." In: Liebert, R. J. and Imershein, A. W. (Eds.) Power, Paradigms and Community Research. Beverly Hills: Sage

Cafferata, G. L. (1979) "Member and Leader Satisfaction with a Professional Association: An Exchange Perspective." Administrative Science Quarterly 24, September

Campbell, R. D. (1981) "Changing Functions of Mass Media in the People's Republic of China." Journal of Communication 4, Autumn

Chadwick-Jones, J. K. (1976) Social Exchange Theory: Its Structure and Influence in Social Psychology. London: Academic Press

Chang, Y. N. (1976) "Early Chinese Management Thought." California Management Review, Winter

Chao, K. (1977) Agrarian Policy of the Chinese Communist Party 1921–1959. New York: Greenwood

Chao, K. (1963) Agrarian Policies of Mainland China. A Documentary Study. Cambridge, Mass.: Harvard University Press

Ch'en, J. (Ed.) (1969) Mao. Englewood Cliffs, N. J.: Prentice-Hall

Chen, P. K. (1984) "Management Professionalization, Responsibility and Democracy." Chinese University of Hong Kong, Working Paper, April

Chen, P. K. (1985) The Labour Movement in China. Hong Kong: Swindon

Child, J. (1977) Organization. A Guide to Problems and Practice. London: Harper and Row

China: A Statistical Survey in 1986 (1986) Hong Kong: Longman

China: A Statistical Survey in 1985 (1985) Beijing: State Statistical Bureau of China

Christensen, P. M. and J. Delman (1983) A Theory of Transitional Society. Mao Zedong and the Shanghai School in China from Mao to Deng. Edited by the Bulletin of Concerned Asian Scholars. New York: M. E. Sharpe, Inc.

Clegg, S. (1979) The Theory of Power and Organization: London: Routledge and Kegan Paul

Clubb, O. E. (1978) 20th Century China. New York: Columbia University Press

Constitution of the Communist Party of China in the Twelfth National Congress of the CPC (1982) Beijing: Foreign Languages Press

Constitution of the People's Republic of China (1982) Produced by the Fifth National People's Congress at Its Fifth Session, December 4, 1982

Croll, E. J. (1982) "The Promotion of Domestic Sideline Production in Rural China (1978–1979)." In: Gray, J. and White, G. (Eds.) China's New Development Strategy. Suffolk, U. K.: Academic Press

Dahl, R. A. (1957) "The Concept of Power." Behavioral Science, pp. 201–205

Deng, Xiaoping (1982) Opening Speech. The Twelfth National Congress of the CPC/September 1982; Chinese Documents. Beijing: Foreign Languages Press

Deng, Xiaoping (1983) "On the Reform of the System of Party and State Leadership." Beijing Review 40

Deng, Xiaoping (1984) Selected Works of Deng Xiaoping. Beijing: Foreign Languages Press

Deng, Xiaoping (1986) On Mao Zedong and Mao Zedong Thought. In: Wenxian Zhong (Ed.) Mao Zedong. Biography – Assessment – Reminiscences. Beijing: Foreign Languages Press, pp. 85–96

Du, R. (1985) "Second-Stage Rural Structural Reform." Beijing Review, June 24

Eberhard, W. (1962) Social Mobility in Traditional China. Leiden: E. J. Brill

Eberhard, W. (1977) A History of China. Bristol: Routledge and Kegan Paul

Egashira, K. (1975) "Chinese-Style Socialism: Some Aspects of Its Origin and Structure." Asian Survey, November

Ekeh, P. P. (1974) Social Exchange Theory. London: Heineman

Emerson, R. M. (1962) "Power-Dependence Relations." American Sociological Review 27, pp. 31–41

Etzioni, A. (1961) A Comparative Analysis of Complex Organizations. New York: Free Press

Field, R. M. (1984) "Changes in Chinese Industry Since 1978." China Quarterly 100, December

Fifth Session of the Fifth National People's Congress (1983) Beijing: Foreign Languages Press

First Session of the Sixth National People's Congress (1983) Beijing: Foreign Languages Press

Franzén, G. (1977) Kinas Väg. Stockholm: Kinapublikationer

French, J. R. R. and B. Raven (1959) "The Bases of Social Power." in: Cartwright, D. (Ed.) Studies in Social Power. Ann Arbor: University of Michigan Press

French, W. (1978) The Personnel Management Process. Boston: Houghton Mifflin

Galbraith, J. R. and D. A. Nathanson (1978) Strategy Implementation: The Role of Structure and Process. St. Paul – New York – Los Angeles – San Francisco: West Publishing

Gao, G. and W. Li (1982) "The Role of Plans in Industrial Enterprises." International Studies of Management and Organization. Summer. Armonk, N. Y.: M. E. Sharpe, Inc.

Gliński, B. (1984) "Variants of the Socialist Economy Management System in Eastern Europe." Paper presented to the Third Workshop on Capitalist and Socialist Organizations, Helsinki, August

Goffman, E. (1982) "On Face-Work: an Analysis of Ritual Elements in Social Interaction." Psychiatry 18/3, pp. 213–231

Gray, J. and White, G. (Eds.) (1982) China's New Development Strategy. Suffolk: Academic Press

Guangmin, L. (1982) "Strengthen and Improve Party Leadership in Enterprise Management." International Studies of Management and Organization XII (2), Summer. Armonk, N. Y.: M. E. Sharpe, Inc.

Guangyuan, Y. (Ed.) (1984) China's Socialist Modernization. Beijing: Foreign Languages Press

Han, Suyin (1968) Kina år 2001. Stockholm: Kinapublikationer

Hardy, C. (1985) "The Nature of Unobtrusive Power." Journal of Management Studies 22 (4), July

Hofstede, G. (1980) Culture's Consequences. International Differences in Work-Related Values. Beverly Hills: Sage

Hofstede, G. (1985) "National Cultures and Organizational Cultures." The Finish Journal of Business Economics 1

Hollander, E. P. (1978) Leadership Dynamics. New York: Free Press

Hollis, M. and E. J. Nell (1975) Rational Economic Man. A Philosophical Critique of Neo-classical Economics. London: Cambridge University Press

Homans, G. C. (1961) Social Behaviour: Its Elementary Forms. New York: Harcourt

Hsueh, Mu-chiao, Su Hsing, and Lin Tse-li (1960) The Socialist Transformation of the National Economy in China. Beijing.

Hultcrantz, G., H. Lindkoff, and J. Valdelin (1974) "Folkrepubliken Kinas ekonomiska och sociala utveckling 1949–1973." Working Paper 6002 EFJ

Hu, Yaobang (1982) Create a New Situation in All Fields of Socialist Modernization, in The Twelfth National Congress of the CPC. Beijing: Foreign Languages Press

IDE, Industrial Democracy in Europe, International Research Group (1981a) Industrial Democracy in Europe. Oxford: Clarendon Press

IDE, International Research Group (1981b) "Industrial Democracy in Europe: Differences and Similarities Across Countries and Hierarchies." Organization Studies 2 (2), pp. 113–130

Kalela, J. (1972) Historian tutkimusprosessi. Helsinki: Oy Gaudeamus

Kerr, C. (1983) The Future of Industrial Societies. Convergence or Continuing Diversity. Cambridge, Mass.: Harvard University Press

King, F. H. H. (1968) A Concise Economic History of Modern China. Bombay: Praeger

Kluckhohn, C. (1951) "The Study of Culture." In: Lerner, D. and Lasswell, H. D. (Eds.) The Policy Sciences. Stanford, Calif.: Stanford University Press

Korpi, W. (1974) "Conflict and the Balance of Power." Acta Sociologica 17 (2)

Kortteinen, M. (1985) "Uusi yhteiskuntamuoto." Sosiologia 2

Kotter, J. P. (1979) Power in management. How to Understand, Acquire and Use It. New York: AMACOM

Kraus, R. C. (1981) Class Conflict in Chinese Socialism. New York: Columbia University Press

Kroeber, A. L. and T. Parsons (1958) "The Concepts of Culture and of a Social System." American Sociological Review 23

Kuan, Ta-tung (1960) The Socialist Transformation of Capitalist Industry and Commerce in China. Beijing

La, G. (1982) "Strengthen and Improve Party Leadership." Enterprise Management and Organization, Summer

Laaksonen, O. (1975) "The Structure and Management of Chinese Enterprises." The Finish Journal of Business Economics 1

Laaksonen, O. (1977) "The Power Structure of Chinese Enterprises." International Studies of Management and Organization. VII (1), Spring, pp. 71–90

Laaksonen, O. (1981) "Resources and Controlling Structures in Comparing Capitalist and Socialist Organizations." Paper presented in Capitalist-Socialist Workshop in Helsinki, May 1981

Laaksonen, O. (1984a) "The Management and Power Structure of Chinese Enterprise During and After the Cultural Revolution." Organization Studies 5 (1), pp. 1–21

Laaksonen, O. (1984b) "Participation Down and Up the Line: Comparative Industrial Democracy Trends in China and Europe." International Social Science Journal XXXVI (2), pp. 299–318

Lammers, C. J. (1967) "Power and Participation in Decision-making in Formal Organizations." American Journal of Sociology. 73, pp. 201–216

Lammers, C. J. and D. J. Hickson (Eds.) (1979) Organizations Alike and Unlike. International and Interinstitutional Studies in the Sociology of Organizations. East Kilbride, Scotland: Routledge and Kegan Paul

Lansbury, R. D., S. H. Ng, and R. B. McKern (1984) "Management at the Enterprise-Level in China." Industrial Relations Journal 15 (4), Winter

Lévi-Strauss, C. (1949) Les Structures élémentaires de la Parante. Paris: Humanities

Lieberthal, K. (1983) "China in 1982: A Middling Course for the Middle Kingdom." Asian Survey XXIII (1), January

Lin, L. (1982) "The Sichuan Experiments: Experiences and Problems." International Studies of Management and Organization, Summer

Lingnan University Research Institute (China) (1982) "Principles of Management in a Socialist Economy." International Studies of Management and Organization, Summer

Lippit, V. (1982) "The People's Communes and China's New Development Strategy in China from Mao to Deng." Bulletin of Concerned Asian Scholars. Armonik, N. Y.: M. E. Sharpe, Inc.

Liu, Zheng (1981) Population Planning and Demographic Theory. In: Liu Zeng,

Song Jian, and others (Eds.) China's Population: Problems and Prospects. Beijing: New World Press

Lockett, M. (1985) "Culture and the Problems of Chinese Management." Unpublished manuscript

Lockett, M. and Littler, C. R. (1983) "Trends in Chinese Enterprise Management 1978–1982." World Development 11 (8)

Loewe, M. (1965) Imperial China. London: George Allen and Unwin

Lu, Dong (1984) "China's Industry on the Upswing." Beijing Review 27 (35)

Lui, A. Y. (1981) The Hanlin Academy. Training Ground for the Ambitious, 1644–1850. Hamden, Conn.: Archon Books

Lukes, S. (1974) Power: A Radical View. London: MacMillan

Ma, Hong (1983) New Strategy for China's economy. Beijing: New World Press

Macrae, N. (1975) "Pacific Century, 1975–2075?" The Economist, January 4, pp. 15–35

Mao Tse-Tung (1975a) Selected Works of Mao Tse-Tung, vol. II. Beijing: Foreign Languages Press

Mao Tse-Tung (1975b) Selected Works of Mao Tse-Tung, vol. III. Beijing: Foreign Languages Press

Mao Tse-Tung (1977a) Selected Works of Mao Tse-Tung, vol. I. Beijing: Foreign Languages Press

Mao Tse-Tung (1977b) Selected Works of Mao Tse-Tung, vol. IV. Beijing: Foreign Languages Press

Maslow, A. H. (1970) Motivation and Personality. New York: Harper

McGregor, D. (1960) The Human Side of Enterprise. New York: McGraw-Hill

McMillan, C. J. (1985) The Japanese Industrial System. Berlin–New York: de Gruyter

Meisner, M. and M. Blecher (1983) "Rural Development, Agrarian Structure, and the County in China." Bulletin of Concerned Asian Scholars; China from Mao to Deng. New York: M. E. Sharpe, Inc.

Mintzberg, H. (1983) Power in and around Organizations. Englewood Cliffs, N. J.: Prentice-Hall

Morgan, M. C. (1981) "Controlling the Bureaucracy in Post-Mao China." Asian Survey XXI (12), December, pp. 1223–1236

Nethercut, R. D. (1982) "Deng and the Gun: Party-Military Relations in the People's Republic of China." Asian Survey XXII (8), August

Olson, M. (1965) The Logic of Collective Action. Cambridge: Harvard University Press

Olve, N.-G. (1984) Challenges for China's Managers. EIASM Working Paper 84–13, October

Orleans, L. A. (1972) Every Fifth Child: The Population of China. Stanford: Stanford University Press

Pan, Cheng-lieh (1980) "Experimentation of Reforming the Economic Management System in the People's Republic of China." Unpublished report (State Economic Commission, PRC), Beijing

Pan, Cheng-lieh (1984) Management Thoughts in Ancient China; in Qiye guanli. Beijing: China Enterprise Management Association, September

Pelzel, J. C. (1972) "Economic Management of a Production Brigade in Post-Leap

China." In: Willmott, W. E. (Ed.) Economic Organization in Chinese Society. Stanford, Calif.: Stanford University Press

Peng, Z. (1982) Report on the Draft at the Revised Constitution of the People's Republic of China in Fifth National People's Congress (November–December 1982). Beijing: Foreign Languages Press

Pfeffer, J. (1981) Power in Organizations. Boston: Pitman

Porter, M. E. (1980) Competitive Strategy. New York: Free Press

Porter, M. E. (1985) Competitive Advantage. New York: Free Press

Provisional Regulations Concerning Congresses of Workers and Staff Members in State-Owned Industrial Enterprises (1981) Beijing: All-China Federation of Trade Unions (October)

Prybyla, J. S. (1970): The Political Economy of Communist China. Scranton, Penn.: Intext

Pugh, D. S., D. J. Hickson, C. R. Hinings, and C. Turner (1968) "Dimensions of Organization Structure." Administrative Science Quarterly 13

Qi, Wen (1979) China. A General Survey. Beijing: Foreign Languages Press

Ramström, D. (1975) "Toward the Information-Saturated Society." In: Leavitt, H., Pinfield, L., Webb, E. (Eds.) Organizations in the Future. New York: Praeger

Redding, S. G. and M. Ng (1982) "The Role of 'Face' in the Organizational Perceptions of Chinese Managers." Organization Studies 3/3, pp. 201–219

Resolution on CPC History (1949–1981) (1981) Beijing: Foreign Languages Press

Rhenman, E. (1972) Menestyvä yritys ja sen ympäristö. Tapiola: Weilin and Göös

Richman, B. A. (1969) Industrial Society in Communist China. New York: Random House

du Rivaux, J.-L. (1974) "A Day in the Life of Li Sheng, Chinese Manager." European Business, Winter/Spring

Rokeach, M. (1973) The Nature of Human Values. New York: Free Press

Rus, V. (1980) "Positive and Negative Power." Organization Studies 1 (1), pp. 3–19

Saarilahti, T. (1960) Suomen lähetysseuran työ Kiinassa vuosina 1901–1926. Helsinki: Kirjapaino Oy Savo

Schran, P. (1975) "On the Yenan Origins of Current Economic Policies." In: Perkins, D. (Ed.) China's Modern Economy in Historical Perspective. Stanford: Stanford University Press

Schurman, F. (1971) Ideology and Organization in Communist China. Berkeley: University of California Press

Selden, M. (1971) The Yenan Way in Revolutionary China. Cambridge, Mass.: Harvard University Press

Simon, H. A. (1957) Administrative Behavior. Chicago: Free Press

Snow, E. (1984) Red Star over China. Toronto–New York–London–Sydney: Grove Press

Staar, R. F. (1985) "Weltkommunismus 1984/85." Osteuropa 7–8

Statistical Yearbook of China 1985 (1985) (English edition), Compiled by the State Statistical Bureau, PRC. Hong Kong: Wing Fat Printing

Stewart, R. (1967) Managers and Their Jobs: A Study of the Similarities and Differences in the Ways Managers Spend Their Time. London: MacMillan

References   361

Su Wenming (Ed.) (1982) "Economic Readjustment and Reform", in China Today
    (3) series. Beijing: Beijing Review
Sung, G. (1965) "China's Regional Politics: A Biographical Approach." Asian
    Survey 15, April
Tannenbaum, A. S. (1968) Control in Organizations. New York: McGraw-Hill
Ten Great Years (1960) New York: AMS Pr
The Tenth, National Congress of the Communist Party of China (Documents)
    (1973). Peking: Foreign Languages Press
Thrasher, M. and D. Dunkerley (1981) "Inter-Governmental Exchange Real-
    tions." Paper presented in Capitalist-Socialist Workshop in Helsinki, May 1981
Tian, Yun (1982) "The Sichuan Experiment: More Authority to Enterprises." In:
    Su, Wenming (Ed.) Economic Readjustment and Reform. Beijing: Beijing Re-
    view
Tinbergen, J. (1961) "Do Communist and Free Economies Show a Converging
    Pattern?" Soviet Studies XII (4), April
Tiusanen, T. (1984) "Konvergenssiteoria ja 1980–luku." Kanava 2
Tregear, T. R. (1965) A Geography of China. Chicago: Elsevier
Tung, R. L. (1982) "Preface: Reforms of the Economic and Management Systems
    in China." International Studies of Management and Organization XII (2),
    pp. 3–19
Twelfth National Congress of the CPC (1982) Beijing: Foreign Languages Press
Wang, R. S. (1975) "Educational Reforms and the Cultural Revolution: The Chin-
    ese Evaluation Process." Asian Survey XV (9), September
Warner, M. (1985) "Enterprise Management and Industrial Training in Chinese
    Firms: An Empirical Study." Working Paper, March, The Management College
    – Henley and Brunel University
Weber, M. (1947) Theory of Social and Economic Organization. New York: Ox-
    ford University Press
Wheelwright, E. L. and B. McFarlane (1970) The Chinese Road to Socialism. New
    York: Monthly Review
White, G. (1983) "Socialist Planning and Industrial Management: Chinese Eco-
    nomic Reforms in the Post-Mao Era." Development and Change 14
Willmott, W. E. (Ed.) (1972) Economic Organization in Chinese Society. Stanford,
    Calif.: Stanford University Press
Wood, S. (1984) "Towards Socialist-Capitalist Comparative Analysis of the Organi-
    zational Problem." Paper presented to the Third Workshop on Capitalist and
    Socialist Organizations, Helsinki, August
Xu, Dixin, et al. (Eds.) (1982) China's Search for Economic Growth. The Chinese
    Economy since 1949. Beijing: New World Press
Xue, Muqiao (1981) China's Socialist Economy. Beijing: Foreign Languages Press
Yeh, K. C. (1984) "Macroeconomic Changes in the Chinese Economy During the
    Readjustment." China Quarterly 100, December
Ylä-Anttila, L. (1983) Organisaatiorakenne ja sen selittyminen. Helsinki. Publica-
    tions of the Helsinki School of Economics
Zhao, Z. (1981) China's Economy and Development Principles. Beijing: Foreign
    Languages Press

Zhao, Z. (1984) Report on the Work of the Government. The Second Session of the Sixth National People's Congress. Beijing: Foreign Languages Press

Zhong, Wenxian (Ed.) (1986) Mao Zedong. Biography – Assessment – Reminiscences. Beijing: Foreign Languages Press

Zhou, Ping (1982) Workers' Congresses: A Step Towards Democratic Management. Economic Readjustment and Reform. Beijing: Beijing Review Special Features Series

Abbreviations

A. D.   After Christ
B. C.   Before Christ
B. R.   Beijing Review
CC   Central Committee of the Communist Party
Ch. D.   China Daily
CPC   Communist Party of China
GDP   Gross Domestic Product
GMD   Guomindang
NPC   National People's Congress
PC   Party Committe
PLA   People's Liberation Army

List of Figures

List of Tables

Subject Index

de Gruyter Studies in Organization

An international series by internationally known authors presenting current research in organization

Vol. 1

The Japanese Industrial System
By *Charles J. McMillan*
2nd revised edition
1985. 15.5 x 23 cm. XII, 356 pages. Cloth. ISBN 3 11 010410 5; 0-89925-005-X (U.S.)

Vol. 2

Political Management
Redefining the Public Sphere
By *H. T. Wilson*
1984. 15.5 x 23 cm. X, 316 pages. Cloth. ISBN 3 11 009902 0

Vol. 3

Limits to Bureaucratic Growth
By *Marshall W. Meyer* in Association with *William Stevenson* and *Stephen Webster*
1985. 15.5 x 23 cm. X, 228 pages. Cloth. ISBN 3 11 009865 2; 0-89925-003-3 (U.S.)

Vol. 4

Guidance, Control and Evaluation in the Public Sector
Edited by *F. X. Kaufmann, G. Majone, V. Ostrom*
1985. 17 x 24 cm. XIV, 830 pages. Cloth. ISBN 3 11 009707 9; 0-89925-020-3 (U.S.)

Vol. 5

International Business in the Middle East
Edited by *Erdener Kaynak*
1986. 15.5 x 23 cm. XVI, 278 pages. Cloth. ISBN 3 11 010321 4; 0-89925-021-1 (U.S.)

Vol. 6

The American Samurai
Blending American and Japanese Managerial Practice
By *Jon P. Alston*
1986. 15.5 x 23 cm. XII, 368 pages. Cloth. ISBN 3 11 010619 1; 0-89925-063-7 (U.S.)

WALTER DE GRUYTER · BERLIN · NEW YORK

Genthiner Straße 13, D-1000 Berlin 30, Phone (0 30) 2 60 05-0, Telex 1 83 027
200 Saw Mill River Road, Hawthorne, N.Y. 10532, Phone (914) 747-0110, Telex 646677

de Gruyter Studies in Organization

Vol. 7

Organizing Industrial Development

Edited by *Rolf Wolff*
1986. 15.5 x 23 cm. XI, 391 pages. Cloth. ISBN 3 11 010669 8; 0-89925-168-4 (U.S.)

Vol. 8

Organization Theory and Technocratic Consciousness

Rationality, Ideology, and Quality of Work
By *Mats Alvesson*
1987. 15.5 x 23 cm. X, 286 pages. Cloth. ISBN 3 11 010574 8; 0-89925-165-X (U.S.)

Vol. 9

Anglo-American Innovation

By *Peter A. Clark*
1987. 15.5 x 23 cm. X, 404 pages. Cloth. ISBN 3 11 010572 1; 0-89925-164-1 (U.S.)

Vol. 10

Unemployment: Theory, Policy and Structure

Edited by *Peder J. Pedersen* and *Reinhard Lund*
1987. 15.5 x 23 cm. XX, 358 pages. Cloth. ISBN 3 11 011071 7; 0-89925-277-X (U.S.)

Vol. 11

Organization of Innovation

East-West-Perspectives
Edited by *John Child* and *Paul Bate*
1987. 15.5 x 23 cm. X, 238 pages. Cloth. ISBN 3 11 010700 7; 0-89925-167-6 (U.S.)

European Approaches to International Management

Edited by *Klaus Macharzina* and *Wolfgang H. Staehle*
1985. 15.5 x 23 cm. XIV, 386 pages. Cloth. ISBN 3 11 009827 X; 0-89925-018-1 (U.S.)

WALTER DE GRUYTER · BERLIN · NEW YORK

Genthiner Straße 13, D-1000 Berlin 30, Phone (0 30) 2 60 05-0, Telex 1 83 027
200 Saw Mill River Road, Hawthorne, N.Y. 10532, Phone (914) 747-0110, Telex 646677